Southern Pamphlets on

Secession,

November 1860–April 1861

CIVIL WAR AMERICA

Gary W. Gallagher, editor

Southern Pamphlets on Se

Edited by Jon L. Wakelyn

The University of North Carolina Press

Chapel Hill & London

cession

November 1860–April 1861

© 1996
The University of North Carolina
Press
All rights reserved
Manufactured in the United States
of America
The paper in this book meets
the guidelines for permanence and
durability of the Committee on
Production Guidelines for Book
Longevity of the Council on
Library Resources.

Library of Congress
Cataloging-in-Publication Data
Southern pamphlets on secession,
November 1860–April 1861 / edited by
Jon L. Wakelyn.
p.   cm. — (Civil War America)
Includes bibliographical references and
index.
ISBN 0-8078-2278-7 (cloth : alk. paper)
1. Secession—Southern States—
Sources.   2. United States—History—
Civil War, 1861-1865—Pamphlets.
I. Wakelyn, Jon L.   II. Series.
E458.1.s68   1996
973.7'13—dc20   95-49492
CIP

00   99   98   97   96
5   4   3   2   1

CONTENTS

973.713
500

PREFACE

During the political crisis of the winter 1860–61, many of the South's most important leaders published and widely disseminated pamphlets in opposition to and support for secession from the Union. Their rhetoric, thoughts, and arguments concerning specific events and issues reveal graphically what was at stake during those frantic days that produced civil war. Although they disagreed over what agitated them, they all discussed the Republican Party's control of the federal government and what would happen to their minority, slave-based section in that fast-growing, dynamic American nation. Fear over the threatened abolition of slavery illustrates just what that system of labor meant to all of their lives. Disagreements about what action to take during that political situation produced deep internal divisions, yet also a growing, near-calm resolution and unity among the majority. Thus, in committing their political and social views and interests to print, those leaders told us much about how political pressures influenced their personal character and, more important, the world in which they lived.

But in spite of the pamphlets' importance to the understanding of that society and its political actions, historians have discussed only a small number of them. To be sure, some excellent older books by fine political historians used a few of them to describe brilliantly the issues and events that led to the Civil War. Modern social historians also have looked at some of those pamphlets to flesh out many facets of Southern slave society, including religious values and attitudes toward slavery. Still, few of those historians of society have applied their findings to the politics of the secession crisis. Perhaps because of these differing approaches to the study of the Old South, this major pamphlet source of both political action and cultural life never has been analyzed systematically. To renew interest in these valuable pamphlets on secession this volume reprints a representative selection of them.

The pamphlets themselves originated as sermons, letters to constituents, speeches, journal and newspaper articles, and a number specifically were written as pamphlets. The authors lived in all of the Southern regions, including the Border, the Upper, and the Lower cotton states. Their works were discussed and reviewed in newspapers and periodicals, and circulated widely throughout the South; some went through many editions, and a few even were sent North. One hundred and twenty of them have been collected, read, and studied, and twenty have been selected to reprint in this volume. Of those included, two antedate the period so as to set in context earlier sectional tensions and secession arguments. Another sixty-five are listed and described to allow the reader to decide which ones complement and add to the arguments of the pamphlets published in this volume.

A few important speeches, letters, sermons, newspaper and periodical articles, and broadsides were never published in pamphlet form but deserve mention. Valuable articles, such as John Randolph Tucker's "The Great Issue," were published in the leading Southern journals of opinion. The secession convention debates and proceedings, as well as written explanations for secession, were published either as books or in newspapers, but not as pamphlets made available for wide use. A *Report on the Debates of the Peace Convention* printed extracts from speeches of Southern Unionists. Many editorials that so inflamed their readers remained locked in the pages of newspapers. Perhaps the most famous secession speech, Alexander Stephens's "Cornerstone Address," although excerpted in the local press and reported on in the North, has never appeared in complete form. (A search through Stephens's papers in the Library of Congress uncovered only notes for the speech.) Because of its importance, the "Cornerstone Address" is printed in an appendix to this volume. The handwritten "Memorial of Free Negroes," which revealed tensions within that group, was not issued as a pamphlet. Those concerned with the South's written arguments over secession should consult these efforts to supplement the published pamphlets.

A chronology of events of those hectic months place issues and grievances discussed in the pamphlets into perspective. The introduction describes the setting for and types of pamphlets included, their audience and circulation, the events they addressed, what the authors claimed caused the secession crisis, and their revelations about the world in which they lived. The pamphlets are arranged chronologically and by region, with those from the Lower South preceding the Upper South. Comments on each of the pamphlets include brief biographical information on the authors' training and careers, a short summary of the salient issues discussed, and a bibliography for further investigation. Footnotes are provided for phrases, names, and events mentioned in the pamphlets to inform the reader how the authors established their arguments. For the sake of space, needless repetition of quotes has been omitted, although footnotes describe their contents. Although every effort has been made to identify the sources of quotations appearing in the pamphlets, in many cases the sources could not be ascertained. When sources could be determined, they are identified in footnotes. Original spelling and punctuation have been retained, except in the few instances where alteration was necessary to clarify meaning. Typographical errors have been corrected. Bracketed material is in the original pamphlets, with the exception of one editorial emendation as noted in the Johnson pamphlet.

This book has been built on the efforts of others who have attempted to understand the elusive Southerners who seemed so willing to risk so much to defend their way of life. Many of my professional colleagues and acquaintances have helped with this project. Eugene D. Genovese, William J. Cooper, William W. Freehling, and Bertram Wyatt-Brown have given me expert advice on whose pamphlets should be included in this book. I hope Gene is pleased that Thornwell got in. Larry Poos read the introduction and did a collocational analysis that set specific ideas in motion. Alan Kraut gave the manuscript a thorough reading. My student Clayton E. Jewett contributed his knowledge of modern technology. Dave Kelly at the Library of Congress made many successful searches. Other staff, alas some now dead, at the archives and libraries where I have looked for sources over many years have been courteous and extremely knowledgeable. I am indebted to the Catholic University of America Research Fund for generous support of this book. To my wife, Joyce Bogardus Walker, for her incalculable assistance, I dedicate this volume.

August 1995
Jon L. Wakelyn
The Catholic University of America

CHRONOLOGY OF EVENTS,

NOVEMBER 1860–APRIL 1861

November 6
   Presidential election
November 7–8
   Southern states receive word of Republican victory
December 3
   United States Congress reconvenes
December 4
   President Buchanan's address to Congress
December 4
   House Committee of Thirty-three appointed
December 11
   Senate Committee of Thirteen appointed
December 13
   Southern address to constituents
December 17
   South Carolina secession convention meets
December 18
   Committee of Thirteen discusses Crittenden Compromise
December 20
   South Carolina secedes
December 26
   Major Robert Anderson moves federal troops to Fort Sumter
December 31
   Committee of Thirteen reports it cannot agree on compromise
January 4
   President Buchanan proclaims National Fast Day
January 5
   President Buchanan sends *Star of West* to relieve Fort Sumter
January 9
   Mississippi secedes
January 11
   Alabama and Florida secede
January 14
   House Committee of Thirty-three report and debate

January 26

    Louisiana secedes

January 28

    Georgia secedes

February 1

    Texas secedes

February 4–27

    Washington Peace Conference

February 4

    Montgomery convention

February 7–March 11

    Provisional Confederate Congress and Constitution

February 28

    U.S. House rejects revised Crittenden Compromise

March 4

    U.S. Senate rejects revised Crittenden Compromise

March 4

    Lincoln inauguration

March 12

    Confederate Commissioners in Washington

April 10

    President Davis demands Fort Sumter surrender

April 12

    Confederates fire on Fort Sumter

April 15

    President Lincoln calls for 75,000 military volunteers

April 17

    Virginia secedes

May 8

    Arkansas secedes

May 21

    North Carolina secedes

June 24

    Tennessee secedes

INTRODUCTION

As word of the Republican victory in the November 1860 presidential election filtered down to the slave states, publicists, preachers, and politicians alike responded with an outpouring of speeches, sermons, letters to constituents, and articles in periodicals and newspapers. All of them discussed the election's meaning for the future of their society. From their pulpits clergy urged their flocks to reject Northern attacks on Southern values. Publicists and other social commentators, many longtime defenders of the "Southern way of life," regarded the national political news as disastrous, yet disagreed over the proper course of action. National, state, and local public figures cautiously analyzed what to expect from the election and called for meetings and conventions to decide future action. As the crisis deepened, those speakers and writers reacted to specific Northern and Southern overtures of compromise and confrontation. Their arguments over how best to protect Southern society generated heated discussion about secession from the Union. In their efforts, secessionist and Unionist alike vividly described what they believed had brought on the crisis, and with great fear, what would happen to their society. In those dire warnings about the future, they revealed much about their interests and what they valued in their culture.

During the months from November 1860 until April 1861, many of the most important of those letters, speeches, sermons, and articles appeared in printed pamphlet form. It is hardly surprising that Southern leaders chose the pamphlet as the best means to communicate with constituents and one another. In fact, use of the pamphlet to influence political activities and to explain values and anxieties dates from early modern Western culture. In the American colonies pamphlets first appeared as clergy warnings of impending doom and later as political grievances with government. The Revolutionary period, as Bernard Bailyn so splendidly has shown, unleashed a full barrage of pamphlets.[1] After the war, during times of intense political conflict such as the debates over the federal Constitution, the War of 1812, the arguments over Missouri statehood in 1819–20, the Nullification controversy of 1828–32, and the sectional confrontations during the 1850s, pamphlets continued to pour forth. Nothing, however, rivaled the

1. Bernard Bailyn, ed., *Pamphlets of the American Revolution* (Cambridge: Harvard University Press, 1965), introduction. Also see Avery O. Craven, *The Growth of Southern Nationalism* (Baton Rouge: Louisiana State University Press, 1953), 406.

torrents that erupted from the presses during the secession crisis of the winter of 1860–61.

The pamphlet was chosen as a means of communication because of its small size, low cost to print, availability in large numbers, and speed with which it could be sent through the mail to specific individuals. Usually no more than twenty to twenty-five pages, in a format of five by eight or four by six inches, bound between colored covers or with just a colored cover page, pamphlets bore titles that conveyed their author's particular concerns. Public figures handily carried them in their pockets, read from them to audiences, and kept many of them in writing desks to use for quotations in their own speeches, writings, and pamphlets. Pamphlets were printed cheaply, some costing as little as $1.00 per 150.[2] Many pamphlets achieved a print run of 50,000 copies or more, and a few went through multiple editions. Newspaper and magazine editors reprinted some of them. In this way authors were able to circulate their views to essential constituents, the local press and other influential publicists, public figures, and cultural and religious leaders.

The audiences and occasions that precipitated those speeches, sermons, and writings, and the groups to whom the pamphlets were sent, reveal their effectiveness during the secession crisis. Early to publish were clergy who had spoken to local audiences in response to the South Carolina governor's call in late November 1860 for a day of fasting and repentance to reflect the graveness of the times. On November 21, the Day of Thanksgiving, a number of Charleston's and Columbia's famous preachers delivered stirring sermons before many of the state's most important leaders.[3] Perhaps the most famous sermon, entitled *Our National Sins*, was delivered by the Presbyterian divine, James Henley Thornwell, who then had it published and distributed throughout the state and the South. It was reprinted in *The Southern Presbyterian Review* and was later selected for a collection of Fast Day sermons published in New York City. Another of Thornwell's pamphlets, *The State of the Country*, which first appeared in a leading Southern periodical, caught the eye of Robert Gourdin, South Carolina's propagandist of secession, and he reprinted it for circulation throughout the entire South.[4]

2. Costs most often were printed at the bottom of the first or last page of the pamphlet.

3. See the pamphlets printed in this volume for further elucidation of the author's points.

4. David B. Chesebrough, ed., *"God Ordained This War": Sermons on the Sectional Crisis* (Columbia: University of South Carolina Press, 1991), 193–96; Benjamin M.

In Louisiana, the governor called for a day of "fasting and humiliation," and the New Orleans Presbyterian minister, Benjamin M. Palmer, responded with a sermon delivered on November 29, 1860. Palmer usually preached "as the spirit moved him," but because of the importance of this particular occasion, he wrote this one, and delivered it in a slow, careful, and, for him, constrained voice. Soon thereafter the New Orleans *Daily Delta* printed a version of it and later published some 30,000 copies as pamphlets; a Mobile, Alabama, newspaper reprinted 5,000. Before the publishing record concluded, some 90,000 pamphlets of Palmer's sermon had been produced, and many were placed in the hands of important leaders. Palmer was quoted by clergy and political leaders alike in their own speeches and pamphlets. Palmer's pamphlet even was discussed in state secession conventions.[5]

Most of those Fast Day sermons were published as pamphlets to comfort parishioners who needed inspiring words of encouragement during troubled times. Printed sermons were useful for political purposes as well. For example, the Rev. George H. Clark of St. John's Episcopal Church in Savannah, Georgia, forwarded a copy of his sermon to a committee of the town's leading citizens. William H. Bullock, who at the time was committed to preserving the Union, insisted Clark's cautionary sermon required long and hard study. He sent copies to Georgians, many of whom soon would declare that state's devotion to the Union.[6] In the midst of those difficult times, President James Buchanan also called for a national day of fasting and thanksgiving. Robert J. Breckinridge, the Unionist Kentucky Presbyterian clergyman, responded, delivering a stirring sermon on January 4, 1861. He immediately published it as a pamphlet, then reprinted it in his Unionist journal, *The Danville Review*. Senator John J. Crittenden, one famous Kentucky Unionist, used Breckinridge's pamphlet in speeches

---

Palmer, *The Life and Letters of James Henley Thornwell* (Richmond: Whittet and Shepperson, 1875), 485–89; James O. Farmer Jr., *The Metaphysical Confederacy: James Henley Thornwell and the Synthesis of Southern Values* (Macon, Georgia: Mercer University Press, 1986), 265–71.

5. See Thomas C. Johnson, *The Life and Letters of Benjamin Morgan Palmer* (Richmond: Presbyterian Committee of Publications, 1906), 206, 220, 222, for printing history; also see Mitchell Snay, *The Gospel of Disunion: Religion and Separatism in the Antebellum South* (New York: Cambridge University Press, 1993), for recent use of these valuable pamphlets.

6. Bullock's request for printing the Clark pamphlet is contained in a letter introducing it. Other letters at the beginning of some pamphlets are most revealing, but they have been omitted because of space constraints.

before Congress.[7] An article written by Rev. James H. Thornwell attacking Breckinridge appeared in *The Southern Presbyterian Review* and was later printed as a pamphlet. Benjamin M. Palmer's reply to Breckinridge, published as *A Vindication of Secession*, served as an excellent summation of the argument for secession. In pamphlet form it circulated among many leaders who also were trying to defend Southern secession.[8]

Another group of pamphlets, the product of the efforts of publicists and politicians who supported the South Carolina secessionist 1860 Association, received wide circulation shortly after the presidential election. The foremost authority on that somewhat mysterious group, believes that Robert G. Gourdin, a Charleston city council member and delegate to the state's secession convention, founded the organization in September 1860. Originally called the "Society of Earnest Men," Gourdin claimed that its object was to function as a "committee of correspondence" to print and distribute pamphlets in support of secession.[9] Gourdin had a wide network of friends from whom he solicited contributions (in the form of articles and speeches) for his effort to force Southern secession. He made certain that influential newspapers, such as Robert B. Rhett Jr.'s *Charleston Mercury*, and periodicals, including James D. B. De Bow's famous *Review*, noticed and even reprinted 1860 Association pamphlets. By late November 1860, some 166,000 pamphlets had appeared in print.[10] To fill a growing demand, second and third editions were issued in rapid order.

Polemicists such as John Townsend and James D. B. De Bow wrote pamphlets for the 1860 Association. Townsend's *The South Alone Should Govern the South* and *The Doom of Slavery in the Union* were discussed in the *Charleston Courier*, which characterized them as "firebells in the night." His *To the People of the South*, specifically addressed to Georgians, was discussed at that state's secession convention. De Bow's *Interest of Non-Slaveowners*

7. Robert J. Breckinridge pamphlet. See comments on Palmer's April 1861 pamphlet in Appendix A.

8. Charles C. Goen, *Broken Churches, Broken Nation: Denominational Schism and the Coming of the Civil War* (Macon, Georgia: Mercer University Press, 1985).

9. May S. Ringgold, "Robert Newman Gourdin and the '1860 Association,'" *Georgia Historical Quarterly* 55 (1971): 501–9; see the constitution of the 1860 Association in John Townsend, *The Doom of Slavery in the Union* (Charleston: Evans and Cogswell, 1860).

10. Charles E. Cauthen, *South Carolina Goes to War, 1860–1865* (Chapel Hill: University of North Carolina Press, 1950), 34–35; Eric H. Walther, *The Fire-Eaters* (Baton Rouge: Louisiana State University Press, 1992).

in Slavery, originally delivered as a speech in Nashville, was printed as an 1860 Association pamphlet and later appeared in his own *Review*.[11] All of these pamphlets circulated among members of the South Carolina secession convention. The Association's last effort, Gabriel Manigault's *Suggestions on the Arming of the State*, was a "comprehensive survey of the military resources of the state." South Carolina's governor used Manigault's pamphlet during his negotiations with Confederate States President Jefferson Davis over what course to take on Fort Sumter.[12]

Other Lower South states lacked organizations like the 1860 Association, and only a small number of pamphlets were issued by their political leaders during the secession crisis. This may have been because they were too preoccupied with the crisis or because time was limited. Nonetheless, a number of Lower South congressmen delivered lectures on secession to constituents and printed them as pamphlets before returning to Washington for the winter 1860–61 term. For example, Congressman Jabez L. M. Curry of Alabama spoke before a large audience in Talledega to influence their actions. "I published," he said, "in pamphlet form and circulated widely." In that address the secession of the state was advised as the only sufficient remedy.[13] Among the Lower South Unionists, former Florida governor Richard K. Call, belatedly addressed a pamphlet, in the guise of a letter to a Northern friend, to the people of the state. He had wanted to keep Floridians from seceding until they had thought through the implications of their actions. In the letter he voiced his frustrations over a North that misunderstood how its attacks on slavery had upset Southerners.[14]

Many national leaders from the Lower South who had remained in Washington during the early deliberations of their states' secession conventions spoke out on issues that had come before Congress. Their speeches, often addressing the events at home as much as those in Washington, were published in pamphlets. For example, Louisiana Senator Judah P. Benjamin's eloquent December 31, 1860, speech, about which Varina Howell Davis confided to her diary in glowing terms as a most able defense of Southern life, was published in a pamphlet and distributed at the

11. Cauthen, *South Carolina Goes to War*, 41; Otis C. Skipper, *J. D. B. De Bow, Magazinist of the Old South* (Athens: University of Georgia Press, 1958), 121.

12. Cauthen, *South Carolina Goes to War*, 43.

13. Jabez L. M. Curry Papers, "Public Life," Library of Congress, Box 11, Notebook B, 83. See also the excellent introduction in William W. Freehling and Craig Simpson, eds., *The Secession of Georgia* (New York: Oxford University Press, 1992).

14. See the Call pamphlet in this volume.

Louisiana convention, reinforcing his support for secession.[15] Likewise, Congressman John H. Reagan tried to get the Texas secession convention to oppose the Unionist governor Sam Houston. Although he claimed to support congressional compromise, in his January 15, 1861, speech on the debate over the report of the House Committee of Thirty-three, Reagan viciously attacked what he called the flawed and weak Northern position on the expansion of slavery, an issue of great importance to the citizens of east Texas. He mailed home 5,000 copies of his speech for the use of Texas secessionists.[16]

Lower South state leaders and publicists made up for the paucity of pamphlets printed for home consumption by sending an avalanche of written material to leaders and people of the Upper South. The correspondence between Robert Gourdin of the 1860 Association and Governor John W. Ellis of North Carolina is most revealing. Gourdin opened the exchange on December 12, 1860, with an offer to provide pamphlets for distribution at the North Carolina convention. He wrote: "We can place ten thousand copies, or even more at the service of North Carolina." On December 17, Governor Ellis replied, "herewith you will find the names and addresses of leading men to whom you may send documents for general circulation." [17] Those pamphlets ended up in the hands of many of North Carolina's political opinion makers who eventually used them to influence voters.

Lower South secession conventions also appropriated funds to send delegates to the Upper South to speak to state legislatures and conventions already in session. Even before his state seceded, Mississippi's A. H. Handy traveled to Maryland to deliver a fiery secession address. It was printed and circulated in Maryland and in Mississippi.[18] Commissioners from Mississippi, Georgia, and South Carolina journeyed to Virginia and spoke eloquently to that state's convention. Over 5,000 pamphlets containing the text of those February 18 and 19, 1861, speeches were distrib-

15. Willie M. Caskey, *Secession and Restoration of Louisiana* (Baton Rouge: Louisiana State University Press, 1938), 22–23.

16. For comments on the speed with which Reagan produced his pamphlet, see Walter F. McCaleb, ed., *Memoirs of John H. Reagan* (New York: The Neale Publishing Co., 1906), 80–82.

17. Noble T. Tolbert, ed., *The Papers of John Willis Ellis*, 2 vols. (Raleigh: State Department of Archives and History), 1:529, 534–35.

18. See comments on the Handy pamphlet in Appendix A. No adequate study of the Lower South delegates sent to the Upper South exists.

uted to the delegates and to the press. Newspaper editors including Fulton Anderson, Henry L. Benning, and John S. Preston, who had longtime ties to Virginia, also contributed to the Virginia secession debates by publishing articles on the substance of the commissioners' speeches.[19] Of course, the pamphlets were also circulated throughout the Lower South.

In the Upper South, vigorous debate over union and secession led to the publication of a number of important and influential pamphlets. Issues raised in those pamphlets informed state leaders' discussions during the secession conventions. Many of the pamphlets, now housed in the Virginia State Library and the Southern Historical Collection, contain underlined passages and written notations made by leaders who were to decide the fate of their states. Local newspapers printed excerpts from those pamphlets and reviewed the best of them, spreading further the Upper South's propaganda war over the merits of secession.[20]

To add to the pamphlet deluge, during January and February 1861, Upper South congressmen engaged in heated debate on compromise versus secession. Speeches made on both sides of the issue were reproduced in pamphlets and posted back home to influence their constituents. Other Upper South congressmen sent letters in the form of pamphlets to their homefolk in order to maintain a high profile on the home front. For example, Thomas L. Clingman's February speech was printed hastily and sent home to North Carolina in hopes of persuading his mountain Unionist constituents to elect secession delegates to the state convention. The Unionist Robert Hatton, a tired and frayed Tennessee congressman who was later to die in service as a Confederate States general, wrote his wife on February 17 that he had sent 12,000 speeches as pamphlets to the folks at home "to define my position." Senator Robert W. Johnson's *Address to the People of Arkansas* was timed to appear in that state on the eve of selection of delegates to the secession convention. The North Carolina Unionist Zebulon B. Vance mailed a pamphlet to *The Citizens of the Eighth Congressional District* in which he apologized for ignoring them. Vance need hardly have worried, since John A. Gilmer, a North Carolina antisecessionist

19. See Dwight L. Dumond, *The Secession Movement, 1860–1861* (New York: Macmillan Co., 1931), 116, 255.

20. See bound pamphlets at the Virginia State Library. The best study of the Virginia pamphlets remains Henry T. Shanks, *The Secession Movement in Virginia, 1847–1861* (Richmond: Garrett and Massie, 1934), 248–61.

congressman, had distributed throughout the state over 10,000 pamphlets printed from the speeches of his fellow North Carolina congressmen.[21]

Aside from using pamphlets to influence events back home and to remain in touch with powerful constituents, Southern congressmen employed the written word to address sectionwide and even national audiences as well. Unionists, one wit allowed, spoke aggressively to the North and soothingly at home. Debates over the Crittenden Compromise, however, forced the Tennessee Unionist, Senator Andrew Johnson, to criticize bitterly his fellow slave state politicians. He seemed to forsake his Southern connections in order to demonstrate loyalty to the Union and to Northern political leaders. The moderate Jefferson Davis of Mississippi spoke on the activities of the Senate Committee of Thirteen in what seemed an attempt to unite his fellow Southerners in Washington. Although too late to influence secession in the Lower South, Davis nevertheless printed the speech and distributed large numbers throughout that region. That pamphlet certainly contributed to his image as a spokesman for the entire slaveholding section. Leaders made statesmanlike farewell addresses to their Washington colleagues, at times more in sorrow than in anger. Many of those last speeches were mailed as pamphlets throughout the nation, although doubtless the primary audience resided in the South.[22]

Southern leaders had widely disseminated tellingly effective pamphlets during the critical months of public debate over secession and union. Few of those efforts, however, were great political speeches or writings, as is demonstrated by the pamphlets' style and contents. Yet most of the authors had been trained in oral and written expression and had had years of experience in public speaking. Many of them even had studied political economics, social theory, and the important works of political thought.[23]

21. Joseph C. Sitterson, *The Secession Movement in North Carolina* (Chapel Hill: University of North Carolina Press, 1939), 206; James Vaux Drake, *Life of General Robert Hatton* (Nashville: Marshall and Bruce, 1867), 321, 323, 342; Daniel W. Crofts, *Reluctant Confederates: Upper South Unionists in the Secession Crisis* (Chapel Hill: University of North Carolina Press, 1989), 4–5.

22. See the Davis and Johnson pamphlets in this volume.

23. See biographical information in the introduction to each pamphlet included in this volume. Also see Bailyn, *Pamphlets of the American Revolution*, introduction; John J. Auer, ed., *Antislavery and Disunion: Studies in the Rhetoric of Compromise and Conflict, 1858–1861* (New York: Harper and Row, 1963), 13; Mary K. Hocksmith, ed., *A History and Criticism of American Public Address*, 3 vols. (New York: Harper and Row, 1965), 3:175–97.

Perhaps the mediocre quality of these pamphlets was a result of the fact that they were hurriedly delivered, hastily written, and clumsily edited. Whatever the reasons, those pamphlets mainly lack clarity of expression, clear organization, and consistent thoughts. Some authors simply piled up multiple and contradictory grievances and over-quoted the works of earlier Southern thinkers. But what they lacked in style and thoughtfulness, they made up for in stridency and force of delivery. Their arguments contain the flourish of hyperbole and the extemporaneity of the moment, but often that resulted in the use of irrational and incautious language. None of them, then, achieved the originality, splendid use of satire, or allegorical power of history's great pamphleteers. Among them one finds no Swift or Defoe, no Charles James Fox or Edmund Burke.

Most of these crude efforts at political and social propaganda, neither well written nor argued brilliantly, were similarly constructed and designed to make convincing arguments for action. Leaders of the various factions in the secession debate delivered speeches and wrote pamphlets in which they responded to specific events and issues during those hectic months. They evaluated in detail the meaning and expected consequences for the South of those events and issues. And, as practical leaders of action, they discussed what had to be done to protect their region; some argued for secession, others favored union, and a few opted for a proposed union of Border states. Most quickly moved from any defense of the right to act to describe their reasons for and the results expected from their decisions. In their comments on events and issues and what actions to take, the authors divulged much about what they valued and what they feared from attacks on their world of slavery.

Not surprisingly, the first and foremost event that precipitated pamphlet response was the presidential election of 1860, which resulted in Republican Party control of the national government. A number of the authors wrote about the Republican Party platform and the postelection pronouncements of the president-elect. Others reacted to Northern state legislatures' passage of personal liberty laws, which repudiated the fugitive slave law. A few, including Judah P. Benjamin on Andrew Johnson and vice versa, and Benjamin M. Palmer on Robert J. Breckinridge, responded to specific issues raised in Congress or published in journal articles. Attempts at compromise, such as those of the House Committee of Thirty-three, produced much debate on the merits of the Crittenden Compromise. Some worried about Northern recalcitrance over the expansion of slavery. Southern Unionists condemned South Carolina secession. Others wrote and spoke about Republican-proposed tariffs and internal improvement bills. The blockade of Southern ports and the mouth of the Mississippi River and federal troops at Fort Sumter in Charleston Harbor were the final events of the period that sparked debate.[24]

The pamphlet writers next turned to the specific meaning of those events for the South. In the opinion of cabinet member Howell Cobb, Lincoln's election meant that a majority of Northerners had turned against the South and that the Republicans could use the federal government to force "Negro equality" on the South. For others, no political means existed to halt majority rule and the corrupt government policies that would follow. Simply put, the Republican majority planned to deny the South equality in the Union, then the general government would move to abolish slavery. Another author insisted that Republicans planned tariff, homestead, and Pacific railroad legislation through the use of bribery and other forms of partisan patronage. If the question of whether Republicans truly dominated the government remained, Jefferson Davis claimed to dispel it with charges that the Republicans planned to finance buildup of the army to defend Fort Sumter.[25]

Despite those Republican actions, a number of Southern leaders hoped that congressional compromise would alleviate the sectional tensions. But the failure of attempts at compromise led Lower South congressmen to assume that Republicans were bent on ending slavery. Even the Unionist Richard K. Call claimed that Northerners had violated public authority by refusing to compromise over the expansion of slavery. He worried that "the consequences of confinement are too terrible to be bourne." For others, the lack of a compromise meant that the North planned to contain slavery within its existing boundaries, which would lead to the "social destruction of society by infusing into it a large free negro population that is most dreaded." Even the Unionist William C. Rives, who insisted that the February 1861 Peace Conference had found a basis for compromise, wondered whether ambitious politicians and antislavery fanatics could support any compromise at all.[26]

24. Pike captured something of how issues raised could be turned into specific accusations. He said, "You must crystallize an abstraction into a fact . . . before you rouse a people to it."

25. Major figures for some time had commented on their opposition to growth of the federal government. See especially comments in the pamphlets of Cobb, Benjamin, Davis, and Clingman in this volume.

26. See Albert D. Kirwin, *John J. Crittenden: The Struggle for the Union* (Lexington: University of Kentucky Press, 1962), 373–90.

The pamphlet writers turned to a discussion of what to do about the crisis over those political events and issues, and their feared results. Inevitably, they questioned the slaveholding states' continued relationship to the federal Union. Benjamin and Pike, as well as a few other students of constitutional law and political theory, argued for the legality of secession. Throughout the antebellum period, those who had calculated the worth of the Union had written about the original constitutional compact and whether the founding fathers had accepted secession as a legitimate right of the states. During the secession winter, pamphlet writers studied those previous efforts with care.[27] But they soon grew bored with arguments about legal rights and turned instead to discussion of how to achieve secession, their reasons for such an act, and the expected results. After all, most of them were political activists rather than deep political thinkers.

Secessionists usually concluded their pamphlets with discussion about the results of their actions. Well aware of what bothered the citizens of Louisiana, for example, Judah Benjamin argued that secession would never result in civil war. Jabez L. M. Curry assured his constituents at the Alabama convention that secession secured "permanent safety in a Southern Confederacy." John H. Reagan asserted that secession was the best route to a self-reliant South, envisioning a future of Southern manufactures, an expanded Gulf Coast land mass, and protection of the economic wealth in slavery. And, as so often in his career, the ambitious Howell Cobb cut through rationalization to say that a separate slaveholding nation was the means to a strong government able to protect Southern society and values from Northern political aggression.[28]

When the Lower South seceded, Upper South secessionists tried to avoid frightening their constituents and friends who continued to hope for compromise on vital issues. Robert Hunter of Virginia suggested that only Northern legal guarantees could derail the secession impetus. In constructing a political scheme to protect the South from the hostile federal government he argued for constitutional reform to include a dual presidency (a notion no doubt taken from the ideas of John C. Calhoun), an end to national party conventions, and a decrease in the frequency of elections. That clever senator left the impression that his diatribe masked a request for the politically impossible. Another Upper South secessionist, North Carolina's Thomas Clingman, simply accepted Lower South action as the

27. Still the most comprehensive study of the right to secede is Jesse T. Carpenter, *The South as a Conscious Minority* (New York: New York University Press, 1930).
28. See the pamphlets of Curry, Reagan, and Cobb.

best means to create a political state able to defend slavery. He admitted that North Carolinians continued to divide over the best course of action but wondered whether the country had already become two nations.[29]

Precipitate actions of the Lower South forced Upper South Unionist pamphlet writers to discuss reasons for support of the Union. Some accused the Lower South of coercion after threats had been made to refuse to buy slaves from the Upper South. For a number of pamphleteers, secession was undesirable because their trade ties with the Union remained strong. Others attacked Lower South leadership for imposing secession on the people. In a long, rambling, and insulting response to those who had attacked him, Andrew Johnson claimed that defense of the laws of the land forced him to support the Union. He insisted that Northerners obeyed the law and would never threaten slavery. Angrily, he accused Lower South leaders of being immune to "government by the people," and of planning to set up a slaveholder aristocracy. In similar blunt fashion, another leader claimed that South Carolina had trampled the liberty and property of other Southerners. Even after the Civil War had started, Anna Carroll of Maryland continued the Unionist pamphlet attack by blaming Lower South leaders, and South Carolina's in particular, for unleashing a rebellion certain to devastate the Border South.[30]

Unlike the committed Unionists, a number of the Upper and Border South pamphlet writers questioned the Republican government's attitude toward slavery but at the same time resisted the so-called protective wing of the new Confederate States of America. Coerced by both sides, they contemplated the united interests of the Upper South and Border and Western states. Maryland's John Pendleton Kennedy denounced a Lower South that had often threatened the Upper South. He suggested that if the radicalized and hostile federal government refused to support the fugitive slave laws, then the Border states had little choice but to form a separate Confederacy. In hopes of dividing Lower South states and building a large border group, Kennedy claimed that Texas and Louisiana had common economic ties to the Border states. He also addressed the issue of slavery expansion, asking whether western Border states would support the re-

29. See William W. Freehling, "The Editorial Revolution, Virginia, and the Coming of the Civil War," *Civil War History* 16 (1970): 71-72.

30. Comments on Carroll's accusation that John C. Breckinridge was fomenting revolution and rebellion in the Border states may be found in Janet L. Coryell, *Neither Heroine Nor Fool: Anna Ella Carroll of Maryland* (Kent, Ohio: Kent State University Press, 1990), 57.

quest from Maryland and Virginia to spread their slave population west. Even the staunch Unionist Robert J. Breckinridge claimed that Border slave and free states had common economic interests. With his at times impenetrable logic, Breckinridge described an immense united coalition of the central states strong enough to fend off the hostile actions of both the radical Northeast and the revolutionary Southeast. Besides, the preacher remarked, if slavery were to survive in the Border free states, those states simply could not remain dependent on the Republican Party.[31]

Clearly, the debates between Unionists and secessionists had aroused such near-pathological fears for the future of slavery that many leaders had been willing to risk rebellion, and even civil war. Most of the opponents of secession had discussed their grievances with both the "cotton" South and Northern radicals and concluded that slavery could remain safe within the Union. But what slavery meant to all of them seemed at times lost in the sheer political rhetoric that those events had generated. Analysis of those hurried, discursive, divisive, and blatantly political printed sources reveals the central importance of slavery in the life and labor of the antebellum South.

As might be expected from a group of political, religious, and cultural speakers and writers conscious of the legality of their actions, the laws of society greatly concerned them. Quite defensive about their support for the rule of law, they made much of supposed Northern violations of it. Those who wrote in favor of rebellion justified it, not as lawlessness, but as an act of self-protection. Rebellion was required, they claimed, because their opponents refused to obey the Constitutional right of peaceful separation due to irreconcilable differences. The secessionist Richard H. Smith, in his pamphlet on the Confederate States Constitution written to satisfy the Upper South of the Lower South's veneration of the law, waxed eloquent on its similarities to the federal Constitution. But the Unionist William C. Rives accused the "cotton" South of anarchy and reminded them that the French Revolution and Mexican independence had resulted in total disregard of the law and eventual destruction of sacred institutions.[32]

31. A view of the Border state Confederacy idea is in Daniel W. Crofts, *Reluctant Confederates: Upper South Unionists in the Secession Crisis* (Chapel Hill: University of North Carolina Press, 1989), but this issue requires much more study.

32. Anne Norton, *Alternative Americas: A Reading of Antebellum Political Culture* (Chicago: University of Chicago Press, 1986), 240–43; James C. Britton, "The Decline and Fall of Nations in Antebellum Southern Thought: A Study of South-

Reverence for the law also was reflected in the pride pamphlet writers expressed in the role the South played in the nation's past. Southerners often cited the ideas of the founding fathers, especially those expressed by the individuals who had represented the slaveholding states, to address their present differences with the North. The pamphlet writers also bragged about Southern deeds and accomplishments, such as personal and financial sacrifices made during the War of 1812 and the Mexican War. But the past also hid, they said, ominous treacheries made against the slave states as well as the reasons for their need to defend themselves against contemporary Northern aggression. Their central focus, as might be expected, was whether the authors of the Constitution had condoned secession. More pointed, however, were the images they conjured of revolutions that had overturned past societies. Thoughts of the French Revolution, Santo Domingo, and others chilled the bones of many who desired rebellion. Many students of earlier revolutions wondered just who might come out on top in the perilous times of 1860–61.[33]

The pamphlet writers' views of history also revealed their enormously personal feelings and sensitivity about honor. Howell Cobb, for example, complained that remarks repudiating the South's equality in the Union had humiliated its people. And the usually calm Judah P. Benjamin recounted insult after insult, reciting "a catalogue of wrongs and outrages" committed by Northern sympathizers. Jefferson Davis insisted that without equality "we are degraded." Even the scholarly Curry believed the North had dishonored the South. Unionists were similarly indignant. For example, Andrew Johnson identified Southern leaders who had attacked his knowledge of history and his educational attainments, and he claimed they had insulted his integrity.[34] Clearly, all of these pamphlet writers had

---

ern Historical Consciousness, 1846–1861" (Ph.D. diss., University of North Carolina, 1988).

33. Mark Tushnet, *American Law of Slavery* (Princeton, N.J.: Princeton University Press, 1981). For further study of the worries about change see Eugene D. Genovese, *The Slaveholder's Dilemma: Freedom and Progress in Southern Conservative Thought, 1820–1860* (Columbia: University of South Carolina Press, 1992), chap. 3; and Jon L. Wakelyn, "The Changing Loyalties of James Henry Hammond," *South Carolina Historical Magazine* (1974): 1–16.

34. The most thorough study of the code of honor is Bertram Wyatt-Brown, *Southern Honor* (New York: Oxford University Press, 1984); but see also Norton, *Alternative Americas*, 270–74.

personalized their grievances and had revealed a keen sensitivity to slights of all sorts.

Personal sensitivity also related to the authors' views of their political system. The issue regarding minority rights in a democratic republic where the majority ruled created much debate. Some secessionists were concerned with the dangers of democratic rule, describing in their pamphlets a North filled with corrupt voting practices and poor quality of leadership. Others insisted that the Republican Party defended majority rights at the expense of regional rights. Still others minced few words rejecting government based on majority rule. Unionists such as Andrew Johnson countered by accusing secessionists of subverting democracy to protect elite control of the Lower South. But Jefferson Davis equated democracy with the rights of a minority to independence, and he worried whether Northern population superiority degraded the equality of white Southerners. None of the secessionists rejected regional majority rule, and all defended the equality of whites, especially, some said, in a slave society, where white rights of equality had to be protected at all costs.[35]

Values including the rule of law, the sanctity of the past, an exaggerated sense of honor, and white equality were distinctly related to slave culture.[36] For example, Jabez L. M. Curry predicted that freed slaves would violate Southern women and murder helpless children, acts that would dishonor Southern civilization and emasculate the menfolk. Howell Cobb's writings echoed this fear when he described the inability of men to protect their families. John Reagan invoked the specter of Santo Domingo, stating shrilly that anarchy and the extinction of the white race was sure to follow if ex-slaves held government office. And Albert Pike spoke for many when he declared he would resist to the death treason "against our children." He envisioned the North creating a swarming Negro population in "which the hungry and discontented light the torches of servile insurrection." Robert

35. See George M. Frederickson, *The Black Image in the White Mind: The Debate on Afro-American Character and Destiny* (New York: Harper and Row, 1971), esp. chap. 3. The most recent attempts to develop the idea of a liberal South are James Oakes, *Slavery and Freedom: An Interpretation of the Old South* (New York: Alfred Knopf, 1990), 180–81, and Lacy Ford, *Origins of Southern Radicalism* (New York: Oxford University Press, 1988).

36. Kenneth S. Greenberg, *Masters and Statesmen: The Political Culture of American Slavery* (Baltimore: Johns Hopkins University Press, 1985), esp. chap. 1.

M. T. Hunter described the destruction of a social system "which is the death of a nation or a people."[37]

Pike and others connected fear of slave rebellion to the consequences of losing the right to expand slavery and the expected resultant growth in the density of the slave population. That may explain why John P. Kennedy insisted that a Border Confederacy would allow slavery to expand. Unionist Rives's adamant need to assure Upper South citizens of compromise on the expansion of slavery was also reflective of this fear. Of course, that many believed a separate Southern Confederacy would open the west to slaves or that they could conquer Mexico betrays only political unreality.[38] But what was not lost on any of the pamphlet writers was the near abject fear their audiences had of Northern abated slave insurrection, especially where slaves dwelt in larger proportion to white folks.

If Southern leaders raised fears of Northern-fomented rebellion, at the same time they attempted calm analysis of the economic consequences of secession for their region. All of them accused the North of economic discrimination and believed that the Republican-controlled government would squeeze them even more. They described the potential wealth of a separate society based on slave labor, which James De Bow insisted would also benefit nonslaveowners. John H. Reagan, an ambitious Southwesterner, wrote of a mixed slave and white working-class labor society freed from the Northern financial yoke, able to diversify its economy. Another pamphleteer claimed that a successful slave labor system kept the South free of "a northern labor system which rests on a volcano." Border state Unionists even hoped to diversify their region's slave economy after it separated from the oppressive staple crop culture of the "cotton" South.[39] In

37. See the pamphlets of Curry, Cobb, Pike, and Hunter. For elaboration on fears for the future see Allan Nevins, *Ordeal of the Union*, 8 vols. (New York: Charles Scribner, 1950–64) 2:470; and Randall C. Jimerson, *The Private Civil War: Popular Thought During the Sectional Conflict* (Baton Rouge: Louisiana State University Press, 1988), 10–11.

38. See Peter Wood, *Black Majority* (New York: Oxford University Press, 1974), for early fears of slave density. The pamphleteers used words such as dispersal, density, confined, and safety valve, and they were obsessed with the need to spread out the slave population.

39. De Bow and Reagan wrote about the economic future of slave society, but also see Kennedy and Breckinridge pamphlets on the Upper South's resistance to Lower South economic oppression.

short, many projected great wealth if only they could get out from under the clutches of their enemies.

Those who discussed their fears about a violent end to slavery, the necessity to expand slavery, and their exploited colonial economy all charged the Republican-controlled federal government with causing their grave anxieties. Jefferson Davis wrote that he had grown fearful of the assumed powers of the "general Government." Another writer insisted that the right of a central authority to tax led to the collection of funds that would be used to abuse the slave states. Thomas Clingman attacked the recent growth of central government power and believed that the slave states would fall victim to legislation that an oppressive North planned to pass. To justify Lower South secession, Benjamin Palmer claimed that the newly empowered Republican federal government had become a threat to everything Southerners valued.[40]

Threats to their values had forced Southerners to consider how best to protect their interests. Secessionists maintained that, had they not left the Union, the Northern government was certain to violate the laws of the land and attempt to destroy slavery. All of the secessionist pamphleteers believed that in secession they had found a way out of an insoluble problem. Eventually, four Upper South states joined in the view that the federal government was dangerous to slavery's future. Only the Southern Unionists insisted to the last that Republican power meant no threat to slavery. Some of them, after all, believed that the Lower South was as much a threat to them as were Northern radicals. But all of the slave state pamphleteers, however they disagreed over what to do, claimed that slavery was central to their culture, its past definition and its future life.

40. Most succinct on this point is Richard F. Bensel, *Yankee Leviathan: The Origins of Central State Authority in America* (New York: Cambridge University Press, 1990), 92–93. Fred Hobson, in *Tell About the South* (Baton Rouge: Louisiana State University Press, 1983), 27, adds, "Their purpose was . . . to persuade, to move to action."

PART I. *Prelude to Secession*

The Quintessence of Long Speeches
Arranged as A Political Catechism . . .

(Charleston: A. E. Miller, 1830)

*Maria Henrietta Pinckney (c. 1782–1836), daughter of Charles Cotesworth Pinck-
ney, was born near Charleston, South Carolina. She lost her mother at an early
age, was educated at home under the tutelage of her famous grandmother, Eliza
Lucas Pinckney, never married, and in later life became the hostess for her father's
household. Pinckney devoted herself to study and writing and is the supposed author of* A Notice of the Pinckneys *(1860), but in an age when women seldom
participated in public life, her enormous knowledge of the law and political theory
must have gone to waste. The pamphlet below, supposedly a catechism for a niece
(none of her siblings had children), written at the height of the Nullification controversy, revealed much about current thought on the rights of state and local
government. In a time when important theorists such as John C. Calhoun and
Robert J. Turnbull wrote at length on Southern rights, Pinckney cut through the
political verbiage to offer a straightforward account of the issues. Published in 1830
and widely circulated, her pamphlet also placed the state's leadership into perspective when she asked rhetorically who would defend the South, and answered,
"the descendants of the patriot band who achieved the Revolution." See George C.
Rogers Jr.,* Charleston in the Age of the Pinckneys *(Norman: University of
Oklahoma Press, 1966), and Frances Leigh Williams,* A Founding Family: The
Pinckneys of South Carolina *(New York: Harcourt Brace, 1978).*

QUESTION – What do we understand by the Federal Union?

ANSWER – It is an agreement between Sovereign States, to forbear exerting their sovereign power over certain defined objects, and to exert
jointly their sovereign power over other specified objects, through the
agency of a General Government. Each State agrees to exert its full sovereign power jointly, for all external purposes; and separately, for all internal
purposes, or State concerns.

Q. Where is this Agreement found?

A. In the bond of Union, or compact between the States, called the Federal Constitution.

Q. What is the nature of the Federal Constitution?

A. It is a compact based upon cautious and jealous specifications. The
distinguished body of men who framed it, guarded and defined every power

that was to be exercised through the agency of the General Government—
and every other power not enumerated in the compact, was to be reserved
and exercised by the States.

Q. Did the States, in forming the Constitution, divest themselves of any
part of their Sovereignty?

A. Of not a particle. The individuality and sovereign personality of the
States was not at all impaired. The States agreed, by the Constitution, that
they would unite in exerting their powers, therein specified and defined,
for the purpose and objects therein designated, and through the agency of
the machinery therein created; but the power exercised by the functionar-
ies of the General Government, is not *inherent* in them, but in the States
whose agents they are. The Constitution is their Power of Attorney, to do
certain acts; and contains, connected with their authority to act, their letter of instruction, as to the manner in which they shall act. They are the
Servants. The power which gives validity to their acts is in their Masters—
the STATES.

Q. Where is the power of Congress during the recess of that body?

A. It possesses no sovereign power—it is but the agent of the Sovereign
States.

Q. Can you illustrate this retention of Sovereignty by the States by any
other example?

A. Suppose an individual, for instance, was to stipulate to transact a
portion of his business by an agent, and the remainder by himself, and to
forbear to exert his moral faculties, and physical energies upon that class of
subjects, which, by his agreement, are to be acted upon by his agent. Has
he by his stipulation lessened, impaired or diminished his moral or physical powers? On the contrary, the validity of the agency depends upon his
retaining those faculties, for if he shall become insane, or die, the agent
cannot act, because the power of his principal has become extinct; so it is
the power, the full subsisting Sovereign Power of the States, which gives
validity to the acts of the General Government. The validity of these acts
does not result from the exercise of a *portion* of the Sovereign Power of
each State.

Q. Why then has it been supposed by some, that when the States formed
the Constitution, they cut the Sovereignty of each State into two parts,
and gave much the larger portion to the General Government?

A. Many erroneous and mischievous opinions proceed from ignorance
of the true meaning of words. Sovereignty, Rebellion, Nullification, &c.
we hear everyday used, without any precise idea being attached to their
signification.

Q. What is the meaning of Sovereignty?

A. It is the will of civil society in the Social Compact, which society is a moral person, whose will, like the will of the human being, cannot be divided without destroying the person; we can conceive the will operating in a thousand various ways, but we cannot conceive its separation into parts; neither can we conceive of the separation of Sovereignty—its unity and life are inseparable.

Q. How do you define Rebellion?

A. It is the resistance of an *inferior* to the lawful authority of a *superior*. A child may rebel against a parent—a slave against his master—citizens against the government, and colonies against the mother-country—but a State cannot rebel; because one Sovereign cannot rebel against another, for all Sovereigns are equal. The Sovereignty of the little State of Delaware is equal to that of New York, or of Russia, though the physical power of those Sovereignties are vastly different. The supposition, therefore, that a Sovereign State can commit Rebellion, Treason, or any crime whatever, is utterly inadmissible in the science of politics. The idea of crime cannot exist where there is no conceivable or possible tribunal, before which the culprit could be arraigned and convicted. Still less can any State be supposed to incur the guilt of rebellion or treason, by resisting an unconstitutional law of the General Government. The General Government is the creature of the States—the offspring of their Sovereign Power. Is the Creator to be governed by the lawless authority of the Creature? We cannot invert the rule of reason and of law upon that subject, and say, that the superior incurs guilt by resisting the inferior, and not the inferior by resisting the superior.

Q. What is the meaning of Nullification?

A. It is the veto of a Sovereign State on an unconstitutional law of Congress.

Q. Are not unconstitutional laws, of course, null and void?

A. Undoubtedly; and an act of Usurpation is not obligatory; it is not law, and resistance is justifiable. In virtue of her Sovereignty, the State is the judge of her own rights, and bound as Sovereign to protect her citizens, which she does by nullifying[1] the obnoxious law, and releasing them from any obligation to obey it.

Q. Has not this right of the State been denied?

---

1. Pinckney often defined her own terms for her own purposes. Most of them are self-explanatory in the text and have therefore been left out of the pamphlet. However, her comment on "nullifying" is important: "It is the right of individuality and sovereign personality of the State which confers the right of Nullification."

A. Only by those who are enemies of State Rights, whose subterfuge is, that they can find Nullification no where in the Constitution. Suppose a State was to make a treaty with a foreign government, to coin money, to grant letters of marque, or assume any power that she had by the compact delegated to the General Government. When Congress should nullify the assumption, would the State have any right to complain that she could not find Nullification in the Constitution. If the implied right is reciprocal, the State possesses the double right to Nullify, for all rights are reserved to her, that are not specified in the Constitution.

Q. Is there no other check upon the General Government, than the one just mentioned of Nullification?

A. The oath, the several legislative, executive and judicial officers of the several States take to support the Federal Constitution, ought to be as effectual security against the usurpation of the General Government, as it is against the encroachments of the State Governments. For the increase of the powers by usurpation, is as clearly a violation of the Federal Constitution, as a diminution of these powers by private encroachments; and that oath obliges the officers of the several States as vigorously to oppose the one as the other.

Q. Could then any collision arise between the States and the Federal Government, were each confined to its proper sphere?

A. The Constitution has left them sufficient space to move harmoniously together; but it is the General Government that is continually wandering out of the sphere of its legitimacy, and usurping powers, that the combined wisdom of the States imagined, they had carefully guarded from all encroachments.

Q. Have the States ever resumed any of the powers they have delegated to the General Government?

A. Never, in a single instance, have they violated, or attempted to violate the Constitution. The enemies of State Rights pretend, that had the States the right to judge of an unconstitutional law of Congress (in other words, of an infringement on their Sovereignty) they would transcend their appropriate sphere, and usurp the powers assigned to the General Government. On the contrary, it is not the interest of the States to resume the powers they have delegated. The same motives which led to the formation of the Union, a conviction of its utility, are as strong now that its beneficial effects have been experienced, as when they were only anticipated. They have evinced from the period of its formation, no sentiment so strong, as an ardent and devoted attachment to the Union. In Union, they take their high station among the nations of the earth; and in Union, the Star Spangled Banner waves over every sea. But there is a principle we should never forget, that the greatest good when perverted becomes the greatest evil. The Union as it was formed—an Union of Free, Sovereign and Independent States—an Union, affording equal protection and mutual benefit to all, will be considered the greatest political good; but as highly as it ought to be valued, it is not the greatest possible good. There is one still better—still more precious—one which is prized infinitely higher—it is LIBERTY—that LIBERTY for which our Fathers toiled and bled. The usurpations and tyranny of Great Britain were not resisted, that the COLONIES might be UNITED, but that the COLONIES might be free, and for the PEOPLE to be FREE, the STATES must be FREE. Whenever the States cease to maintain their Sovereignty unimpaired, and become vassals of the General Government, the duration of the Union will then, indeed, be problematical. It is, therefore, on the friends of the State Rights—on the supporters of State Rights—on those who cling to State Rights, as to the palladium of their liberties, that we must rely for the maintenance and perpetuity of the Union, and not on the enemies of State Rights.[2] The weak—the timid— the apathetic, and the ambitious, who raise the cry of disunion to palsy the unity of action, that would emancipate us from the chains of usurpation— these are the real disunionists, and to these and these only, will be attributed, the evils arising from the dissolution of the Union.

Q. What is the new version of the Constitution by Messrs. Webster & Co.?

A. They have discovered that the Constitution was not formed by the States in their Sovereign capacity—that it is not a compact between the States—but that it is a Government formed by the people, *en masse*, that is, by the people collected into one nation—that this nation brought the Government into existance—established it, and hath hitherto supported it for the very purpose, among others, of imposing certain salutary restraints

2. Pinckney comments: "State rights,—There is a test by which the real State Right Party may at once be distinguished from the counterfeit, who assume their name to conquer under false colours. The real State Right Party hold as their Cardinal Doctrine that, as guardian of its reserved rights, each State is the judge for itself, of an infringement of them; that there is, under the Union, as peaceable mode of redress, when the Constitution has been violated, and that every State is bound by a political necessity to maintain its Sovereignty unimpaired, as essential to the liberty of the people, and preservation of the Union."

on State Sovereignties. That in forming this National Government, the people conferred upon the Supreme Court, the power of imposing these certain salutary restraints upon the Sovereignty of the States.

Q. How did they contrive to convert the people of thirteen distinct States into one people?

A. A short analysis of the process by which a State is formed, will demonstrate the impossibility. The discussion of the elements of Government is dull, as is all abstract discussion. But if we undertake to talk politics, we must undertake to know about what we talk, and we cannot understand the nature of our Government, without referring to first principles.

Q. By what process are States formed?

A. There are but two conditions of mankind—the one national, and the other artificial. In a state of nature, there is no government. The laws of nature are the only rules of human conduct, and each individual is his own expounder of those laws. He is the arbiter of his own rights, and the avenger of his own wrongs. There is no power (that is, no moral power) in one man to direct, control, or govern another; all are equally free. The evils inseparable from this condition, induce those who are suffering from it to escape to the artificial state. The transition from a state of nature to that of civil society, is effected by an agreement among all who compose the society, that each and his concerns, shall be directed by the understanding, and protected by the power of all. The agreement is reciprocal. The right which each man possessed, in a state of nature, to direct himself, is voluntarily surrendered by him to the society, and he agrees, that he and his concerns shall henceforth be subject to the will of the society. This contract is either expressed or understood. The power to govern can be obtained upon no other supposition. It is denominated the social compact. It is the charter by which it acquires personality and unity; by which the action of all the people, is considered as the action of a moral agent, of a single person. This moral agent is, in reference to its own condition, called a state, probably, from the fixed and stable condition of the people, compared with their unstable and fluctuating condition in a state of nature. The people compressed or compacted by the social compact into the unit, called a State, remains unchanged under all the changes of its Government, which accident may produce, or war or convulsion may inflict. If a Republic becomes a Monarchy, or a Monarchy a Republic, or if compacts are formed with other States, these are but changes of Government, the Civil Society or State remains unchanged, and is Sovereign, while ever it manages its own affairs by its own will. It is upon this principle that States are not absolved from their debts by revolution, The State and not the Government is the contracting party, and nothing but the dissolution of the social compact and consequent extinction of the State, can absolve it from its payment. Much confusion has arisen from the indiscriminate use of the word State. State means the people in their political capacity, and never their government. By this reference to first principles, we find from the existing state of things—as there were thirteen distinct States at the time the Constitution was formed—that it must of necessity have been formed by the States, not by the people consolidated into one nation, for in no other way could they have been collected into one, but by first absolving themselves from their allegiance to their respective States, and dissolving the compacts by which they were formed into States. Civil Societies have been destroyed by earthquakes, by deluge, and by the exterminating ravages of war; they have often been subdued into vassalage or reduced by usurpation to the condition of provinces, but we have no account in history of a people voluntarily dissolving the social compact. Messrs. Webster & Co's discovery, therefore, is a proof that there is no absurdity too great for those who are determined to accomplish their views on particular subjects.

Q. Does not the Supreme Court also contend that the Constitution was formed by the people, collectively?

A. The Supreme Court is the creature of the General Government, and has with a constancy and silence, like the approaches of death, adhered to a construction that has increased its own power—enlarged that of the General Government, and thrown chains over State Rights—chains never dreamed of at the formation of the Constitution.

Q. Upon what does the Supreme Court and Messrs. Webster & Co. found their discovery?

A. Upon the preamble to the Constitution—it is in these words: "We the people of the United States, to form a more perfect Union," &c. To the people of common understanding, black actually means black, and white really white; but to Messrs. Webster & Co. it means just the reverse, "We the people of the United States" means according to them—"We the people *not* of the United States, but the people collectively."

Q. When the States formed the Constitution, under which kind of government were they?

A. They were united by the Confederation. To form a more perfect Union of the States already united, to consolidate their Union, was the object of the present Constitution, and not to unite the people, for it was impossible to unite them more perfectly by a Constitution than they were already united by the social compact.

Q. What is the nature of the Supreme Court, that according to Messrs.

Webster & Co. has the power of imposing salutary restraints upon State Sovereignty?

A. The epithet of supreme which gives importance to the Court and imposes on the ignorant, is entirely relative, and imports only that appellative jurisdiction which it may exercise over the subordinate Courts of the *General Government*. The appellative Court, or Court of Appeals of every State, is just as supreme for the same reason — it also exercises jurisdiction over the inferior Courts. It is not called supreme, in reference to the other departments of the Government, nor has it any supremacy in reference to the States. The power accorded it is *purely judicial*. It is the umpire in all cases of law and equity arising under the Constitution. But questions of sovereignty, policy, or expediency, are unsusceptible of its judicial cognizance and decision. The power to declare a law of Congress, or any of the States, unconstitutional, was never intended to be conferred on the Supreme Court as a *direct* power. The exercise of the power is merely *incidental* in exercising the judicial power. The Constitutionality of a law may be *incidentally* decided, in deciding the law and justice of a case. But the decision must be given in the exercise of merely judicial, and not of political power. Can it be believed that the great men who framed the Constitution, and guarded each specification with such zealous care, ever intended to subject the whole to the control of a judicial Oligarchy? The power asserted for the Supreme Court, is superior to that of imperial Rome in her proudest days. The conquests of Rome were achieved at an incalculable expense of blood and treasure. But the Supreme Court may vassal twenty-four Sovereign States, without expending one cent or shedding one drop of blood.

If the States were but true to themselves, and faithful in the discharge of their high duties, they would move on in the majesty of their sovereign power, and maintain with a steady and equal hand both their Governments within its appropriate sphere, and not permit the mere modicum of judicial power which they have granted to the Supreme Court, to control them in the exercise of their sovereign power.

Q. Why have the States allowed the Constitution, the sacred legacy of the combined wisdom of their fathers, to be violated by sacrilegious hands?

A. Because that self interest is the governing principle of three-fourths of mankind. The North, East, and West acquiesced in the usurpation of the General Government, because it was for their exclusive benefit, while the South was passive through apathy and sleep. The North and East bribed the West by internal improvement, and by donations of the public lands — and the West in her turn, bribed the North and East with the Tariff. Internal improvements and a Tariff of protection, are twin born abominations unknown to the Constitution. The South, whose vital interests and almost her existence depended on the inviolability of the Constitution, scarcely awakened from her dream of sovereignty, finds herself the vassal province of a Consolidated Central Government, without limitation to its power, but the will of the majority to legislate for the general welfare—the very government by usurpation, that the Supreme Court and Messrs. Webster & Co. discovered was established by the people. The usurped power is a virtual abrogation of the Constitution, and consequently leave the minority to ruin and degradation. This minority is the South.

Q. What is the remedy for these evils, according to the submission men, [or Tories of the Revolution?]

A. To shut our eyes—hold our tongues, and fold our arms.

Q. What is the greatest anomaly at present in the Union?

A. It is, that the South, whose *beau ideal* was LIBERTY, who sacrificed to it as to the God of their idolatry, is now in vassalage to the North, East and West.

Q. To what may the patriotism of many here be likened?

A. To the philanthropists, whose charity is too exalted to relieve the misery at their own door, but are willing to bestow it on three-quarters of the globe.

Q. What is the feeling that Carolina's real sons cherish for her at this moment?

A. That feeling so touchingly and beautifully expressed by the Beaufort Orator on the last anniversary of independence. "If, in celebrations like this, the name of Carolina was unmentioned by her Orators, the omission was altogether unmarked—why was it when now you can think only of her? It was, because she had not yet been depressed into notorious inequality from the level of the majority of her Sister States. She was not yet in full possession of that deepest and most touching attractiveness, with which misfortune and the world's persecution never fail to invest a beloved object in the contemplation of the generous and brave; you had not yet felt in the cold and cutting blast of federal unkindness the necessity of cherishing and warming her in your hearts. She had been prosperous and affluent, and you but rejoiced that she was your State—she had been honoured—and you were but proud of her, as your section of the Union; but when she was injured and insulted, we felt that she was our country! And when she was most insolently trampled, we clung to her most fondly, and when they called her weakest, our hearts beat strongest in her cause." [3]

3. Possibly this is reference to a speech of Robert Y. Hayne, who was brought

Q. What is the attitude Carolina should assume at the present crisis?

A. She must at once appeal to her sovereignty, and decide whether she shall herself exert the protecting power of Nullification through the organs of her Legislature, or assuming her highest attitude of sovereignty, through that of a Convention.

Q. What will be the result of this resistance on the part of the State to the obnoxious usurpation?

A. The first result will be, the preservation of her sovereignty—the next result, the General Government, no longer relying on the supineness of the State, will be driven back to the sphere of its legitimacy.

Q. But if one of these results should not follow, must the state forbear to resist the aggression upon her rights?

A. No—decidedly no. She must maintain her sovereignty at every hazard, and every means within her power. She is good for nothing—worse than good for nothing—without it.

Q. Will this not lead to civil war—to war between the State, and the General Government?

A. No: The General Government would not put itself so completely in the wrong, as to consecrate its Usurpation by the blood of those it shall have attempted to oppress. If the State is led by apprehensions of this kind to submit to oppression, there is then an end of shaking off her fetters. Fear is a bad counsellor of even an individual, it should never be consulted by a Sovereign State. The strength and powers of Usurpation consist wholly in the fear of resisting it. Let the State only will to be free, and the General Government must recede from its pretensions.

Q. But if the General Government does not recede?

A. Then let the State send a solemn embassy to the bar of Congress, and demand as a Sovereign State, one of the parties to the compact, a redress of her grievances, or an appeal to the ultimate arbiter, provided by the fifth article in the Constitution. Three-fourths of the States compose this august tribunal. The State does not compromise her dignity, by referring to them questions of Sovereignty being themselves Sovereign, but she cannot without violating every principle of self-respect, submit a question in relation to her sovereignty to one of her subalterns, the Supreme Court. It is in the power of this tribunal to define anew the relations between the State and the General Government; if it does not concur in admitting the contested power or shall not pronounce that it already exists, the General

---

up in Beaufort. See William W. Freehling, *Prelude to Civil War* (New York: Harper and Row, 1967), 103.

Government will at once be constrained to abandon the exercise of it, for no new power could have been granted without the concurrence of this tribunal.

Q. But if three-fourths of the States, the ultimate arbiter, decide the question against the State, whose vital interest is at stake, does acquiescence become a duty?

A. The State must then calculate the value of the Union; she has always the right of secession, but we will not, even in idea, "fathom the abyss, until we have descended the precipice of disunion."

Q. On whom must Carolina depend in her hour of peril?

A. On the descendants of the patriot band who achieved the Revolution. On the descendants of those brave and generous foreigners who united with us in that arduous and glorious struggle. On the proprietors of the soil—and on those whose motto is "MILLIONS FOR DEFENCE, NOT A CENT FOR TRIBUTE."

WILLIAM HENRY TRESCOT

The Position and Course of the South

(Charleston: Walker and James, 1850)

William Henry Trescot (1822–98) was born in Charleston, South Carolina, at-
tended local private schools, and graduated in 1842 from the College of Charles-
ton. He read law and was admitted to the bar in 1843, but rather than practicing
law, he turned to writing history and to managing a family plantation. He wrote
important historical studies in diplomacy, including The Diplomacy of the
American Revolution *(1852) and* Diplomatic History of the Administration
of Washington and Adams *(1857). Trescot served as secretary of the legation*
in London and in 1860 became assistant secretary of state, a post from which he
resigned in December of that year. During the Civil War he was a member of
the South Carolina state legislature and joined the staff of Governor Andrew G.
McGrath. An ardent secessionist, Trescot wrote a number of pamphlets in support
of Southern rights. His most famous were An Oration Delivered Before the
South-Carolina Historical Society *(1859), in which he claimed that slavery*
had created a society of equals "by elevating all citizens of the State to the condition
of a privileged class" (p. 21), and the pamphlet reproduced below. This pamphlet,
which was published in 1850, represents well South Carolina's and Southernwide
radical views about the Compromise of 1850 and the necessity for a new generation
of Southern leaders to consider a destiny for the South separate from the rest of
the nation. For further study see David Moltke-Hansen, "The Contexts and Con-
tents of William Henry Trescot's Orations," Proceedings of the South Carolina Historical Association *50 (1981): 120–32, and Robert Nicholas Olsberg,*
"A Government of Class and Race: William Henry Trescot and the South Caro-
lina Chivalry, 1860–1865" (Ph.D. diss., University of South Carolina, 1972). The
Library of Congress has a collection of Trescot's letters.

If history teaches any one lesson more emphatically than another,
it is, that political institutions are never destroyed by influences foreign to
themselves. Wherever, therefore in the history of government, there have
been two contending classes, the success of the one has been achieved by
the inconsistency of the other. The reformation was begun by a Catholic
Priest. The feudal system was destroyed by absolute monarchs. The revolution of 1688 was the work of the whig aristocracy, as was the reform bill
of a later period—and the French revolution, so often misquoted, was the
joint labour of infidel Priests and democrat nobles.

And the warning which points this universal lesson, assumes a special significance at times like the present, when the marked characteristic of political life is the violent and uncompromising antagonism of great interests. Look to what quarter you may of the civilized world, and everywhere, government which should be almost judicial in its decision upon the complicated claims of national interests, has become simply the executive expression of a triumphant class. And every where great and contending interests struggle for power, not as a trust, but as a monopoly. In governments, the most consolidated populations the most homogeneous, this truth is illustrating itself with destructive energy. What, for example, is now the great political difficulty in England, but that there two classes, two great interests are contending for legislative power—the landholder and the manufacturer. The one reasons thus: The feudal system carved England into great estates—to the crown—to the church—to the nobles each its share. The fundamental relation from the king to the crown, was that of landlord and tenant—of owner and occupier. The revenues of the crown came from the land and the landholders represented the productive power of the nation. From this system proceded the whole past history of England. Thence sprung that magnificent Common Law, broad and sure in its foundations as the soil, and as varied and prolific in its rich results— thence rose that life of exquisite civilization, the product of past energy and present cultivation, and thence only can come the power to preserve whence came the vigour to create. If England is to be the free monarchy of its past history, it must be the England of landholders. And the logical consequences are limited representation, and the corn laws. The other reasons thus: England has falsified the conditions of feudal life—the basis of her empire is no longer English soil—her colonial territories represent no connection of landlord and tenant—the crown no longer draws its revenue from royal forests—the sails of Liverpool, and the looms of Manchester, symbolize the relation of capital and labour. From this new relation must England's future history flow; thence must spring the controlling power of foreign markets; the mighty trade of England's wider empire; and thence only can come the vigour to create, whence comes the power to conceive. If England is to be an empire of the future, she must be the England of manufacturers. And the logical consequences are the reform bill and the repeal of the corn laws. But fatal as is such a struggle to the efficiency and character of national action, even in its mildest shape, there are conditions of political society in which the conflict of vast and sectional interests, concentrates into the portentous issue of a mortal strife. The confederacy of the United States has reached this period in its history. The legislation of the present Congress has effected a political revolution. It has destroyed old relations and rejected established compromises. Basing its action upon a principle recognized only by a portion of its constituency; the government, in becoming the exponent of one class, becomes necessarily also the enemy of the other. And having, in violation of traditional faith and constitutional securities, achieved its purpose, it foists an unknown language into its commentary upon the constitution, and forces upon half the commonwealth the bitter alternative of becoming subject or rebels. The California bill and its kindred measures have been passed; the policy of the federal government firmly and distinctly declared, and the institution of slavery so far as by any possibility of constitutional construction it can be compassed, is outlawed. Under these circumstances, whether the South recognizes or rejects recent Congressional enactments, we are called on to review our position. For if we remain in the Union, we are bound by new conditions; stand in a very altered attitude, and should, at our earliest opportunity, learn to know our place. The object of these pages is, therefore, simply to ascertain what is the position of the South, and what course of action it behoves us to follow in the discharge of our duties as a slaveholding people.

The vindication of slavery is no part of our purpose. We know that Providence has placed us in the midst of an institution which we cannot, as we value national existence, destroy. It has solved for us in the wisest manner, that most dangerous of social questions, the relation of labour to capital, by making that relation a moral one. It has developed the physical wealth of the country in its highest, that is, its agricultural branch, in unprecedented proportion. It has created a civilization combining in admirable measure energy and refinement. It informs all our habits of thought, lies at the basis of our political faith and of our social existence. In a word, for all that we are, we believe ourselves, under God, indebted to the institution of slavery—for a national existence, a well ordered liberty, a prosperous agriculture, an exulting commerce, a free people, and a firm government. And where God has placed us, there, without argument, are we resolved to remain, between the graves of our fathers and the homes of our children. The only questions open now for our discussion are, what are the dangers we have to meet, and what are our means of meeting them. As historical truths, affording prompt answers to these questions, we submit to the attention of every Southern man who desires to do his duty at this perilous crisis, the following propositions:

1. That all legitimate government is but the larger development of the same principles which underlie the social institutions of a nation, and that therefore the test of national health is a perfect sympathy between national government and popular institutions.

2. That the institutions of the slaveholding States are peculiar in their nature, differing in most essential features of political character from the political system of the rest of the country.

3. That this difference has excited a sectional jealousy, which, in the political history of the country has deepened into sectional hostility, and that by recent legislation, the Federal Government has declared itself the ally of the North and North-west against the institutions of the South.

4. That in such a political crisis the only safety of the South is the establishment of a political centre within itself; in simpler words, the formation of an independent nation.

We shall include the two first propositions under one head, as the one is, in a great measure, but the illustration of the other.

An effort, in a practical political discussion, to resort to first principles, is always difficult, if not dangerous. For scarcely a human action, and none of the great events of history, can be traced to the simple working of a single principle. And, in the varied process of investigation, terms originally clear and definite, assume necessary and sometimes strange modifications, in order to meet the exigencies of a complicated argument. The word government is a fertile illustration of these difficulties of definition. It is applied alike to the absolutism of Russia and to the republicanism of America; although this mutual application to subjects, different not in degree, but in kind, is irreconcilable with truth. As at present used, it must mean one of two very contradictory things; either a power above and beyond the people, shaping their fortunes according to its wisdom—and it is easy to conceive such a power, deriving its origin from peculiar circumstances in national history, and thus possessed of a historical legitimacy, which a conservative philosophy would anxiously respect—or the mere administrative machinery, by which a people regulate the economical necessities of political life, and execute the resolutions of the national will. Administrations like these are widely different, and when they are loosely comprehended under the same name, it can only be, because the latter, in the exercise of necessary power, too often seeks justification in the analogies of a doubtful political generalization. It is not difficult to understand how a power like the first, independent of, and elevated above, local interest, might, with energy and wisdom, guide the course of a nation composed of very dissimilar material. Indeed, to a certain extent the empires of Russia and Austria furnish an illustration. But where the administration is, as in the latter case, the representative of conflicting interests, the decided strength of any one great interest must, of necessity, explode the machine, or re-adjust its arrangements. It is, then, to governments of the latter character, that we more especially refer our remarks. To say of such a government, that it depends for its existence upon its conformity to popular ideas, seems almost a truism. To attempt gravely to prove that a democracy like New-York would never tolerate a House of Lords, or that a commercial people like New-England would never grant peculiar privileges to landholders, would be a waste of words and time. And the general proposition would never be questioned, were there in the country an unity of political opinion, or were the national interests divided into many classes, singly too small for preponderance, and equally scattered over the whole national territory. Unfortunately, however, the most striking feature of our physical history, is the marked development of great geographical sections; and the most important event in our industrial progress, is the creation of vast interest, bounded in their field of action by these ineradicable geographical lines. It is true that science has achieved, over space and time, triumphs almost miraculous, but it has not annihilated them. It is true that the panting of the steam-engine and the tremor of the magnetic wire indicate an unwearied material activity, but still mountain ranges rear their heads in unbroken ruggedness—rivers roll their ceaseless currents, and oceans heave their world of waters, in discharge, now as ever, of God's great commission—to divide the nations. It is almost impossible to conquer nature. A dozen bridges across the Rhine would not identify the Frenchman and the German; a tunnel through the Alps would scarcely reconcile the Italian to the Austrian; and it is idle to suppose that the mere speed and facility of communication between distant geographical sections, will entirely counteract those national peculiarities, which it is an unerring law of Providence that those divisions shall of necessity develope.

"It was not," says a recent traveller, "until I had sailed a few miles from Lutrarki, and observed the greater clearness with which the Parnassian ranges came out, that I realized the fact, that Corinth and Delphi, two cities morally so opposed to each other as Washington and Mecca, were yet physically so close, that the laughter of the midnight revellers might almost have met the hymns of the priests midway on the waters. What again could be more different that the character of Boetia—sacerdotal, traditionary, unchanging—the Hellenic Austria, and that of the inventive and mercurial Attica? And yet, from the same ridge of Parnes, the shepherd descried the capitals of both. How remote from each other, in character, were Sparta—in which the whole life of man was perpetual-military discipline—and Athens, in which every one went on his own business, after his own fashion. Yet the mariner ran across, in perhaps a day's sail, from the one territory to the other, passing on his way communities unlike both."

In examining, then, the conflicting characters of two great sections, it is no unfavourable introduction to such an investigation, to discover that nature herself has drawn deeply the sectional lines. Now, if a map of the settled portion of the North American continent be prepared, indicating only the great mountain ranges and the large rivers, the most superficial review would mark three grand divisions—the north, the south, the west. The north and south this side of the Alleghanies; the west beyond it, having its Pacific border, its bold headlands looking out on Asia; its capacious harbors and its own rivers, riding, running, emptying beyond the mountains, even their sources separated by immense territories from the heights of Atlantic commerce; wealth, unbounded wealth, for its inheritance and independence, the necessary condition of its future life. Upon this side of the mountains, two great sections, divided by the Ohio and the Potomac, from the Mississippi to the Atlantic; the north possessing in the lakes and the St. Lawrence, a channel of commercial communication, reaching from Wisconsin to Maine, and the South enjoying in the Mississippi the same connection from Missouri to Florida. Not only has nature drawn these lines, but history, in the action of its providential instinct, has followed their guidance. In the colonization of this continent, who has not been struck with the marvellous parallel? The antithesis of Plymouth and Jamestown did not end with their settlement. The growth of the two great sections, radiated from different centres, diverged in distant directions, were developed from differing principles, and perfected through dissimilar experiences. For every point of likeness in the history of the two plantations, points of difference might be multiplied, and from the quaint freshness of the old chronicles might be drawn, passage after passage, expressing, in language of the most strongest symbolism, their ancient, continued, and present variance. Nor does the argument stop here. As the country has filled up, internal improvements have spread through the land, in obedience to laws hardly perhaps recognized by those who planned, and have developed, in process of completion, well defined sectional systems.

With these preparations for great national differences, no philosophical inquirer would be surprised to discover a wide distinction of sentiment and institution; and the student of political principles would anticipate the impossibility of the consistent action of a single government. What are the facts?

There is one relation, lying at the basis of all social and political life, the shifting character of which fairly indicates the national progress in wealth and civilization—the relation of labour to capital. In the history of the world, this relation has, so far, always taken one of three shapes—serfdom, slavery, or service that is voluntary labour for wages. In the two first, the relation is a moral one, or labour is a duty; in the latter, the relation is a legal one, or labour is the execution of a contract. But which ever of these shapes it has taken, the history of all that is great in achievement— all that is glorious in art—all that is wise in law, proves that the best interests of humanity require, first, that labour should be subordinate to, and controlled by capital; and second, that the interests of the two should by that very dependence be as closely as possible identified. It may safely be asserted, that wherever the relation has been one of contract, the first condition only has been obtained, and that the interests of labour and capital can never be permanently or properly reconciled, except under the institution of slavery; for it stands to reason, that wherever the political theory of government recognizes the equality of labour and capital, while the great reality of society shows the one in hopeless and heartless dependance on the other, there will exist between the two a constant jealousy and a bitter strife, the weaker demanding its rights with impotent cursing, or enforcing them with revolutionary fierceness. Look for a moment at the condition of the operatives of England and France. In both the population is free, labour and capital are politically equal; while, in fact, capital tyrannizes with selfish power, holding labour to its terrible bond—the obligation a life of barely sustained toil—the penalty death by starvation. There is no moral relation between them, and the working classes who comprehend political theories only in practical results, rebel against the powers that be. In England, the chartist calls for equal representation, denounces the aristocratic institutions within which capital strives to entrench itself, and demands logically enough, we must say, that the nation should abandon the palpable inconsistency of free labour and a privileged class.[1] In France, with still stricter and more unscrupulous logic, the socialist demonstrates that if labour and capital are equal in principle, they should be equal in practice, and that all property is theft. That this should be, reason suggests—that it ever has been, experience confirms. For while history teems with rebellions of free labour against royal power, and feudal prerogative and class privilege—revolutions which have overthrown dynasties and changed constitutions, we challenge a solitary example in the whole scope of the world's record, where slave labour has risen in successful protest against national authority, or even forced from privileged power a single political conces-

1. Reference to the English Chartist Movement of the 1840s for better working conditions and the expansion of suffrage. See Dorothy Thompson, *Chartism* (London: MacMillan, 1971).

sion. The Hebrew commonwealth, in the progress of its Divine mission, spread into the proportion of a magnificent monarchy, and again shrunk into the insignificance of a scattered people, and the foundations of its slave institutions were unshaken. The kingdoms of Greece sprung struggling from their cradles, but in the perpetual strife which strengthened their manhood, the institution of slavery never perplexed their economy, nor escaped their control. The Roman governed the world, and his million of slaves never changed an Emperor, nor lost him a province. In the ancient world, the relation of labour and capital took the shape of slavery, and what disturbance did it work? In the modern world, it has taken the shape of service, and what civil commotion, what parliamentary perplexity has it not wrought? What political question is so terrible to English statesmen as the condition of England question? What combination more fearful for French politicians than the organization of labour? Without dwelling on this truth, which is capable of an infinity of illustration, we have arrived at the first great contradiction between the institutions of the North and the South. At the North, the relation of labour and capital is voluntary service; at the South it is involuntary slavery. At the North, labour and capital are equal; at the South, labour is inferior to capital. At the North, labour and capital strive; the one, to get all it can; the other, to give as little as it may—they are enemies. At the South, labour is dependant on capital, and having ceased to be rivals, they have ceased to be enemies. Can a more violent contrast be imagined. The political majority of the North represents labour—the political majority of the South represents capital— can the latter suffer the power of legislation in the hands of the former? Free labour hates slave labour—capital, at the mercy of labour, is jealous of capital owning labour—where are their points of sympathy?

And it requires but ordinary sagacity to see that this difference of relation between labour and capital, necessitates for the North and South the development of two individual and inconsistent systems both of representation and taxation. If representation be adjusted according to the Northern principle of equality of labour and capital, the foundation of the social and political state of the South—the subordination of labour which is slave to capital, which is master, is at once overturned. If on the other hand, representation be based upon the Southern principle of property, the support of the Northern society, the equal right of every individual constituent of the Commonwealth, is stricken away, and in order to maintain political existence, the North would be forced to the creation of a privileged class from individuals claiming equal rights. And it may be here remarked that, wherever labour and capital have been recognised as theoretically, equal society has been forced in self-preservation, to the creation of artificial privileged classes. Equality of rights and privileges can, in the nature of things, exist only where the participants of political power form a separate class, and the labour of the country is subjected to it. Where this separation of labour and capital is adjusted between people of the same race, there will be more or less of struggle—but where the separation is drawn with the distinctness of colour, the political necessities of this antagonism, assume the character of providential arrangements, and execute themselves in harmony with the highest and purest moral feeling.

That this strife has not yet developed itself in fierce commotion, is owing to circumstances which are fast vanishing; that it must come, the whole history of Northern politics declares, and society is busy in preparing the elements generated between the two extremes. Now these two systems are irreconceivable either in their principles or their practice, reason and experience pronounce that can never be joined together.

In the Constitution of the United States, they have both been comprehended—time has changed a compromise of interests into a conflict of sections, and the submission of one, or the separation of both is the only alternative. And not only does this antagonism between the two systems of labour and capital exist in the two sections, but it is aggravated by the mode in which that labour and capital is employed. The progress of time has materially altered the great national relations which form the staple of the world's political history. Consumer and producer are now the great regulating terms of political results, and, although there never has been an age in which commercial interests have not entered as influencing elements into considerations of national policy, yet never has the civilized world been so dictatorially governed by the power of trade. Facility of transport, and the immense capabilities of manufacturing invention have not merely stimulated traffic to unparalleled activity, but have knit the nations together by a chain work of universal extent, and exquisite sensitiveness—and not only so, but like the nervous system of the human body, this subtle and all pervading conductor ramify as it may, spreads from one great centre—the cotton trade. The power which controls this trade, holds to a very great extent the fortunes of the world in its hand. The London Times for September 7, 1850, speaks thus, in its leader on the Diplomatic necessities of Great Britain: "What the circumstances are which would make it requisite to have an able officer representing England, in a particular country can easily be conceived. A country may have by its position and power, a great influence upon our well being, or it may be intimately connected with us by commercial relations. Two countries in the world peculiarly represent these classes, France and the United States. France has in past times occupied the first place in our regard because we have for ages been at war with her, our nearest and most powerful neighbour on the Continent. American is of far more importance commercially. The commerce of France is of little importance, that with America transcends all others." Now where has nature placed the great controlling power of American commerce? In the South and as an unavoidable inference, does it follow that the industrial economy and the system of foreign relations of the nation, so far as based on commercial principles, should spring from, and be controlled by the cotton growing States. Why is it otherwise, but that in the nation there is another section supported by interests antagonist to these, in other words, a section which is in fact, a foreign power. We have shown that in the vital principle of political organization, the relation of labour and capital, the North and the South are irreconceivably hostile, that their social and political systems cannot co-exist—that the one in the nature of things wages internecine war against the other. Now we need not attempt to prove that cotton can be produced in quantities sufficient for the world's wants, only where labour and capital stand in the relation of master and slave. Experience has decided that question if it has settled no other. What is the result? Why that throwing aside the variance in the systems of representation and taxation above referred to—the North and South are diametrically opposed to each other of those most essential political relations which govern the wealth, the civilization, the national existence of the South. More than this—the vast extent and pre-eminent influence of the cotton trade divide the commercial nations of the world into two classes—those who produce cotton and those who manufacture it. They are, it is true, mutually dependant; but according to that principle of selfishness which God has for wise purposes implanted in every breast, they are each bent on using the other at the lowest remuneration—each wishes to have the best of the bargain, and between foreign nations this is all right; this competition has served, and will serve wise purposes. Now to which class does the northern section of this confederacy belong? What greater sympathy does the North feel for us as a cotton growing section than is felt by England? Does a cotton bale meet any more fraternal regard in the way of prices in New-York than it does in Liverpool? What more sympathy is there between the southern planter and the abolition manufacturer of Lowell, than exists between him and the spinner of Manchester? We speak the same language with both— our historical associations cluster upon English soil with more fervour and frequency than upon the coast of Dutch Manhattan—our transactions with the Englishman count up in larger ciphers? What makes the one less a foreigner than the other, but the assumed right of our northern brother to meddle that he may mar? And we say boldly that it would be as wise, as safe, as honourable, to trust our domestic institutions and our foreign interests to the Parliament of Great Britain as to a Congress with a northern majority. Nay, wiser and safer, for her colonial experience has taught England never again to sacrifice her profits to her philanthropy.

Again. Our foreign relations are every day assuming growing and graver importance. And here the same antagonism of interest developes itself. The two principles of the foreign system of the great Northern section, as expressed by their statesmen and leading journals, being, 1. The extension of their commercial interests in foreign markets, bringing them into active diplomatic rivalry with Great Britain; and, 2. The manifestation of a spirit of propagandist license, inspiring them to intermeddle in the domestic struggles of every foreign nation, where there arises a contest between constituted authority and revolutionary restlessness. The annexation of Canada, which is fast becoming from a remote speculation, a matter of party policy. The hasty welcome to the socialist government of France — a government which signalized its brief history by colonial emancipation and domestic bankruptcy — the demagogue denunciation of the Austrian court — are all significant indications of popular sentiment and national systems. Now look at the position of the South — cultivated by a slave population — supplying the staple of the world's manufacture, and ranged in imposing strength around the Gulf of Mexico, so as to command the trade of the Isthmus connection — what should be the foundation principles of her foreign relations. 1. A close alliance with the few great manufacturing nations, an anxiety to see them creating markets and multiplying their production; and 2. An unchangeable resolution to leave the interior affairs of other nations to their own discussion, and a careful abstinence from all legislative reflection on foreign institutions, which, like our own, may be censured only because they are not comprehended. With these two basis of foreign action, and the command of the Gulf and the cotton trade, the South would be, in the maturity of her strength, the guardian of the world's commerce — the grave and impartial centre of that new balance of power, which, at no distant day, will be adjusted by the experience of the old and the energy of the new world, working together for the best interests of humanity.

It would be easy to illustrate, in a more special manner and in fuller detail, these sectional differences in social systems — in industrial interests — in foreign policy. But such an analysis would run too parallel with party history, which it is our anxious desire to avoid, and our conclusions upon which, we are afraid, would be acceptable to none. But, surely enough has been said to indicate the grounds upon which we may justly, and with no exaggeration, conclude that the Institutions of the two sections are diametrically opposed. If it can be proved that the government is with the Northern section of the Confederacy, the utter want of sympathy between that Government and the South, is, as a consequence, established—the due relation between the two is broken, and we must look for safety at home. What, then, is the position of the Government? Our answer is very brief: The sense of wrong is too strong for the elaboration of syllogisms. There never yet was an honest feeling that did not spring from a correct thought. We feel that we are weak—it cannot take us long to think out the same conclusion. We will avoid metaphysico political discussion on the checks of the Constitution. The experience of the last twenty years, from General Jackson downwards, has proved that the President, as has been admirably said, "is a demagogue by position"—that the House of Representatives represent popular passions and interests—that in the Senate only is to be found the conservative element of government. Now the representative majority is Northern—the Presidential electoral majority is Northern—and since the admission of California, the Senatorial majority is Northern. Can a multiplication table work out results more certain. If the government obeys the popular spirit which creates and sustains it, what must it do but reflect Northern sentiment, sustain Northern interests, impersonate Northern power. For argument sake, we will admit that the admission of California is right—that a savage greediness for gold is the purest of social bonds—that a State is admirably adapted to influence national legislation, where its heads are the shrewdest of speculators and its body the outcasts of every population under heaven. We will admit that Texas ought to pocket, in an extravagance of jockeying triumph, her ten millions, and chuckle at the market price of patriot blood and State pride—she may have more to spare, and she has found a generous customer. We will admit that Virginia and Maryland are but intruders in the District of Columbia, and if not acceptable, should be removed without even notice to quit; they gave the land to their Northern brethren—what more have they to do with it.[2] We will admit, with Mr. Toombs, that the South has nothing at all to complain of, but as we do not know what we may have to censure, we earnestly ask every Southern man to take a list of the States and having separated the two sections, make the simplest of calculations, and then, with neither

2. Clay offered compromise legislation on the territorial question and the tensions over fugitive slaves. See Holman Hamilton, *The Compromise of 1850* (Lexington: University of Kentucky Press, 1964).

the fear nor favour of party before his eyes, answer the question, What is the position of the South? In case—and we may in argument imagine so improbable a thing—in case our rights should be attacked, where is our constitutional protection? The mournful but indignant echo from the past answers—where? If, then, the lessons of experience are worth the reading—if the political events of the last few months are not illusions—if the expression of outraged feeling all through our Southern land, be any thing by the wild ravings of wicked faction—it is time for the South to act firmly, promptly, and for ever. But one safe path is open to her honour, and that is, Secession and the formation of an Independent Confederacy. Another plan has indeed been proposed and sanctioned by great names, but to us it seems either impracticable or identical with the first. It is a readjustment of the constitutional compact, so as to recognize the independence of each section as to its domestic policy. The formation of a Union somewhat analogous to the German confederation, by which a Zollverein should regulate our industrial policy and a Diet control our foreign relations. That this can be obtained from the North without force, we do not believe, and the only circumstances under which such an arrangement could be effected, would be the absolute national independence of the two sections and their willingness to enter into treaty stipulations with each other, as to such interests as might be common between them. So far, then, this scheme implies secession. But we do not honestly think that the elements of our political constitution could be combined after such a fashion, and with this reference we leave the subject. What are the objections to the first course of action? They shall be stated as strongly as we have been able to find them—in the language too of Southern men. At a meeting of the citizens of Bibb county, in Georgia, on Sept. 28, 1850, a report was adopted, which uses the following language:

"The dangers that would attend a dissolution of the Union, we regard as palpable and imminent. In our opinion, it would be followed by the most disastrous consequences.

"1. It will gain for the South no additional guaranties for her cherished institutions. It will not check the spirit of fanaticism at the North, nor secure the extension of slavery into California.

"2. It will result in a civil, perhaps servile war, which would absorb all our resources, force us into a system of direct taxation, and render our property less secure than at present, both in Georgia and in the border States.

"3. It would compel the slaveholders in the border States to push their negroes into the Southern markets, and thus force the planters of Georgia and adjoining States to *pay* Virginia, Kentucky and Maryland for manumitting their slaves.

"4. It would force the more southern States ultimately to *secede again* from the new confederacy, or to fall back upon separate organizations, and thus give to the South a set of petty States, without either power or respectability.

"5. Under such circumstances, the people of the South would have neither men nor money with which to carry slavery into California. They would not be able to retain it at home, much less to force it across to the shores of the Pacific.

"6. All these causes, operating conjointly, would limit the area of slavery to a few of the South Atlantic and Gulf States—where the lands would soon become exhausted—where slave labour would cease to remunerate—where the slaves themselves would be worthless, and the institution become a *tax* upon the people.

"7. The final result of the whole matter would be, that the owners would be compelled to *abolish slavery* in self-defence—because the property itself will become valueless, and they would have no means left to support it!

"Here, then are some of the curses of dissolution; and, in our candid opinion, if the Union is severed, it will not require a quarter of a century to consummate this grand scheme of mischief and ruin."

Our analysis of these objections will divide them into two classes: 1. That a secession of the Southern States cannot be effected without war, civil or servile—perhaps both. 2. That, if effected, it would not answer the purposes of its formation.

The first objection is not a legitimate one. It is simply a selfish unwillingness to suffer, in order to succeed. If the rights in question are worth a struggle, the necessity of the conflict is no argument against the propriety of action. If the duty of the citizen is clear, the perils of the strife become patriotic privileges, and the fact that war is inevitable only proves to what an extent we have endured before we have ventured to resist—only demonstrates the power of that unrighteous authority against which we are forced to arm. We say nothing in mitigation of the unimaginable horrors of civil war—dangers are not disarmed by self-deception, and if these terrors lie direct in our path, look at them full but firmly; but there are more terrible disasters than war, and in the perpetual cry of peace, peace, there is as much selfishness as sense. This world is not one of peace—its wisest and highest teacher brought into its troubled life "not peace but a sword," and nothing of national greatness or individual good has been achieved without sacrifice and sorrow. It is a truth of history, untouched by an exception, that no nation has ever yet matured its political growth without the stern and scarring experience of civil war. The God of this world's history is indeed the God of Hosts, and he who shrinks, in the plain path of duty, from that last appeal to arms, is not more holy than he is wise. But, while prepared for any consequence, where is the probability of civil war resulting from Southern secession? In the first place, what motive would influence the North to an invasive war? If there be any truth in the protests of our Northern brethren—if slavery be a burden to their consciences, why interfere against an Exodus which would carry with it the plague—why not let the South and slavery go together? It can only be because the industrial prosperity of the North is, to a great degree, dependent upon Southern labour and Southern consumption. If this be so—and every financial document proves it— if this be so, the question submitted to Northern statesmen may be stated thus: As a nation, we draw our wealth, in great measure, from the Southern production of cotton and the Southern consumption of our manufactured cotton. Federal legislation enabled us to benefit by that production and to control the remuneration on that consumption. The South has seceded, our relations are broken; in what way can they be restored? Shall we fight? To do so we must make up our minds to stop our manufactories; to give up our supply of cotton; to surrender our Southern market, for a time at least, to English rivals—bear up against the financial embarrassments necessary on such a state of things, and undertake, at the same time, the maintenance of a costly army and navy, and the support of a distant war; for we must act offensively. Will this pay, if it succeeds, and is success certain? The present army and navy would, to a large extent, be unofficered, the whole body of Southern officers having resigned—among them experienced, efficient, able men, fitted to organize Southern forces. Then the war of the revolution and the war of 1812 have proved that Southern armies subsist themselves on their own soil, with half the trouble and expense that foreign forces must employ. The military experience of the country points to the South and emphatically the region of soldiers; and lastly, can such a war be protracted for a period sufficient to affect Southern prosperity or Southern spirit, without the interference of those great foreign powers whose commerce is controlled by the cotton manufacture, and who would be most materially injured by a suspension of American trade? Who can, for a moment, doubt the conclusion at which Northern sagacity would arrive? If the South acts unitedly, the apprehension of civil war is the idlest of fears. As to a servile war, we have scarcely patience to refer to it. We do not believe that any man, born and bred at the South, reared among negroes and familiar with their habits, ever entertained such an idea. We have passed through two wars, and we have yet to read the record of one servile insurrection of any military consequence, and may in all justice decline reply to an argument which cannot base itself on even a respectable probability.

So much for the first class of objections. Now let us look at the second, viz: that Southern secession, if successful, would not effect its purposes. And the first point to be settled is, what are those purposes? Why should we secede? We honestly believe that much of the unwillingness that does undoubtedly exist in some quarters, to concerted Southern action, springs from a misconception on this point. Many think that we are called upon to rebel against practical oppression—to overturn some special congressional enactment—and we are in consequence met by such replies as, "How am I oppressed?["]—you cannot un-State California. If Texas chooses to sell her lands how can we complain?

The true position of the South is this:—From the formation of the government there have existed, in the two great sections of the Union, political systems, opposed in principle. Recent events have developed into excited hostility these contradictions, and just at the time when sectional interests are most antagonistic, the government, by the admission of California, has destroyed the balance of power between the two sections, and placed the South, its interests, and its institutions, in helpless dependence upon Northern majorities. Will not the establishment of a Southern confederacy, with a homogeneous population, and an united government, relieve the South from this false and dangerous situation, enable her to control her own fortunes, and use, to the best advantage, the strength of her natural position.

The prime element of national Southern strength, is commerce; the peculiar character of the Southern staple identifying agriculture and commerce more completely than in any other national experience. It is in relation to commercial questions, that the South would come in contact with foreign powers, and by her industrial policy, that she would influence remote countries. Rivalry, on these points, with foreign nations, exists only in the northern section of the republic. The formation of an independent Southern confederacy, would give to the South the control of its industrial policy and its commercial connection; thus arming it, at the very outset of its national career, with diplomatic power, and at the same time, from the character of those interests propitiating all foreign jealousy, and inviting the cordial alliance of European powers. The advantages of such a position are incalculable, and the most selfish interests of the foreign world would be prompted to a speedy recognition of our national independence.

William Henry Trescot   [29

When we consider too, that completion of the Isthmus connection promises to make the Gulf of Mexico the theatre of a mightier commerce than that which, in the days of ancient Rome, civilized the classic shores of the Mediterranean, and gave the provincial city of Alexandria a place among the capitals of history, or that which illuminated with its treasure the pages of Venetian and Genoan story, we must acknowledge that the formation of a Southern confederacy, at least so far as regards its foreign relations, bids fair to place the South, an equal among the nations of the earth.

If then secession fails in its purpose, it can only be in respect to its domestic policy. What do we expect in this regard? That a homogeneous people, governed by the same sentiment and acting upon the same interests, will give to their government unity of character, and thus that parties will be formed by a fair difference of opinion on national measures, and not upon theoretical differences as to the nature of the government itself. That the government placed in immediate and active sympathy with popular institutions, will devote itself to the practical perfection of those institutions, and will cut off all extraneous agitation. Of course we can no more present the expression of northern sentiment at the North, than we can check the eloquence of Exeter Hall in London, but then the agitation at the North will affect us only in the same degree. As to the expression of opinion, the world may think as it pleases, and say what it thinks. We do not complain of Northern sentiment, except where having achieved political representation, it undertakes to act in Congress. Through the national councils only does it reach us, and there only do we protest against it. England and Massachusetts—Lord Palmerston and Gov. Briggs—both think the law of South-Carolina, imprisoning colored seamen, a very unfeeling measure. They are both opposed to it in sentiment. But when the practical action of that State brought the question before the British Parliament, Lord Palmerston very wisely said that nothing could be done, foreign powers made their own police law. When the same question came before the Massachusetts Legislature, Gov. Briggs appealed to the constitution, and sent an ambassador to dispute our rights on our own soil. To this extent, then, at least, an independent government could and would check agitation; would suppress that of which only we complain, *legislative agitation*. But, says the report above quoted, all this may be true as to the body of the confederacy, but you must sacrifice the border States; and of course as this abandonment of the border States will only make new states on the narrowed border, there will follow another series of sacrifices, and the great Southern confederacy will be thus border on to destruction. This may be witty, it is scarcely wise. We have been so long accustomed to have the ocean on one side, and a blank wildness on the other, that the sense of neighborhood with certain politicians, is a fearful experience. They cannot realize that two nations can be at peace in each other's presence. With them, 'tis distance that gives safety to the view. Now, in the first place, as agitation would be expected on these borders, it would be guarded against, and if the price of liberty is eternal vigilance, we would not complain of paying the same price for slavery. But, in the next place, agitation would be very cautious how it crossed the line, when on the other side it had no common constitution to appeal to, and realized the risk of trial by the laws of the offending party. Even fanaticism is not reckless of its own safety. Again, there are two sides to this same border difficulty. If Virginia and Maryland and Kentucky are border states, so are Ohio and Pennsylvania. Now, if the argument be that these first States will be more exposed to the spoliation of their property, Ohio and Pennsylvania would allow their borders to be infested by a set of miscreants, whose action would be to draw on these States the evils of a perpetual border warfare. Indeed, if selfishness has not lost its cunning, the border States of a Northern confederacy would be the safest neighbours for their border brethren of the South. The arguments of the report as to the deterioration of the value of slaves, is of course based upon the successful result of this agitation. If, therefore, there be any justice in our argument, that not only will the South have the power, but that it will be the direct interest of the Northern border States, to suppress agitation, the whole force of the report on this head is broken. The weakness of this position could be demonstrated from other points of view, but they would not come within the scope of the present argument. Enough of the report and its resolutions.

One more objection, and we have done. There are many men who have grown old in the Union, who feel an honest and pardonable regret at the thought of its dissolution. The enthusiasm of their boyhood, the hopes of their manhood, the calm honours of their age belong to the completed circle of the past. They have felt themselves parties to the great experiment of political self-government, they have prided themselves on the successful demonstration of that great problem, and they feel that the dissolution of the Union, proclaims a mortifying failure. But it is not so. The vital principle of political liberty is representative government, and when federal arrangements are discarded, that lives in original vigor—it has become the characteristic of our race, to spread with our emigrant millions over continents, and into the hidden isles of distant seas. Who does not consider the greatest triumph of the British constitution, the facility with which it adapted itself to the altered condition of its colonies—the vigour with which under slight modifications, it developed into the great republican government, under which we have accomplished our national progress.

And so it will be with our own constitution; the elements of constitutional liberty, may be slightly varied in their action under different governments; but they will act with energy for they have been incorporated into the national character. The experiment instituted by our fathers will receive its highest illustration and a continent of great republics, equal, independent, and allied, will demonstrate to the world the capabilities of republican, constitutional government. That the dissolution of the Union must come, even without the present agitation, at no distant day, is almost a historical necessity; for the history of the world is the record of the aggregation and dissolution of great empires. National individuality seems to be the agent of Providence in the conduct of the world, and having, in the extension of our territories to the extremest Western verge accomplished the first part of our destiny, we are about to fulfil the second in creating those separate national interests and individual national peculiarities, to the attrition of which is due the varied and brilliant civilization of modern times.

We have thus endeavoured to suggest the elements of the present discussion. The question is the gravest that can well be imagined—it is invested with a solemn responsibility, and rises above the flippant passion and uncertain temper of ordinary politics. We believe that the interests of the southern country demand a separate and independent government. We believe that the time has come when such a government can be established temperately, wisely, strongly. But in effecting this separation, we would not disown our indebtedness, our gratitude to the past. The Union has redeemed a continent to the christian world—it has fertilized a wilderness, and converted the rude force of nature into the beneficient action of a civilized agriculture. It has enriched the world's commerce with the untold wealth of a new and growing trade. It has spread over the vast territories of this new land the laws, the language, the literature of the Anglo-Saxon race. It has developed a population with whom liberty is identical with law, and in training thirty-three States to manhood, has fitted them for the responsibility of independent national life. It has given to history sublime names, which the world will not willingly let die—heroic actions which will light the eyes of a far-coming enthusiasm. It has achieved its destiny. Let us achieve ours.

PART II. *The Lower South*

The Perils and Duty of the South, . . . Speech Delivered in Talladega, Alabama, November 26, 1860

(Washington: Lemuel Towers, 1860)

> *Jabez L. M. Curry (1825–1903) was born in Georgia, raised in Alabama, and educated at Franklin College (later the University of Georgia) and the Harvard Law School. He practiced law in Alabama, served in the Mexican War, gained election to the Alabama state legislature, and in 1857 entered the U.S. House of Representatives. A secessionist, upon his resignation from Congress on January 21, 1861, he was elected to the Provisional Confederate States Congress, where he assisted in drafting the Constitution, and the first Confederate Congress. After the war, Curry became a Baptist preacher, an agent for the Peabody Education fund, and a noted historian of the causes of the Civil War. One of his finest works was* The Legal Justification of the South in Secession *(1899). In his congressional speech of March 14, 1860, "The Constitutional Rights of the States," he claimed that the federal government "prohibited the South that equality of condition, without which the Government could not and ought not have been established" (p. 2). Curry's contribution herein, which was delivered in the Talladega Methodist Church, recounted Southern grievances against the North, maintained that all Alabamians were united, called for secession, and promised his audience to influence his Washington colleagues on secession. For details of Curry's career see Jesse Pearl Rice,* J. L. M. Curry: Southerner, Statesman and Educator *(New York: King's Crown Press, 1949). J. Mills Thornton,* Politics and Power in a Slave Society: Alabama, 1800–1860 *(Baton Rouge: Louisiana State University Press, 1978), makes a case for Curry's role in Alabama's secession. Curry's papers are in the Library of Congress, and his pamphlet collection (including a few of those included in this volume) is located in the Alabama Department of Archives and History in Montgomery.*

The Presidential election, with its hopes, its excitements, its banners, its candidates, its alienations, its divisions, is past. What is unprecedented in party warfare there is no rejoicing over local victories; we are overwhelmed with the intelligence of Abolition success. The appalling danger looms up in terrible distinctness before us. The black flag will soon wave over the Federal Capitol. The crimson dagger of fanaticism has been deliberately plunged into the very vitals of the Constitution. Men of all parties in the South are combining for defence and security. Religious conventions speaking out solemn convictions, and indignant protests against wrong to their section have been wrung from reluctant lips. "Darkness visible" wraps the future, and the imperiled South calls upon every son and daughter to do their duty.

CHARACTER OF THE GOVERNMENT

The Declaration of Independence in 1776, and the treaty of peace in 1783, with Great Britain, recognized the freedom and independence of the colonies as separate States. As independent sovereignties they entered upon the work of forming the Union. Instead of subjecting themselves to the dominion and authority of a centralized and consolidated government, they ordained a constitutional compact, "to form a more perfect union, establish justice, insure domestic tranquility, provide for the common defense, and promote the general welfare." The end and purpose were to preserve, protect, and perpetuate a community and reciprocity of rights as between sovereign and co-equal States. A confederacy of States, and not a consolidated nation, was established. The people were not blended into one undistinguishable mass, but their separateness as citizens of particular States was jealously preserved. "The Union is a union of States as communities, and not a union of individuals." The Constitution was not ordained by the American people collectively, but by independent States. As such they represented themselves in the Convention; as such they voted in the Convention. When the Constitution was adopted it was not submitted for ratification to the people of the United States *en masse*, but to the people of each State. The ratification was by each State for itself, each doing what it alone could do, binding its citizens, and the Constitution was to be binding only between the States so ratifying. Certain specified powers were delegated to the Government, so formed, and prohibited to the States, while the great residuary mass of undelegated, unprohibited and undescribed powers were reserved to each State respectively and the people *thereof.* The Government is but the agent of the States, "constituted to execute their joint will, as expressed in the Constitution." It is one of well-defined limitations and restrictions, and in every part of the compact the States, the contracting parties, evinced the most jealous care of their separate sovereignty and independence, and refused to delegate any power which would infringe upon their equality, or surrender the right to determine the nature and extent of the agreement they made, not with the Government, their creature, but with one another.

At the time of the formation of the Constitution, slavery had been abolished in Massachusetts, and other northern States were planning measures for the prospective emancipation of the increase of the few slaves in their midst. In the Convention a serious difference of opinion, threatening disaster to the project of forming a new government, disclosed itself in reference to the recognition and guaranty of slavery, and the relation which should subsist between the white and black races. This difference of opinion developed a future diversity of interests, which interposed a serious obstacle to success and harmony. Mr. Madison, in a speech before the body, said "the difference of interests lay not between the large and small, but between the northern and southern States. The institution of slavery and its consequences formed the line of discrimination." Moderate counsels prevailed, and in seeking to secure the blessings of liberty to themselves and their posterity, our fathers wisely recognized the relation of dependance and servitude on the part of the blacks, left the whole subject of slavery in the States to the separate and uncontrolled judgment of each State, and refused to the General Government any power to prohibit slavery in any of the public domain under its jurisdiction. By compromise, after many efforts, it was provided that representatives and direct taxes should be apportioned among the States according to their respective numbers, and that, in ascertaining the number of each, three-fifths of the slaves should be included. Next, that Congress should not prohibit the African slave trade prior to 1808. Next, that slaves escaping to States, where slavery did not exist, should not be discharged from servitude, but should be delivered up on claim of the owner. Next, that no capitation or direct tax should be laid but in proportion to federal numbers. And next, that the States should be protected by the United States against invasion or domestic violence. Most of these provisions were adopted with unanimity; all of them were satisfactory. Judge Baldwin, in the case of Johnson vs. Tompkins and others, said: "The foundations of the Government laid and rest on the right of property in slaves."[1] The framers of the Government indulged in no such sickly sentimentality or false philosophy as Lincoln and the Chicago platform avow. They found in the country 600,000 african slaves, and they made no pretence of emancipating them or giving them

1. Johnson v. Tompkins, settled in the circuit court in Baldwin, Pennsylvania, concerned local laws that allowed a slave owner to recapture his fugitive slave. The owner could remove his slave without appeal to local authority. See John Codman Hurd, *The Law of Freedom and Bondage in the United States* (Boston: Little, Brown: 1858–62), 2:44. I am indebted to Max Bloomfield for this citation.

the rights of citizenship. They never dreamed that the Declaration of Independence included negroes, and that the negroes were entitled to freedom without reference to place, time, or circumstance.

BLACK REPUBLICAN PARTY SECTIONAL AND HOSTILE

In the progress and administration of the government there have necessarily been parties pervaded by some leading ideas, and drawing the political elements into two or more divisions. Until recently those parties have derived unity, consistency, and personality from variant views of constitutional construction, and the advocacy of different governmental policies as applied to trade, finance, manufactures expenditures, territorial extension, &c. These parties have alike existed in every State, and in every county of every State. They were national, coextensive with the Union, and the success or defeat of either was welcomed or deplored in every part of the Republic. Candidates for the highest offices were chosen from all sections. Electoral tickets for them were formed in every State, and political discussions elicited the merits or defects appertaining to all. Now, how changed! The Republican party is an anomaly in our federative system, and you cannot characterize it save by what Washington in his farewell address termed a geographical discrimination. It exists only in the northern States, and for the first time in our history a partisan organization, exclusively and intensely sectional, has obtained ascendency in our Government. Its majorities, so large and fearful, were obtained in one section. In a large portion it has neither majorities nor minorities. In the South it has no practical existence. The Government is to be with the North. There is an impulsive tendency in human nature to maintain power when acquired, and secure and fortify the means of its acquisition. There must inevitably be a want of sympathy between the Government and the South. Lincoln and the Republican party must obey the law of their being. They cannot assume new positions, and liberate themselves from the trammels of opinions and associations which have carried them into power. The bond of brotherhood between the North and the South, so far as political parties are concerned, is broken. Where is the security of the South, and what is her position in the Union? If history furnishes any lessons of wisdom or experience, she must rely upon herself for protection and safety.

The party which has the supremacy is not only sectional and geographical, but it is based upon opinions which will subvert, if unresisted, the foundations of the social structure of the fifteen southern States. Its fundamental idea is hostility to the South and her peculiar property, and it arrays the eighteen northern against the fifteen southern States of the confederacy. The recent election has consolidated and made permanent a political revolution, which has for several years been in process of establishment. Sectional and hostile candidates, by the popular voice of a sectional majority, have been elected President and Vice-President. Abolitionism has triumphed. Former relations of fraternity and mutuality of interests between confederated States have been destroyed. What our fathers, by patriotism and common sympathy, wrought, in the Constitution, into a compromise of interests, has been changed into a conflict of sections; and at the North, love and good will have degenerated into jealousy and hostility. The North has sectionalized itself, and is controlled by principles and ideas adverse to our equality and property. The Government "in becoming the exponent of that one section, necessarily becomes the enemy of the other." Future public policy is authoritatively and unmistakably declared. The *vox populi* which created and must uphold Lincoln's administration will still have the mastery, and require obedience, and compel the support of northern interests, the development of northern ideas, the security of northern power, and the destruction of African slavery. The institution of slavery is put under the ban, proscribed, and outlawed. Southern States and citizens of those States, because of the possession of slave property, are stigmatized and *pilloried* and reduced to inferiority.

WHAT ABOLITIONISM HAS DONE
AND PROPOSES TO DO

The progress of anti-slaveryism, with its gigantic and God-defying assumptions, may well awaken serious apprehensions. It has been progressive and aggressive. With the remorseless insatiety of the two daughters of the horse-leech, no concessions have satisfied its cormorant appetite, and no compromises have imposed obligation on its seared conscience. In 1852 the Whig and Democratic parties, in national conventions, resolved the "compromise measures" of 1850 into "a finality"; but the Whig party was overthrown in the effort, while the Democratic party was crippled, and has since been riven in twain, if not destroyed forever. It is idle to attribute the growth and power of abolitionism to the Kansas bill, the repeal of the Missouri restriction, or to any recent cause. Prior to that time parties had been denationalized, and the strong ties which bound kindred ecclesiastical organizations of the same faith and order had been loosened or snapped asunder. Ten States in 1847 passed resolutions, through their legislatures, in favor of excluding the South from the Territories, held in trust for common use and enjoyment. Through the school room, the public lecture, the pulpit, the political convention, the legislature, and the thousand-tongued press, the northern mind has been educated *down* to this devil-born fanaticism. To attempt to arrest or eradicate by mild persuasion or appeal to brotherly love, would be as vain as the attempt to summon back a moment of time from the great ocean of the past into which it has just been engulphed.

It is difficult to enumerate, without shame of southern spirit, what antislaveryism has done and proposes to do. I need not tire you with a recital of the agitation persistently kept up for years against slavery as found in our midst; of the shameless aspersions of our good name and character, at home and abroad; of the denunciation of slavery, as a relic of barbarism, equiponderant in infamy with polygamy; of the felonious running away of thousands of slaves by underground railroads; of the emissaries sent in our midst to excite insurrection; of fire-brand publications transmitted through the mails; of sending Sharpe's rifles and emigrants to Kansas; of the invasion of Virginia by John Brown and his murderous confreres; or of the sympathy and honors showered upon his remains. These may be objected to as exceptional ebullitions of individual fanaticism. Unfortunately, we are not wanting in proofs of hostility of higher grade. With utter disregard of oaths and constitutional obligations, with sneering contempt for southern chivalry, the Constitution — "the only bond of the Union of these States" — is openly violated. Ingenious devices have been invented by northern States to embarrass the execution of the fugitive-slave law, and render nugatory one of the plainest provisions of the federal covenant. Eleven states have made the prosecution of the Master's claim to a runaway or stolen negro a *crime*, and prohibit their officers and citizens from aiding the execution of the law; some deny the use of their jails and public buildings in aid of the master; some provide legal defence for the runaway, and some impose fines and imprisonment on the owner or his agent.[2]

Judge Story, not friendly to slavery, in one of his decisions (Prigg *vs.* Pennsylvania) said, speaking of the constitutional provision for the recovery of fugitive slaves, which has been so grossly nullified: "Historically, it is well known that the object of this clause was to secure to the citizens of the slaveholding States the complete right and title of ownership in their slaves, as property, in every State of the Union into which they might escape from the State wherein they were held in servitude." "The

2. Southerners resisted the personal freedom laws that had been recently passed in some Northern states that violated the Fugitive Slave Law of 1850.

full recognition of this right and title was indispensable to the security of this species of property in all the slaveholding States, and, indeed, was so vital to the preservation of their interests and institutions, that *it cannot be doubted that it constituted a fundamental article, without the adoption of which the Union would not have been formed.*" "The clause was of the last importance to the safety and security of the southern States, and could not be surrendered by them without endangering their whole property in slaves."

Daniel Webster, in a speech at Capon Springs, Virginia, in 1851, said: "I do not hesitate to Say and repeat that if the northern States refuse wilfully and deliberately to carry into effect that part of the constitution which respects the restoration of fugitive slaves, the South would no longer be bound to observe the compact. A bargain broken on one side is broken on all sides."

Caleb Cushing, than whom Massachusetts has not a purer patriot or abler statesman, says, in a recent letter, that "the violation of the fundamental compact of association by one of the contracting parties, serves in morality, as well as law, to release the others."

Such conduct as I have described, on the part of a foreign nation, would justify war, and was one of the chief causes of the Peloponnesian war. Those States which have defeated the execution of this federal law by State laws,—which, in the language of Cushing, are "scandalously false in their profession of purpose and tyrannical in their domestic and treasonable in their federal relations,"—have broken the bargain, have assumed a treasonable and revolutionary attitude against the Constitution, and are in rebellion against the supreme law of the land. The recent election justifies the treason, vindicates the rebellion, unblushingly sanctions the violation of the compact; and we are counselled to submit to "the perpetration of the enormous crime which has placed this Government in the hands of the revolutionary chiefs" of a hostile section.

Having shown the character of the Republican party and some of its wrong-doings, it is appropriate to pursue the discussion by an inquiry into its aims and policy, now that it will soon obtain possession of the Government. The animating principle of the party is hostility to slavery. It champions the idea of the natural, inherent, inalienable right of the Africans to freedom, and to the rights, privileges, and immunities of citizenship. It wages an unceasing crusade against our civilization. It educates the northern people to alienation, bitterness, strife, and hate. It denounces the "barbarism" of our institutions, and us as "barbarians." It has overwhelmed and crushed out the conservative elements of the North. It has ostracized the Fillmores, and Everetts, and Winthrops, on the one side, and the Lanes, the Dickinsons, the Halletts, and the Fitchs, on the other, and promoted in their stead the Sumners, the Wilsons, the Sewards, the Wades, the Lovejoys. It seeks the extinction of African slavery at the South—the liberation of the negroes in our midst. "It threatens," says a northern writer, "with fire and sword every southern hearth, with death every southern man, and with dishonor every southern female, amid a saturnalia of blood."

Coming into power on the flood-tide of popular fanaticism, grown insolent by repeated submissions on the part of the South, it behooves us to ascertain their purposes and to understand the dangers which imperil us. Denying to the South equality in the enjoyment of the common Territories, they seek to circumscribe the South, to prevent her growth and expansion, and localize slavery in the present States of its existence. Proceeding one step further, the inter-State and coast-wise slave trade is to be prohibited; slaves are not to be transported for sale beyond the limits of any State, nor shopped from Baltimore to Charleston, from Norfolk to Savannah, from New Orleans to Galveston. The saleable or transferable value is to be diminished, and the institution localized and made less profitable in the particular States which allow it. Advancing still further in the work of destruction, slavery is to be abolished in the District of Columbia and other places subject to federal jurisdiction, and those points made the citadels of constant attack upon our peace and property. No more unexceptionable testimony of the objects of the Republicans can be adduced than the avowals of their representative men. In 1858 Mr. Lincoln said: "I believe this Government cannot endure permanently half slave and half free. I do not expect the Union to be dissolved, . . . but I do expect it will cease to be divided. It will become all one thing or all the other. Either the *opponents of slavery will* arrest the farther spread of it, and *place it* where the public mind shall rest in the belief that it is *in the course of ultimate extinction*; or its advocates will push it forward till it shall become alike lawful in all the States." Later in the same year Mr. Seward adopted and popularized the "irrepressible conflict" theory, and avowed the "one idea" of his party to be "resistance to slavery and devotion to freedom." In the same speech, he declared that the secret of assured success lay in the fact that it was a party of one idea—"the idea of equality—the equality of *all men* before human tribunals and human laws." At Albany, while stigmatizing southern citizens as "an oligarchy," a "privileged class," he says that slavery "will be overthrown, either peacefully and lawfully under the Constitution, or it will work the subversion of the Constitution, together with its own overthrow. Then the slaveholders would perish in the struggle. The change can now be made without violence, and *by the agency of the ballot-box*. . . . We must restore the principle of equality among the members of the States—the principle of the sacredness of the absolute and inherent rights of man." At Lansing, advocating the election of Lincoln, he says: "You, then, come to the great question of the irrepressible conflict between freedom and slavery. Those who think that a nation can be wise and prosperous and happy that retains slaves will have another opportunity at the next Presidential election to secure the machinery by which it can be done. On the other hand, all of us who have enlisted in this great civic contest, on which the eyes of the whole world are set, will then find that all we have to do is to take care that we do not suffer differences among ourselves or any other cause to divide us, and *one single administration will settle this question finally and forever.*"

In the same speech, he says, "I will favor as long as I can, within the limits of constitutional action, the decrease and diminution of African slavery *in all the States.*" At an earlier day, in a speech in Ohio, he says that slavery "can and *must be abolished,* and you and I must do it." Similar quotations might be multiplied *ad nauseam* from Greeley, Lovejoy, Sumner, and others, but I close this branch of the argument by referring you to the Chicago platform—the magna charta of Republicanism—which reaffirms the "self-evident" truths of the Declaration of Independence; makes the maintenance of the principles "essential to the preservation of our Republican Institutions"; declares the normal condition of the Territories to be free-soil, and denies the authority of Congress, of a territorial legislature or of *any individuals,* to give *legal existence to slavery* in *any* territory of the United States.[3] The Republicans, in the use of general phrases, always include the slave. When they speak of "equality" and "freedom" and "liberty," they mean the equality and freedom of southern slaves. I close the volume of irrefragable testimony, and if any one in this audience now doubts that the Republicans, with Lincoln at their head, intend to abolish slavery in the States, he would not believe though one rose from the dead.

CONSEQUENCES OF ABOLITIONISM

It would be supererogation to paint, if I had the power, the consequences of emancipation. To the negro it would be savage cruelty. At the North, driven into poverty and vice, he stands a perishing monument of the incapacity of his race and of the heartless selfishness which conferred liberty and starvation. The white man is stimulated to labor by its re-

3. Reference to the much-discussed Republican Party presidential platform of 1860, which was written in Chicago.

turns. The black man will not work save by compulsion, and pauperism and crime are the results of his unhindered idleness. The West India islands furnish a conclusive refutation of all anti-slavery theories. In Lewis' West Indies, written before emancipation, it is said, "as to the free blacks, they are almost uniformly lazy and improvident; most of them half starved and only anxious to live from hand to mouth. . . . As to a free negro hiring himself out for plantation labor, no instance of such a thing was ever known in Jamaica." Six hundred and thirty-three thousand blacks were liberated in the West Indies at an expense of $100,000,000, yet the products have nearly ceased except what arises from the substituted labor of the Coolies. Nearly a fourth part of the population of Trinidad are returned in 1852 as living in idleness.

INTEREST OF NON-SLAVEHOLDERS IN SLAVERY

Unreflecting partisans have sometimes insinuated, rather than openly expressed the opinion, that non-slaveholders are not interested in the institution of slavery. No greater or more mischievous mistake could be made, and a few suggestions will show it. The most perplexing problem to modern governments is the relation between labor and capital. Nothing is so terrible to England, nothing so fearful to France, nothing awakens such serious apprehensions with the thoughtful and far-seeing in the populous portions of the North. Laws are passed regulating labor, fixing wages, restricting capital and lubricating the friction between clashing labor and capital. Between the two opposing forces in free society, there is a constant tendency to collision. In Europe standing armies, and restricted suffrage, and artificial privileged classes, and sumptuary laws, and perpetual governmental interference, keep the interests of labor in subordination. In the North, facility of emigration to the fertile and unoccupied West and the conservative influence of slavery have mitigated the severity of the conflict, significant premonitions of the irrepressibility of which are occasionally heard in the "strikes" of the operatives and the bated whisperings of "bread or blood." Where slavery does not exist, the antagonism between labor and capital is everywhere felt, and it is mitigated or aggravated by the mode of employment of both. The warfare "between opposing and enduring forces" is inseparable from the unadjusted relation. There is no sympathy, no recognized and felt moral relation between the combatting forces and capital tyrannizes over labor, depriving it of political rights, of personal freedom and wresting from its hard earnings all but a scanty subsistence.

The difficult problem finds a solution in African slavery, and here labor and capital are identified. The two are blended in harmony and political irreconcilability is adjusted by the providential and predestined distinction of color. Profits and wages in our social organization are blended. The slaveholder, owning both capital and labor in the negro, is interested in receiving for his labor a remunerating return, and hence the wages of mechanics and field-laborers in the South are higher than at the North. Besides, no matter how the price of produce may fluctuate, the slaveholder makes his largest possible crop, as his negroes must be clothed and subsisted. Labor is not turned loose adrift in times of pecuniary depression, and thus all classes of the community and every profession, the lawyer, the merchant, the overseer, the mechanic, the physician, the preacher, are interested in the products of slave labor. In the North, social distinctions are defined by the rich and the poor. In the South, color draws the ineffaceable line of separation. In Europe, to preserve the wall of partition, privileged classes are created and voting is confined to a favored few or prohibited altogether. In the North, like distinctions would be made but for connection with the South. Putting out of view, in the event of abolition, the abhorrent degradation of social and political equality, the probility of a war of extermination between the races or the necessity of flying the country to avoid the association, it is susceptible of demonstration, that those whom the abolitionists stigmatize as "the poor whites of the South" are more interested in the institution than any other portion of the community. Thank God, they cannot be duped by the wiles of their enemies, and none are more ready when the occasion demands to

> "Strike for their altars and their fires,
> Strike for the green graves of their sires,
> God and their native land."

OBJECTIONS TO RESISTANCE

A plea is interposed by some hopeful southern men against resistance, that the President elect and his party in Congress, being sworn, will administer the Government in accordance with the Constitution. Did it never occur to such persons, that, without State remedies, the Constitution is what the President and majority in Congress determine it to be; that the standard of rights and measure of obligations are their will and discretion; that different rules of interpretation prevail; that a "higher" and more imperative law than the Constitution is recognized; that State legislators of the same party, equally sworn, have nullified the Constitution; that the constitutionality of property in the labor of a slave is denied; that the Constitution is said to be based upon the Declaration of Independence which affirms the inalienable right of black and white men to freedom; that slavery is so peculiar and sensitive, it cannot long survive the active hostility of the Government, "even though the hostile action be confined to a systematic use of the powers of the Government for the purposes of its destruction, and to a systematic abdication of the powers of protection"; that numerous clauses of the Constitution under Black Republican torture can be perverted by hate or interest to authorize direct interference in the States; and that some means, sooner or later, will be found of "striking a fatal blow at slavery in spite of the Constitution and of the independent power of the States over the subject."

Another more plausible objection to resistance is found in the fact, that Lincoln has been elected by a popular majority, in accordance with the forms of law and the Constitution. A constitution implies fundamental rules as the guaranties of the rights and liberties of a free people. It means something more than lifeless formalities—than words without life-giving power. The outward form may be preserved while the spirit is extinct. Tyranny of the worst character may be perpetrated with its machinery and technicalities. The forms of the Roman Commonwealth were retained after the Government had become a hated despotism, and the image of liberty was stamped on the coins of Nero. Madame Roland, when led to the guillotine, exclaimed, O Liberty, how many crimes are committed in thy name! Empty technicalities will not preserve freedom. The Constitution interpreted and administered by our enemies may become the instrument of oppression. It may be the sword of justice or the sword of vengeance. Seward, in one of his speeches, suggests the power of amendment, which may be made under the "forms" of the Constitution, as a mode of accomplishing abolition through the agency of the Constitution.

It is suicidal to defer action until the commission of what is not very intelligibly termed "an overt act." The Republican party is a standing menace. Its success is a declaration of war against our property and the supremacy of the white race. The election of Lincoln is the overt act. The law justifies the taking of life in advance of injury, when the killer was under such apprehensions as would influence a reasonable mind. The like rule of self-preservation applies to a people endangered.

The possession of the Government by a hostile, sectional party, places our destinies under the control of another and distinct people. To the slaveholding States it is a *foreign government*, which understands not our condition, defers not to our opinions, consults not our interests, and has no sympathy with our peculiar civilization. The South had no agency in putting the administration in power, its public opinion will not be represented. It will be organized and throw its patronage in opposition to an institution that enters into the very texture of our social and political being. It is just such a government as incited the Revolutionary patriots to throw off British allegiance. They denied the right of a foreign people, of the same blood, language, religion and government, to legislate for them. They spurned the mockery of a partial representation in Parliament, remembering the condition of Ireland, and knowing that every separate community, every minority interest, must have within its own control some self-protecting power. From the origin of this Government, there have existed in the North and South opposing political principles. The ideas of the duties and powers of the Government are essentially different. They have divided not merely upon policy of measures, but upon the theory and nature of our political system. Ordinarily a Southern Whig was nearer to a Southern Democrat than to a Northern Whig, and *vice versa*. Our social institutions are peculiar and affect our political character. Our productions are different and require different legislation. In our intercourse with foreign nations, the same antagonism of interests exhibits itself. The election of Lincoln "has developed into excited hostility" and made apparent these contradictions, and the South—her social institutions, her peculiar property, her political ideas, her interests, domestic and international—is placed in entire and helpless dependence upon hostile Northern majorities. Our industrial policy and commercial connexions and foreign relations are dependent on the will of a people separate from and hostile to us.

Black-Republican ascendancy is not a sudden and unpremeditated attack upon us. It is deliberate and with forewarning, and "in contempt for the obligation of law and security of compacts, evincing a deadly hostility to the rights and institutions of the Southern people and a settled purpose to effect their overthrow." Nor have we "been wanting in attentions to our Northern brethren. We have warned them, from time to time, of attempts made by their legislatures to extend an unwarrantable jurisdiction over us. We have reminded them of the circumstances" of our Union and the solemnity of their engagements. "We have appealed to their native justice and magnanimity, and we have conjured them by the ties of our common kindred to disavow these usurpations, which would inevitably interrupt our connexions and correspondence." We have said in all the forms in which the declaration could be made, that we would not submit to the election of an Abolitionist to the Presidency. Our public men and presses have repeated it, in and out of season. Our legislatures, in more solemn modes, have declared it. What have we not done to make known to the North our fixed purpose not to submit to the humiliation, dishonor, and ultimate ruin of allowing our Government to pass into the hands of a sectional party, whose bond of union is a hatred of our institutions and a determination to destroy them? "They have been deaf to the voice of justice and consanguinity." They have responded to these declarations with sneers, ridicule, defiance, contemptuous insults, grosser violations of the Constitution, and now, as the very culmination of insult and injury, by electing an Abolitionist to the Presidency. Federal officers are to be appointed in all the Southern States, who will first be apologists for Lincoln, then palliate and justify and approve, and then become little centres or nuclei for Republican organizations. For one, I shall never acquiesce in the insult and degradation. I would pay millions for defence, and dare everything earthly, before I would voluntarily submit to such dishonor.

The Legislature of Alabama, with patriotic unanimity, declared that "to permit such seizure of the Government by those whose unmistakeable aim is to pervert its whole machinery to the destruction of a portion of its members, would be an act of suicidal folly and madness almost without a parallel in history," and therefore they "deemed it their solemn duty to provide, in advance, the means by which they may escape such peril and dishonor," and accordingly authorized the Governor to call a Convention upon the happening of the election of a Black Republican. All honor to our General Assembly for the thoughtful sagacity and patriotism which provided for averting the peril and dishonor!

DECISIVE ACTION IMPERATIVE

Lord Bacon said, that "it were better to meet some danger half-way, though they come nothing near, than to keep too long a watch upon their approaches, for if a man watch too long, it is odds he will fall asleep." Instead of meeting half-way, we have tarried long and sought to avert danger by argument and appeal and remonstrance, and have essayed to overthrow at the ballot-box. In all these we have failed. The remedy of appeal to fraternal feeling and constitutional obligation—made under the most advantageous circumstances, with a fusion of the opposition to Abolition in every doubtful State—has proved inefficacious; and now decisive measures are more politic, and "from the nettle, *danger*, we may pluck the flower, *safety*." It would be uncandid to conceal the opinion, that there may be dangers and probable sufferings ahead. Submission involves inequality with the North, oppressive taxation, foreign rule, emancipation of negroes and equality with them at the South. Resistance may bring temporary depreciation of property, commercial depression, and possibly the casualties of war. The heroes of '76 encountered all these and more to prevent the domination of a foreign people. It was attempted to stave off the war of 1812 by dilatory restrictive and embargo measures, but the people demanded a declaration of war to protect New England men and New England property, and preserve national honor. When duty is plain, "perils are privileges," and if Federal coercion be attempted (as is threatened), and war ensue, "it only proves to what an extent we have submitted before we venture to resist—only demonstrates the power of that unrighteous authority against which we are forced to arm."

Resistance, however, to the last resort, involves less evils than many conjure up. There is no true analogy between such a procedure on our part and revolution, even bloodless, in Great Britain or France. As each nation is there consolidated into one government, there must be a suspension of authority and usurpation of power. Provisional, temporary, and irregular governments must be established to prevent anarchy and social disorder. Here, we have not a consolidated nation, but distinct, sovereign States, fully equipped with all the machinery of regularly and lawfully constituted governments, and wholly independent of the Federal agency at Washington. We have in Alabama an Executive, a Legislature, a Judiciary, an Army, and internal order will be preserved by local authorities, which are not in subordination to Federal, and are alone responsible to the people of the State. Of all fantasies that ever disturbed an excited brain, the most ridiculous is the idea, that Liberty is dependent upon the continuance of this Government, and that dissolution will be succeeded by despotism. Practical political liberty has its highest illustration and best security in representation, and this vital principle, while it may be modified by external circumstances, is too thoroughly ingrained in the national character to be surrendered without a contest such as the world has never witnessed.

In this connection it may be pertinent to examine into the operations of
the Federal Government, and of northern connection, and ascertain how
much the South is annually drained and depleted by what is paid to the
North. The facts prove that the southern States have been to the North
as the conquered province were to Rome, when the tributes exacted from
them were sufficient to defray the whole expenses of the Government. A
report of the Secretary of the Treasury for 1838 shows that, in the five years,
1833-'37, out of $102,000,000 of expenditure, only $37,000,000 were in the
slave States; yet, during the same years, they paid $90,000,000 of duties
to $17,500,000 paid by the free States. The amount of customs collected,
says Kettell, in the past seventy years, reaches eleven hundred millions of
dollars, a large portion of which was disbursed at the North.[4] Bounties to
fisheries have amounted to over $13,000,000, and have been paid mostly to
Maine and Massachusetts. Like unjust inequalities are exhibited in the appropriation of public lands, in the light-house system, in the collection of
customs, in the internal improvement system, in the erection of court and
custom houses, and hospitals and post offices. An intelligent writer says,
that the heads of federal expenditure show that while the South has paid
seven-ninths of the taxes, the North has had seven-ninths of their disburse-
ments. The North furnishes, in great degree, our carriers, importers, merchants, bankers, brokers, and insurers. One of the ablest statisticians and
political economists in America, Mr. Kettell, a northern man, estimates the
annual amount of means sent North by southern owners and producers, as
the sum of their dealing with the North, at $462,560,394. The South fur-
nishes six-sevenths of the freight for the shipping of the country, while the
North supplies one-seventh. The South pays $36,000,000 per annum to
the shipping interest for the transportation of the products of slave labor.
"All the profitable branches of freighting, brokering, selling, banking, in-
surance, &c., that grow out of southern products, are enjoyed in New York.
The profits that importers, manufacturers, bankers, factors, jobbers, ware-
housemen, carmen, and every branch of industry connected with merchan-
dizing, realize, from the mass of goods that pass through northern cities,
are paid by southern consumers." The same careful authority approximates

4. Kettell was a Northern economist with pro-Southern views; see Thomas
Prentiss Kettell, *Southern Wealth and Northern Profits* (New York: G. W. and J. A.
Wood, 1860).

the annual load which southern industry, dependent on southern labor, is required to carry, at $231,500,000, and distributes among bounties to fishermen, customs, importers, manufacturers, shippers, agents, travellers, &c. It is this North grown rich from the earnings of slave labor, dependent for its prosperity and profits upon southern wealth, that has placed Lincoln and them that "hate us to rule over us." Jeshurun has waxed fat and kicked.

The South has more elements of strength and wealth, more ability to sustain herself as a separate government than any country of equal size in the world. In territorial area she has 850,000 square miles, more than the United States, prior to the acquisition of Louisiana, and as large as Great Britain, France, Spain, Prussia, and Austria. Her population is four times as large as that of the colonies at the commencement of the Revolutionary war, and is sixty per cent greater than that of the whole United States, when we entered upon the war of 1812. She has 9,000 miles of railroad, which has been mainly built with her own capital. In the sixth year ending 1860 the South built more miles of railroad than the West, but did not exhaust her means in their reconstruction. The West was prostrate while the South was never in a better condition; and in the crash of 1857 we saved the North from ruin by sending her 1,600,000 bales of cotton, which were sold for $65,000,000.

The strength of a people consists in their wealth — in the excess of production over consumption. For the fiscal year ending June 30, 1860, the United States exported to foreign countries $316,220,610, excluding specie and foreign merchandize re-exported. Of this amount $214,322,880 are the exclusive products of the South, that are not and cannot be raised at the North; $5,071,434 were furnished by free, and $96,826,299 by free and slave States. Adding one-third of the $96,826,299, the joint product of free negro and slave States, the South furnished $246,598,313 of the aggregate exports. The commerce of this country is based upon southern productions, and exports are the basis of imports. One article alone, cotton — of which we exported last year $191,806,555 — is said to be King. Through the Crimean war, the late and present war in Italy, and the revulsion of 1857, cotton has maintained a steady and reinunerating price, while other articles have undergone violent fluctuations. The manufacturing interest of the world is dependent upon it; and every man who wears a shirt is interested in slave labor, because cotton cannot be produced sufficient for the world's wants without African slavery. The capital invested in the cotton trade, in Great Britain, is between $300,000,000 and $350,000,000. She consumes annually $120,000,000 worth of cotton goods, and one-third of her entire exports consists of cotton goods and yarns.

Mr. Kettell, to whom I am so much indebted, speaking of the dealings between the North and the South, says: "If we were to penetrate beyond a rupture, and imagine a peaceable separation, by which the North and South should be sundered without hostilities, we might contemplate the condition and prospects of each. From what has been detailed, as revealed from the returns of the census, it is quite apparent that the North, as distinguished from the South and West, would alone be permanently injured. Its fortune depends upon manufacturing and shipping; but it neither raises its own food nor its own raw material, nor does it furnish freights for its own shipping. The South, on the other hand, raises a surplus of food, and supplies the world with raw materials. Lumber, hides, cotton, wool, indigo — all that the manufacturer requires — is within its own circle. The requisite capital to put them in action is rapidly accumulating; and in *the long run, it would lose* — after recovering from first disasters — *nothing by separation.* The North, on the other hand, will have food and raw materials to buy, in order to employ its labor. . . . Both the South and West have vast natural resources to be developed, and the time for that *development is only retarded by the present profit that the North derives* from supplying each with those things that they will soon cease to want. The North has no future natural resources. In minerals, both the other sections surpass it; in metals, it is comparatively destitute; of raw materials, it has none. Its ability to feed itself is questionable. Its commerce is to the whole country what that of Holland once was to the world, viz., living on the trade of other people."

Upon the muster rolls the South has a million of militia, which would make the most effective military force in the world, as during a war slaves would produce the means of subsistence. Apprehension of general and successful revolt on the part of the slaves is a dreamy chimera. History furnishes no single instance of a successful protest by slave labor against lawful authority, while wars have been numerous and bloody between struggling labor and grinding capital, in other systems of society. During the existence of the Hebrews as a separate nation, whether as a commonwealth, a monarch, or as scattered tribes, their slave institutions were uninjured. Greece, amid all her conflicts, was never perplexed by slavery. Rome governed the world, and "the millions of slaves never changed an emperor nor lost a province." In our revolutionary war, the war of 1812, and Indian wars, slaves did not embarrass or impede, but rather strengthened our military operations.

Should the southern States be driven to the necessity of forming a government, adapted to the condition of the society on which it is to operate, war will only result from a tyrannical attempt to coerce or subjugate. The southern States will commit no aggressions upon the North. They will simply withdraw from the dominion of a government which has become hostile and foreign, and has failed to subserve the purposes of its creation. The first Federal gun fired against a seceding State will touch a chord that will vibrate in every southern heart. The craven southern Congressman, who votes for a dollar or a musket or a law for such a purpose, will have an infamy akin to that of Arnold and Judas combined.

An election for delegates to a State Convention is to be held on the 24th of December. You should send your best men, combining wisdom, prudence, firmness, patriotism, and a stern determination never to submit to abolition domination. Can't we unite as has so happily been done in Montgomery and Dallas? Can't we bury the hatchet of party discord in the presence of the portentous cloud, black with fury and common ruin? Can't Bell men and Douglas men and Breckinridge men unite on three Delegates, to whom every citizen of this county will be willing to entrust his rights and his honor? As one, I should be willing to support men combining the characteristics I have described without requiring from them, in advance, any pledges as to the precise mode of resistance, leaving that to be decided by the circumstances, which shall exist, when the Convention meets. In assenting to this I make large concessions. My opinion, deliberate and carefully formed, is that Alabama owes it to her safety, her peace, her honor, to withdraw from the Government and provide new securities for the protection of her people. Cooperation will be had, but a convention of irresponsible delegates from the southern States to lay down the Georgia platform, as an ultimatum, will be taking steps backward from the position of all parties in 1850, and will result, in my judgment, in disastrous submission. With a full knowledge of all contained in that ultimatum, the North has "precipitated" this contest upon us; and, besides, the ultimatum suggested leaves untouched and unremedied the obnoxious legislation of Northern States which render impotent and valueless the fugitive slave law. To make a formal appeal to northern State to repeal those laws nullifying the Constitution would be an empty farce. They were passed with a full knowledge and in contemptuous disregard of the Constitution and our wishes, and are not likely, at our dictation and request, to be removed from the statute-books. The Vermont Legislature has recently, by an overwhelming majority, refused to abandon nullification and repeal the personal-liberty bill of that State. The New York *Tribune*, the most potent organ of abolitionism, pronounces the difference between the two sections on the question of the surrender of runaway negroes to be "radical, fundamental, irrepressible," and truly says that "any stipulation, however precise and solemn, that the fugitives who escape from slavery shall be generally caught and returned, will be a deception and a sham." New constitutional guaranties cannot be plainer, and will not be more effective, than the present ones. These temporizing expedients stick in the bark, and do not remedy the disease. The people are tired of this incessant agitation and strife, and properly demand a settlement which will be permanent, final, and not subject to speedy revisal.

My advice to Alabama is to act for herself, and seek the simultaneous co-operation of neighboring States, who will join her, not to propose terms to our enemy, but to secure permanent safety in a Southern Confederacy. I go from among you to fight your battles on another theatre—to vindicate your honor—to sustain the Constitution. God grant that the telegraphic wires may bring to me no such humiliating intelligence as that Alabama, in meek submission, has bowed the neck to abolition subjugation! What will be said in the future, if we eat our words and succumb to the foul wrong? How can I, as your representative, hold up my head and talk of southern honor, southern wrongs, southern rights? With what pitiful emptiness would all such gasconade fail upon the ears of our abolition rulers and masters! No, no, no! I rely with strong confidence the State of my allegiance and affections, and can say of her:

> "My heart, my hopes, are all with thee;
> My heart, my hopes, my prayers, my tears,
> My faith triumphant o'er my fears,
> Are all with thee—are all with thee."

A Sermon, Delivered in St. John's Church, Savannah, On Fast Day, Nov. 28, 1860

(Savannah: George N. Nichols, 1860)

Rev. George Henry Clark (1819–1906) was born and received his early educa-tion in Massachusetts, graduated in 1843 from Yale College, attended the Virginia Theological Seminary in Alexandria, and was ordained an Episcopal priest in 1846. He served as Rector of All Saints in Worcester, Massachusetts, from 1846–49; of St. John's, in Savannah, Georgia, from 1854–61; and of Christ Church, in Hartford, Connecticut, from 1861–67. Clark became a famous preacher, and many of his sermons were published. He also wrote about history, including a well-received biography of Oliver Cromwell (1893). In his sermon included in this volume Clark described fierce civil divisions that had occurred in the world throughout history to show the horrors that could result from the dissolution of the Union, but he concluded that if there was no other solution, he would support se-cession. The loyalties of this kindly and highly regarded preacher were to his native North, and he soon left for Hartford. For more information about the Church in Savannah see Henry Thompson Malone, The Episcopal Church in Georgia, 1733-1957 *(Atlanta: Protestant Episcopal Church, 1960). No biography of Clark exists, but he is profiled in* Twentieth Century Biographical Dictionary of Notable Americans *(Boston, Mass.: James H. Lamb Co., 1900–1903), vol. 1.*

"THEY SHALL LOOK UNTO THE EARTH, AND
BEHOLD TROUBLE AND DARKNESS"
— Isaiah: Chap. VIII., verse XXII.

People of the North, forgetting that slavery has come to the Afri-can as a blessing, and has raised a most degraded race in every way, physi-cally, socially, intellectually and morally; and overlooking the necessity of its continuance, not only for our protection and our prosperity, but for the preservation and welfare of those, to whom they would entrust the danger-ous gift of liberty, have entered a crusade against the institution, and are bending their energies to sweep it from the land. They propose, they can propose, no plan beyond that of giving freedom to those to whom freedom would not come as a blessing. They ignore the rights, and they invade the privileges of those with whom they have entered into a solemn contract for the common benefit of all. They would trample beneath their feet that

Constitution, which was created by the wisdom, and sealed by the blood of our fathers. Urged on by unscrupulous politicians and by ignorant demagogues, they have refused, by their suffrages, to preserve to the South her just prerogatives, and have recklessly attempted to undermine her possessions. What we regard as a necessity, they look on as a curse. What we know to be a benefit, they assume to be an evil; and looking at the subject with passions heated, they have, by their numerical power, raised to the highest position, which a citizen can hold, one whose antecedents would indicate, that he will look, in the high place which he is to occupy, to the interests of a section and a party, rather than to the interests of the whole country.

And to what has this agitation brought our land? It has brought it to a position of extreme peril. The horizon is dark on every side, and storms of which no statesman can see the consequences, are impending over us.

It is under such circumstances that we are called, by the Governor of our State, to gather here for humiliation and for prayer.[1] Instead of coming together, as in years gone by, for joy and gratitude and thanksgiving, we meet in sorrow and in fear. A country rich in physical resources of every character; a country locked together in all its parts, by mighty rivers, and by iron roads, intended, it would seem, by God and man, to be forever one and inseparable; a country containing a people who speak the same language and profess the same religion; a country over which the banners of liberty have proudly waved for nearly a century, and to whose shores exiles from tyranny and despotism have come for refuge and for shelter; a country where commerce has accomplished its noblest triumphs, and where science has achieved her grandest victories; a country whose rapid progress in wealth, in population, and in art, has given the promise of a marvellous future; a country, which has cemented itself socially, fraternally, in the hallowed rites of marriage by that love, which is the purest and holiest of earth, is now rent with faction and with discord: already the sound of conflict reaches us, which, if the history of the past teaches any lessons, is but the distant rumbling, on the far horizon, of a tempest, which shall sweep with terrific power, and with universal desolation, over the length and breadth of the land; already that flag, whose stars have shone for eighty years, as fixed and constant as the constellations of the heaven, and which in the ice bound Arctic, and on the broad Pacific, under the rocks of Gibraltar, and in the waters of the British Channel, we have watched with pride

1. Georgia governor Joseph E. Brown had called for a day of fasting and thanksgiving for the clergy to preach on and discuss the secession crisis. A number of Clark's parishioners had asked him to print his sermon.

and admiration, waving over our commerce, and over our peaceful ships of war, is trailing in the dust, and is stamped on as the emblem of a glory no longer worth preserving. God of our fathers, we need to bow ourselves! God of nations, have mercy on us!

But all this, some of you tell me, will pass away. We are too prosperous, too great, too civilized for war; science, and art, and a thousand industrial interests, make that an impossibility. It cannot be, that such a country can be permanently checked in its prosperity. Did not the people of Babylon, doubtless, think the same, at the time that mighty Empire extended from Armenia to the deserts of Arabia, and from the Euphrates to the boundaries of Egypt, and her capital, sixty miles in circumference, with its eight story buildings, and its vast trade, and its hewn stone bridges, and its immense towers, shone with so much splendor, when they first knew that Cyrus was looking to a war? Did they think then, that so wide and so rich an empire would be merged into Persia? Did they think, that in five centuries their superb capital would become a mass of ruins, and that, at some distant epoch, men would search her grass covered mounds for relics of her greatness?

Did not the people of Carthage, doubtless, think the same, just before the third Punic war, when this metropolis is said to have contained seven hundred thousand inhabitants, and when her territories stretched from Egypt to Gibraltar? She, then, held supremacy over the seas. Her docks contained shipping, on which her merchant princes looked with pride. Mago wrote twenty-eight books on her agriculture. "She had a commerce," says McPherson, "which, by its unrivalled extent, and judicious management, relieved all nations of their superfluities, supplied all their wants, and everywhere dispensed plenty and comfort." How little did those seven hundred thousand prosperous inhabitants of Carthage dream of what their destiny would involve; that, out of seven hundred thousand strong men, and gentle women, and fair children, in three short years, only fifty thousand would be left to surrender in despair before the armies of Rome; how little did they dream, that those magnificent docks, which they had excavated for their ships, would no longer hold their magnificent commerce; that those splendid gardens, which stretched away, for a score of miles in the country around, and in which music, and beauty, and love, had mingled their fascinations, would all be turned into a desert; and that, one day, some earnest voyager would land on that shore, and search, in vain, for the ruins of its proud capital.

Passing over a hundred lessons of history of a similar character, and coming nearer to our own times, I ask, did not the people of Prussia think

somewhat the same, when their third Frederick, to gratify his personal ambition, began to make havoc on the kingdoms around him. Did they see,
that a seven years defensive war was coming? Did they believe that their
population would be decimated? that whole villages would be depopulated?
that for lack of men, delicate women would be driven to the fields to dig for
bread? and that it would take ages to restore what so ruthlessly had been
lost? No. The previous reign had been a peaceful one, and they expected
peace to continue. People slowly come to the conviction that a great calamity is near them; it is on them, often, before they begin to realize it.

Floating down the crimsoned currents of history, we come to France.
I would like to know who of her Statesmen or Philosophers, in August,
seventeen hundred and eighty-nine, when the revolution was inaugurated,
had prophetic vision of seventeen hundred and ninety-three. What far-
seeing Peer, what keen-sighted Legislator, throwing his possessions on
the "altar of fatherland" and proclaiming the rights, but not the duties of
man, penetrated through the labyrinths of those four years? Who thought
then, of the rushing downward to destruction? Who thought then, of the
Revolutionary Tribunal and the axe of the guillotine? Who thought then,
that the cradle of fraternity would, so soon, be exchanged for the death
cart, bearing grey headed philosophers, and eloquent advocates, and lovely
women to an ignominious end? Who thought then, that the demon of anarchy, under the very shadow of the statue of Liberty, would drink the
blood of the virtuous and the beautiful? that the hospital where brothers
languished, would be crushed down, and its sick inmates be buried alive;
that spies would be lurking everywhere, and private enmity have the power
to carry men from the tribunals of injustice to their tombs; that day after
day, and week after week, wagon loads of the most harmless people in the
land would be driven along the streets of Paris to the place of execution;
that captives would be swept down by grape shot, and boys and girls, by
vessel loads, be sunk in the rivers, for no other crime, than the expression
of opinions, adverse to the government, and perhaps not even under that
accusation, but only for the inheritance of gentle blood. "O! Liberty!"
said one of the noblest and most beautiful of the victims of the revolution, looking up at the statue, which represented Liberty, on her way to
the guillotine, "O! Liberty, what things are done in thy name."

But it will be said, Why dwell *now* on the past? *Because the past repeats
itself.* Human nature is unchangeable. Those, who took a prominent part
in this tragedy were men of high cultivation; men of science and learning; many of them were amiable and honest men; they thought, they were
doing right; they thought, that their country demanded such mighty sac-

rifices. We think, having so much knowledge, so deep a sense of justice, and such stupendous interests at stake, that our people cannot allow their passions to plunge the nation into war, and never could become so lost to reason, as to permit lawlessness and violence to desolate the land. Many believe, having so vast a country, and such immense resources, that the tide of our prosperity cannot, by any possible calamities, be turned back. It may be so; but this I know, that as regards war, these States are an exception in the history of the last three thousand years, and that it would be in analogy with the past, notwithstanding all that Christianity has done, and all that it promises, for the country to be, for centuries to come, the theatre of perpetual strife; and in analogy with the past, for trade, and wealth, and prosperity, to occupy new localities; perhaps the eastern coast of the Pacific, perhaps the magnificent and fertile valleys of South America. Just consider, if you think these statements extravagant or unfounded, the fate of all the ancient nations, excepting China, and one or two despotisms in Eastern Asia; remember Egypt, Assyria, Persia, Greece, Rome, Tyre, Carthage, Venice, Genoa, Spain, with her vast possessions in the sixteenth century, Holland, which three hundred years ago, possessed the commerce of the world; and you will not doubt that, in the event of the breaking up of this Confederacy, collisions, at no distant period, are almost inevitable; and the diversion of traffic, and with traffic, the diversion of population, wealth, learning, science and art, not at all improbable.

I have dwelt on this subject, believing the consideration of it in harmony with the Proclamation of the Governor of our State, and calculated to lead us to weigh seriously the questions which are now at issue. It is not wisdom to ignore the experiences of the past. It is not wisdom to shut our eyes before the lights of history. We need the calmest deliberation, and we need the wisest counsel. The country may have reached its point of culmination; its star, this very year, may pass the meridian and begin to descend; and hereafter, of her destiny, it may be said, as a friend of mine once said of Carthage: "As one by one the lights that she has kindled along the coasts of the world were extinguished, the wail of her miserere rose up through the vaulted galleries and the still cloisters of the past, and then dumb with inarticulate woe, she lay like the transient mist of the morning along the borders of the desert, till it is drunk up by the sunbeams and dissipated forever."

And now, let me ask, what, in this crisis, is a christian man's *duty*, looked at from the stand point of the Bible?

I reply first: obedience to law. In this requisition, it is not my purpose to deny the right of *revolution*, but only to indicate the necessity of conformity to the obligations, which men are under to society and to government. The duty of obedience to human law is plainly and emphatically stated in the Scriptures; but this does not touch the right or the propriety of using lawful means to punish offenders, and to guard one's privileges. How beautifully, and how truly is it said, by the great Richard Hooker, "Of law, there can be no less acknowledged, than that her seat is the bosom of God, her voice the harmony of the world; all things in heaven and earth do her homage, the very least as feeling her care, and the greatest as not exempted from her power; both angel and men, and creatures of what condition soever, each in different sort and manner, admiring her as the mother of their peace and joy."[2] Let then, no individuals in their individual capacity, attempt to take the law into their own hands. It is unwise. It is hazardous. It is unchristian. It will, if persisted in, lead to confusion and to anarchy. Let society relieve itself, but let it relieve itself by legitimate means; let its dangerous elements be removed, but let them be removed *by law*, not in violation of it. This not only would be in harmony with Justice, and for the welfare of Society, but in harmony with the spirit of the Gospel.

Once more, it seems to me, to be the duty of a christian man, notwithstanding the facts to which I alluded in the introduction of this discourse, even now to attempt to preserve this confederation of States, in the hope that fanaticism may yet be checked, and that wisdom may, hereafter, guide the people in their suffrages, and in their legislative councils. Perhaps it is too late to entertain this expectation; but considering how ignorant the great majority of voters are, and how they have been urged on by their political leaders; considering, too, those rules of love, which our divine Master has left for our guidance, and contemplating the great social and moral evils, which must be the result of antagonism, does it not appear to be the part of duty to suspend, for a short time, a final decision on the dissolution of those bonds, which, for so long a period, have held together the various parts of our country.

And now, in closing these remarks, let me urge on you the duty of prayer to Almighty God in this, the great necessity and peril of our land.

2. Richard Hooker, *Of the Laws of Ecclesiastical Polity* (London: H. Mortlock, 1705). No doubt Clark, and later Bishop Thomas Atkinson of North Carolina, cited Hooker, a late Elizabethan Anglican priest and political theorist, because Hooker tried to negotiate a compromise between Rome and the emerging Puritan religious spirit. His name symbolized the spirit of moderation for the perilous secession times.

"Our help is in the Lord." He is our Preserver in calamity, and it is He who can give us "songs of deliverance." Though he hath showed us sore troubles, because of our sins, yet, by our faith, and our love, and our obedience, shall He "bring us up again from the depths of the earth." "Come and let us return unto the Lord, for He hath torn and He can heal us; He hath smitten and He can bind us up." "God is our refuge and strength, a very present help in trouble." Pray, then, my christian hearer, to the God of your fathers. Pray to that God who hath watched over this nation, and showered down upon it peace, love, and plenty. If but one hope remains that we may yet preserve the rich, I had almost said, sacred legacy, which our fathers have bequeathed to us, O pray, that that hope may not be extinguished. If but one hope remains that this once strong and mighty ship of state, which has sailed on so tranquilly and prosperously for more than three quarters of a century, may yet be saved, may not sink into that ocean in which so many great empires lie buried, O pray, that that hope may not be lost; pray that light may be poured into men's darkened minds; that faction may be arrested; that God may be pleased to direct the consultation of our rulers to the advancement of His glory, and the safety, honor and welfare of his people; that "peace and happiness, truth and justice, religion and piety, may be established among us, for all generations."

My hearers, my heart trembles, and the blood thrills through my veins, when I contemplate the dissolution of these States. The destruction of such a nation, lightly as some may hold it, will be no common calamity; its death struggles will present no common spectacle. I see, springing up from the battered dust of the fair and beautiful Statue of Liberty, under which we and our fathers have reposed, a hundred headed monster, waving his black flags, and brandishing his blood red weapons, age after age, over the homes of our children and our children's children; crushing his iron feet, now on some sovereign State, where democracy staggers and reels, and now on some griping despotism, where power desolates everything it touches; at one period of his long dominion, blighting with his touch, commerce, agriculture, manufactures, art, science, and religion; at another, laughing, with infernal gladness, over the clashing masses of men, who once were friends and brothers; in one century, exulting in commemoration of a shattered Republic, in the next, beholding, with demoniacal joy, the *fragments* of that Republic "scattered and peeled"; and off, in the distance, amid the mists that hang there, I see it only by the lights which come gleaming up from the past, I see that hundred headed monster, with his ghastly fingers, writing one more name among the epitaphs of nations.

Men, citizens, christians, reflect long, labor faithfully, pray earnestly to God for help, before you make your *last* decision; and then, if there *be no remedy*, in darkness and in gloom, in sackcloth and in ashes, looking up to heaven for light to guide our sons, for mercy to protect our daughters, we will sing the requiem of these United States.

The South: Her Peril and Her Duty

(New Orleans: Office of True Witness & Sentinel, 1860)

Benjamin Morgan Palmer (1818–1902) was born in Charleston, South Carolina, and educated at Waterloo Academy in South Carolina. He attended and was later expelled from Amherst College in Massachusetts and in 1839 graduated from Franklin College. He then studied under the renowned James H. Thornwell at the Columbia Theological Seminary in South Carolina. He served as Presbyterian minister in Savannah, Georgia, then in Columbia, where he helped found The Southern Presbyterian Review *and taught at the Theological Seminary, then moved permanently to a famous pulpit in New Orleans, Louisiana. During the Civil War Palmer became the first moderator of the Confederate States Presbyterian Church and gave many important sermons on behalf of the Confederate cause, including a famous funeral address in December 1862 for General Maxcy Gregg. Palmer wrote six books and published many pamphlets and was considered one of the South's most brilliant religious leaders. His Thanksgiving Day Sermon of November 29, 1860, printed here, was widely circulated and became a famous contribution to the secession cause.[1] In it he linked religious principles to Southern patriotism, defended slavery as part of the South's social fabric and as a matter of self-preservation, and claimed he would not shrink from civil war. For an account of his life see Thomas Cary Johnson,* The Life and Letters of Benjamin Morgan Palmer *(Richmond: Presbyterian Committee of Publications, 1906); for comments on his sermon see Mitchell Snay,* The Gospel of Disunion: Religion and Separatism in the Antebellum South *(New York: Cambridge University Press, 1993), 175–81, and Wayne C. Eubank, "Benjamin Morgan Palmer's Thanksgiving Sermon, 1860," in J. Jeffrey Auer, ed.,* Antislavery and Disunion: Studies in the Rhetoric of Compromise and Conflict, 1858–1861 *(New York: Harper and Row, 1963), 291–309. Palmer also wrote an attack on the Kentucky Unionist Rev. Robert J. Breckinridge in which he also summed up the reasons for secession. See Palmer, "A Vindication of the South,"* Southern Presbyterian Review *14 (April, 1861): 162–75.*

Psalm XCIV, 20.—Shall the throne of iniquity have fellowship with thee, which frameth mischief by law?

Obadiah 7.—All the men of thy confederacy have brought thee even

---

1. In addition to appearing in New Orleans, Palmer's pamphlet was published in Mobile, Alabama, and elsewhere. Altogether, some 60,000 copies appeared in print.

to the border; the men that were at peace with thee have deceived thee, and prevailed against thee; they that ate thy bread have laid a wound under thee; there is none understanding him.

The voice of the Chief Magistrate has summoned us to-day to the house of prayer.[2] This call, in its annual repetition, may be too often only a solemn state-form; nevertheless it covers a mighty and a double truth.

It recognizes the existence of a personal God whose will shapes the destiny of nations, and that sentiment of religion in man which points to Him as the needle to the pole. Even with those who grope in the twilight of natural religion, natural conscience gives a voice to the dispensations of Providence. If in autumn "extensive harvests hang their heavy head," the joyous reaper, "crowned with the sickle and the wheaten sheaf," lifts his heart to the "Father of Lights from whom cometh down every good and perfect gift." Or, if pestilence and famine waste the earth, even pagan altars smoke with bleeding victims, and costly hecatombs appease the divine anger which flames out in such dire misfortunes. It is the instinct of man's religious nature, which, among Christians and heathen alike, seeks after God—the natural homage which reason, blinded as it may be, pays to a universal and ruling Providence. All classes bow beneath its spell especially in seasons of gloom, when a nation bends beneath the weight of a general calamity, and a common sorrow falls upon every heart. The hesitating skeptic forgets to weigh his scruples, as the dark shadow passes over him and fills his soul with awe. The dainty philosopher, coolly discoursing of the forces of nature and her uniform laws, abandons, for a time, his atheistical speculations, abashed by the proofs of a supreme and personal will.

Thus the devout followers of Jesus Christ, and those who do not rise above the level of mere theism, are drawn into momentary fellowship; as under the pressure of these inextinguishable convictions they pay a public and united homage to the God of nature and of grace.

In obedience to this great law of religious feeling, not less than in obedience to the civil ruler who represents this commonwealth in its unity, we are now assembled. Hitherto, on similar occasion, our language has been the language of gratitude and song. "The voice of rejoicing and salvation was in the tabernacles of the righteous." Together we praised the Lord "that our garners were full, affording all manner of store; that our sheep brought forth thousands and ten thousands in our streets; that our oxen were strong

2. The governor of Louisiana had called for a day of fasting and thanksgiving in the early stages of debate over secession.

to labor, and there was no breaking in nor going out, and not complaining was in our streets," As we together surveyed the blessing of Providence, the joyful chorus swelled from millions of people, "Peace be within thy walls and prosperity within thy palaces." But, to-day, burdened hearts all over this land are brought to the sanctuary of God. We "see the tents of Cushan in affliction, and the curtains of the land of Midian do tremble." We have fallen upon times when there are "signs in the sun, and in the moon, and in the stars; upon the earth distress of nation, with perplexity; the sea and the waves roaring; men's hearts failing them for fear and for looking after those things which are coming" in the near yet gloomy future. Since the words of this proclamation were penned by which we are convened, that which all men dreaded, but against which all men hoped, has been realized; and in the triumph of a sectional majority we are compelled to read the probable doom of our once happy and united confederacy. It is not to be concealed that we are in the most fearful and perilous crisis which has occurred in our history as a nation. The cords which, during four-fifths of a century, have bound together this growing republic are now strained to their utmost tension; they just need the touch of fire to part asunder forever. Like a ship laboring in the storm and suddenly grounded upon some treacherous shoal—every timber of this vast confederacy strains and groans under the pressure. Sectional divisions, the jealousy of rival interests, the lust of political power, a bastard ambition which looks to personal aggrandizement rather than to the public weal, a reckless radicalism which seeks for the subversion of all that is ancient and stable, and a furious fanaticism which drives on its ill-considered conclusions with utter disregard of the evil it engenders—all these combine to create a portentous crisis, the like of which we have never known before, and which puts to a crucifying test the virtue, the patriotism and the piety of the country.

You, my hearers, who have waited upon my public ministry and have known me in the intimacies of pastoral intercourse, will do me the justice to testify that I have never intermeddled with political questions. Interested as I might be in the progress of events, I have never obtruded, either publicly or privately, my opinion upon any of you; nor can a single man arise and say that, by word or sign, have I ever sought to warp his sentiments or control his judgment upon any political subject whatsoever. The party questions which have hitherto divided the political world, have seemed to me to involve no issue sufficiently momentous to warrant my turning aside, even for a moment, from my chosen calling. In this day of intelligence, I have felt there were thousands around me more competent to instruct in statesmanship; and thus, from considerations of modesty no less than prudence, I have preferred to move among you as a preacher of righteousness belonging to a kingdom not of this world.

During the heated canvass which has just been brought to so disastrous a close, the seal of a rigid and religious silence has not been broken. I deplored the divisions amongst us as being, to a large extent, impertinent in the solemn crisis which was too evidently impending. Most clearly did it appear to me that but one issue was before us; an issue soon to be presented in a form which would compel the attention. That crisis might make it imperative upon me as a Christian and a divine to speak in language admitting no misconstruction. Until then, aside from the din and strife of parties, I could only mature, with solitary and prayerful thought, the destined utterance. That hour has come. At a juncture so solemn as the present, with the destiny of a great people waiting upon the decision of an hour, it is not lawful to be still. Whoever may have influence to shape public opinion, at such a time must lend it, or prove faithless to a trust as solemn as any to be accounted for at the bar of God.

Is it immodest in me to assume that I may represent a class whose opinions in such a controversy are of cardinal importance? The class which seeks to ascertain its duty in the light simply of conscience and religion; and which turns to the moralist and the Christian for support and guidance. The question, too, which now places us upon the brink of revolution, was in its origin a question of morals and religion. It was debated in ecclesiastical councils before it entered legislative halls. It has riven asunder the two largest religious communions in the land; and the right determination of this primary question will go far toward fixing the attitude we must assume in the coming struggle. I sincerely pray God that I may be forgiven if I have misapprehended the duty incumbent upon me to-day; for I have ascended this pulpit under the agitation of feeling natural to one who is about to deviate from the settled policy of his public life. It is my purpose — not as your organ, compromitting you, whose opinions are for the most part unknown to me, but on my sole responsibility — to speak upon the one question of the day; and to state the duty which, as I believe, patriotism and religion alike require of us all. I shall aim to speak with a moderation of tone and feeling almost judicial, well befitting the sanctities of the place and the solemnities of the judgement day.

In determining our duty in this emergency it is necessary that we should first ascertain the nature of the trust providentially committed to us. A nation often has a character as well defined and intense as that of the individual. This depends, of course, upon a variety of causes operating through a long period of time. It is due largely to the original traits which distinguish the stock from which it springs, and to the providential training which has formed its education. But, however derived, this individuality of character alone makes any people truly historic, competent to work out its specific mission, and to become a factor in the world's progress. The particular trust assigned to such a people becomes the pledge of the divine protection; and their fidelity to it determines the fate by which it is finally overtaken. What that trust is must be ascertained from the necessities of their position, the institutions which are the outgrowth of their principles and the conflicts through which they preserve their identity and independence. If then the South is such a people, what, at this juncture, is their providential trust? I answer, that it is *to conserve and to perpetuate the institution of domestic slavery as now existing.* It is not necessary here to inquire whether this is precisely the best relation in which the hewer of wood and drawer of water can stand to his employer; although this proposition may perhaps be successfully sustained by those who choose to defend it. Still less are we required, dogmatically, to affirm that it will subsist through all time. Baffled as our wisdom may now be, in finding a solution of this intricate social problem, it would nevertheless be the height of arrogance to pronounce what changes may or may not occur in the distant future. In the grand march of events Providence may work out a solution undiscovered by us. What modifications of soil and climate may hereafter be produced, what consequent changes in the products on which we depend, what political revolutions may occur among the races which are now enacting the great drama of history; all such inquiries are totally irrelevant because no prophetic vision can pierce the darkness of that future. If this question should ever arise, the generation to whom it is remitted will doubtless have the wisdom to meet it, and Providence will burnish the lights in which it is to be resolved. All that we claim for them and for ourselves is liberty to work out this problem guided by nature and God, without obtrusive interference from abroad. These great questions of Providence and history must have free scope for their solution; and the race whose fortunes are distinctly implicated in the same is alone authorized, as it is alone competent, to determine them. It is just this impertinence of human legislation, setting bounds to what God only can regulate, that the South is called this day to resent and resist. The country is convulsed simply because "the throne of iniquity frameth mischief by a law." Without, therefore, determining the question of duty for future generations, I simply say, that for us, as now situated, the duty is plain of conserving and transmitting the system of slavery, with the freest scope for its natural development and extension. Let us, my brethren, look our duty in the face. With this institution assigned to our keeping, what reply shall we make to those who say that its days are numbered? My own conviction is, that we should at once lift ourselves, intelligently, to the highest moral ground and proclaim to all the world that we hold this trust from God, and in its occupancy we are prepared to stand or fall as God may appoint. If the critical moment has arrived at which the great issue is joined, let us say that, in the sight of all perils, we will stand by our trust; and God be with the right!

The argument which enforces the solemnity of this providential trust is simple and condensed. It is bound upon us, then, by the *principle of self-preservation*, that "first law" which is continually asserting its supremacy over all others. Need I pause to show how this system of servitude underlies and supports our material interests? That our wealth consists in our lands and in the serfs who till them? That from the nature of our products they can only be cultivated by labor which must be controlled in order to be certain? That any other than a tropical race must faint and wither beneath a tropical sun? Need I pause to show how this system is interwoven with our entire social fabric? That these slaves form parts of our households, even as our children; and that, too, through a relationship recognized and sanctioned in the Scriptures of God even as the other? Must I pause to show how it has fashioned our modes of life, and determined all our habits of thought and feeling, and moulded the very type of our civilization? How then can the hand of violence be laid upon it without involving our existence? The so-called free States of this country are working out the social problem under conditions peculiar to themselves. These conditions are sufficiently hard, and their success is too uncertain, to excite in us the least jealousy of their lot. With a teeming population, which the soil cannot support—with their wealth depending upon arts, created by artificial wants—with an eternal friction between the grades of their society—with their labor and their capital grinding against each other like the upper and nether mill-stones—with labor cheapened and displaced by new mechanical inventions, bursting more asunder the bonds of brotherhood; amid these intricate perils we have ever given them our sympathy and our prayers, and have never sought to weaken the foundations of their social order. God grant them complete success in the solution of all their perplexities! We, too, have our responsibilities and trials; but they are all bound up in this one institution, which has been the object of such unrighteous assault through five and twenty years. If we are true to ourselves we shall, at this critical juncture, stand by it and work out our destiny.

This duty is bound upon us again *as the constituted guardians of the slaves themselves*. Our lot is not more implicated in theirs, than is their lot in ours, in our mutual relations we survive or perish together. The worst foes of the black race are those who have intermeddled in their behalf. We know better than others that every attribute of their character fits them for dependence and servitude. By nature the most affectionate and loyal of all races beneath the sun, they are also the most helpless; and no calamity can befall them greater than the loss of that protection they enjoy under this patriarchal system. Indeed the experiment has been grandly tried of precipitating them upon freedom which they know not how to enjoy; and the dismal results are before us in statistics that astonish the world. With the fairest portions of the earth in their possession, and with the advantage of a long discipline as cultivators of the soil, their constitutional indolence has converted the most beautiful islands of the sea into a howling waste. It is not too much to say that if the South should, at this moment, surrender every slave, the wisdom of the entire world, united in solemn council, could not solve the question of their disposal. Their transportation to Africa, even if it were feasible, would be but the most refined cruelty; they must perish with starvation before they could have time to relapse into their primitive barbarism.[3] Their residence here, in the presence of the vigorous Saxon race, would be but the signal for their rapid extermination before they had time to waste away through listlessness, filth and vice. Freedom would be their doom; and equally from both they call upon us, their providential guardians, to be protected. I know this argument will be scoffed abroad as the hypocritical cover thrown over our own cupidity and selfishness; but every Southern master knows its truth and feels its power. My servant, whether born in my house or bought with my money, stands to me in the relation of a child. Though providentially owing me service, which, providentially, I am bound to exact, he is, nevertheless, my brother and my friend; and I am to him a guardian and a father. He leans upon me for protection, for counsel, and for blessing; and so long as the relation continues no power, but the power of Almighty God, shall come between him and me. Were there no argument but this, it binds upon us the providential duty of preserving the relation that we may save him from a doom worse than death.

It is a duty which we owe, farther, *to the civilized world*. It is a remarkable fact that during these thirty years of unceasing warfare against slavery, and while a lying spirit has inflamed the world against us, that world has grown

3. Palmer decried attempts to colonize slaves and free blacks and regarded the movement as death to blacks who went back to what he believed to be primitive African culture. For the history of that movement see Philip J. Staudenraus, *The African Colonization Movement* (New York: Columbia University Press, 1961).

more and more dependent upon it for sustenance and wealth. Every tyro know that all branches of industry fall back upon the soil. We must come, every one of us, to the bosom of this great mother for nourishment. In the happy partnership which has grown up in providence between the tribes of this confederacy, our industry has been concentrated upon agriculture. To the North we have cheerfully resigned all the profits arising from manufacture and commerce. Those profits they have, for the most part, fairly earned, and we have never begrudged them. We have sent them our sugar and bought it back when refined; we have sent them our cotton and bought it back when spun into thread or woven into cloth. Almost every article we use, from the shoe-lachet to the most elaborate and costly article of luxury, they have made and we have bought; and both sections have thriven by the partnership, as no people ever thrived before since the first shining of the sun. So literally true are the words of our text, addressed by Obadiah to Edom, "All the men of our confederacy, the men that were at peace with us, have eaten our bread at the very time they have deceived and laid a wound under us." Even beyond—this the enriching commerce, which has built the splendid cities and marble palaces, of England as well as of America, has been largely established upon the products of our soil; and the blooms upon Southern fields gathered by black hands, have fed the spindles and looms of Manchester and Birmingham not less than of Lawrence and Lowell. Strike now a blow at this system of labor and the world itself totters at the stroke. Shall we permit that blow to fall? Do we not owe it to civilized man to stand in the breach and stay the uplifted arm? If the blind Samson lays hold of the pillars which support the arch of the world's industry, how many more will be buried beneath its ruins than the lords of the Philistines? "Who knoweth whether we are not come to the kingdom for such a time as this?"

Last of all, in this great struggle, *we defend the cause of God and Religion.* The abolition spirit is undeniably atheistic. The demon which erected its throne upon the guillotine in the days of Robespierre and Marat, which abolished the Sabbath and worshipped reason in the person of a harlot, yet survives to work other horrors, of which those of the French revolution are but the type. Among a people so generally religious as the American, a disguise must be worn; but it is the same old threadbare disguise of the advocacy of human rights. From a thousand Jacobin clubs here, as in France, the decree has gone forth which strikes at God by striking at all subordination and law. Availing itself of the morbid and misdirected sympathies of men, it has entrapped weak consciences in the meshes of its treachery; and now, at last, has seated its high priest upon the throne, clad in the black garments of discord and schism, so symbolic of its ends. Under this specious cry of reform, it demands that every evil shall be corrected, or society become a wreck—the sun must be stricken from the heavens, if a spot is found upon his disc. The Most High, knowing His own power which is infinite, and His own wisdom which is unfathomable, can afford to be patient. But these self-constituted reformers must quicken the activity of Jehovah or compel his abdication. In their furious haste, they trample upon obligations sacred as any which can bind the conscience. It is time to reproduce the obsolete idea that Providence must govern man, and not that man should control Providence. In the imperfect state of human society, it pleases God to allow evils which check others that are greater. As in the physical world, objects are moved forward, not by a single force, but by the composition of forces; so in his moral administration, there are checks and balances whose intimate relations are comprehended only by himself. But what reck they of this—these fierce zealots who undertake to drive the chariot of the sun? Working out the single and false idea which rides them like a nightmare, they dash athwart the spheres, utterly disregarding the delicate mechanism of Providence; which moves on, wheels within wheels, with pivots and balances and springs, which the great designer alone can control. This spirit of atheism, which knows no God who tolerates evil, no Bible which sanctions law, and no conscience that can be bound by oaths and covenants, has selected us for its victims, and slavery for its issue. Its banner-cry rings out already upon the air—"liberty, equality, fraternity," which simply interpreted, means bondage, confiscation and massacre. With its tricolor waving in the breeze—it waits to inaugurate its reign of terror. To the South the high position is assigned of defending, before all nations, the cause of all religions and of all truth. In this trust, we are resisting the power which wars against constitutions and laws and compacts, against Sabbaths and sanctuaries, against the family, the state, and the church; which blasphemously invades the prerogatives of God, and rebukes the Most High for the errors of His administration; which, if it cannot snatch the reins of empire from His grace, will lay the universe in ruins at His feet. Is it possible that we shall decline the onset?

This argument, then, which sweeps over the entire circle of our relations, touches the four cardinal points of duty *to ourselves, to our slaves, to the world, and to Almighty God.* It establishes the nature and solemnity of our present trust, to *preserve and transmit our existing system of domestic servitude, with the right, unchallenged by man, to go and root itself wherever Providence and nature may carry it.* This trust we will discharge in the face of the worst possible peril. Though war be the aggregation of all evils, yet, should the madness of the hour appeal to the arbitration of the sword, we will not shrink even from the baptism of fire. If modern crusaders stand in serried ranks upon some plain of Esdraelon, there shall we be in defense of our trust. Not till the last man has fallen behind the last rampart, shall it drop from our hands; and then only in surrender to the God who gave it.

Against this institution a system of aggression has been pursued through the last thirty years. Initiated by a few fanatics, who were at first despised, it has gathered strength from opposition until it has assumed its present gigantic proportions. No man has thoughtfully watched the progress of this controversy without being convinced that the crisis must at length come. Some few, perhaps, have hoped against hope, that the gathering imposthume might be dispersed, and the poison be eliminated from the body politic by healthful remedies. But the delusion has scarcely been cherished by those who have studied the history of fanaticism in its path of blood and fire through the ages of the past. The moment must arrive when the conflict must be joined, and victory decide for one or the other. As it has been a war of legislative tactics, and not of physical force, both parties have been maneuvering for a position; and the embarrassment has been, whilst dodging amidst constitutional forms, to make an issue that should be clear, simple, and tangible. Such an issue is at length presented in the result of the recent Presidential election. Be it observed, too, that it is an issue made by the North, not by the South; upon whom, therefore, must rest the entire guilt of the present disturbance. With a choice between three national candidates, who have more or less divided the votes of the South, the North, with unexampled unanimity, have cast their ballot for a candidate who is sectional, who represents a party that is sectional, and the ground of that sectionalism, prejudice against the established and constitutional rights and immunities and institutions of the South. What does this declare—what can it declare, but that from henceforth this is to be a government of section over section; a government using constitutional forms only to embarrass and divide the section ruled, and as fortresses through whose embrasures the cannon of legislation is to be employed in demolishing the guaranteed institutions of the South? What issue is more direct, concrete, intelligible than this? I thank God that, since the conflict must be joined, the responsibility of this issue rests not with us, who have ever acted upon the defensive; and that it is so disembarrassed and simple that the feeblest mind can understand it.

The question with the South today is not what issue shall *she* make, but how shall she meet that which is prepared for her? Is it possible that we can hesitate longer than a moment? In our natural recoil from the perils of revolution, and with our clinging fondness for the memories of the past, we may perhaps look around for something to soften the asperity of this issue, for some ground on which we may defer the day of evil, for some hope that the gathering clouds may not burst in fury upon the land.

It is alleged, for example, that the President elect has been chosen by a fair majority under prescribed forms. But need I say, to those who have read history, that no despotism is more absolute than that of an unprincipled democracy, and no tyranny more galling than that exercised through constitutional formulas? But the plea is idle, when the very question we debate is the perpetuation of that constitution now converted into an engine of oppression, and the continuance of that union which is henceforth to be our condition of vassalage. I say it with solemnity and pain, this Union of our forefathers is already gone. It existed but in mutual confidence, the bonds of which were ruptured in the late election. Though its form should be preserved, it is, in fact, destroyed. We may possibly entertain the project of reconstructing it; but it will be another union, resting upon other than past guarantees. "In that we say a new covenant we have made the first old, and that which decayeth and waxeth old is ready to vanish away" — "as a vesture it is folded up." For my self I say that, under the rule which threatens us, I throw off the yoke of this Union as readily as did our ancestor the yoke of King George III, and for causes immeasurably stronger than those pleaded in their celebrated declaration.

It is softly whispered, too, that the successful competitor for the throne protests and avers his purpose to administer the government in a conservative and national spirit. Allowing him all credit for personal integrity in these protestations, he is, in this matter, nearly as impotent for good as he is competent for evil. He is nothing more than a figure upon the political chess-board — whether pawn or knight or king, will hereafter appear — but still a silent figure upon the checkered squares, moved by the hands of an unseen player. That player is the party to which he owes his elevation; a party that has signalized its history by the most unblushing perjuries. What faith can be placed in the protestations of men who openly avow that their consciences are too sublimated to be restrained by the obligation of covenants or by the sanctity of oaths? No! we have seen the trail of the serpent five and twenty years in our Eden; twined now in the branches of the forbidden tree, we feel the pangs of death already begun as its hot breath is upon our cheek, hissing out the original falsehood, "Ye shall not surely die."

Another suggests that even yet the Electors, alarmed by these demonstrations of the South, may not cast the black ball which dooms their country to the executioner. It is a forlorn hope. Whether we should counsel such breach of faith in them or take refuge in their treachery — whether such a result would give a President chosen by the people according to the constitution—are points I will not discuss. But that it would prove a cure for any of our ills who can believe? It is certain that it would, with some show of justice, exasperate a party sufficiently ferocious; that it would doom us to four years of increasing strife and bitterness, and that the crisis must come at last under issues possibly not half so clear as the present. Let us not desire to shift the day of trial by miserable subterfuges of this sort. The issue is upon us; let us meet it like men and end this strife forever.

But some quietest whispers, yet further, this majority is accidental and has been swelled by accessions of men simply opposed to the existing administration; the party is utterly heterogeneous and must be shivered into fragments by its own success. I confess, frankly, this suggestion has staggered me more than any other, and I sought to take refuge therein. Why should we not wait and see the effect of success itself upon a party whose elements might devour each other in the very distribution of the spoil? Two considerations have dissipated the fallacy before me. The first is, that however mixed the party, abolitionism is clearly its informing and actuating soul; and fanaticism is a blood-hound that never bolts its track when it has once lapped blood. The elevation of their candidate is far from being the consummation of their aims. It is only the beginning of that consummation; and, if all history be not a lie, there will be cohersion enough till the end of the beginning is reached, and the dreadful banquet of slaughter and ruin shall glut the appetite. The second consideration is a principle which I cannot blink. It is nowhere denied that the first article in the creed of the now dominant party is the restriction of slavery within its present limits. It is distinctly avowed by their organs, and in the name of their elected chieftain; as will appear from the following extract from an article written to pacify the South and to reassure its fears: "There can be no doubt whatever in the mind of any man, that Mr. Lincoln regards slavery as a moral, social, and political evil, and that it should be dealt with as such by the Federal Government, in every instance where it is called upon to deal with it at all. On this point there is no room for question—and there need be no misgivings as to his official action. The whole influence of the Executive Department of the Government, while in his hands, will be thrown against the extension of slavery into the new territories of the Union, and the re-opening of the African slave trade. On these points he will make no compromise nor yield one hair's breadth to coercion from any quarter or in any shape. He does not accede to the alleged decision of the Supreme Court, that the Constitution places slaves upon the footing of other property, and protects them as such wherever its jurisdiction extends, nor will he be, in the least degree, governed or controlled by it in his executive action. He will do all in his power, personally and officially, by the direct exercise of the powers of his office, and the indirect influence inseparable from it, to arrest the tendency to make slavery national and perpetual, and to place it in precisely the same position which it held in the early days of the Republic, and in the view of the founders of the Government."[4]

Now, what enigmas may be concluded in this last sentence—the sphinx which uttered them can perhaps resolve; but the sentence in which they occur is as big as the belly of the Trojan horse which laid the city of Priam in ruins.

These utterances we have heard so long that they fall stale upon the ear; but never before have they had such significance. Hitherto they have come from Jacobin conventicles and pulpits, from the rostrum, from the hustings, and from the halls of our national Congress; but always as the utterance of irresponsible men or associations of men. But now the voice comes from the throne; already, before clad with the sanctities of office, ere the anointing oil is poured upon the monarch's head, the decree has gone forth that the institution of Southern slavery shall be constrained within assigned limits. Though nature and Providence should send forth its branches like the Banyan tree, to take root in congenial soil, here is a power superior to both, that says it shall wither and die within its own charmed circle.

What say you to this, to whom this great providential trust of conserving slavery is concerned? "Shall the throne of iniquity have fellowship with thee, which frameth mischief by a law?" It is this that makes the crisis. Whether we will or not, this is the historic moment when the fate of this institution hangs suspended in the balance. Decide either way, it is the moment of our destiny—the only thing affected by the decision is the complexion of that destiny. If the South bows before this throne she accepts the decree of restriction and ultimate extinction, which is made the condition of her homage.

As it appears to me, the course to be pursued in this emergency is that which has already been inaugurated. Let the people in all the Southern States, in solemn council assembled, reclaim the powers they have delegated. Let those conventions be composed of men whose fidelity has been approved—men who bring the wisdom, experience and firmness of age to support and announce principles which have long been matured. Let these conventions decide firmly and solemnly what they will do with this great trust committed to their hands. Let them pledge each other in sacred cove-

4. From William Cullen Bryant, New York *Evening Post*, November 18, 1860.

nant, to uphold and perpetuate what they cannot resign without dishonor and palpable ruin. Let them further take all the necessary steps looking to separate and independent existence; and initiate measures for framing a new and homogeneous confederacy. Thus, prepared for every contingency, let the crisis come. Paradoxical as it may seem, if there be any way to save, or rather to re-construct, the union of our forefathers, it is this. Perhaps, at the last moment, the conservative portions of the North may awake to see the abyss into which they are about to plunge. Perchance they may arise and crush out forever the abolition hydra, and cast it into a grave from which there shall never be a resurrection.

Thus, with restored confidence, we may be rejoined a united and happy people. But, before God, I believe that nothing will effect this but the line of policy which the South has been compelled in self-preservation to adopt. I confess frankly, I am not sanguine that such an auspicious result will be reached. Partly, because I do not see how new guarantees are to be grafted upon the Constitution, nor how, if grafted, they can be more binding than those which have already been trampled under foot; but chiefly, because I do not see how such guarantees can be elicited from the people at the North. It cannot be disguised, that almost to a man, they are antislavery where they are not abolition. A whole generation has been educated to look upon the system with abhorrence as a national blot. They hope, and look, and pray for its extinction within a reasonable time, and cannot be satisfied unless things are seen drawing to that conclusion. We, on the contrary, as its constituted guardians, can demand nothing less than that is should be left open to expansion, subject to no limitations save those imposed by God and nature. I fear the antagonism is too great, and the conscience of both parties too deeply implicated to allow such a composition of the strife. Nevertheless since it is within the range of possibility in the Providence of God, I would not shut out the alternative.

Should it fail, what remains but that we say to each other, calmly and kindly, what Abraham said to Lot: "Let there be not strife, I pray thee, between me and thee, and between my herdmen and thy herdmen, for we be brethren: Is not the whole land before thee? Separate thyself, I pray thee, from me — if thou will take the left hand, then I will go to the right, or if thou depart to the right hand, then I will go to the left." Thus, if we cannot save the Union, we may save the inestimable blessings it enshrines; if we cannot preserve the vase, we will preserve the precious liquor it contains.

In all this I speak for the North no less than for the South; for upon our united and determined resistance at this moment depends the salvation of the whole country—in saving ourselves we shall save the North from the ruin she is madly drawing down upon her head.

The position of the South is at this moment sublime. If she has grace given her to know her hour she will save herself, the country, and the world. It will involve, indeed, temporary prostration and distress; the dykes of Holland must be cut to save her from the troops of Philip. But I warn my countrymen the historic moment once passed, never returns. If she will arise in her majesty, and speak now as with the voice of one man, she will roll back for all time the curse that is upon her. If she succumbs now, she transmits that curse as an heirloom to posterity. We may, for a generation, enjoy comparative ease, gather up our feet in our beds, and die in peace; but our children will go forth beggared from the homes of their fathers. Fishermen will cast their nets where your proud commercial navy now rides at anchor, and dry them upon the shore now covered with your bales of merchandise. Sapped, circumvented, undermined, the institutions of your soil will be overthrown; and within five and twenty years the history of St. Domingo will be the record of Louisiana. If dead men's bones can tremble, ours will move under the muttered curses of sons and daughters, denouncing the blindness and love of ease which have left them an inheritance of woe.

I have done my duty under as deep a sense of responsibility to God and man as I have ever felt. Under a full conviction that the salvation of the whole country is depending upon the action of the South, I am impelled to deepen the sentiment of resistance in the Southern mind, and to strengthen the current now flowing towards a union of the South, in defense of her chartered rights. It is a duty which I shall not be called to repeat, for such awful junctures do not occur twice in a century. Bright and happy days are yet before us; and before another political earthquake shall shake the continent, I hope to be "where the wicked cease from troubling and where the weary are at rest."

It only remains to say, that whatever be the fortunes of the South, I accept them for my own. Born upon her soil, of a father thus born before me—from an ancestry that occupied it while yet it was a part of England's possessions—she is in every sense my mother. I shall die upon her bosom—she shall know no peril, but it is my peril—no conflict, but it is my conflict—and no abyss of ruin, into which I shall not share her fall. May the Lord God cover her head in this her day of battle!

JAMES D. B. DE BOW

The Interest in Slavery of the Southern Non-Slaveholder

(Charleston: Evans & Cogswell, 1860)

James D. B. De Bow (1820–67) came from a poor Charleston family, attended Cokesbury Institute in South Carolina, studied at the College of Charleston on a scholarship, graduated number one in his class in 1843, and then read law. A poor speaker, he soon realized that the law was not for him and instead began to write for The Southern Quarterly Review, *an intellectual and political periodical in Charleston. In 1845 De Bow moved to New Orleans, Louisiana, where he founded the business magazine* De Bow's Review, *became a professor of political economy at the University of New Orleans, gained fame as head of the Louisiana Bureau of Statistics, and served as superintendent of the 1850 U.S. Census. Ardent about defending the South, he published many important political and economic articles on the sectional crisis. During the presidential election in 1860 he traveled in the Gulf states and the Southeast to meet with secession leaders and to give speeches in support of secession. His most famous speech, which became the pamphlet printed below,[1] was a reply to Hinton R. Helper's* Impending Crisis of the South *(New York: Burdick Brothers, 1857), in which he refuted Helper's views on the decline of the Southern economy and the damage that the slave culture did to poor whites. De Bow blamed the problems of Southern agriculture on a conspiracy of Northern manufacturers and shippers, as he attempted to unite all Southerners in defense of slavery and secession. During the Civil War he held posts in the Confederate Treasury Department and as a Confederate cotton agent. For information about his life see Otis Clark Skipper,* J. D. B. De Bow: Magazinist of the Old South *(Athens: University of Georgia Press, 1958); interested readers should peruse the pages of* De Bow's Review *(1846–67).*

When in charge of the national census office, several years since, I found that it had been stated by an abolition Senator from his seat, that the

1. This pamphlet originated as a speech on December 5, 1860, in Nashville, Tennessee. It created such a stir that Robert Gourdin of the South Carolina 1860 Association asked De Bow if he could reprint it as pamphlet number five of his secession pamphlets. De Bow also reprinted the speech in *De Bow's Review* 30 (January 1861): 67–76. For a study of the 1860 Association see Charles Edward Cauthen, *South Carolina Goes to War, 1860–1865* (Chapel Hill: University of North Carolina Press, 1950).

number of slaveholders in the South did not exceed 150,000. Convinced that it was a gross misrepresentation of the facts, I caused a careful examination of the returns to be made, which fixed the actual number at 347,255, and communicated the information, by note, to Senator Cass, who read it in the Senate. I first called attention to the fact that the number embraced slaveholding families, and that to arrive at the actual number of persons, which the census showed to a family. When this was done, the number swelled to about 2,000,000.

Since these results were made public, I have had reason to think, that the separation of the schedules of the slave and the free, was calculated to lead to omissions of the single properties, and that on this account it would be safe to put the number of families at 375,000, and the number of actual slaveholders at about two million and a quarter.

Assuming the published returns, however, to be correct, it will appear that one-half of the population of South Carolina, Mississippi, and Louisiana, excluding the cities, are slaveholders, and that one-third of the population of the entire South are similarly circumstanced. The average number of slaves is nine to each slave-holding family, and one-half of the whole number of such holders are in possession of less than five slaves.

It will thus appear that the slaveholders of the South, so far from constituting numerically an insignificant portion of its people, as has been malignantly alleged, make up an aggregate, greater in relative proportion than the holders of any other species of property whatever, in any part of the world; and that of no other property can it be said, with equal truthfulness, that it is an interest of the whole community. Whilst every other family in the States I have specially referred to, are slaveholders, but one family in every three and a half families in Maine, New Hampshire, Massachusetts and Connecticut, are holders of agricultural land; and, in European States, the proportion is almost indefinitely less. The proportion which the slaveholders of the South, bear to the entire population is greater than that of the owners of land, of houses, agricultural stock, State, bank, or other corporation securities anywhere else. No political economist will deny this. Nor is that all. Even in the States which are among the largest slaveholding, South Carolina, Georgia and Tennessee, the land proprietors outnumber nearly two to one, in relative proportion, the owners of the same property in Maine, Massachusetts and Connecticut, and if the average number of slaves held by each family throughout the South be but nine, and if one-half of the whole number of slaveholders own under five slaves, it will be seen how preposterous is the allegation of our enemies, that the slaveholding class is an organized wealthy aristocracy. *The poor men of the South are the holders of one to five slaves, and it would be equally consistent with truth and justice, to say that they represent, in reality, its slaveholding interests.*

The fact being conceded that there is a very large class of persons in the slaveholding States, who have no direct ownership in slaves; it may be well asked, upon what principle a greater antagonism can be presumed between them and their fellow-citizens, than exists among the larger class of non-landholders in the free States and the landed interest there? If a conflict of interest exists in one instance, it does in the other, and if patriotism and public spirit are to be measured upon so low a standard, the social fabric at the North is in far greater danger of dissolution than it is here.

Though I protest against the false and degrading standard, to which Northern orators and statesmen have reduced the measure of patriotism, which is to be expected from a free and enlightened people, and in the name of the non-slaveholders of the South, fling back the insolent charge that they are only bound to their country by its "loaves and fishes," and would be found derelict in honor and principle and public virtue in proportion as they are needy in circumstances; I think it be easy to show that the interest of the poorest non-slaveholder among us, is to make common cause with, and die in the last trenches in defence of, the slave property of his more favored neighbor.

The non-slaveholders of the South may be classed as either such as desire and are incapable of purchasing slaves, or such as have the means to purchase and do not because of the absence of the motive, preferring to hire or employ cheaper white labor. A class conscientiously objecting to the ownership of slave-property, does not exist at the South, for all such scruples have long since been silenced by the profound and unanswerable arguments to which Yankee controversy has driven our statesmen, popular orators and clergy. Upon the sure testimony of God's Holy Book; and upon the principles of universal polity, they have defended and justified the institution. The exceptions which embrace recent importations into Virginia, and into some of the Southern cities from the free States of the North, and some of the crazy, socialistic Germans in Texas, are too unimportant to affect the truth of the proposition.

The non-slaveholders are either urban or rural, including among the former the merchants, traders, mechanics, laborers and other classes in the towns and cities; and among the latter, the tillers of the soil in sections where slave property either could, or could not be profitably employed.

As the *competition of free labor with slave labor is* the gist of the argument used by the opponents of slavery, and as it is upon this that they rely in support of a future social *conflict* in our midst, it is clear that in cases where the competition cannot possibly exist, the argument, whatever weight it might otherwise have, must fall to the ground.

Now, from what can such competition be argued in our cities? Are not all the interests of the merchant and those whom he employs in necessity upon the side of the slaveholder? The products which he buys, the commodities which he sells, the profits which he realizes, the hopes of future fortune which sustain him; all spring from this source, and from no other. The cities, towns, and villages of the South, are but so many agencies for converting the product of slave labor into the product of other labor obtained from abroad, and as in every other agency the interest of the agent is, that the principal shall have as much as possible to sell, and be enabled as much as possible to buy. In the absence of every other source of wealth at the South, its mercantile interests are so interwoven with those of slave labor as to be almost identical. What is true of the merchant is true of the clerk, the drayman, or the laborer whom he employs—the mechanic who builds his houses, the lawyer who argues his causes, the physician who heals, the teacher, the preacher, etc., etc. If the poor mechanic could have ever complained of the competition, in the cities, of slave labor with his, that cause or complaint in the enormous increase of value of slave property has failed, since such increase has been exhausting the cities and towns of slave labor, or making it so valuable that he can work in competition with and receive a rate of remuneration greatly higher than in any of the non-slaveholding towns or cities at the North. In proof of this, it is only necessary to advert to the example of the City of Charleston, which has a larger proportion of slaves than any other, at the South, where the first flag of Southern independence was unfurled, and where the entire people, with one voice, rich and poor, merchant, mechanic and laborer, stand nobly together. Another illustration may be found in the city of New York, almost as dependent upon Southern slavery as Charleston itself, which records a majority of nearly thirty thousand votes against the further progress of abolitionism.

As the competition does not exist in the cities it is equally certain that it does not exist in those sections of the South, which are employed upon the cultivation of commodities, in which slave labor could not be used, and that there exists no conflict there except in the before states cases of Virginia and Texas, and some of the counties of Missouri, Maryland and Kentucky. Theses exceptions are, however, too unimportant to affect the great question of slavery in fifteen States of the South, and are so kept in check as to be incapable of effecting any mischief even in the communities referred to. It would be the baldest absurdity to suppose that the poor farmers of South Carolina, North Carolina and Tennessee, who grow corn, wheat, bacon and hogs and horses, are brought into any sort of competition with the slaves of these of other States, who, while they consume these commodities, produce but little or none of them.

The competition and conflict, if such exist at the South, between slave labor and free, is reduced to the single case of such labor being employed side by side, in the production of the same commodities and could be felt only in the cane, cotton, tobacco and rice fields, where almost the entire agricultural slave labor is exhausted. Now, any one cognizant of the actual facts, will admit that the free labor which is employed upon these crops, disconnected from and in actual independence of the slaveholder, is a very insignificant item in the account, and whether in accord or in conflict would affect nothing the permanency and security of the institution. It is a competition from which the non-slaveholder cheerfully retires when the occasion offers, his physical organization refusing to endure that exposure to tropical suns and fatal miasmas which alone are the condition of profitable culture and any attempt to reverse the laws which God had ordained, is attended with disease and death. Of this the poor white foreign laborer upon our river swamps and in our southern cities, especially Mobile and New Orleans, and upon the public works of the South, is a daily witness.

Having then followed out, step by step, and seen to what amounts the so much paraded competition and conflict between the non-slaveholding and slaveholding interests of the South; I will proceed to present several general considerations which must be found powerful enough to influence the non-slaveholders, if the claims of patriotism were inadequate, to resist any attempt to overthrow the institutions and industry of the section to which they belong.

1. *The non-slaveholder of the South is assured that the remuneration afforded by his labor, over and above the expense of living, is larger than that which is afforded by the same labor in the free States.* To be convinced of this he has only to compare the value of labor in the Southern cities with those of the North, and to take note annually of the large number of laborers who are represented to be out of employment there, and who migrate to our shores, as well as to other sections. No white laborer in return has been forced to leave our midst or remain without employment. Such as have left, have immigrated from States where slavery was less productive. Those who come among us are enabled soon to retire to their homes with a handsome com-

petency. The statement is nearly as true for the agricultural as for other interests, as the statistics will show. . . .[2]

2. *The non-slaveholders, as a class, are not reduced by the necessity of our condition, as is the case in the free States, to find employment in crowded cities and come into competition in close and sickly workshops and factories, with remorseless and untiring machinery.* They have but to compare their condition in this particular with the mining and manufacturing operative of the North and Europe, to be thankful that God has reserved them for a better fate. Tender women, aged men, delicate children, toil and labor there from early dawn until after candle light, from one year to another, for a miserable pittance, scarcely above the starvation point without hope of amelioration. The records of British free labor have long exhibited this and those of our own manufacturing States are rapidly reaching it and would have reached it long ago, but for the excessive bounties which in the way of tariffs have been paid to it, without an equivalent by the slaveholding and non-slaveholding laborer of the South. Let this tariff cease to be paid for by a single year and the truth of what is stated will be abundantly shown.

3. *The non-slaveholder is not subjected to that competition with foreign pauper labor, which has degraded the free labor of the North and demoralized it to an extent which perhaps can never be estimated.* From whatever cause, it has happened, whether from climate, the nature of our products or our own labor, the South has been enabled to maintain a more homogenous population and show a less admixture of races than the North. This the statistics show.

	Ratio of Foreign To Native Population
Eastern States	12.65 in every 100
Middle States	19.84 " "
Southern States	1.86 " "
South-western States	5.34 " "
North-western States	12.75 " "

Our people partake of the true American character, and are mainly the descendants of those who fought the battles of the Revolution, and who understand and appreciate the nature and inestimable value of the liberty

2. Here De Bow printed a comparison of daily wages among bricklayers, carpenters, and day laborers in major Northern and Southern cities. He also looked at agricultural labor and found it "highest in the Southwest, the lowest in the Northeast, the South and North differing very little. . . ."

which it brought. Adhering to the simple truths of the Gospel and the faith of their fathers, they have not run hither and thither in search of all the absurd and degrading isms which have sprung up in the rank soil of infidelity. They are not Mormons or Spiritualist, they are not Owenites, Fourierites, Agrarians, Socialists, Free-lovers or Millerites. They are not for breaking down all the forms of society and of religion and reconstructing them; but prefer law, order and existing institutions to the chaos which radicalism involves. The competition between native and foreign labor in the Northern States, has already begotten rivalry and gearburning, and riots; and lead to the formation of political parties there which have been marked by a degree of hostility and proscription to which we have known none of this, except in two or three of the larger cities, where the relations of slavery and freedom scarcely exist at all. The foreigners that are among us at the South are of a select class, and from education and example approximate very nearly to the native standard.

4. *The non-slaveholder of the South preserves the status of the white man, and is not regarded as an inferior or a dependant.* He is not told that the Declaration of Independence, when it says that all men are born free and equal, refers to the negro equally with himself. It is not proposed to him that the free negro's vote shall weigh equally with his own at the ballot-box, and that the little children of both colors shall be mixed in the classes and benches of the school-house, and embrace each other filially in its outside sports. It never occurs to him, that a white man could be degraded enough to boast in a public assembly, as was recently done in New York, of having actually slept with a negro. And his patriotic ire would crush with blow the free negro who would dare, in his presence, as is done in the free States, to characterize the father of the country as a "scoundrel." No white man at the South serves another as a body servant, to clean his boots, wait on his table, and perform the menial services of his household. His blood revolts against this, and his necessities never drove him to it. He is a companion and an equal. When in the employ of the slaveholder, or in intercourse with him, he enters his hall, and has a seat at his table. If a distinction exists, it is only that which education and refinement may give, and this is so courteously exhibited as scarcely to strike attention. The poor white laborer at the North is at the bottom of the social ladder, whilst his brother has ascended several steps and can look down upon those who are beneath him, at an infinite remove.

5. *The non-slaveholder knows that as soon as his savings will admit, he can become a slaveholder, and thus relieve his wife from the necessities of the kitchen and the laundry, and his children from the labors of the field.* This, with ordinary

frugality, can, in general, be accomplished in a few years, and is a process continually going on. Perhaps twice the number of poor men at the South own a slave to what owned a slave ten years ago. The universal disposition is to purchase. It is the first use for savings, and the negro purchased is the last possession to be parted with. If a woman, her children become heir-looms and make the nucleus of an estate. It is within my knowledge, that a plantation of fifty or sixty persons has been established, from the descendants of a single female, in the course of the lifetime of the original purchaser.

6. *The large slaveholders and proprietors of the South begin life in great part as non-slaveholders.* It is the nature of property to change hands. Luxury, liberality, extravagance, depreciated land, low prices, debt, distribution among children, are continually breaking up estates. All over the new States of the South-west enormous estates are in the hands of men who began life as overseers or city clerks, traders or merchants. Often the overseer marries the widow. Cheap lands, abundant harvests, high prices, give the poor man soon a negro. His ten bales of cotton bring him another, a second crop increases his purchases, and so he goes on opening land and adding labor until in a few years his draft for $20,000 upon the merchant becomes a very marketable commodity.

7. *But should such fortune not be in reserve for the non-slaveholder, he will understand that by honesty and industry it may be realized to his children.* More than one generation of poverty in a family is scarcely to be expected at the South, and is against the general experience. It is more unusual here for poverty than wealth to be preserved through several generations in the same family.

8. *The sons of the non-slaveholder are and have always been among the leading and ruling spirits of the South; in industry as well as in politics.* Every man's experience in his own neighborhood will evince this. He has but to task his memory. In this class are the McDuffies, Langdon Cheves, Andrew Jacksons, Henry Clays, and Rusks, of the past; the Hammonds, Yanceys, Orrs, Memmingers, Benjamins, Stephens, Soules, Browns of Mississippi, Simms, Porters, Magraths, Aikens, Maunsel Whites, and an innumerable host of the present; and what is to be noted, these men have not been made demagogues for that reason, as in other quarters, but are among the most conservative among us.[3] Nowhere less in the world have intelligence and virtue disconnected from ancestral estates, the same opportunities for advancement, and nowhere else is their triumph more speedy and signal.

3. Some of these sons of nonslaveowners certainly disagreed with De Bow's classification of them.

9. *Without the institution of slavery, the great staple products of the South would cease to be grown, and the immense annual results, which are distributed among every class of the community, and which give life to every branch of industry, would cease.* The world furnishes no instances of these products being grown upon a large scale by free labor. The English now acknowledge their failure in the East Indies. Brazil, whose slave population nearly equals our own, is the only South American State which has prospered. Cuba, by her slave labor, showers wealth upon old Spain, whilst the British West India Colonies have now ceased to be a source of revenue, and from opulence have been, by emancipation, reduced to beggary. St. Domingo shares the same fate, and the poor whites have been massacred equally with the rich. . . .[4]

10. *If emancipation be brought about as will undoubtedly be the case, unless the encroachments of the fanatical majorities of the North are resisted now, the slaveholders, in the main, will escape the degrading equality which must result, by emigration, for which they would have the means, by disposing of their personal chattels: whilst the non-slaveholders, without these resources, would be compelled to remain and endure the degradation.* This is a startling consideration In Northern communities, where the free negro is one in a hundred of the total population, he is recognized and acknowledged of as a pest, and in many cases even his presence is prohibited by law. What would be the case in many of our States, where every other inhabitant is a negro, or in many of our communities, as for example the parishes around and about Charleston, and in the vicinity of New Orleans where there are from twenty to one hundred negroes to each white inhabitant? Low as would this class of people sink by emancipation in idleness, superstition and vice, the white man compelled to live among them, would by the power exerted over him, sink even lower, unless as is to be supposed he would prefer to suffer death instead.

In conclusion . . . I must apologize to the non-slaveholders of the South, of which class, I was myself until very recently a member, for having deigned to notice at all the infamous libels which the common enemies of the South have circulated against them, and which our everyday experience refutes; but the occasion seemed a fitting one to place them truly and rightly before the world. This I have endeavored faithfully to do. They fully understand the momentous questions which now agitate the land in all their relations. They perceive the inevitable drift of Northern aggression, and know that if necessity impel to it, as I verily believe it does at

4. De Bow listed U.S. exports for 1859 to show the financial wealth of the South.

this moment, the establishment of a Southern confederation will be a sure refuge from the storm. *In such a confederation our rights and possessions would be secure, and the wealth being retained at home, to build up our towns and cities, to extend our railroads, and increase our shipping, which now goes in tariffs or other involuntary or voluntary tributes, to other sections; opulence would be diffused throughout all classes, and we should become the freest, the happiest and most prosperous and powerful nation upon earth.*[5]

5. In his concluding remarks in which he responds to Robert Gourdin's request for the speech, De Bow cited Kettell, *Southern Wealth and Northern Profits*, to show that the "annual drain in profits which is going to the North" was nearly $250 million.

Letter . . . to the People of Georgia

(Washington: Lemuel Towers, 1860)

Howell Cobb (1815–68), who was a member of a prominent Georgia political family, graduated from Franklin College and became a successful lawyer in Athens, Georgia. He entered public life as solicitor general of the western district of Georgia, gained election to the U.S. House of Representatives, eventually became Speaker of the House, and served as governor of Georgia. Regarded as a major figure in national Democratic Party politics, he served President James Buchanan as secretary of the treasury, an office he resigned on December 8, 1860. Cobb chaired the proceeding of the Montgomery convention, which formed the Confederate States government. During the Civil War he eschewed government service to become brigadier general and later major general in the Confederate army. In December 1860 Cobb wrote the open letter that follows to his many worried Georgia constituents, in which he attempted to expose the Republican Party as under control of abolitionists bent on using the growing powers of the federal government to destroy slavery. He also attacked Northern institutions including state government and churches as hostile to all Southern interests. There is no adequate biography of Cobb, but see John Eddins Simpson, Howell Cobb: The Politics of Ambition *(Chicago: University of Chicago Press, 1973); his papers are at the University of Georgia, and an excellent collection of his letters is in Ulrich B. Phillips, ed.,* Correspondence of Robert Toombs, Alexander H. Stephens, and Howell Cobb *(Washington: American Historical Association, 1911).*

The whole subject may properly be considered in the discussion of the following inquiry. Does the election of Lincoln to the Presidency, in the usual and constitutional mode, justify the Southern States in dissolving the Union?

The answer to this enquiry involves a consideration of the principles of the party who elected him, as well as the principles of the man himself.

The Black Republican party had its origin in the anti-slavery feeling of the North. It assumed the form and organization of a party for the first time in the Presidential contest of 1856. The fact that it was composed of men of all previous parties, who then and still advocate principles directly antagonistic upon all other questions except slavery, shows beyond doubt or question that hostility to slavery, as it exists in the fifteen Southern States, was the basis of its organization and the bond of its union.

Free-trade Democrats and protective-tariff Whigs, internal improvement and anti-internal improvement men, and indeed all shades of partizans, united in cordial fraternity upon the isolated issue of hostility to the South, though for years they had fought each other upon all other issues. The fact is important because it illustrates the deep-rooted feeling which could thus bring together these hostile elements. It must be conceded that there was an object in view of no ordinary interest which could thus fraternize these incongruous elements. Besides, at the time this party organized there was presented no bright promise of success. All the indications of the day pointed to their certain defeat. So deep however was this anti-slavery planted in their hearts that they forgot and forgave the asperities of the past, the political differences of the present, and regardless of the almost certain defeat which the future had in store for them, cordially embraced each other in the bonds of anti-slavery hatred, preferring defeat under the banner of abolition to success, if it had to be purchased by a recognition of the constitutional rights of the South. The party has succeeded in bringing into its organization all the Abolitionists of the North except that small band of honest fanatics who say, and say truly, that if slavery is the moral curse which the Black Republicans pronounce it to be, they feel bound to dissolve their connection with it, and are therefore for a dissolution of the Union. Such I may denominate the *personnel* of the Black Republican party, which, by the election of Lincoln has demonstrated its numerical majority in every Northern State except New Jersey. . . .[1]

There is one dogma of this party which has been so solemnly enunciated, both by their national conventions and Mr. Lincoln that it is worthy of serious consideration. I allude to the doctrine of negro equality. The stereotyped expression of the Declaration of Independence that "All men are born equal," has been perverted from its plain and truthful meaning, and made the basis of a political dogma which strikes at the very foundations of the institution of slavery. Mr. Lincoln and his party assert that this doctrine of equality applies to the negro, and necessarily there can exist no such thing as property in our equals. Upon this point both Mr. Lincoln and his party have spoken with a distinctness that admits of no question or equivocation. If they are right, the institution of slavery as it exists in the Southern States is in direct violation of the fundamental principles

1. Quotations from and Cobb's comments on the 1860 Republican Party platform are omitted, as are long quotes from speeches of Abraham Lincoln, William H. Seward, Charles Sumner, and other Republicans.

of our Government; and to say that they would not use all the power in their hands to eradicate the evil and restore the Government to its *"ancient faith,"* would be to write themselves down self-convicted traitors both to principle and duty. These principles have not only been declared in the impassioned language of its advocates and defenders, but have at length found their way into the statute books of ten of the Northern States.

Every good citizen, North and South, admits that the Constitution of the United States in express terms requires our fugitive slaves to be delivered up to their owners, when escaping into another State. Congress has discharged its duty in passing laws to carry out this constitutional obligation; and, so far, every Executive has complied with his oath of office, to see this law duly executed. The impediments thrown in the way by lawless mobs, the threats of violence to which the owner has been on different occasions subjected, and the expense to which both the Government and the owner have been put are matters of small consideration compared with the more pregnant fact that ten sovereign States of the Union have interposed their strong arm to protect the thief, punish the owner, and confiscate the property of a citizen of a sister State. Such are the laws passed by these Northern States to defeat the fugitive slave act of Congress and annul a plain provision of the Constitution of the United States.[2]

These laws are the legitimate fruit of the principles and teachings of the Black Republican party, and have therefore very naturally made their appearance upon the statute books of States under the control and in the hands of that party. Their existence cannot and should not be overlooked by those who are desirous of knowing what this party will do on the subject of slavery whenever they have the power to act. I call attention to them not only as an important item in the evidence I am offering of the principles and objects of the Black Republican party, but for the more important purpose of presenting a plain and palpable violation of the constitutional compact by ten of the sovereign parties to it. These very States are among the loudest in their demands for unconditional submission on the part of the South to the election of Lincoln. The inviolability of the Union is the magic word with which they summon the South to submission. The South responds by holding up before them a Constitution basely broken—a compact wantonly violated. That broken Constitution and violated compact formed the only Union we ever recognized; and if you would still have us

2. Cobb was referring to the Southern hatred for the personal liberty laws being passed by Northern state legislatures in repudiation of the Fugitive Slave Law.

to love and preserve it, restore to it that vital spirit of which it has been robbed by your sacrilegious hands, and make it again what our fathers made it—a Union of good faith in the maintenance of constitutional obligations. Do this, and the Union will find in all this land no truer or more devoted supporters than the ever-loyal sons of the South. This, however, the Black Republicans will not do, as the facts I am now developing will show beyond all doubt or question.

In the election which just transpired, the Black Republicans did not hesitate to announce, defend and justify the doctrines and principles which I have attributed to them. During the progress of the canvass I obtained copies of the documents which they were circulating at the North, with a view of ascertaining the grounds upon which they were appealing to the people for their support and confidence. With the exception of a few dull speeches in favor of a protective tariff, intended for circulation in Pennsylvania and New Jersey, and still fewer number of pitiful appeals for squandering the public lands, the whole canvass was conducted by the most bitter and malignant appeals to the anti-slavery sentiment of the North. Under the sanction of Senators and Representatives in Congress the country was flooded with pamphlets and speeches holding up slave-holders as "barbarians, more criminal than murderers," and declaring unhesitatingly in favor of immediate and unconditional abolition in every State in the Confederacy where it now exists—doctrines which are the necessary and legitimate consequences of the universally recognized dogmas of the Black Republican party. It is worse than idle to deny that such are the doctrines and principles of their party because all of them have not reached that point of boldness and honesty which induce men to follow principles to their legitimate conclusions. One thing at least is certain: The managers of the canvass believed that such doctrines were popular, or they would not have spent both their time and money in giving them such general circulation to the exclusion of all other matter. The election of Lincoln in response to such appeals show that these men properly understood popular sentiment of their section, to whom alone they appealed for votes to elect their candidate.

From these doctrines, principles and acts of the Black Republican party I propose to extract the aims and object of the party. It will be borne in mind, that I rely upon the declaration of their principles: 1st. As made by their national convention. 2d. As contained in the deliberate and repeated declarations of their successful candidate for the Presidency. 3d. As announced by their most honored and trusted leaders in the Senate of the United States. I invite attention to the following propositions, as the plain and legitimate objects proposed to be carried out to the extent of their power:

First. That slavery is a moral, social and political evil; and that it is the duty of the Federal Government to prevent its extension.

Second. That slavery is not recognized by the Constitution of the United States; and that the Federal Government is in nowise committed to its protection.

Third. That property in slaves is not entitled to the same protection at the hands of the Federal Government with other property.

Fourth. That so far from protecting, it is the duty of the Federal Government, wherever its power extends, to prohibit it, and therefore it is the duty of Congress by law to prevent any Southern man from going into the common territories of the Union with his slave property.

Fifth. That slavery is such an evil and curse, that it is the duty of everyone, to the extent of his power, to contribute to its ultimate extinction in the United States.

Sixth. That there is such a conflict between slave and free labor that all the states of the Union must become either slave or free; and as all Black Republicans are opposed to slavery and slave States their policy and doctrines look to all these States becoming free, as not only the natural but desired result of the "irrepressible conflict."

Seventh. That the Declaration of Independence expressly declares and the Constitution recognizes the equality of the negro to the white man; and that the holding of the negro in slavery is violative of his equality as well as of that *"ancient faith,"* which Mr. Lincoln says is violated in the present relation of master and slave in the Southern States.

Eighth. That the Southern States do not stand upon an equality with the non-slaveholding States, because, whilst it is the recognized duty of the General government to protect the latter in the enjoyment of all their rights of property and would especially be required to protect their citizens from any act of confiscation in the common territories of the Union, it would be the duty of the same General government not only to withhold such protection from the citizen of a Southern State with his slave property in the common domain, but to exercise that power for his exclusion from that common territory.

Ninth. That the admission of more slave States into the Union is rendered a moral if not a physical impossibility.

To appreciate the full import of these doctrines and principles of the Black Republican party, they should be looked at in connection with the constitutional rights and guarantees claimed by the Southern States. They are briefly:

1. That the Constitution of the United States recognizes the institution of slavery as it exist in the fifteen Southern States.

2. That the citizens of the South have the right to go with their slave property into the common territories of the Union, and are entitled to protection for both their persons and property from the General Government during its territorial condition.

3. That by the plain letter of the Constitution the owner of a slave is entitled to reclaim his property in any State into which the slave may escape, and that both the General and State Governments are bound under the Constitution to the enforcement of this provision; the General government by positive enactment, as has been done; and the State governments by interposing no obstacle in the way of the execution of the law and other Constitution.

I decline to enumerate other constitutional rights, equally clear, because I prefer to confine myself in this argument to those which have been fully recognized by the highest judicial tribunal in the country. No law and Constitution-abiding man will deny that the rights here enumerated are within the clear provisions of the Constitution, and that the South is fully justified in demanding their recognition and enforcement. Otherwise we are asked to pay tribute and give allegiance to a government which is wanting either in the will or power to protect us in the enjoyment of undoubted rights. I apprehend it is equally clear that the antagonism between these recognized rights and the doctrines and principles of the Black Republican party is plain, direct and irreconcilable. The one or the other must give way. Surely no right-minded man who admits the existence of the rights claimed by the South will say that she ought to yield. It only remains to enquire whether the Black Republican party will recede from its position and thus end the "irrepressible conflict" which their doctrines have inaugurated. Those who indulge the hope that such will be the case are, in my honest judgment, greatly deluded. The boldness and earnestness with which this party have avowed their principles, the sacrifices they have made to secure their triumph, the deliberation with which their position has been taken, the clear and emphatic committals of their conventions, their candidate and all their leading men; the solemn acts of their State Legislatures—all indicate with unerring certainty that there is no reasonable hope of such a result.

I know that there are those who say and believe that this party is incapable of exercising the power it has obtained without breaking to pieces, and they look confidently to its overthrow at an early period. It may be that a cool philosophy located at a safe distance from the scene of danger may reason plausibly upon the chances of overthrowing a party so utterly unworthy of public confidence; but men looking to the security of property, and fathers and husbands anxious for the safety of their families, require some stronger guarantee than the feeble assurance of partisan speculations to quiet their apprehensions and allay their fears. This may be the case; but unfortunately for the future peace and security of the South, the causes which may lead to its dissolution and defeat arise outside of the slavery question. So far from the question of slavery leading to such a result, it is the only subject upon which the party thoroughly harmonizes. Hostility to slavery is the magic word which holds them together; and when torn to pieces by other dissensions, hatred to the South and her institutions swallows up all other troubles and restores harmony to their distracted ranks. On this point we are not left to mere conjecture; the history of the party in the ten nullifying States affords practical proof of the fact. In which of these States did the Black Republican party lose power in consequence of their acts repudiating the fugitive-slave law and nullifying the Constitution of the United States? So far from their anti-slavery legislation being an element of weakness, it has proven in all these States the shibboleth of their strength. In New York and Pennsylvania the corruptions of this party were so palpable and infamous that their own press cried out against it. Those of the party who made pretension of honesty felt the shame and humiliation brought upon them; and yet, when the Presidential battle was won, hatred to the South and her institutions swallows up all, and these acts of fraud and corruption were forgotten and forgiven in the greater and more absorbing feeling of hostility and hatred to the South and her institutions. Shall we close our eyes to these historical facts and indulge the vain hope that these men will play a different part, simply because they are transferred to a new theatre of action? I do not doubt that the Black Republican party will be guilty of similar and greater frauds in the Federal government; nor do I doubt that their wrangling and quarrels over the offices and patronage will plant in their party the seeds of strife and dissension which would lead ordinarily to their speedy downfall and overthrow; but I feel assured by the teachings of the past that the magic word of anti-slavery will again summon them to a cordial and fraternal reunion to renew and continue the war upon slavery, until they shall have accomplished the great object of their organization—"its ultimate extinction."

What are the facts to justify the hope that the Black Republicans will recede from their well defined position of hostility to the South and her institutions? Are they to be found in the two millions of voters who have deliberately declared in favor of these doctrines by their support of Lincoln? Is the hope based upon the fact that an overwhelming majority of the people of every Northern state save one cast their vote for the Black Republican candidate? Is it drawn from the fact that on the fourth of March next the chair of Washington is to be filled by a man who hates the institution of slavery as much as any other abolitionist, and who has not only declared but used all the powers of his intellect to prove that our slaves are our equals and that all laws which hold otherwise are violative of the Declaration of Independence and at war with the law of God—a man who is indebted for his present election to the Presidency alone to his abolition sentiments—and who stands pledged to the doctrine of "the irrepressible conflict," and indeed claims to be its first advocate? Or, shall we look for this hope in the whispered intimation that, when secure of his office, Lincoln will prove faithless to the principles of his party and false to his own pledges, or in his emphatic declaration of May, 1859, that he would "oppose the lowering of the Republican standard by *a hair's breadth*," or in the public announcement made by Senator Trumbull of Illinois, since the election, *in the presence* of Mr. Lincoln, that he, Lincoln, would *"maintain and carry forward the principles on which he was elected,"* at the same time holding up the military power of the United States as the instrumentality to enforce obedience to the incoming abolition administration, should any Southern State secede from the Union; or in the prospect of a more efficient execution of the fugitive slave law, when the marshals' offices in all the Northern States shall have been filled with Lincoln's abolition appointees; or in the refusal of Vermont, since the election of Lincoln, by the decisive vote of more than two to one in her Legislature to repeal the Personal Liberty Bill of that State; or shall we look for it in the doctrine of negro equality which finds among its warmest supporters the brightest lights of the Black Republican party; or in the announcements solemnly made by conventions, speakers, papers, and all other organs of the party that the recognized rights of the South to equality and protection of slave property shall never be tolerated; or in the fact that the party is not only sectional in its principles but sectional in its membership, thereby giving to the South the promise of such boon as she may hope to receive from Black Republicans in their newly assumed character of guardians and masters; or in the warning voice of their ablest statesmen that the decisions of the Supreme Court in favor of our constitutional rights are to be met not with reason and argument for reversal but with the more potent and practical remedy of "reorganization of the Court," by adding a sufficient number of abolitionists to reverse existing decisions; or in the pregnant fact developed by the census returns now coming in, that the numerical majority of the North is steadily and rapidly increasing, with the promise of still further increase by the addition of more free States carved out of that common territory from which the South is to be excluded by unjust and unconstitutional legislation; or in such manifestations of Northern sentiment as led to the nomination by this party of John A. Andrew for Governor of Massachusetts after he had declared his sanction and approval of the John Brown raid;[3] or in the election of that same Andrew to that office by seventy thousand majority after he had declared in his anxiety to abolish slavery that "he could not wait for Providence" to wipe it out, but must himself undertake that duty with the aid of his Black Republican brethren; or shall we be pointed to the defiant tones of triumph which fill the whole Northern air with the wild shouts of joy and thanksgiving that the days of slavery are numbered and the hour draws nigh when the "higher law" and "hatred of slavery and slave holders" shall be substituted for "the Constitution" and the spirit of former brotherhood; or to the cold irony which speaks through their press of the "*inconvenience*" of negro insurrections, arson, and murder which may result in the South from the election of Lincoln. In none of these, nor of the other facts to which I have before referred, can anything be found to justify the hope suggested by those confiding friends who in this hour of gloom and despondency are disposed to hope against hope.

Turning from these indications in the political world to the more quiet and peaceful walks of social and religious life, let us pause for a moment and look to the pulpit, the Sunday schools, and all the sources of Christian influence, for one cheering beam of light. Unfortunately wherever you find the presence of Black Republicanism it is engaged in this work of educating the hearts of the people to hate the institution of slavery. The pulpit forgets every other duty and doctrine to thunder its anathemas against this institution whilst the Sunday-school room is made the nursery of youthful Abolitionists. This hope we are asked to adopt will find in these sources no encouragement or support. On the contrary nothing has contributed more to the creation of that bitter feeling of hatred which now pervades the two sections of the country than the religious teachings of the North. It has broken social relations, severed churches, and now threatens, in company with its political handmaid, Black Republicanism, to overthrow our once happy and glorious Union.

3. Not only did governor-elect Andrew of Massachusetts sanction John Brown's raid on Harpers Ferry, but other leading political, religious, and intellectual leaders, including Henry David Thoreau, Ralph Waldo Emerson, and Theodore Parker, supported Brown's actions as well.

I refer to one other source upon which the South is asked to rely, and will then close the argument. We are expected, in view of all these facts, to rely for our safety and protection upon an uncertain and at best trembling majority in the two Houses of Congress, and told, with an earnest appeal for further delay, that with a majority in Congress against him Lincoln is powerless to do us harm. I doubt not the sincerity of those who present this appeal against Southern action; but their confidence in its merit only shows how superficial has been their consideration of the subject. It is true that without a majority in Congress Lincoln will not be able to carry out *at present* all the aggressive measures of his party. But let me ask if that feeble and constantly-decreasing majority in Congress against him can arrest that tide of popular sentiment at the North against slavery which, sweeping down all the barriers of truth, justice and constitutional duty, has borne Mr. Lincoln into the Presidential chair? Can that Congressional majority, faint and feeble as it is known to be, repeal the unconstitutional legislation of those ten nullifying States of the North? Can it restore the lost equality of the Southern States? Can it give to the South its constitutional rights? Can it exercise its power in one single act of legislation in our favor without the concurrence of Lincoln? Or can it make Christians of Beecher, Garrison, Cheever and Wendell Phillips, or patriots of Seward, Chase and Webb? Can that majority in Congress control the power and patronage of President Lincoln? Can it stay his arm when he wields the offices and patronage of the Government to cement and strengthen the anti-slavery sentiment which brought his party into existence and which alone can preserve it from early and certain dissolution? Can it prevent the use of that patronage for the purpose of organizing in the South a band of apologists—the material around which Black republicanism hopes during his four years to gather an organization in Southern States to be the allies of this party in its insidious warfare upon our family firesides and altars?[4] True but over-confiding men of the South, may catch at this congressional majority straw, but it will only be to grasp and sink with it.

The facts and considerations which I have endeavored to bring to your view present the propriety of resistance on the part of the South to the election of Lincoln in a very different light from the mere question of resisting the election of a President who has been chosen in the usual and constitutional mode. It is not simply that a comparatively obscure aboli-

4. For more about this fear of a Southern Republican Party see Michael Johnson, *Toward a Patriarchal Republic* (Baton Rouge: Louisiana State University Press, 1977).

tionist, who hates the institutions of the South, has been elected President, and that we are asked to live under the administration of a man who commands neither our respect or confidence, that the South contemplates resistance even to disunion. Wounded honor might tolerate the outrage until by another vote of the people the nuisance could be abated; but the election of Mr. Lincoln involves far higher considerations. It brings to the South the solemn judgement of a majority of the people of every Northern State—with a solitary exception—in favor of doctrines and principles violative of her constitutional rights, humiliating to her pride, destructive of her equality in the Union, and fraught with the greatest danger to the peace and safety of her people. It can be regarded in no other light than a declaration of the purpose and intention of the people of the North to continue, with the power of the Federal Government, the war already commenced by the ten nullifying States of the North upon the institution of slavery and the constitutional rights of the South. To these acts of bad faith the South has heretofore submitted, though constituting ample justification for abandoning a compact which had been wantonly violated. The question is now presented whether longer submission to an increasing spirit and power of aggression is compatible either with her honor or her safety. In my mind there is no room for doubt. The issue must now be met, or forever abandoned. Equality and safety in the Union are at an end; and it only remains to be seen whether our manhood is equal to the task of asserting and maintaining independence out of it. The Union formed by our fathers was one of equality, justice and fraternity. On the fourth of March it will be supplanted by a Union of sectionalism and hatred. The one was worthy of the support and devotion of freemen—the other can only continue at the cost of your honor, your safety, and your independence.

Is there no other remedy for this state of things but immediate secession? None worthy of your consideration has been suggested, except the recommendation of Mr. Buchanan, of new constitutional guarantees—or rather, the clear and explicit recognition of those that already exist. This recommendation is the counsel of a patriot and a statesman. It exhibits an appreciation of the evils that are upon us, and at the same time a devotion to the Constitution and its sacred guarantees. It conforms to the record of Mr. Buchanan's life on this distracting question—the record of a pure heart and a wise head. It is the language of a man whose heart is overwhelmed with a sense of the great wrong and injustice that has been done to the minority section, mingled with an ardent hope and desire to preserve that Union to which he has devoted the energies of a long and patriotic life.

The difficulty is, there will be no response to it from those who alone have it in their power to act. Black Republicanism is the ruling sentiment at the North, and by the election of Lincoln has pronounced in the most formal and solemn manner against the principles which are now commended to the country for its safety and preservation. As a matter of course they will spurn these words of wisdom and patriotism, as they have before turned their back upon all the teachings of the good and true men of the land, or else they will play with it in their insidious warfare to delude the South into a false security, that they may the more effectually rivet their iron chains and thereby put resistance in the future beyond our power. They have trampled upon the Constitution of Washington and Madison, and will prove equally faithless to their own pledges. You ought not—cannot trust them. It is not the Constitution and the laws of the United States which need amendment, but *the hearts* of the northern people. To effect the first would be a hopeless undertaking, whilst the latter is an impossibility. If the appeal of the President was made to *brethren* of the two sections of the country, we might hope for a different response. Unfortunately, however, Black Republicanism has buried brotherhood in the same grave with the Constitution. We are no longer "brethren dwelling together in unity." The ruling spirits of the North are Black Republicans—and between them and the people of the South there is no other feeling than that of bitter and intense hatred. Aliens in heart, no power on earth can keep them united. Nothing now holds us together but the cold formalities of a broken and violated Constitution. Heaven has pronounced the decree of divorce, and it will be accepted by the South as the only solution which gives to her any promise of future peace and safety.

To part with our friends at the North who have been true and faithful to the Constitution will cause a pang in every Southern breast; for with them we could live forever, peaceably, safely, happily. Honor and future security, however, demand the separation, and in their hearts they will approve though they may regret the act.

Fellow-citizens of Georgia, I have endeavored to place before you the facts of the case, in plain and unimpassioned language; and I should feel that I had done injustice to my own convictions, and been unfaithful to you, if I did not in conclusion warn you against the dangers of delay and impress upon you the hopelessness of any remedy for these evils short of secession. You have to deal with a shrewd, heartless and unscrupulous enemy, who in their extremity may promise anything, but in the end will do nothing. On the 4th day of March, 1861, the Federal Government will pass into the hands of the Abolitionists. It will then cease to have the slightest claim either upon your confidence or your loyalty; and, in my honest judgement, each hour that Georgia remains thereafter a member of the Union will be an hour of degradation, to be followed by certain and speedy ruin. I entertain no doubt either of your right or duty to secede from the Union. Arouse, then, all your manhood for the great work before you, and be prepared on that day to announce and maintain your independence out of the Union, for you will never again have equality and justice in it. Identified with you in heart, feeling and interest, I return to share in whatever destiny the future has in store for our State and ourselves.

JUDAH P. BENJAMIN

The Right of Secession

(Washington: Lemuel Towers, 1861)

Judah P. Benjamin (1811–84) was born in the West Indies and was later brought to Savannah, Georgia. He attended Fayetteville Academy in North Carolina and Yale College. Young Benjamin traveled widely and then settled in New Orleans, Louisiana, where he taught school, studied law, and became a wealthy lawyer and planter. A brilliant legal mind, Benjamin soon entered the state legislature, wrote part of the Louisiana constitutional revisions of 1845, and gained election to the U.S. Senate, from which he subsequently resigned on February 4, 1861. In his farewell speech to the Senate he promised that there would be no civil war. During the Civil War he served his close friend President Jefferson Davis as attorney general in the Provisional Government, and as secretary of war, and later as secretary of state. Benjamin fled the United States at the war's end and eventually became a famous barrister in England. He began the pamphlet below[1] with a defense of the constitutional right of secession but quickly turned to the secession of South Carolina as representative of the rest of Southern opinion, as he recounted Southern grievances against the Northern-controlled government for its attacks on slavery. The most recent biography of this fascinating political survivor is Eli N. Evans's Judah P. Benjamin *(New York: Free Press, 1988); also see Rollin G. Osterweis,* Judah Benjamin *(New York: G. P. Putnam, 1933).*

When I took the floor at our last adjournment, I stated that I expected to address the Senate to-day in reference to the critical issue now before the country. I had supposed that by this time there would have been some official communications to the Senate, in reference to the fact now known to all, of the condition of affairs in South Carolina. I will assume, for purposes of the remarks that I have to make, that those facts have been officially communicated, and address myself to them. Probably never had a deliberative assembly been called upon to determine questions calculated to awaken a more solemn sense of responsibility than those that now address themselves to our consideration. We are brought at last sir, directly forced, to meet promptly an issue produced by an irresistible course of events whose inevitable results some of us, at least, have foreseen for years.

1. This pamphlet's text was delivered as a speech in the U.S. Senate on December 31, 1860, to wild cheers and support from Southerners.

Nor, sir, have we failed in our duty of warning the Republicans that they were fast driving us to a point where the very instincts of self-preservation would impose upon us the necessity of separation. We repeated those warnings with a depth of conviction, with an earnestness of assertion that inspired the hope that we should succeed in imparting at least some faint assurance of our sincerity to those by whose aid alone could the crisis be averted. But, sir, our assertions were derided, our predictions were scoffed at; all our honest and patriotic efforts to save the Constitution and the Union sneered at and maligned, as dictated, not by love of country, but by base ambition for place and power. . . .[2]

Alas, the feelings and sentiments expressed since the commencement of this session, on the opposite side of this floor, almost force the belief that a civil war is their desire; and that the day is full near when American citizens are to meet each other in hostile array; and when the hands of brothers will be reddened with the blood of brothers.

The State of South Carolina, with a unanimity scarcely with parallel in history, has dissolved the union which connects her with the other States of the confederacy, and declared herself independent. We, the representatives of those remaining States, stand here to-day, bound either to recognize that independence, or to overthrow it; either to permit her peaceful secession from the confederacy, or to put her down by force of arms. That is the issue. That is the sole issue. No artifice from an excited or alarmed public, can suffice to conceal it. Those attempts are equally futile and disingenuous. As for the attempted distinction between coercing a State, and forcing all the people of the State, by arms, to yield obedience to an authority repudiated by the sovereign will of the State, expressed in its most authentic form, it is as unsound in principle as it is impossible of practical application. Upon that point, however, I shall have something to say a little further on.

If we elevate ourselves to the height from which we are bound to look in order to embrace all the vast consequence that must result from our decision, we are not permitted to ignore the fact that our determination does not involve the State of South Carolina alone. Next week, Mississippi, Alabama, and Florida, will have declared themselves independent; the week after, Georgia; and a little later, Louisiana; soon, very soon, to be followed by Texas and Arkansas. I confine myself purposely to these eight States, because I wish to speak only of those whose action we know with positive certainty, and which no man can for a moment pretend to controvert.

2. Omitted is a lengthy quote from a speech Benjamin made in the Senate on May 2, 1856, in which he attacked Republican "violence to the Constitution."

I designedly exclude others, about whose action I feel equally confident, although others may raise a cavil.

Shall we recognize the fact that South Carolina has become an independent State, or shall we wage war against her! And first as to her right. I do not agree with those who think it idle to discuss that right. In a great crisis like this, when the right asserted by a sovereign State is questioned, a decent respect for the opinions of mankind at least requires that those who maintain it. If, in the discussion of this question, I shall refer to familiar principles, it is not that I deem it at all necessary to call the attention of members here to them; but because they naturally fall within the scope of my argument, which might otherwise prove unintelligible.

From the time that this people declared its independence of Great Britain, the right of the people to self-government in its fullest and broadest extent has been a cardinal principle of American liberty. None deny it. And in that right, to use the language of the Declaration itself, is included the right whenever a form of government becomes destructive of their interests or their safety, "to alter or to abolish it, and to institute a new government, laying its foundation on such principles and organizing its powers in such form as to them shall seem most likely to effect their safety and happiness." I admit that there is a principle that modifies this power, to which I shall presently advert; but leaving that principle for a moment out of view, I say there is no other modification which, consistently with our liberty, we can admit, and that the right of the people of one generation, in convention duly assembled, to alter the institutions bequeathed by their fathers is inherent, inalienable, not susceptible of restriction; that by the same power under which one Legislature can repeal the act of a former Legislature, so can one convention of the people duly assembled; and that it is in strict and logical deduction from this fundamental principle of American liberty, that South Carolina has adopted the form in which she has declared her independence. She has in convention duly assembled in 1860, repealed an ordinance passed by her people in convention duly assembled in 1788. If no interests of third parties were concerned, if no question of compact intervened all must admit the inherent power—the same inherent power which authorizes a Legislature to repeal a law, subject to the same modifying principle, that were the rights of other than the people who passed the law are concerned, those rights must be respected and cannot be infringed by those who descend from the first Legislature or who succeed them. If a law be passed by a Legislature impairing a contract, that law is void, not because the Legislature under ordinary circumstances would not have the power to repeal a law of its predecessor, but because by repealing a law of its predecessor involving a contract, it exercises rights in which third persons are interested, and over which they are entitled to have an equal control. So in the case of a convention of the people assuming to act in repeal of an ordinance which showed their adherence to the Constitution of the United States, the power is inherently in them, subject only to this modification: that they are bound to exercise it with due regard to the obligations imposed upon them by the compact with others. . . .[3]

We have then in the case of South Carolina, so far as the duly organized convention is concerned, the only body that could speak the will of this generation in repeal of the ordinance passed by their fathers in 1788; and I say again, if no third interests intervened by a compact binding upon their faith, the power to do so is inherent and complete. But there is a compact, and no man pretends that the generation of to-day is not bound by the compacts of the fathers; but to use the language of Mr. Webster, a bargain broken on one side is a bargain broken on all; and the compact is binding upon the generation of to-day only if the other parties to the compact have kept their faith.

This is no new theory, nor is practice upon it without precedent. I say that it was precisely upon this principle that this Constitution was formed. I say that the old Articles of Confederacy provided in express terms that they should be perpetual; that they should never be amended or altered without the consent of all the States. I say that the delegates of States unwilling that the Confederation should be altered or amended, appealed to that provision in the convention which formed the Constitution, and said: "If you do not satisfy us by the new provisions, we will prevent your forming your new government, because your faith is plighted, because you have agreed that there shall be no change in it unless with the consent of all." This was the argument of Luther Martin, as was the argument of Paterson, of New Jersey, and of large numbers of other distinguished members of the convention. Mr. Madison answered it. . . .[4]

I need scarcely ask if anybody has found in the Constitution of the United States any article providing, by express stipulation, that force shall be used to compel an offending member of the Union to discharge its duty.

Acting on that principle, nine States of the Confederation, seceded from the Confederation, and formed a new Government. They formed it upon

3. Omitted is a quote from Daniel Webster on the power of the people to choose their own kind of government.

4. Quotes, as did so many, came from James Madison, *Debates in the Federal Convention*, 5 vols. (Philadelphia: J. B. Lippincott, 1836–59); see especially vol. 5, 206–7.

the express ground that some of the States have violated their compact. Immediately after, two other States seceded and joined them. They left two alone, Rhode Island and North Carolina. After this Government had been organized; after every department had been in full operation for some time; after you had framed your navigation laws, and provided what should be considered as ships and vessels of the United States, North Carolina and Rhode Island were still foreign nations, and so treated by you, so treated by you in your laws; and in September, 1789, Congress passed an act authorizing the citizens of the States of North Carolina and Rhode Island to enjoy all the benefits attached to owners of ships and vessels of the United States up to the 1st of the following January—gave them that much more time to come into the new Union, if that thought proper; if not, they were to remain as foreign nations. Here is the History of the formation of this Constitution, so far as it involves the power of the States to secede from a Confederation, and to form new confederacies to suit themselves.

Now there is a difficulty in this matter, which was not overlooked by the framers of the Constitution. One State may allege that the compact has been broken, and others may deny it; who is to judge? When pecuniary interests are involved, so that a case can be brought up before the courts of justice, the Constitution has provided a remedy within itself. It has declared that no act of a State, either in convention or by Legislature, or in any other manner, shall violate the Constitution of the United States, and it has provided for a supreme judiciary to determine cases arising in law or equity which may involve the construction of the Constitution or the construction of such laws.

But suppose infringements on the Constitution in political matters, which from their very nature cannot be brought before the court? That was a difficulty not unforeseen; it was debated upon propositions that were made to meet it. Attempts were made to give power to this Federal Government in all its departments, one after the other, to meet the precise case, and the convention sternly refused to admit any.

It was proposed to enable the Federal Government, through the action of Congress, to use force. That was refused.

It was proposed to give the President of the United States the nomination of State Governors, and to give them a veto on State laws, so as to preserve the supremacy of the Federal Government. That was refused.

It was proposed to make the Senate the judge of difficulties that might arise between States and the General Government. That was refused.

It was finally proposed to give Congress a negative on State legislation interfering with the powers of the Federal Government. That was refused.

At last, at the very last moment, it was proposed to give that power to Congress by a vote of two-thirds of each branch; and that, too, was denied. . . .[5]

Now if we admit, as we must, that there are certain political rights guaranteed to the States of this Union by the terms of the Constitution itself—rights political in their character, and not susceptible of judicial decision—if any State is deprived of any of those rights, what is the remedy: for it is idle to talk to us at this day in a language which shall tell us we have rights and no remedies. For the purpose of illustrating the argument upon this subject, let us suppose a clear, palpable case of violation of the Constitution. Let us suppose that the State of South Carolina having sent two Senators to sit upon this floor, had been met by a resolution of the majority here that, according to her just weight in the Confederacy, one was enough, and that we had directed our Secretary to swear in but one, and to call but one name on our roll as the yeas and nays are called for voting. The Constitution says that each State shall be entitled to two Senators, and each Senator shall have one vote. What power is there to force the dominant majority to repair that wrong? Any court? Any tribunal? Has the Constitution provided any recourse whatever? Has it not remained designedly silent on the subject of that recourse? And yet, what man will stand up in this Senate and pretend that if, under these circumstances, the State of South Carolina had declared, "I entered into a Confederacy or a compact by which I was to have my rights guaranteed by the constant presence of two Senators upon your floor; you allow me but one; you refuse to repair the injustice; I withdraw"; what man would dare say that was a violation of the Constitution on the part of South Carolina? Who would say that that was a revolutionary remedy? Who would deny the plain and palpable proposition that it was the exercise of a right inherent in her under the very principles of the Constitution, and necessarily so inherent for self-defence?

The North if it has not a majority here to-day will have it very soon. Suppose these gentlemen from the North with the majority think that it is no more than fair; inasmuch as we represent here States in which there are large numbers of slaves, that the northern States should have each three Senators, what are we to do? They swear them in. No court has the power of prohibition, of *mandamus* over this body in the exercise of its political powers. It is the exclusive judge of the elections, the qualifications, and the

5. Quoted from "leading members of the (Constitutional) Convention on these propositions to subject the States . . . to any power of the General Government. . . ."

returns of its own members, a judge without appeal. Shall the whole fifteen southern States submit to that, and be told that they are guilty of revolutionary excess if they say, we will not remain with you on these terms; we never agreed to it? Is that revolution, or is it the exercise of clear constitutional right?

Suppose this violation occurs under circumstances where it does not appear so plain to you, but where it does appear equally plain to South Carolina; then you are again brought back to the inevitable point, who is to decide? South Carolina says, you forced me to the expenditure of my treasure, you forced me to the shedding of the blood of my people, by a majority vote, and with my aid you acquired territory; now I have a constitutional right to go into that territory with my property, and to be there secured by your laws against its loss. You say, no, she has not. Now, there is this to be said; that right is not put down in the Constitution in quite so clear terms as the right to have two Senators; but it is a right which she asserts with the concurrent opinion of the entire South. It is a right which she asserts with the concurrent opinion of one-third or two-fifths of your own people interested in refusing it. It is a right that she asserts, at all events, if not in accordance with the decision — as you may say no decision was rendered — in accordance with the opinion expressed by the Supreme Court of the United States; but yet there is not tribunal for the assertion of that political right. Is she without a remedy under the Constitution? If not, then what tribunal? If none is provided, then natural law and the law of nations tells you that she and she alone, form the very necessity of the case, must be the judge of the infraction and the mode and measure of redress. . . .⁶

But the President of the United States tells us that he does not admit this right to be constitutional, that it is revolutionary. I have endeavored thus far to show that it results from the nature of their compact itself; that it must necessarily be one of those reserved powers which was not abandoned by it, and therefore grows out of the Constitution, and is not in violation of it. If I am asked how I will distinguish this from revolutionary abuse, the answer is prompt and easy. These States, parties to the compact, have a right to withdraw from it, by virtue of its own provisions are violated by the other parties to the compact, when either powers not

6. Benjamin cites the Virginia and Kentucky Resolutions of Jefferson and Madison and shows how Northern states early on repudiated the rights of states. He praised the early efforts to find ways to redress grievances against the "National Government."

granted are usurped, or rights are refused that are especially granted to the States. But there is a large class of powers granted by this Constitution, in the exercise of which a discretion these admitted powers might be so perverted and abused as to give cause of complaint, and, finally, to give the right to revolution; for under those circumstances there would be no other remedy. Now, taking again the supposition of a dominant northern majority in both branches, and of a sectional President and Vice President, the Congress of the United States then, in the exercise of its admitted powers, and the President to back them, could spend the entire revenue of the Confederation in that section which had control, without violating the words or the letter of the Constitution; they could establish forts, light-houses, arsenals, magazines, and all public buildings of every character in the northern States alone, and utterly refuse any to the South. The President, with the aid of his sectional Senate, could appoint all officers of the Navy and of the Army, all the civic officers of the Government, all the judges, attorneys, and marshals, all collectors and revenue officers, all post-masters—the whole host of public officers he might, under the forms and powers vested by the Constitution, appoint exclusively from the northern States, and quarter them in the southern States, to eat out the substance of our people, and assume an insulting superiority over them. All that might be done in the exercise of admitted constitutional power; and it is just that train of evils, of outrages, of wrongs, of oppression long continued, that the Declaration of Independence says a people preserves the inherent right of throwing off by destroying their government by revolution.

I say, therefore, that I distinguish the rights of the States under the Constitution into two classes; on resulting from the nature of their bargain; if the bargain is broken by the sister States, to consider themselves freed from it on the ground of breach of compact; if the bargain be not broken, but the powers be perverted to their wrong and their oppression, then, whenever that wrong and oppression shall become sufficiently aggravated, the revolutionary right—the last inherent right of man to preserve freedom, property, and safety—arises, and must be exercised, for none other will meet the case.

But suppose South Carolina to be altogether wrong in her opinion that this compact has been violated to her prejudice, and that she has, therefore, a right to withdraw; take that for granted—what then? You will have the same issue to meet, face to face. You must permit her to withdraw in peace, or you must declare war. That is, you must coerce the State itself, or you must permit her to depart in peace. There is nothing whatever that can render for an instant tenable the attempted distinction between coercing a State itself, and coercing all the individuals in the manner now proposed. . . .[7]

If there was anything in this idea in theory, you might reduce it to practice; but what can be more absurd, more vague, more fanciful, than the suggestions put out by gentlemen here? You are going now, observe, to declare no war and to coerce no State; you are simply going to execute the laws of the United States against individuals in the State of Carolina. That is your proposition. Is it serious? One gentleman says he will hang for treason. Ah, where is the marshal to seize, and where is the court to try, where is the district attorney to prosecute, and where is the jury to convict? Are you going to establish all these by arms? Perhaps you tell me you will remove him elsewhere for trial. Not so; our fathers have not left our liberties so unguarded and so unprotected as that. The Constitution originally provided that no man could be brought to trial for an offence out of the State where he committed it. The fathers were not satisfied with it, and they added an amendment that he should be brought to trial out of the district even in which he had committed it. You cannot take him out of the district. You have got no judge, no marshal, no attorney, no jurors, there; and suppose you had: who is to adjudge, who is to convict? His fellow-citizens, unanimously in opinion with him, determine that he has done his duty, and has committed no guilt. That is the way you are going to execute the laws against treason!

What next? Oh, no, says the Senator from Ohio (Mr. Wade), this is what we will do; we will execute the laws to collect revenue by blockading your ports, and stopping them up. At first blush this seems a very amusing mode of collecting revenue in South Carolina, by allowing no vessels to come in on which revenue can be collected. It is the strangest of all possible fancies that that is the way of collecting revenue there, enforcing the laws in the States against the individuals. But first you are to have no war. And what is blockade? Does any man suppose that blockade can exist by a nation at peace with another; that it is a peace power; that it can be exercised on any other ground then that you are at war with the party whose ports you blockade, and that you make proclamation to all the Governments of the earth that their vessels shall not be authorized to enter into these ports, because you are reducing your enemy by the use of regular constituted,

7. As did others who defended the rights of states for so many years, Benjamin invoked the work of Emmerick De Vattell (1714–67), *Laws of Nations*, 2 vols. (Philadelphia: T. and J. W. Johnson, 1854). Jesse T. Carpenter, *The South as a Conscious Minority* (New York: New York University Press, 1930), remains the best study of how Southerners used Vattell.

recognized, warlike means? Oh, but perhaps it is not a blockade that you will have; you will have an embargo, that is what you mean. We are guarded here again. The Constitution heads you off at every step in the Quixotic attempt to go into a State to exercise your laws against her whole citizens without shutting up all; the Constitution itself from forcing a vessel bound to or from one State to enter or clear or pay duties in another, or from making any regulations of commerce whatever, giving any preference to the ports of one State over the ports of another; and you have no more right to blockade or close the ports of South Carolina by embargo, even by act of Congress, that you have to declare that a sovereign State shall have no right to have more than one Senator on this floor. Your blockade is impracticable, unconstitutional, out of the power of the President.

What is the idea of executing the laws by armed force against individuals? Gentlemen seem to suppose—and they argue upon the supposition— that it is possible, under the Constitution of the United States, for the President to determine when laws are not obeyed and to force obedience by the sword, without the interposition of courts of justice. Does any man have such an idle conceit as that? Does he suppose that, by any possible construction, the power of the Federal Congress to call out the militia, and to use the Army and the Navy to suppress insurrection and to execute the laws, means that the President is to do it of his own violation and without the intervention of the civil power? The honorable Senator from Tennessee (Mr. Johnson), the other day, called upon us to look at the examples of Washington, who put down rebellion in Pennsylvania. He said well that he was no lawyer, when he cited that precedent. General Washington called forth the militia of Pennsylvania and of other States to aid in executing the laws only upon a requisition by a judge of the Supreme Court of the United States certifying to him that the marshall was unable to carry out the judgements of the court. . . .[8]

We cannot go to war; we are not going to war; we are not going to coerce a State. "Why," says the Senator from Illinois, "who talks of coercing a State: you are attempting to breed confusion in the public mind; you are attempting to impose upon people by perverting the question; we only mean to execute the laws against individuals." Again, I say, where will be the civil process which must precede the action of the military force? Surely, surely it is not at this day that we are to argue that neither the Presi-

8. What followed was an angry exchange between Benjamin and Andrew Johnson in which Benjamin accused Johnson of violating the rights of individual citizens.

dent, nor the President and Congress combined, are armed with the powers of a military despot to carry out the laws, without the intervention of the courts, according to their own caprice and their own discretion, to judge when laws are violated, to convict for the violation, to pronounce sentence, and to execute it. You can do nothing of the kind with your military force.

But it is suggested, and the President is weak enough to yield to the suggestion, that you will collect your revenue by force—by the action of the powers of the Federal Government on individuals. Has anybody followed this out practically? Is it possible? I remember that Mr. Webster once, as mere figure of rhetoric, in his debate on the Foote resolutions, used some such threat as this against this same State of South Carolina; but it was looked upon as a mere beautiful figure of speech. No man ever paid any attention to it as really a threat of the use of constitutional power. You will put your collector on board of a vessel in the harbor. It shall be a man of war; it is in the port; and there you will make everybody pay duties before the goods are loaded. That is the next proposition, that nobody sees any practical difficulty about. But, sir, it is totally impracticable—totally impossible. Take a case. A citizen of New York owns a vessel which loads at Liverpool with a cargo of assorted merchandise, part free, part owing duty, and consigns it to Charleston. He enters the harbor. Under the law he is obliged to make entry of his vessel, to produce his manifest, to go through certain other formalities. He goes on board your ship-of-war, sees the collector, and complies with the orders. What next? There are no duties paid yet, and the man who has a right to the free goods has no duties to pay. You cannot prevent him from going to the wharf and discharging them. There is no law to be executed there against an individual. But I will take it for granted that the whole cargo is a duty-paying cargo, and all belongs to one man, who does not mean to pay your duties. You are no better off. The man declines to enter his cargo. What is the law? The master of the vessel wants to go away. He is entitled by law to report to the collector that he is ready to deliver his cargo, that nobody is there to enter it, and that he may go upon his new voyage; and you cannot change that, unless you change the law for all the ports of the United States. Or he may go further: the importer may go to the collector, and say, "I want to enter my cargo in warehouse"; and he gives a bond signed by himself and a solvent fellow-citizen, that they will pay the duty when he takes the goods out of the warehouse. Then you must let him put those goods into the custom-house warehouse; and you cannot change the law either, without changing it for the whole United States; because you cannot, under the Constitution, by any regulation of commerce, give any preference to the ports of one State over those of another.

Mind you, you are at peace; you are not coercing a State; you are merely executing the laws against individuals. You cannot do it without breaking up your whole warehouse system; you cannot do it without breaking up your whole commercial system in every port of the Confederacy. Your goods are ashore; they are in Government warehouses; but you have not got the duties. A rush upon the warehouse, and the goods are taken out. You have got a bond, but you have no court to sue it in; and if you had, you would have no jury to forfeit it, because the jury would be told by the court, or at all events by the lawyers in behalf of the defendant, that the Government had no right to collect that bond; that it was a usurpation which required him to give the bond.

This whole scheme, this whole fancy, that you can treat the act of sovereign State, issued in an authoritative form, and in her collective capacity as a State, as being utterly out of existence; that you can treat the State as still belonging collectively to the Confederacy, and that you can proceed, without a solitary Federal officer in the State, to enforce your laws against private individuals, is as vain, as idle, and delusive as any dream that ever entered into the head of man. The thing cannot be done. It is only asserted for the purpose of covering up the true question, than which there is no other; you must acknowledge the independence of the seceding State, or reduce her to subjection by war.

I desire not to enter in any detail into the dreary catalogue of wrongs and outrages by which South Carolina defends the position that she has withdrawn from this Union because she has a constitutional right to do so, by reason of prior violations of the compact by her sister States. Before, however, making any statement—that statement to which we have been challenged, and which I shall make in but very few words—of the wrongs under which the South is now suffering, and for which she seeks redress, as the difficulty seems to arise chiefly from a difference in our construction of the Constitution. . . . [9]

You, Senators of the Republican party, assert, and your people whom you represent assert, that under a just and fair interpretation of the Federal Constitution it is right that you deny that our slaves, which directly and indirectly involve a value of more than four thousand million dollars, are property at all, or entitled to protection in Territories owned by the common Government.

You assume the interpretation that it is right to encourage, by all pos-

9. Again Benjamin cites Vattell, *Laws of Nations*, vol. 2, chap. 15, for support of his position.

sible means, directly or indirectly, the robbery of this property, and to legislate so as to render its recovery as difficult and dangerous as possible; that it is right and proper and justifiable, under the Constitution, to prevent our mere transit across a sister State, to embark with our property on a lawful voyage, without being openly despoiled of it.

You assert, and practice upon the assertion, that it is right to hold us up to the ban of mankind, in speech, writing, and print, with every appliance of publicity, as thieves, robbers, murderers, villains, and criminals of the blackest dye, because we continue to own property which we owned at the time we all signed the compact.

That it is right that we should be exposed to spend our treasure in the purchase, or shed our blood in the conquest, of foreign territory, with no right to enter it for settlement without leaving behind our most valuable property, under penalty of its confiscation.

You practically interpret this instrument to be that it is eminently in accordance with the assurance that our tranquility and welfare were to be preserved and promoted, that our sister States should combine to prevent our growth and development; that they should surround us with a cordon of hostile communities, for the express and avowed purpose of accumulating in dense masses, and within restricted limits, a population which you believe to be dangerous, and thereby force the sacrifice of property nearly sufficient in value to pay the public debt of every nation in Europe.

This is the construction of the instrument that was to preserve our security, promote our welfare, and which we only signed on your assurance that that was its object. You tell us that this is a fair construction—not all of you, some say one thing, some another; but you act, or your people do, upon this principle. You do not propose to enter into our States, you say, and what do we complain of? You do not pretend to enter into our States to kill or destroy our institution by force. Oh, no. You imitate the faith of Rhadamistus: you propose simply to close us in an embrace that will suffocate us. You do not propose to fell the tree; you promise not. You merely propose to girdle it, that it die. And then, when we tell you that we do not understand this bargain this way, that your acting upon it in this spirit releases us for the obligation that accompany it; that under no circumstances can we consent to live together under the interpretation, and say: "we will go from you; let us go in peace"; we are answered by your leading spokesmen: "Oh, no; you cannot do that; we have no objection to it personally, but we are bound by our oaths; if you attempt it, your people will be hanged for treason. We have examined this Constitution thoroughly; we have searched it out with a fair spirit, and we can find warrant in it for releasing ourselves from the obligation of giving you any of its benefits, but our oaths force us to tax you; we can dispense with everything else; but our conscience we protest upon our souls will be sorely worried if we do not take your money." (Laughter.) That is the proposition of the honorable Senator from Ohio, in plain language. He can avoid everything else under the Constitution, that stands in the way of secession; but how is he to get rid of the duty of taking our money he cannot see. (Laughter.)

Now, Senators, this picture is not placed before you with any idea that it will act upon any one of you, or change your views, or alter your conduct. All hope of that is gone. Our committee has reported this morning that no possible scheme of adjustment can be devised by them all combined. The day for the adjustment has passed. If you would give it now, you are too late.

And now, Senators, within a few weeks we part to meet as Senators in one common council chamber of the nation no more forever. We desire, we beseech you, let this parting be in peace. I conjure you to indulge in no vain delusion that duty or conscience, interest or honor, impose upon you the necessity of invading our States or shedding the blood or our people. You have no possible justification for it. I trust it is in no craven spirit, and with no sacrifice of the honor or dignity of my own State, that I make this last appeal, but from far higher and holier motives. If, however, it shall prove vain, if you are resolved to pervert the Government framed by the fathers for the protection of our rights into an instrument for subjugating and enslaving us, then, appealing to the Supreme Judge of the universe for the rectitude of our intention, we must meet the issue that you force upon us as best becomes freemen defending all that is dear to man.

What may be the fate of this horrible contest, no man can tell, none pretend to foresee; but this much I will say: the fortunes of war may be adverse to our arms; you may carry desolation into our peaceful land, and with torch and fire you may set our cities in flames; you may even emulate the atrocities of those who, in the war of the revolution, hounded on the blood-thirsty savage to attack upon the defenseless frontier; you may, under the protection of your advancing armies, give shelter to the furious fanatics who desire, and profess to desire, nothing more than to add all the horrors of a servile insurrection to the calamities of civil war; you may do all this—and more, too, if more there be—but you never can subjugate us; you never can convert the free sons of the soil into vassals, paying tribute to your power; and you never, never can degrade them to the level of an inferior and servile race. Never! Never!

Remarks on the Special Message on Affairs in South Carolina. *Jan. 10, 1861*

(Baltimore: John Murphy & Co., 1861)

Jefferson Davis (1808–89) was born in Kentucky and raised in Mississippi. He attended St. Thomas College and Transylvania College in Kentucky as well as Jefferson College in Mississippi, and he graduated from the U.S. Military Academy. His successful brother gave him a cotton plantation in Mississippi. Davis entered public life as a U.S. congressman, served as a colonel during the Mexican War, and became a U.S. senator before taking office as President Franklin Pierce's secretary of war. A moderate during the secession crisis, Davis again entered the Senate, where he was a member of the Senate Committee of Thirteen and supported the Crittenden Compromise over slavery in the territories; he resigned from the Senate on January 21, 1861. He became president of the Confederate States of America and served throughout the Civil War. Arrested at war's end he languished in prison for some time and spent the last years of his life revising history in his version of the secession crisis, The Rise and Fall of the Confederate Government, 2 vols. *(New York: D. Appleton and Co., 1881). In the pamphlet printed below, the text of which was taken from his speech in congress, Davis reacted vehemently to the Northern government's threatened use of force over Fort Sumter, and he rejected its powers to coerce a state. In this discursive speech, Davis also blamed Northern congressmen for the failure of the Crittenden Compromise, stated that the 1860 Republican presidential platform "denies . . . us equality," and most important, claimed that Lincoln's election represented the full force of the Northern majority's antagonism toward slavery. Much is being written about Davis, but the best recent study remains Clement Eaton,* Jefferson Davis *(New York: Free Press, 1977). Rice University is publishing a twenty-volume edition of Davis's letters and papers.*

When I took the floor yesterday, I intended to engage somewhat in the argument which has heretofore prevailed in the Senate upon the great questions of the constitutional right, which have divided the country from the beginning of the Government. I intended to adduce some evidences, which I thought were conclusive, in favor of the opinions which I entertain; but events, with a current hurry on as it progresses, have borne me past the point where it would be useful for me to argue, by the citing of authorities, the question of rights. To-day, therefore, it is my purpose to deal with events. Abstract argument has become among the things that are past. We have to deal now with facts; and in order that we may meet those facts and apply them to our present condition, it is well to inquire what is the state of the country. The Constitution provides that the President shall, from time to time, communicate information on the State of the Union. The message which is now under consideration gives us very little, indeed, beyond that which the world, less, indeed, than reading men generally, knew before it was communicated.

What, Senators, to-day is the condition of the country? From every quarter of it comes the wailing cry of patriotism pleading for the preservation of the great inheritance we derived from our fathers. Is there a Senator who does not daily receive letters appealing to him to use even the small power which one man here possesses to save the rich inheritance our fathers gave us? Tears now trickling down the stern face of man; and those who have bled for the flag of their country, and are willing now to die for it, stand powerless before the plea that the party about to come into power laid down a platform, and that come what will, though ruin stare us in the face, consistency must be adhered to, even though the Government be lost.

In this state of the case, then, we turn and ask, what is the character of the Administration? What is the executive department doing? What assurance have we there for the safety of the country? But we come back from that inquiry with a mournful conviction that feeble hands now hold the reins of State; that drivelers are taken in as counselors not provided by the Constitution; that vacillation is the law; and the policy of this great Government is changed with every new phase of causeless fear. In this state of the case, after complications have been introduced into the question, after we were brought to the verge of war, after we were hourly expecting by telegraph to learn that the conflict had commenced, after nothing had been done to insure the peace of the land, we are told in this late hour that the question is thrown at the door of Congress, and here rests the responsibility.

Had the garrison at Charleston, representing the claim of the Government to hold the property in a fort there, been called away thirty days, nay, ten days ago, peace would have spread its opinions over this land, and calm negotiation would have been the order of the day. Why was it not recalled? No reason yet has been offered, save that the Government is bound to preserve its property; and yet look from North to South, from East to West, wherever we have constructed forts to defend States against a foreign foe, and everywhere you find them without a garrison, except at a few points where troops are kept for special purposes; not to coerce or to threaten a State, but stationed in sea-coast fortifications there merely for the purpose of discipline and instruction as artillerists. You find all the other forts in the hands of fort keepers and ordinance sergeants, and before a moral and patriotic people, standing safely there as the property of the country.[1]

I asked in this Senate weeks ago "what causes the peril that is now imminent at Fort Moultrie; is it the weakness of the garrison?" and then I answered, "no, it is the presence, not its weakness." Had an ordnance sergeant there represented the Federal Government; had there been no troops, no physical power to protect it, I would have pledged my life upon the issue that no question ever would have been made as to its seizure. Now, not only there, but elsewhere, we find movements of troops further to complicate this question, and probably to precipitate us upon the issue of civil war; and worse than all, this Government, strong in the affections of the people; this Government (I describe it as our fathers made it) is now furtively sending troops to occupy positions lest "the mob" should seize them. When before in the history of our land was it that a mob could resist the sound public opinion of the country? When before was it that an unarmed magistrate had not the power, by crying, "I command the peace," to quell a mob in any portion of the land? Yet now we find, under cover of night, troops detached from one position to occupy another. Fort Washington, standing in its lonely grandeur, and overlooking the home of the Father of his Country, near by the place where the ashes of Washington repose, built there to prevent a foreign foe from coming up the Potomac with armed ships to take the capital—Fort Washington is garrisoned by marines sent secretly away from the navy-yard at Washington. And Fort McHenry, memorable in our history as the place where, under bombardment, the star-spangled banner floated through the darkness of night, the point which was consecrated by our national song—Fort McHenry, too, has been garrisoned by a detachment of marines, sent from this place in an extra train, and sent under cover of the night, so that even the mob should not know it.

Senators, the responsibility is thrown at the door of Congress. Let us take it. It is our duty in this last hour to seize the pillars of our Government and uphold them, though we be crushed in the fall. Then what is our policy? Are we to drift into war? Are we to stand idly by and allow war to be precipitated upon the country? Allow an officer of the Army to make war? Allow an unconfirmed head of a Department to make war? Allow a

1. Refers to events surrounding the removal of federal troops from Fort Moultrie to Fort Sumter in Charleston harbor. The best account of this much-studied event is David M. Potter, *The Impending Crisis* (New York: Harper and Row, 1976), chap. 20.

general of the Army to make war? Allow a President to make war? No, sir. Our fathers gave to Congress the power to declare war, and even to Congress they gave no power to make war upon a State of the Union. It could not have been given, except as a power to dissolve the Union. When, drifting into a war between the United States and an individual State, does it become the Senate to sit listlessly by and discuss abstract questions, and read patch-work from the opinions of men now mingled with the dust? Are we not bound to meet events at they come before us, manfully and patriotically to struggle with the difficulties which now oppress the country?

In the message yesterday we were even told that the District of Columbia was in danger. In danger of what? From whom comes the danger? Is there a man here who dreads that the deliberations of this body are to be interrupted by an armed force? Is there one who would not prefer to fall with dignity at his station, the representative of a great and peaceful Government, rather than to be protected by armed bands? And yet the rumor is—and rumors seem now to be so authentic that we credit them rather then other means of information—that companies of artillery are to be quartered in this city to preserve peace where the laws have heretofore been supreme, and that this District is to become a camp, by calling out every able-bodied man within its limits to bear arms under the militia law. Are we invaded? Is there an insurrection? Are there two Senators here who would not be willing to go forth as a file, and put down any resistance which showed itself in this District against the Government of the United States? Is the reproach meant against these, my friends from the South, who advocate southern rights and State rights? If so, it is a base slander. We claim our rights under the Constitution; we claim our rights reserved to the States; and we seek by no brute force to gain any advantage which the law and the Constitution do not give us. We have never appealed to mobs. We have never asked for the Army and the Navy to protect us. On the soil of Mississippi, not the foot of a Federal soldier has been impressed since 1819, when, flying from the yellow fever, they sought refuge within the limits of our State; and on the soil of Mississippi their breathes not a man who asks for any other protection than that which our Constitution gives us, that which our strong arms afford, and the brave hearts of our people will insure in every contingency.

We are rapidly drifting into a position in which this is to become a Government of the Army and Navy; in which the authority of the United States is to be maintained, not by the law, not by constitutional agreement between the States, but by physical force; and will you stand still and see this policy consummated? Will you fold your arms, the degenerate descendants of those men who proclaimed the eternal principle that government rests on the consent of the governed; and that every people have a right to change, modify, or abolish a Government when it ceases to answer the ends for which it was established, and permit this Government imperceptibly to slide from the moorings where it was originally anchored, and become a military despotism? It was well said by the Senator from New York, whom I do not now see in his seat [Mr. Seward], well said in a speech, wherein I found but little to commend, that this Union could not be maintained by force, and that a Union of force was despotism. It was a great truth, come from what quarter it may. That was not the Government instituted by our fathers; and against it, so long as I live, with heart and hand, I will rebel.

This brings me to consider a passage in the message, which says:

> "I certainly had no right to make aggressive war upon any State; and I am perfectly satisfied that the Constitution has wisely withheld that power even from Congress";—

Very good.

> ". . . But the right and the duty to use military force defensively against those who resist the Federal officers in the execution of their legal functions, and against those who assail the power of the Federal Government, is clear and undeniable."

Is it so? Where does he get it? Our fathers were so jealous of a standing army, that they scarcely would permit the organization and maintenance of any army. Where does he get the "clear and undeniable" power to use the force of the United States in the manner he there proposes? To execute a process, troops may be summoned as a *posse comitatus*; and here, in the history of our Government, it is not to be forgotten that in the earlier, and, as it is frequently said, the better days of the Republic—and painfully we feel that they were better indeed—a President of the United States did not recur to the Army; he went to the people of the United States. Vaguely and confusedly, indeed, did the Senator from Tennessee [Mr. Johnson] bring forward the case of the great man, Washington, as one in which he has used a power which, he argued was equivalent to the coercion of a State; for he said that Washington used the military power against a portion of the people of a State; and why might he not as well have used it against the whole State? Let me tell that Senator that the case of General Washington has no application, as he supposes. It was a case of insurrection within the State of Pennsylvania; and the very message from which he read communicated the fact that Governor Mifflin thought it necessary to call the militia of adjoining States to aid him. President Washington cooperated with Governor Mifflin; he called the militia of adjoining States to cooperate with those of Pennsylvania. He used the militia, not as a standing army. It was by the consent of the Governor; it was by his advice. It was not the invasion of the State; it was not the coercion of the State; but it was aiding the State to put down insurrection, and in the very manner provided for in the Constitution itself.

But, I ask again, what power has the President to use the Army and the Navy except to execute process? Are we to have drum-head courts substituted for those which the Constitution and laws provide? Are we to have sergeants sent over the land instead of civil magistrates? Not so thought the elder Adams; and here, in passing, I will pay him a tribute he deserves, as the one to whom, more than any other man among the early founders of this Government, credit is due for the military principles which prevail in its organization. Associated with Mr. Jefferson originally, in preparing the rules and articles of war, Mr. Adams reverted through the long pages of history back to the empire of Rome, and drew from that foundation the very rules and articles of war which now govern in our country to-day, and drew them thence because he said they had brought two nations to the pinnacle of glory—referring to the Romans and the Britons, whose military law was borrowed from them. Mr. Adams, however, when an insurrection occurred in the same State of Pennsylvania, not only relied upon the militia, but his orders, through Secretary McHenry, required that the militia of the vicinage should be employed; and, though he did not order mounted troops from Philadelphia, he required the militia of the northern counties to be employed as long as they were able to execute the laws; and the orders given to Colonel McPherson, then in New Jersey, were, that Federal troops should not go across the Jersey line except in the last resort. I say, then, when we trace our history to its early foundation, under the first two Presidents of the United States, we find that this idea of using the Army and the Navy to execute the laws at the discretion of the President, was one not even entertained, still less acted upon, in any case.

Then we are brought to consider passing events. A little garrison in the harbor of Charleston now occupies a post which, I am sorry to say, is gained by the perfidious breach of an understanding between the parties concerned; and here, that I may do justice to one who had not the power on this floor, at least, to right himself—who has no friend here to represent him—let me say that remark does not apply to Major Anderson; for I hold that, though his order were not so designed, as I am assured, they did empower him to go from one post to another, and to take his choice of the posts in the harbor of Charleston; but, in so doing, he committed an act of hostility. When he dismantled Fort Moultrie, when he burned the carriages and spiked the guns bearing upon Fort Sumter, he put Carolina in the attitude of an enemy of the United States; and yet he has not shown any just cause for apprehension. Vague rumors had reached him — and causeless fear seems now to be the impelling motive of every public act — vague rumors of an intention to take Fort Moultrie. But, sir, a soldier should be confronted by an overpowering force before he spikes his guns and burns his carriages. A soldier should be confronted by a public enemy before he destroys the property of the United States lest it should fall into the hands of such an enemy. Was that fort built to make war upon Carolina? Was an armament put into it for such a purpose? Or was it built for the protection of Charleston harbor; and was it armed to make that protection complete? If so, what right had any soldier to destroy that armament lest it should fall into the hands of Carolina?

Some time since I presented to the Senate resolutions which embodied my views upon this subject, drawing from the Constitution itself the date on which I based those resolutions. I then invoked the attention of the Senate in that form to the question as to whether garrisons should be kept within a State against the consent of that State. Clear was I then, as I am now, in my conclusion. No garrison should be kept within a State against the consent of that State. Clear was I then, as I am now, in my conclusion. No garrison should be kept within a State during a time of peace, if the State believes the presence of that garrison to be either offensive or dangerous. Our Army is maintained for common defense; our forts are built out of the common Territory, to which every State contributes; and they are perverted form the purpose for which they were erected whenever they are garrisoned with a view to threaten, to intimidate, or to control a State in any respects.

Yet we are told this in no purpose to coerce a State; we are told that the power does not exist to coerce a State; but the Senator from Tennessee [Mr. Johnson] says it is only a power to coerce individuals; and the Senator from Ohio [Mr. Wade] seems to look upon this latter power as a very harmless power in the hands of the President, though such coercion would be to destroy the State. What is a State? Is it land and houses? Is it taxable property? Is it the organization of the local government? Or is it all these combined, with the people who possess them? Destroy the people, and yet not make war upon the State! To state the proposition is to answer it, by reason of its very absurdity. It is like making desolation, and calling it peace.

There being, as it is admitted on every hand, no power to coerce a State,

I ask what is the use of a garrison within a State where it needs no defense? The answer from every candid mind must be, there is none. The answer from every candid mind must be, peace requires, under all such circumstances, that the garrison should be withdrawn. Let the Senate to-day, as the responsibility is thrown at our door, pass those resolutions, or others which better express the idea contained in them, and you have taken one long step towards peace, one long stride towards the preservation of the Government of our fathers.

The President's message of December, however, had all the characteristics of a diplomatic paper, for diplomacy is said to abhor certainty, as nature abhors a vacuum; and it was not within the power of man to reach any fixed conclusion from that message. When the country was agitated, when opinions were being formed, when we are drifting beyond the power ever to return, this was not what we had a right to expect from the Chief Magistrate. One policy or the other he ought to have taken. If a federalist, if believing this to be a Government of force, if believing it to be a consolidated mass and not a confederation of States, he should have said: no State has a right to secede; every State is subordinate to the Federal Government, and the Federal Government must empower me with the physical means to reduce to subjugation the State asserting such a right. If not, if a State-rights man and a Democrat—as for many years it has been my pride to acknowledge our venerable Chief Magistrate to be—then another line of policy should have been taken. The Constitution gave no power to the Federal Government to coerce a State; the Constitution gave an army for the purposes of common defense, and to preserve domestic tranquility; but the Constitution never contemplated using that army against a State. A State exercising the sovereign function of secession is beyond the reach of the Federal Government, unless we woo her with the voice of fraternity, and bring her back to the enticements of affection. One policy or the other should have been taken; and it is not for me to say which, though my opinion is well know; but one policy or the other should have been pursued. He should have brought his opinion to one conclusion or another, and to-day our country would have been safer than it is.

What is the message before us? Does it benefit the case? Is there a solution offered here? We are informed in it of propositions made by commissioners from South Carolina. We are not informed even as to how they terminated. No countervailing proposition is presented; no suggestion is made. We are left drifting loosely, without chart or compass.

There is, in our recent history, however, an event which might have suggested a policy to be pursued. When foreigners, having no citizenship within the United States, declared war against it, and made war upon it; when the inhabitants of a Territory disgraced by institutions offensive to the law of every State of the Union held this attitude of rebellion; when the Executive there had power to use troops, he first sent commissioner of peace to win them back to their duty. When South Carolina, a sovereign State, resumes the grants she had delegated; when South Carolina stands in an attitude which threatens within a short period to involve the country in a civil war, unless the policy of the Government be changed—no suggestion is made to us that this Government be changed—no suggestion is made to us that this Government might send commissioners to her; no suggestion is made to us that better information should be sought; there is no policy of peace, but we are told the Army and the Navy are in the hands of the President of the United States, to be used against those who assail the power of the Federal Government.

Then, my friends, are we to allow events to drift onward to this fatal consummation? Are we to do nothing to restore peace? Shall we not, in addition to the proposition I have already made, to withdraw the force which complicates the question, send commissioners there in order that we may learn what this community desires, what this community will do, and put the two Governments upon friendly relations?

I will not weary the Senate by going over the argument of coercion. My friend from Ohio [Mr. Pugh], I may say, has exhausted the subject. I thank him, because it came appropriately from one not identified by his position with South Carolina. It came more effectively from him than it would have done from me, had I (as I have not) a power to present it as forcibly as he has done. Sirs, let me say, among the painful reflections which have crowded upon my heart that the reflection that our separation severs the ties which have so long bound us to our northern friends, of whom we are glad to recognize the Senator as a type.

Now let us return a moment to consider what would have been the state of the case if the garrison at Charleston had been withdrawn. The Fort would have stood there—not dismantled, but unoccupied. It would have stood there in the hands of an ordinance sergeant. Commissioners would have come to treat of all questions with the Federal Government, of these forts as well as others. They would have remained there to answer the ends for which they were constructed—the ends of defense. If South Carolina was an independent State, then she might hold to us such a relation as Rhode Island held the dissolution of the Confederation and before the formation of the Union, when Rhode Island appealed to the sympathies existing between the States connected in the struggles of the Revolution, and asked that a commercial war should not be waged upon her. These forts would have stood there then to cover the harbor of a friendly State; and if the feeling which once existed among the people of the State had subsisted still, and that fort had been attacked, brave men from every section would have rushed to the rescue, and there imperiled their lives in the defense of a State identified with their early history, and still associated in their breasts with affection; and the first act of this time would have been one appealing to every generous motive of those people again to reconsider the question of how we could live together, and through that bloody ordeal to have brought us into the position in which our fathers left us. There could have been no collision; there could have been no question of property which that State was not ready to meet. If it was a question of dollars and cents, they came here to adjust it. If it was a question of covering an interior State, their interests were identical. In whatever way the question could have been presented, the consequence would have been to relieve the Government of the charge of maintaining the fort, and to throw it upon the State which had resolved to be independent.

Thus we see that no evil could have resulted. We have yet to learn what evil the opposite policy may bring. Telegraphic intelligence, by the man who occupied the seat on the right of me in the old Chamber, was never relied on. He was the wisest man I ever knew—a man whose prophetic vision foretold all the trials through which we are now passing; whose clear intellect, elaborating everything, borrowing nothing from anybody, seemed to dive into the future, and to unveil those things which are hidden to other eyes. Need I say I mean Calhoun? No other man than he would have answered this description. I say, then, not relying upon telegraphic dispatches, we still have information enough to notify us that we are on the verge of civil war; that civil war is in the hands of men irresponsible, as it seems to us; their act unknown to us; their discretion not covered by any existing law or usage; and we now have the responsibility thrown upon us, which justifies us in demanding information to meet an emergency in which the country is involved.

Is there any point of pride which prevents us from withdrawing that garrison? I have heard it said by a gallant gentleman, to whom I make no special reference, that the great objection was an unwillingness to lower the flag. To lower the flag! Under what circumstances? Does any man's courage impel him to stand boldly forth to take this life of his brethren? Does any man insist upon going upon the open field with deadly weapons to fight his brother on a question of courage? There is no point of pride. These are your brethren; and they have shed as much glory upon that flag as any equal number of men in the Union. They are the men, and that is the locality, where the first Union flag was unfurled, and where was fought a gallant battle before our independence was declared—not the flag with thirteen stripes and thirty-three starts, but a flag with a cross of St. George, and the long stripes running through it. When the gallant Moultrie took the British Fort Johnson, and carried it, for the first time, I believe, did the Union flag fly in the air; and that was in October, 1775. When he took the position and threw up a temporary battery with palmetto logs and sand, upon the site called Fort Moultrie, that fort was assailed by the British fleet, and bombarded until the old logs, clinging with stern tenacity to the enemy that assailed them, were filled with balls, the flag still floated there, and, though many bled, the garrison conquered. Those old logs are gone; the eroding current is even taking away the site where Fort Moultrie stood; the gallant men who held it, now mingled with the earth; but their memories live in the hearts of gallant people, and their sons yet live, and they, like their fathers, are ready to bleed and to die for the cause in which their father triumphed. Glorious are the memories clinging around that old fort which now, for the first has been abandoned—abandoned not even in the presence of a foe, but under the imaginings that a foe might come; and guns spiked and carriages burned where the band of Moultrie bled, and, with an insufficient armament, repelled the common foe of all the colonies. Her ancient history compares proudly with the present.

Can there, then, be a point of pride upon so sacred a soil as this, where the blood of the fathers cries to Heaven against civil war? Can there be a point of pride against laying upon that sacred soil to-day the flag for which our fathers died? My pride, Senators, is different. My pride is that that flag shall not set between contending brothers; and that, when it shall no longer be the common flag of the country, it shall be folded up and laid away like a vesture no longer used; that it shall be kept as a sacred memento of the past, to which each of us can make a pilgrimage, and remember the glorious days in which we were born.

In the answer of the commissioners, which I caused to be read yesterday, I observed that they referred to Fort Sumter as remaining a memento of Carolina faith. It is an instance of the accuracy of the opinion which I have expressed. It stood without a garrison. It commanded the harbor, and the fort was know to have the armament in it capable of defense. Did the Carolinians attack it? Did they propose to seize it? It stood there safe as public property; and there is might have stood to the end of the negotiations without a question, if a garrison had not been sent into it. It was the faith on which they lost the advantage they would have had in seizing it when unoccupied. I think that something is due to faith as well as fraternity; and I think one of the increasing and accumulative obligations upon us to withdraw the garrison from that fort is from the manner in which it was taken—taken, as we heard by the reading of the paper yesterday, while Carolina remained under the assurance that the *status* would not be violated; while I was under that assurance, and half a dozen other Senators now within the sound of my voice felt secure under the same pledge, that nothing would be done until negotiations had terminated, unless it was to withdraw the garrison. Then we, the Federal Government, broke the faith; we committed the first act of hostility; and from this first act of hostility arose all those acts to which reference is made in the message as unprovoked aggressions—the seizing of forts elsewhere. Why were they seized? Self-preservation is the first law of nature; and when they no longer had confidence that this Federal Government would not seize the forts constructed for their defense, and use them for their destruction, they only obeyed the dictates of self-preservation when they seized the forts to prevent the enemy from taking possession of them as a means of coercion, for they then were compelled to believe this Federal Government had become an enemy.

Now, what is the remedy? To assure them that you do not intend to use physical force against them is your first remedy; to assure them that you intend to consider calmly all the propositions which they make, and to recognize the rights of the Union was established to secure; that you intend to settle with them upon a basis in accordance with the Declaration if Independence and the Constitution of the United States. When you do that, peace will prevail over the land, and force become a thing that no man will consider necessary.

I am here confronted with a question which I will not argue. The position which I have taken necessarily brings me to its consideration. Without arguing it, I will merely state it. It is the right of a State to withdraw from the Union. The President says it is not a constitutional right. The Senator from Ohio [Mr. Wade] and his ally, the Senator from Tennessee, argued it as no right at all. Well, let us see. What is meant by a constitutional right? It is meant to be a right derived from the Constitution—a grant made in the Constitution? If that is what is meant, of course we all see at once we do not derive it in that way. It is intended that it is not a constitutional right, because it is not granted in the Constitution? That shows, indeed, but a poor appreciation of the nature of our Government. All that is not granted in the Constitution belongs to the States; and nothing but what is granted in the Constitution belongs to the Federal Government; and keeping this distinction in view, it requires but little argument to see the conclusion at which we necessarily arrive. Did the States surrender their sovereignty to the Federal Government? Did the States agree that they never could withdraw from the Federal Union?

I know it has been argued here, that the Confederation said the Articles of Confederation were to be a perpetual bond of Union, and that the Constitution was made to form a more perfect Union, that is to say, a Government beyond perpetuity, or one day, or two or three days after doomsday. But that has no foundation in the Constitution itself; it has no basis in the nature of our Government. The Constitution was a compact between independent States; it was not a national Government; and hence Mr. Madison answered with such effectiveness to Patrick Henry, in the convention of Virginia, which ratified the Constitution, denying his proposition that it was to form a nation, and stating to him the conclusive fact, that "we sit here as a convention of the States to ratify or reject that Constitution; and how then can you say that it forms a nation, and is adopted by the mass of the people." It was not adopted by the mass of the people, as we all know, historically; it was adopted by each State; and each State voluntarily ratifying it, entered the Union; and that Union was formed whenever nine States should enter it; and in abundance of caution, it was stated in the resolutions of ratification of three States, that they still possessed the power to withdraw the grants which they had delegated, whenever they should be used to their injury or oppression. I know it is said that this meant the people of all the States; but that is such an absurdity that I suppose it hardly necessary to answer it; or to speak of an elective government rendering itself injurious and oppressive to the whole body of the people by whom it is elected is such an absurdity, that no man can believe it; and to suppose that a State convention, speaking for a State, having no authority to speak for anybody else, would say that it was declaring what the people of the other States would do, would be an assumption altogether derogatory to the sound sense and well-known sentiments of the men who formed the Constitution and ratified it.[2]

In the name of common sense, I ask how are we to fight in the Union? We take an oath of office to maintain the Constitution of the United States. The Constitution of the United States was formed for domestic tranquil-

2. Refers to Benjamin's December 31, 1860, speech (see above) that invoked the Constitutional Convention as the source for protection against the coercion of a state. Davis also quoted from Benjamin's attack on Andrew Johnson's comments on the increase in militia around Washington, D.C., and his tawdry statement that the Southern states should remain in the Union and fight the "battle like men."

lity; and how, then, are we to fight in the Union? I have heard the proposition from others; but I have not understood it. I understand how men fight when they assume attitudes of hostility; but I do not understand how men remaining connected together in a bond as brethren, sworn to mutual aid and protection, still propose to fight each other. I do not understand what the Senator means. If he chooses to answer my question, I am willing to hear him, for I do not understand how we are to fight in the Union. . . .[3]

I received the answer from the Senator, and I think I comprehend now that he is not going to use any force, but it is a sort of fighting that is to be done by votes and words; and I think, therefore, the President need not bring artillery and order out the militia to suppress them. I think, altogether, we are not in danger of much bloodshed in the mode proposed by the Senator from Tennessee.

I am entirely satisfied that the answer of the Senator shows me he did not intend to fight at all; that it was a mere figure of speech, and does not justify converting the Federal capital into a military camp. But it is a sort of revolution which he proposes; it is a revolution under the forms of the Government. Now, I have to say, once for all, that, as long as I am a Senator here, I will not use the powers I possess to destroy the very Government to which I am accredited. I will not attempt, in the language of the Senator, to handcuff the President. I will not attempt to destroy the Administration by refusing any officers to administer its functions. I should vote, as I have done to Administrations to which I stood in nearest relation, against a bad nomination; but I never would agree, under the forms of the Constitution, and with the powers I bear as a Senator of the United States, to turn those powers to the destruction of the Government I was sworn to support. I leave that to gentlemen who take the oath with a mental reservation. It is not my policy. If I must have revolution, I say let it be a revolution such as our fathers made when they were denied their natural rights.

So much for that. It has quieted apprehension; and I hope that the artillery will not be brought here; that the militia will not be called out; and that the female schools will continue their sessions as heretofore. [Laughter.] The authority of Mr. Madison, however, was relied on by the Senator from Tennessee; and he read fairly an extract from Mr. Madison's letter to Mr. Webster, and I give him credit for reading what it seems to me destroys his whole argument. It is this clause:

3. Andrew Johnson interrupted and replied to Davis: "I meant that the true way to fight the battle was for us to remain here and occupy the places assigned to us by the Constitution of the country."

"The powers of the Government being exercised, as in other elective and responsible Governments, under the control of its constituents, the people, and the Legislatures of the States, and subject to the revolutionary rights of the people in the extreme cases."

Now, sir, we are confusing language very much. Men speak of revolution; and when they say revolution, they mean blood. Our Fathers meant nothing of the sort. When they spoke of revolution, they spoke of an inalienable right. When they declared as an inalienable right the power of the people to abrogate and modify their form of Government whenever it did not answer the ends for which it was established, they did not mean that they were to sustain that by brute force. They meant that it was a right; and force could only be invoked when that right was wrongfully denied. Great Britain denied the right in the case of the colonies; and therefore our revolution for independence was bloody. If Great Britain had admitted the great American doctrine, there would have been no blood shed; and does it become the descendants of those who proclaimed this as the great principle on which they took their place among the nations of the earth, not to proclaim, if that is a right, it is one which you can only get as the subjects of the Emperor of Austria may get their rights, by force overcoming force? Are we, in this age of civilization and political progress, when political philosophy has advanced to the point which seemed to render it possible that the millennium should now be seen by prophetic eyes; are we now to roll back the whole current of human thought, and again to return to the mere brute force which prevails between beasts of prey, as the only method of settling questions between men?

If the Declaration of Independence be true (and who here gainsays it?) every community may dissolve its connection with any other community previously made, and have not other obligation than that which results from the breach of any alliance between States. Is it to be supposed; could any man reasoning *a priori* come to the conclusion that the men who fought the battles of the Revolution for community independence—that the men who struggled against the then greatest military Power on the face of the globe in order that they might possess those inalienable rights which they had declared—terminated their great efforts by transmitting posterity to a condition in which they could only gain those rights by force? If so, the blood of the Revolution was shed in vain; no great principles were established; for force was the law of nature before the battles of the Revolution were fought.

I see, then—if gentlemen insist on using the word "revolution" in the sense of a resort to force—a very great difference between their opinion and that of Mr. Madison. Mr. Madison put the rights of the people over and above everything else; and he said this was the Government *de facto*. Call it what name you will, he understood ours to be a Government of the people. The people never have separated themselves from those rights which our fathers had declared to be inalienable. They did not delegate to the Federal Government the powers which the British Crown exercised over the colonies; they did not achieve their independence for any purpose so low as that. They left us to the inheritance of freemen, living in independent communities, the States united for the purposes which they thought would bless posterity. It is the exercise of this reserved right as defined by Mr. Madison, as one to which all the powers of Government are subject, that the people of a State in convention have claimed to resume the functions which in like manner they have made to the Federal Government.

I pass from the argument of this question, which I have previously said I did not intend to enter into at large, to ask, why is the right denied? It is part of the history of our times, it is part of the condition of the country, that the right is denied, because this conflict between sections, in which one was struggling for domination, the other for existence, has been brought to the point where the dominant section insists that it will hold the other for its purposes; where it claims that we shall not go in peace, nor remain with our rights; and if the attempt be made to hold that position by force, we accept the wager of battle.

Mississippi, in her brief history, claims to have shown at Pensacola and New Orleans something of the spirit of the freemen who achieved our independence. I was reared in a country where, when the soil of a neighboring State was invaded by a powerful foe, the draft was who should stay at home, not who should go. I also have the satisfaction to know that the present generation have not derogated from the history of those who went before it. From many a bloody field, both in foreign and Indian war, has ascended the proud spirit of a Mississippian enshrined in glory, whence they look down upon us to vindicate the honorable fame of our State; and every heart beats true to the impulse of pride and the dictate of duty. If this right were admitted, we should have less cause to exercise it than we have. If admitted, then there would be less danger from a dominant section than there is; there would be less tendency to use power, when it was acquired, to the injury of others. The denial of the right is a grievance inflicted on all who fear that power will be used for aggression. The concession of the right might delay its exercise; and at the same time would restrain the dominant section from abusing its power so as to drive others to resort to it. Why is the right denied? It is an impractical question at best. If you take us out of the history of our country, throw us into a broad discussion of the natural rights of man, we may answer by the facts which are being enacted. States have gone out; and what is the use of arguing their rights? The only questions which remain are for yourselves: first, have you the right to coerce them back? and secondly, have you the power?

My friend from Louisiana, in closing his remarks, referred to the disastrous scenes which might be occasioned by the invasion of the South. He did not offer the other side of the picture; and yet I have seen that, in northern papers, he has been criticized for saying even what he did. There is, however, another side to the picture. An army with banners would do but little harm in marching through a country of plantations. They would have but little power to subsist themselves in a sparsely settled region. They would find it hard to feed the army with which they invaded, and would have no power to bring away prisoners and fugitives. How stands it on the other side? In a country of populous cities, of manufacturing towns, where population is gathered from the country into towns and villages, the torch and sword can do their work with dreadful havoc, and starving millions would weep at the stupidity of those who had precipitated them into so sad a policy.

We do not desire these things. We seek not the injury of any one. We seek not to disturb your prosperity. We, at least to a great extent, have from time to time looked to our agricultural labor as that to which we prefer to adhere. We have seen, in the diversity of the occupations of the States, the bond of Union. We have rejoiced in your prosperity. We have sent you our staples, and purchased your manufactured articles. We have used your ships for the purpose of transport and navigation. We have gloried in the extension of American commerce everywhere; have felt proud as yourselves in every achievement you made in art; on every sea that you carried your flag in regions to which it had hitherto not been borne; and, if we must leave you, we can leave you still with the good-will which would prefer that your prosperity should continue. If we must part, I say we can put our relations upon that basis which will give you the advantage of a favored trade with us, and still make the intercourse mutually beneficial to each other. If you will not, then it is an issue from which we will not shrink; for, between oppression and freedom, between the maintenance of right and submission to power; we will invoke the God of battles, and meet our fate, whatever it may be.

I was reading, a short time ago, an extract from the speech of the Senator from Tennessee which referred to the time when "we"—I suppose it means Tennessee—would take the position which it was said to be an absurdity for South Carolina to hold. How can the change of names thus affect the question; and who is to judge in the case? Tennessee still was put, in the same speech, in the attitude of a great objector against the exercise of the right of secession. Is there anything in her history which thus places her? Tennessee, born of secession, rocked in the cradle of revolution, taking her position before she was matured, and claiming to be a State because she had violently severed her connection with North Carolina, and through an act of secession and revolution, claimed to have become a State. I honor her for it. I honor the gallant old Sevier for maintaining the rights of which North Carolina attempted to deprive him, and I admired the talent which made recruits from every army which was sent to subdue him. Washington and Jackson, too, are often presented as authority against it—Washington, who led the army of the Revolution; Washington, whose reputation rests upon the fact that with the sword he cut the cord which bound the Colonies to Great Britain, they not having the justification of the sovereign attributes belonging to States; Washington, who presided when the States seceded from the Confederation, and formed the Union, in disregard of the claims of the States not agreeing to it; and Jackson, glorious old soldier, who, in his minority, upon the sacred soil of South Carolina, bled for the cause of revolution and the overthrow of a Government which he believed to be oppressive; who, through his whole life, indicated the same cast of character, standing in an attitude which to-day would be called rebellion and treason, when he opposed the Federal Government, denied their power, contemned their orders to disband his troops, threatened to put any officer in irons who came into his camp to recruit, and marched his force, the Tennessee militia, back from Washington in Mississippi, to the place whence they had started. Bad authorities are these for our opponents; yet they are names under the shadow of which we can safely repose!

If we were reduced to arguing the question on the ground of expediency; if we had to convince the dominant section that it was good for them that their best customers should leave them; if we had to convince them that they should not any longer have the power to tax us, that they should not collect the revenue which fills the Treasury and builds ups their vast public works, I fear we are of no advantage to them; if they look upon the southern States as a burden; if they think we require their protection, then, we are ready to relieve them.

The question which now presents itself to the country is, what shall we do with events as they stand? Shall we allow this separation to be total? Shall we render it peaceful, with a view to the chance that when hunger shall brighten the intellects of men, and the teachings of hard experience shall have tamed them, they may come back, in the spirit of our fathers, to the task of reconstruction? Or will they have that separation partial; will they give to each State all its military power; will they give to each State its revenue power; will they still preserve the common agent; and will they thus carry on a Government different from that which now exists, yet not separating the States so entirely as to make the work of reconstruction equal to a new creation; not separating them so as to render it utterly impossible to administer any functions of the Government in security and peace?

I waive the question of duality, considering that a dual Executive would be the institution of a king-lord. I consider a dual legislative department would be to bring into antagonism the representatives of two different countries, to war perpetually, and thus to continue, not union, but the irrepressible conflict. There is no duality possible (unless there be two Confederacies) which seems to me consistent with the interests of either or both. It might be that two Confederacies could be so organized as to answer jointly many of the ends of our present Union; it might be that States, agreeing with each other in that internal polity—having a similarity of interests and an identity of purpose—might associate together; and that these two Confederacies might have relations to each other so close as to give them a united power in time of war against any foreign nation. These things are possibilities; these things it becomes us to contemplate; these things it devolves on the majority section to consider now; for with every motion of that clock is passing away your opportunity. It was greater when we met on the first Monday in December than it is now; it is greater now then it will be on the first day of next week. We have waited long; we have come to the conclusion that you mean to do nothing. In the committee of thirteen, where the resolutions of the Senator from Kentucky [Mr. Crittenden] were considered, various attempts were made, but no prospect of any agreement on which it was possible for us to stand, in security for the future, could be matured. I offered a proposition, which was but the declaration of that which the Constitution announces; but that which the Supreme Court had, from time to time, and from an early period, asserted; but that which was necessary for equality in the Union. Not one single vote of the Republican portion of that committee was given for the proposition.

Looking then upon separation as inevitable, not knowing how that separation is to occur, or at least what States it is to embrace, there remains to us, I believe, as the consideration which is most useful, the inquiry, how can this separation be effected so as to leave to us the power, whenever we shall have the will, to reconstruct? It can only be done by adopting a policy of peace. It can only be done by denying the Federal Government all power to coerce. It can only be done by returning to the point from which we started, and saying, "This is a Government of fraternity, a Government of consent; and it shall not be administered in a department from those principles."

I do not regard the failure of our constitutional Union, as very many do, to be the failure of self-government; to be conclusive in all future time of the unfitness of man to govern himself. Our State governments have charge of nearly all the relations of person and property. This Federal Government was instituted mainly as a common agent for foreign purposes, for free trade among the States, and for common defense. Representative liberty will remain in the States after they are separated. Liberty was not crushed by the separation of the colonies from the mother country, then the most constitutional monarchy and the freest Government known. Still less will liberty be destroyed by the separation of theses States to prevent the destruction of the spirit of the Constitution by the maladministration of it. There will be injury—injury to all; differing in degree, differing in manner. The injury to the manufacturing and navigating States will be to their internal prosperity. The injury to the southern States will be to their internal high pride and power which belong to the flag now representing the greatest Republic, if not the greatest Government, upon the face of the globe. I would that it still remained to consider what we might calmly have considered on the first Monday in December—how this could be avoided; but events have rolled past that point. You would not make propositions when they would have been effective. I presume you will not make them now; and I know what effect they would have if you did. Your propositions would have been most welcome if they had been made before any question of coercion, and before any vain boasting of power; for pride and passion do not often take counsel of pecuniary interest, at least among those whom I represent. But you have chosen to take the policy of clinging to words, in disregard of events, and have hastened them onwards. It is true, as shown by the history of all revolutions, that they are most precipitated and intensified by obstinacy and vacillation. The want of a policy, the obstinate adherence to unimportant things, have brought us to a condition where I close my eyes, because I cannot see anything that encourages me to hope.

In the long period which elapsed after the downfall of the great Republic of the East, when despotism seemed to brood over the civilized world, and only here and there constitutional monarchy even was able to rear its head; when all the great principles of republican and representative government had sunk deep, fathomless, into the sea of human events; it was then that the storm of our Revolution moved the waters. The earth, the air, and the sea, became brilliant; and from the foam of ages rose the constellation which was set in the political firmament as a sign of unity and confederation and community independence, coexistent with confederate strength. That constellation has served to bless our people. Nay, more; its light has been thrown on foreign lands, and its regenerative power will outlive, perhaps, the Government as a sign for which it was set. It may be pardoned to me, sir, who, in my boyhood, was given to the military service, and who have followed under tropical suns, and over northern snows, the flag of the Union, suffering from it as it does not become me to speak it, if I here express the deep sorrow which always overwhelms me when I think of taking a last leave of that object of early affection and proud association, feeling that henceforth it is not to be the banner which, by day and by night, I am ready to follow, to hail with the rising and bless with the setting sun. But God, who knows the hearts of men, will judge between you and us, at whose door lies the responsibility of this. Men will see the efforts I have made, here and elsewhere; that I have been silent when words would not avail, and have curbed an impatient temper, and hoped that conciliatory counsels might do that which I know could not be effected by harsh means. And yet the only response which has come from the other side has been a stolid indifference, as though it mattered not, "let the temple fall, we do not care." Sirs, remember that such conduct is offensive, and that men may become indifferent event to the objects of their early attachments.

If our Government shall fail, it will not be the defect of the system, though its mechanism was wonderful, surpassing that which the solar system furnishes for our contemplation; for it has had no center of gravitation; each planet was set to revolve in an orbit of its own, each moving by its own impulse, and all attracted by the affections which countervailed each other. It has been the perversion of the Constitution, it has been the substitution of theories of morals for principles of government; it has been forcing crude opinions about things not understood upon the domestic institutions of other men, which has disturbed these planets in their orbit; it is this which threatens to destroy the constellation which, in its power and its glory, had been gathering one after another, until, from thirteen, it had risen to thirty-three stars.

If we accept the argument of to-day in favor of coercion as the theory of our Government, its only effect will be to precipitate men who have pride and self-reliance into the assertion of the freedom and independence to which they were born. Our fathers would never have entered into a confederate Government which had within itself the power of coercion. I would not agree to remain one day in such a Government after I had the power to get out of it. To argue that a man who follows the mandate of his State, resuming her sovereign jurisdiction and power, is disloyal to his allegiance to the United States, which allegiances he only owed through his State, is such a confusion of ideas as does not belong to an ordinary comprehension of our Government. It is treason to the principle of community independence. It is to recur to that doctrine of passive obedience which, in England, cost one monarch his head, and drove another into exile; a doctrine which, since the revolution of 1688, has obtained nowhere where men speak the English tongue; and yet all this it is needful to admit before we accept this doctrine of coercion, which is to send an Army and a Navy to do that which there are no courts to perform; to execute the law without a judicial decision, and without an officer to serve process. This, I say, would degrade us to the basest despotism under which man could live; the despotism of a many-headed monster, without the sensibility or regardful consideration which might belong to a hereditary king. . . .[4]

There are two modes, however, of dissolving the Union. One alone has been contemplated. It was that which proceeded from States separating themselves from those to whom they are united. There is another. It is by destroying the Constitution; by pulling down the political temple; by forming a consolidated Government. Union, in the very meaning of the word, implies the junction of separate States. Consolidation would be the destruction of the Union, and far more fatal to popular liberty than the separation of the States. But, if fanaticism and sectionalism, like the blind giant of old, shall seize the pillars of the temple to tear them down, in order that they may destroy its inmates, it but remains for us to withdraw, and it will be our purpose to commence the erection of another one on the same plan on which our fathers built this. We share no such common ruin as falls upon a people by consolidation and destruction of the principles of liberty contained in the Constitution, by interference with community and social rights; and we go out of such a Government whenever it takes that form, in accordance with the Constitution, and in defense of the principles on which that Constitution rests. We have warned you for many years that you would drive us to this alternative, and you would not heed.

4. Davis questioned Andrew Johnson's accusation that Senator Alfred Iverson of Georgia supported a constitutional monarchy for the South. Iverson stated, "there is not one man in a million . . . in the State of Georgia, or elsewhere in the South, who would be in favor of any such principle."

I believe that you still look upon it as a mere passing political move, as a device for some party end, knowing little of the deep struggle with which we have contemplated this as a necessity, not as a choice, when we have been brought to stand before the alternative—the destruction of our community independence, or the destruction of that Union which our fathers made. You would not heed us. You deemed our warning to be merely to the end of electing a candidate for the miserable spoils of office, of which I am glad to say I represent a people who have had so little indeed that they have never acquired and appetite for them. Yet you have believed—not looking to the great end to which our eyes were directed—that it was a mere political resort, by which we would intimidate some of your own political resort, by which we would intimidate some of your own voters. You have turned upon those true friends of ours at the North who have vindicated the Constitution, and pointed out to you the danger of your course, and held them responsible for the censure you received, as though you had not, in fact aggressed. Even at this session, after forty years of debate, you have asked us what was the matter.

Your platform on which you elected your candidate denies us equality. Your votes refuse to recognize our domestic institutions which preexisted the formation of the Union, or property which was guarded by the Constitution. You refuse us that equality without which we should be degraded if we remained in the Union. You elect a candidate upon the basis of sectional hostility; one who, in his speeches, now thrown broadcast over the country, made a distinct declaration of war upon our institutions. We care not whether that war be made by armies marching for invasion, or whether it be by proclamation, or whether it be by indirect and covert process. In both modes, however, you have declared your hostility. The leading members of that party, some of them now before me, making speeches in various portions of the country during the last summer, even after the election was over, when no purpose of the canvass remained still to excite them, announcing the triumph which had been achieved, as the downfall of our domestic institutions; and still you ask us to make specifications, to file an indictment as though we intended to arraign you before a magistrate's court. Our fathers united with yours on the basis of equality, and they were prompted to form a union by the fraternity which existed between them. Do you admit that equality? Do you feel that fraternity? Do your actions show it? They united for the purpose not only of domestic tranquillity, but for common defense; and the debates in the convention which formed the Constitution set forth that the navigation and manufacturing interests of one section, and the better defense in the other, were the two great objects which drew them together. Are you willing now to fulfill the conditions on which our fathers agreed to unite?

When you use figurative language, its harshness indicates the severity of your temper and the bitterness of your hate. When you talk about having your heel on the slave power and grinding it into dust; when you talk about the final triumph; when you talk about the extinction of slavery, and institution with which you have nothing to do and of which you know nothing, is this the fraternity, is this the Union, to which we were invited? Is that the administration of the Government under which we can live in safety? Is this a condition of things to which men, through whose veins flows blood of the Revolution, can stoop without acknowledging that they had sunk from their birthright of freedom to become slaves!

I care not to read your platform; I care not to read from the speeches of your President elect. You know them as I do; and the man who is regarded over this country as directing intellect of the party to which he belongs, the Senator from New York [Mr. Seward] has, with less harshness of expression than others, but with more of method, indicated this same purpose of deadly hostility in every form in which it could be portrayed. Did we unite with you in order that the powers of the General Government should be used for destroying our domestic institutions? Do you believe that now, in our increased and increasing commercial as well as physical power, we will consent to remain united to a Government exercised for such a purpose as this?

What boots it to tell me that no direct act of aggression will be made? I prefer direct to indirect hostile measures which will produce the same result. I prefer it, as I prefer an open to a secret foe. Is there a Senator upon the other side who to-day will agree that we shall have equal enjoyment of the Territories of the United States? Is there one who will deny that we have equally paid in their purchases, and equally bled in their acquisition in war? Then, is this the observance of your compact? Whose is the fault if the Union be dissolved? Do you say that there is one of you who controverts either of these positions? Then I ask you, do you give us justice; do we enjoy equality? If we are not equals, this is not the Union to which we were pledged; this is not the Constitution you have sworn to maintain, nor this the Government we are bound to support.

There is much, too, which is exceedingly offensive in the speculations you make upon our servants when you talk about negro insurrection. Governments have tampered with slaves; bad men have gone among the ignorant and credulous people, and incited them to murder and arson; but of themselves—moving by themselves—I say history does not chronicle a case of negro insurrection. San Domingo, so often referred to, and so little understood, is not a case where black heroes rose and acquired a Government. It was a case in which the French Government, trampling upon the rights and safety of a distant and feeble colony by sending troops among them, brought on a revolution, first of the mulattoes, and afterwards of the blacks. Their first army was not even able to effect this. It required a second army, and that army to be quartered on the plantations; nay, after all, it required that the master should be arrested on the charge of treason and taken to France, before the negroes could be aroused to insurrection.

Do you wonder, then, that we pause when we see this studied tendency to convert the Government into a military despotism? Do you wonder that we question the right of the President to send troops to execute the laws whenever he pleases, when we remember the conduct of France, and that those troops were sent with like avowal, and quartered on plantations, and planters arrested for treason—just such charges as are made to-day against southern men—and brought away that insurrection might be instigated among their slaves?

I seek not to exasperate or intensify the causes of difficulty. It is needful that we should understand each other. I thought we had done so before, and was surprised to hear the question asked, "What is the matter?" The last canvass, I thought, had expressed the feelings and the opinions of the southern States. The State of Mississippi gave warning in solemn resolutions passed by her Legislature. Those resolutions were printed elsewhere, and were generally known. She declared her purpose to take counsel with her southern sister States whenever a President should be elected on the basis of sectional hostility to them. With all this warning, you paused not. The quarrel was not of our making. Our hands are stainless; you aggressed upon our rights and our homes, and, under the will of God, we will defend them. . . .[5]

I have heard, with some surprise, for it seemed to me idle, the repetition of the assertion heretofore made that the cause of the separation was the election of Mr. Lincoln. It may be a source of gratification to some gentlemen that their friend is elected; but no individual had the power to product the existing state of things. It was the purpose, the end; it was the

5. The Mississippi senator joined many Southern pamphleteers in comparing Northern behavior in 1860 to that of England in 1775. Edmund Burke became a Southern hero in part because of his defense of the colonists during the American Revolution.

declaration by himself and his friends, which constitute the necessity of providing new safeguards for ourselves. The man was nothing, save as he was the representative of the opinions, of a policy, of purposes, of power, to inflict upon us those wrongs to which freemen never tamely submit.

I have spoken longer than I desired. I had supposed it was possible, avoiding argument and not citing authority, to have made to you a brief address. It was thought useless to argue a question which now belongs to the past. The time is near at hand when the places which have known us as colleagues laboring together, can know us in that relation no more forever. I have striven to avert the catastrophe which now impends over the country, unsuccessfully; and I regret it. For the few days which I may remain, I am willing to labor in order that the catastrophe shall be as little as possible destructive to public peace and prosperity. If you desire at this last moment to avert civil war, so be it; it is better so. If you will but allow us to separate from you peaceably since we cannot live peaceable together, to leave with the rights we had before we were united, since we cannot enjoy them in the Union, then there are many relations which may still subsist between us, drawn from the associations of our struggles from the revolutionary era to the present day, which may be beneficial to you as well as to us.

If you will not have it thus; if in the pride of power, if in contempt of reason and reliance upon force, you say we shall not go, but shall remain as subjects to you, then, gentlemen of the North, a war is to be inaugurated the like of which men have not seen. Sufficiently numerous on both sides, in close contact with only imaginary lines of division, and with many means of approach, each sustained by productive sections, the people of which will give freely both of money and of store, the conflicts must be multiplied indefinitely; and masses of men, sacrificed to the demon of civil war, will furnish hecatombs, such as the recent campaign in Italy did not offer. At the end of all this, what will you have effected? Destruction upon both sides; subjugation upon neither; a treaty of peace leaving both torn and bleeding; the wail of the widow and the cry of the orphan substituted for those peaceful notes of domestic happiness that now prevail throughout the land; and then you will agree that each is to pursue his separate course as best he may. This is to be the end of war. Through a long series of years you may waste your strength, distress your people, and get at last to the position which you might have had at first, had justice and reason, instead of selfishness and passion, folly and crime, dictated your course.

Is there wisdom, is there patriotism in the land? If so, easy must be the solution of this question. If not, then Mississippi's gallant sons will stand like a wall of fire around their State; and I go hence, not in hostility to you, but in love and allegiance to her, to take my place among her sons, be it for good or for evil.

I shall probably never again attempt to utter here the language either of warning or of argument. I leave the case in your hands. If you solve it not before I go, you will have still to decide it. Towards you individually, as well as to those whom you represent, I would that I had the power now to say there shall be peace between us forever. I would that I had the power now to say the intercourse and the commerce between the States, if they cannot live in one Union, shall still be uninterrupted; that all the social relations shall remain undisturbed; that the son in Mississippi shall visit freely his father in Maine, and the reverse; and that each shall be welcomed when he goes to the other, not by himself alone, but also by his neighbors; and that all that kindly intercourse which has subsisted between the different sections of the Union shall continue to exist. It is not only for the interests of all, but it is my profoundest wish, my sincerest desire, that such remnant of that which is passing away may grace the memory of a glorious, though too brief, existence.

Day by day you have become more and more exasperated. False reports have led you to suppose there was in our section hostility to you with manifestations which did not exist. In one case, I well remember when the Senator from Vermont [Mr. Collamer] was serving with me on a special committee, it was reported that a gentleman who had gone from a commercial house in New York had been inhumanly treated at Vicksburg, and this embarrassed a question which we then had pending. I wrote to Vicksburg for information, and my friends could not learn that such a man had ever been there; but if he had been there, no violence certainly had been offered to him. Falsehood and suspicion have thus led you on a step by step in the career of crimination, and perhaps has induced to some part of your aggression. Such evil effects we have heretofore suffered, and the consequences none have their fatal culmination. On the verge of war, distrust and passion increase the danger. To-day it is the power of two bad men, at the opposite ends of the telegraphic line between Washington and Charleston, to precipitate the State of South Carolina and the Unites States into a conflict of arms without other cause to have produced it.

And still will you hesitate; still will you do nothing? Will you sit with sublime indifference and allow events to shape themselves? No longer can you say the responsibility is upon the Executive. He has thrown it upon you. He has notified you that he can do nothing; and you therefore know he will do nothing. He has told you the responsibility now rests with Congress; and I close as I began, but invoking you to meet that responsibility, bravely to act the patriot's part. If you will, the angel of peace may spread her wings, though it be over divided States; and the sons of the sires of the Revolution may still go on in friendly intercourse with each other, ever reviewing the memories of common origins, the sections, by the diversity of their products and habits, acting and reacting beneficially, the commerce of each may swell the prosperity of both, and the happiness of all be still interwoven together. Thus may it be; and thus it is in your power to make it. [Applause in the galleries.] 6

6. Davis concluded his speech with a heated exchange with Senator Lyman Trumbull of Illinois over just which section caused the impending crisis over Fort Sumter.

JOHN H. REAGAN

State of the Union. Speech . . . Delivered in the House of Representatives, Jan. 15, 1861

(Washington: W. H. Moore, 1861)

John H. Reagan (1818–1905) was born in Tennessee, attended private schools, moved to Texas to survey Western lands, studied law, and developed a successful legal practice. He gained election to the state legislature, served as a district judge, and entered the U.S. House of Representatives in 1857. Upon his withdrawal from Congress, Reagan became a delegate to the Texas secession convention, helped to draft the Confederate States constitution, and during the Civil War served as Confederate postmaster general. At first disfranchised after the war, he later served in the U.S. House and had a distinguished career in the U.S. Senate. In the pamphlet below, reprinted from a speech during the debate over the House Committee of Thirty-three report, Reagan stated that there was no time left to argue over the right of secession but he wanted to explain why Southern states had seceded. For him, slave property was at stake, and firsthand experience had taught him how abolitionists stirred slave violence. Reagan also insisted that Southerners were willing to fight to protect their border and their investments. For information about his life see Ben H. Proctor, Not Without Honor: The Life of John H. Reagan *(Austin: University of Texas Press, 1962); Walter F. McCaleb, ed.,* Memoirs of John H. Reagan *(New York: The Neale Publishing Co., 1906) provides the best insights into his life and work.*

We stand in the presence of great events. When Congress assembled some weeks ago, the control of the condition of the country was in its hands. I came here with a full knowledge of the deep discontent that prevailed in a portion of the States, and I felt then satisfied—as all must be satisfied now—that they intended to insist unconditionally and unalterably upon being secured in their constitutional rights in the Union, or on going out of it for the sake of self-preservation. I came here with the hope that such measures might be brought forward by those who had the power to control this question, as would assure the people of the South that they might expect future security for their rights in the Union. I believe that if the Republican members had manifested, at the beginning of this session of Congress, a purpose to respect simply the constitutional rights of all the States and of their people, all these difficulties might before this time, have been settled. I do not mean to be understood, in making that remark, as indicating that it would have been necessary for them to have acceded to any extravagant or unreasonable demands. Such demands would not have been made, unless they deem it extravagant and unreasonable to insist upon plain, specific guarantees of those rights which were assuredly secured to us under the present Constitution as it was formed, and which have been secured to us by the action of all departments of the Federal Government down to this time. This, I believe, was the condition of things when Congress assembled at the beginning of this session. In view of the fact that Republican members of Congress have held sullenly back, and have neither proposed nor accepted any compromise, but have declared that they have none to make, four States are now out of the Union; and many others are in rapid motion to go out. Unless something can now be done to arrest this movement there will be but few southern States, if any, acknowledging allegiance to the Federal Government on the 4th of March next.[1]

This state of things having been produced, what can change it? I cannot say now that it is possible to arrest the movement. It is certainly all but impossible now to arrest it. It is my duty to speak on this occasion as I would speak in the presence of the future—as I would speak in the presence of the calamities invoked on this people by the action of this Congress, and by a portion of the States of the Union. No men on the face of this earth, at any period of the world's history, were ever charged with a more solemn responsibility than that which rests to-day on the American Congress. It calls not for passion, but for calm deliberation; not for the maintenance of mere partisan supremacy, but for the ascendancy of patriotism; not for the domination of the one party and the overthrow of the other, but for a constitutional Union based on the action of the people, and on the support of a Government friendly to all its parts; not nurturing and fostering the one and hostile to the other, but just and fair to all alike. These are the great principles which should animate our action if we intend to preserve the Union. On the other hand, if fifteen States come here—minority as they may be in Congress, in the popular masses, in wealth and power—telling you of their discontents, and the cause of them, and if you tender no olive branch, no conciliation, but sternly deny them their constitutional rights, and tender them on the one hand submission to ruin, and on the other powder and ball, who is it that does not know what decision will be whatever may be the consequences?

Is there a cause for this discontent? It has been interrogatively sug-

1. Reagan was referring to presidential inauguration day, when the Republican Party would assume control of the federal government.

gested that there was none. It has been partially admitted by others that there is some cause. This is no time to come here and suppose that, by special pleading and ingenious statements of the cause of controversy, we can change the judgements of posterity as to the attitude of public affairs in these times. It is beneath the dignity of the statesman; it is beneath the dignity of the men who control events, to resort now to special pleading to misrepresent the cause of the grievances which now exist. History will tell what those causes are. All of you know to-day what they are. For twenty years the anti-slavery strength has been growing in the free States of this Confederacy. In recent years it has become aggressive. The question tendered to the people of the South is well expressed in the language of the President elect—that this agitation must go on until the northern mind shall rest in the belief that slavery is put in a condition of ultimate extinction. That was his sentiment. That is the sentiment of the great leaders of that party. I presume that few members of that party would to-day, in their place deny that such was its purpose. I take it for granted, that we may act on the presumption that that is its purpose. What justice is there in that? Let us, for one moment, revert to the history of the Government to know whether it is just in it to assume the responsibility of so grave an act. I need hardly say that, at the date of the Declaration of Independence, each of the thirteen colonies of the Union was slaveholding. At the date of the formation of the Federal Constitution, twelve years after that, twelve of the thirteen States of the Union were slaveholding States. Is it to be presumed that twelve out of thirteen States made a Constitution which was intended to recognize slaves as freemen and equals? It would be asking too much of human credulity to believe such a proposition. If anything were necessary to repel the idea, it is supplied by the bare fact that the convention which framed this Constitution, and gave it to us as the charter of our rights and liberties, provided in it for keeping open the African slave trade for twenty years after the formation of that Constitution, so that the white race might go on under authority of the Constitution and acquire a larger amount of property in negro slaves. The interests of a portion of the States disposed of their negroes, not so numerous then, it is true, as they were in some of the more southern States. Then they made their States what they call free States. The southern States raised no objection, and had no right to raise any objection, that these States had chosen for themselves to exclude negro slavery; but they had rights under the Federal Constitution—the right to protection and security—which it was their duty to insist upon. That is all they have done.

I cannot dwell longer upon this portion of our history; but I will ask attention to another feature of this question. I invoke the attention of Republicans for a moment, to what would be the result of the success of their doctrines if they will not cease this agitation until they can rest in the belief that negro slavery is put in process of extinction. But, before I do it, I wish to make one remark, not altogether connected with my argument, but which may not be unserviceable. We have for years back heard of what is termed the irrepressible conflict. It has emanated from men who have been eulogized for their statesmanship and their learning. It rested on the idea of irrepressible hostility between the interests and institutions of States of the Union. It has been invoked for partisan success and for sectional prejudice. It has culminated too soon for its authors. And here, to-day, behold the fruits of the irrepressible conflict. Every man who looks forward with an eye to the interests and hopes of the country, has foreseen what the irrepressible conflict meant—that it meant subjugation and humiliation of the South, or the dissolution of the Union. You have reached now its logical end. Are you, then, longer prepared to eulogize a doctrine, and eulogize its authors, which has brought upon us so precipitately such fruits as these?

But to the point to which I was calling attention. I ask Republicans to-day—and I would to God I could throw my voice to every city and town and village and hamlet in the whole North, and could be heard by every citizen there, and answered by all—to trace the history of the African race through all the centuries of the past, in every country and every clime, from their native barbarism in Africa to slavery in Brazil and the West Indies, and everywhere else that you find them, and then come to the southern States, and compare the condition of the negroes there with their condition anywhere else, and answer me if they are not in the enjoyment of more peace, more blessings, and everything that gives contentment and happiness, than any other portion of that race, bond or free, at any age or in any other portion of the world? Will any man deny that they are? And if they are, is it the part of philanthropy to turn them back to the condition of the rest of their race, and, in doing so, destroy the hopes and the social and political future of fifteen States of this Confederacy? Then, again I would ask this other question: Suppose these slaves were liberated: suppose the people of the South would to-day voluntarily consent to surrender $3,000,000,000 of slave property, and send their slaves at their expense into the free States, would you accept them as freemen and citizens in your States? You dare not answer me that you would. You would fight us with all the energy and power of your States for twenty years, before you would submit to it. And yet you demand of us to liberate them, to surrender this $3,000,000,000 of slave property, to dissolve society, to break up social-order, to ruin our commercial and political prospects for the future, and still to retain such an element among us.

Again: I ask you, do you believe, one of you—does any Republican in this Union believe this day that, if you could purchase a separate Territory, occupied by no human being, if you could liberate all the slaves to-day, take them to that Territory, frame a government for them, and give them money to start it—do you believe that, for one year, or in any future period, those negroes could maintain a government in peace, giving security to life and person, and prosperity and repose to society? I venture to say there is not a Republican in this Union who would hazard his reputation by answering that question in the affirmative. And yet, in religion's name, in God's name, in the name of justice and humanity, you are invoking every feeling that can stir the hearts of the people to press on with your irrepressible conflict; never halting, never stopping to consider, as all statesmen must consider, the relative condition and capacities of the races; and what is to be the end of the conflict which you invoke, with the certainty, on your part, that it must result in breaking up this Republic, or in the subjugation and the infliction upon the South of the worst despotism that can be forced upon any country. I address you with all the earnestness of my nature; I address you in the name of humanity, in the name of our common country, and of the cause of civil liberty.

Again: if I wanted experience to prove the truth of my supposition that such would be the calamitous effect of carrying your principles to their ultimate results, the history of the past furnishes that experience. In 1793, when red republicanism assumed its reign in France, and the wild delusion of unrestrained liberty seized upon the minds of the masses, there was a wretched fanatic who undertook to proclaim the equality of every human being, and he proposed the liberation of the slaves in the French West India colonies. The ideal chimed in with the popular delusions of the day, and a decree was passed that all the slaves should be free. The colonies would not accept the decree, and did not until the army of France was brought into requisition, and the slaves were set at liberty. But, what was the result to the colonies? Great Britain, catching the contagion from France, determined upon the policy of liberating the slaves in her West India colonies; but she was a little more humane and liberal. She did make compensation to the owners of the slaves liberated, to the amount of, perhaps, one-eighth of their value. But what was the fruit of those decrees to the colonies interested? What was the result of conferring the boon of freedom upon the African race in these colonies? What was the condition of these colonies prior to the execution of these decrees? They were the homes of civilization, contentment, prosperity, and happiness; their farms were cultivated, their cities were alive with business, their ports were covered with the canvass of the fleets of all nations, bearing to and from the commerce of the world.

Those decrees were passed. What followed? The white race was exterminated by all the implements and modes of cruelty and torture that ingenuity and barbarism could invent. Yes, sir, exterminated. The fields then glowing under the hand of industry soon went back into jungle, inhabited by the wild beasts of the forest; grass grew in the streets of their cities, and ships departed from their ports to return no more. And they have gone on in this experiment of liberty from revolution to revolution, carnage succeeding carnage, until at this time they have relapsed into and present a spectacle of savage African barbarism. Gentlemen of the Republican party, are you now prepared to go on in your aggressions until you have inaugurated the same scenes for your southern brethren? I say your brethren, for hundreds and thousands of them are your own common kindred, living in the enjoyment of the blessings of the same system of Government, and enjoying the prosperity common to our people. Are you prepared to inaugurate a system which can only end in such a result? Are you prepared to attempt to force us by fire and sword to submit to such a fate as this?

Your people have lived in the habitual violation of the Constitution and laws of Congress, for many years, to our serious injury, and we have never invoked the doctrine of Federal coercion against your States. Your Legislatures have passed laws nullifying a provision of the Federal Constitution which ought to have secured protection to our rights. The members of your Legislature had to commit official perjury in voting for these laws. And your Governors had to do the same thing in signing and approving them. And a number of your States have passed laws to fine and imprison their own citizens if they should aid in executing the fugitive slave law—a law passed in conformity with the requirements of the Federal Constitution, and which had been adjudged to be constitutional and binding on all, by the Supreme Court of the United States.

During all the time your States have stood in open rebellion against the Constitution and laws of the country—and this in carrying out your aggressive and hostile policy against us—we have heard nothing of Federal coercion, not even from our northern friends who are now so ready to turn the Federal bayonets against us. But now that the southern States have determined that they can stand these lawless and hostile aggressions on their right no longer; now that they have determined not to live under a Government for their common good, but which are to be used under Republican rule for their ruin, we hear continually from Republicans of the treason and rebellion of the South; and they are loud and seemingly sincere in their demands for the *enforcement of the laws* by Federal guns. And I regret to see that northern Democrats, some of them, seem to be equally forgetful of our wrongs and of abolition aggressions on our rights, and equally anxious for this gun-powder enforcement of the laws, against the authority of States sovereignty in the exercise of their highest and most sacred duties— the protection and defense of the rights of their own citizen, who can no longer look for security or protection under a Government to be administered by hostile enemies under a violated Constitution.

But again: I wish to call your attention to another point. What is to be the effect upon the material prosperity, not of the South alone, but upon the North, upon Great Britain, and upon the whole of continental Europe, from the success of your policy? Let me ask you to consider—for it would not seem that you have contemplated it for yourselves—this fact: during the last year, the foreign exports from the southern States amounted to $250,000,000. Of this amount $200,000,000 consists in the exportation of the single article of cotton. That cotton supplies the material for your northern manufacturers of cotton goods. It employs the millions of capital engaged in that business. It employs the time and services of hundreds of thousands of operatives who work there. It employs the investments made in your northern cities in the shipping in our coastwise trade and foreign commerce. It employs the untold millions of English capital engaged in the manufacture of cotton goods. It employs the millions of English capital engaged in the transportation of cotton, manufactured and unmanufactured. It supplies with bread the hundreds of thousands of operatives employed in the manufacture of these goods in England.

Now, suppose you succeed in striking down African slavery in the United States: you strike down not only our prosperity in the South, and inaugurate instead all the horrors of Africanized barbarism under which the French and British West India colonies now suffer; you strike down all the investments made in the manufacture of cotton goods; you bankrupt your capitalists; you beggar your operatives; you bankrupt Great Britain; you beggar millions there; you inaugurate starvation and famine in Great Britain to an extent ten-fold beyond that which will be suffered here. You require of us unconditional submission; and if that is not rendered, you propose to imply all the force of the Army and Navy to subjugate us.

You contemplate, as a part of the means of your operations, the blockade of our ports. Well, I grant that you have the ships, and you could blockade our ports if none but ourselves were concerned. But let me warn you in advance, that like a distinguished general of a former war, you will find a fire in the rear as well as in front when you undertake to do it. Your own people will not permit you to do it. Your commercial cities will not permit you to do it. Your manufacturers will not permit you to do it. But suppose your people should be so demented as to allow you to destroy their interests; do you think Great Britain would permit it? Will she permit you to bankrupt her capitalists engaged in the manufacture of cotton goods, and in the commerce growing but of cotton, and to starve her millions of operatives? If your own interests, and all the dictates of humanity and justice, will not induce you to forbear from the madness and folly which must produce such results, Great Britain and continental Europe will promptly require you to raise the blockade of our ports.

Gentlemen, I mention these things, and you can consider them if you think they are worth considering. We are dealing with questions which involve not only our interests, but the interests of all the civilized and commercial world.

You are not content with the vast million of tribute we pay you annually under the operation of our revenue laws, our navigation laws, your fishing bounties, and by making your people our manufacturers, our merchants, our shippers. You are not satisfied with the vast tribute we pay you to build up your great cities, your railroads, your canals. You are not satisfied with the millions of tribute we have been paying you on account of the balance of exchange which you hold against us. You are not satisfied that we of the South are almost reduced to the condition of overseers of northern capitalists. You are not satisfied with all this; but you must wage a relentless crusade against our rights and institutions. And now you tender us the inhuman alternative of unconditional submission to Republican rule on abolition principles, and ultimately to free negro equality and a Government of mongrels or a war of races on the one hand, or on the other secession and a bloody and desolation civil war, waged in an attempt by the Federal Government to reduce us to submission to these wrongs. It was the misfortune of Mexico and Central and South America, that they attempted to establish governments of mongrels, to enfranchise Indians and free negroes with all the rights of freemen, and invest them, so far as their numbers went, with the control of those governments. It was a failure there; it would be a failure here. It has given them an uninterrupted reign of revolution and anarchy there; it would do the same thing here. Our own Government succeeded because none but the white race, who are capable of self-government, were enfranchised with the rights of freemen. The *irrepressible conflict* propounded by abolitionism has produced now its legitimate fruits—disunion. Free negro equality, which is its ultimate object, would make us re-enact the scenes of revolution and anarchy we have so long witnessed and deplored in the American Government to the south of us.

We do not intend that you shall reduce us to such a condition. But I can tell you your folly and injustice will compel us to do. It will compel us to be free from your domination, and more self-reliant than we have been. It will compel us to assert and maintain our separate independence. It will compel us to manufacture for ourselves, to build up our own commerce, our own great cities, our own railroads and canals; and to use the tribute money we now pay you for these things for the support of a government which will be friendly to all our interests, hostile to none of them. Let me tell you to beware lest your abolitionism and *irrepressible conflict* statesmanship produce these results to us, and calamities to you of which you dream not now.

The question again recurs, what has brought about the perilous condition of the country? Why, sir, to hear the taunts that are made to the South; to hear the epithets of "treason," "rebellion," "revolt"; to hear the declarations and pretensions made in the North, one would think that the people of the South were a reckless, wayward people, seeking only to do wrong. How? In what? Let the question be echoed and re-echoed all over the Union—all over the civilized world. How? In what have the South done wrong? Have they sought to violate the Federal Constitution? Have they sought to violate the laws? Have they asked you to sacrifice any material interest? Have they asked you to sacrifice any principle that is not in conflict with the Federal Constitution and laws? I wish this question could go everywhere and sink into every heart, and be answered by every human being. How have we done wrong? In what have we wronged you? History is to answer the question; and it is to answer it in the face of the consequences which must follow.

I stand here to-day to say that if there be a southern State, or a southern man even, who would demand, as a condition for remaining in this Union, anything beyond the clearly specified guarantees of the Constitution of the United States as they are, I do not know of it. I can speak for my own State. I think I have had intimate association enough with her people to declare that they have never dreamed of asking more than their constitutional rights. They are, however, unalterable determined never to submit to less than their constitutional rights; never, never sir!

I regret that in the course of this discussion an assumption is made, and arguments are predicated upon it, that it was simply a question of whether we have the right to rebel against the Federal Government. Those arguments have seemed to go upon the hypothesis that we neither knew or appreciated the blessings of this Union; but, on the contrary, we hated and wished to destroy it. And here I must say that, on yesterday, I was deeply pained to hear certain arguments advanced by the distinguished gentlemen from Illinois and Ohio. Their arguments seemed to proceed upon the assumption I have stated. I was the more pained, sir, because I have seen the gallant battles they have fought against the abolitionists and the "irrepressible conflict." I know, sir, that they are representative men of a great and gallant party. I felt profound regret to see such arguments, proceeding upon such an assumption, come from those gentlemen.

Now, if I can I will correct some of the errors upon which the arguments advanced against us predicated. We do rightly estimate the value of the Union. We do rightly estimate the value of the blessings of this Government. We have loved and cherished the Union. Nobody has a better right that I have, although I say to myself, to make that declaration. I have loved the Union with an almost extravagant devotion. I have fought its battles whenever they were to be fought in my section of the country. I have met every sectional issue, at home in my section, and in my State particularly, which was attempted to be forced upon the public mind, and which I thought would mar the harmony of the Democratic party. I have fought the battles of the Union without looking forward to the consequences. I have fought them in times when the result for the Union seemed hopeless. If I could believe we could have security for our rights within the Union, I would go home and fight the battles of the Union in the future with the same earnestness and energy that I have done in times past.

While those gentlemen tender us war as the alternative, if we do not submit, yet, sir, not one word is said in the way of rebuke to those of the Republican party who have created the present storm; no demand is made of the Republican party to relinquish their unconstitutional encroachments—to give up pretension inconsistent with our system of government and our political rights. There, appeal ought to be made, that our rights should be given to us, and that we should be secured in the enjoyment of them. Let that be done, and no arm and no voice will be raised against the Federal Union. Deny us our rights, and we will face your messengers of death, and show you how freemen can die, or living, how they can maintain their rights. Mark that, sir? . . .[2]

They have not repealed the personal liberty bill. That was my statement; and that statement is not denied. I do not believe that they will repeal

2. What followed was a short exchange and debate about which Northern states actually have adopted personal liberty laws.

them in the northern States. It does not lie in the mouths of our northern friends to ask us to believe them until they can promise with certainty that those laws will be repealed. We know that delay is death. We have already experienced some of the fruits of delays.

We want to avert civil war if we can. Yet no effort has been made to give us what, under the Constitution, we ought to have. It is not proposed to give us what will reasonable make the southern people believe that they will have security in the Union. No such proposition can be made and sustained; because, to give us our rights is to disband the Republican party. The existence of that party depends upon violating the Federal Constitution; and in making war upon the institutions of the South. There is now an irrepressible conflict; and either the Federal Government or the Republican party must end. I am not here to paliate or to dodge one of the inevitable dangers that beset us. I am ready, for one, to face them all; and I think that that is the better course for us all to pursue. When we all do that, then we will have a just understanding of our relative positions. You all know that we cannot, and dare not, live in this Union, with our rights denied by the Republican party. Its ascendancy is our destruction; and, sir, its destruction this day is the only salvation for the Union.

I will now, for a moment, refer to the arguments of the distinguished gentlemen from Illinois and Ohio. As one member of this House, I want to give them an assurance that the anticipations they entertain, and upon which they base their arguments, can never be realized. I have been taught, from my earliest instruction in the theory and practice of our Government, that this is a Government of consent and agreement, as contradistinguished from a Government of force or a military despotism. It is bound to be one or the other. Which is it? It is a voluntary association of free, republican States, upon terms of equality or it is a military despotism, in which the Federal arm, through its Army and Navy, can subdue the States at will, and force them to submit to any grievance which may emanate from the Federal Government, has the right to bind the States in all things; they go upon the hypothesis that their interests and position will require them to command the outlet to the Gulf of Mexico and the forts upon the coast of Florida. I do not rise for the purpose of denying the right of passage to the Gulf; but I must express my regrets that they talk in advance of cleaving their way to the Gulf by armies with banners, before one man from all that country has ever said that they should have any cause of war. No one has ever intended to deprive them of the benefits of the navigation of the Mississippi. No one intends it to-day; so that if we are trampled upon by force, let me proclaim to them and to the country, that they must place their action upon a different ground, because we intend that they shall never have cause of war upon that account. . . .[3]

Our interest is peace, and our hopes are for peace. War is in opposition to all our interests and our hopes. We want no war; and we intend to give no just cause for war, unless the attempt to separate ourselves peaceably from despotism, and to take care of our rights under a friendly government — and they would be destroyed under a hostile government — is a cause for war. We declare in advance that we will not interfere with your navigation of the Mississippi river. We know that is necessary for you; but we cannot, because there may possibly be some conflict of interest between us, consent to surrender our liberties rather than assume the responsibility of organizing a government which will cover the lower part of that river and the capes of Florida.

I have but one word more to say. I live far to the South. We have a long Mexican boundary, and a long Indian frontier, infested by hostile savages throughout its whole extent; and yet this Government has refused for years to defend us against them. We have a long coast, open to the approaches of naval force, and we know the consequences of our acts, and we know what may follow an attempt to take care of ourselves and our liberty; but we remember, at the same time, the history of the past. Less than twenty-five years ago Texas stood a province of Mexico, with a population of not more than thirty thousand, entitled to the privileges of Mexican citizens, including all ages and sexes. We lived under the Mexican Constitution of 1824, which the Texans fought to sustain. That Constitution was subverted by a military despot; and our liberties were trampled in the dust. That despot came against us with invading armies for our subjugation. He intended to overawe us by display of military power, as the President and General Scott are now attempting to do with the southern States. The thirty thousand people of Texas resisted that power for the sake of liberty and those rights to which we were entitled, trusting to the God of battles and the justice of their cause. In that great struggle companies and battalions fell to rise no more. They stand nobly for freedom, as freemen will sink again for her cause whenever you shall tender to us that alternative. Upon the field of San Jacinto they won their liberty by the brave hearts and their stalwart arms. They vindicated that liberty for ten or twelve years after; and then as a pledge of their love to this Union, and their confidence in its principles,

3. Congressman John A. McClernand of Illinois, a constitutional Unionist, maintained that he resisted the actions of both radical parties and was determined to support constitutional guarantees for the South.

and desire for its prosperity and its happiness, that the people tendered Texas, a free and voluntary offering, to come in as one of the States of the Union, upon terms of equality with the other States.

But we were told yesterday that we sold ourselves. The gentleman did not mean exactly what his language would imply; but he must see how offensive such kind of remarks must be to those who do not appreciate the use he intended to make of the argument. Texas cost this Government not one cent. She vindicated her liberty by her arms; and rendered to civil and religious liberty a country as large as six New England States, and New York, Pennsylvania, Maryland, Ohio, and Indiana, all put together. She redeemed it from Catholic priestcraft, and military despotism, and has covered it over with five hundred thousand freemen, and prosperous and happy people; and they are prepared to vindicate their liberties when they are encroached upon again by a despotism of one or of many men.

It is true, that war grew out of the annexation of Texas; and I suppose it is that with which the gentleman charges Texas. But this government knew what it was doing when it was acquiring dominion over that country, and adding to the United States to aid in building up its commercial, agricultural, and manufacturing interests. But they also acquired New Mexico and Utah, and the great golden State of California, by that war, and extended their power and dominion to the Pacific ocean. And that is it was the gentleman from Ohio, and the friends of those measures, now sneeringly refer to in their reference to the purchase of Texas, I was sorry to hear it.

Allusion has also been made to the fact that $10,000,000 were subsequently paid for a portion of the domain of Texas, to some of which, it is said, she had not title. I have no time to enter into an argument upon that question. The Federal Government took upon our quarrel for that boundary. As our agent, she obtained the title deed for us. No lawyer will say that it lay with her to dispute our title. She then offered us $10,000,000 for a part of this land—eighty or a hundred thousand square miles of it. Texas accepted the offer: Shall the representatives of the Federal Government now taunt us with the statement that Texas has been bought for a price and paid for? Why, this government only bought a portion of Texas. She has that now. It is not in the jurisdiction of Texas. This Government proposed the trade. Texas assented to it. Was there anything in this to call for contemptuous taunts? We made no sale to this Government, freely and voluntarily, her sovereignty and the dominion of all her vast and fertile domain, and ought to be exempt from the contemptuous charge of having been bought. It is wholly untrue, and self-respect should prevent the making of such a charge.

There are other subjects which I had hoped to discuss this morning, but I will not trespass on the patience of the House by discussing them now. I have to say in the end, that yet, almost hopeless as it seems, I would be glad to see an effort made towards conciliation. Above all things I stand here to invoke members to look upon this question as one which involves the interests and destiny of States; to warn them that they are making advances against fifteen States; with thirteen million people, and with more than two thirds of the exports of the country; against a people who understand all these questions, and who are not to be misled or deceived by special pleading; a people who never intended or wished to raise their voice against the Federal Government, and who never would have done so if they had been let alone. Remember that we only ask you to let us alone—nothing else. Give us security in the Union. Respect our rights in the common Territories. So act among yourselves as to let us know that we need no longer live under continual fear of the consequences of your action.

I must say that the very State from which I came, the very district which I represent, has had some painful experience during the last summer, growing out of the doctrines of abolitionism. We found, for the last two or three years, that the members of the Methodist Church North, and others, living in Texas, were propagating abolition doctrines there. We warned them not to carry on their schemes of producing disaffection among our negroes; but they persisted, and did not cease until they had organized a society called the "Mystic Red." Under it auspices, the night before the last of August election the towns were to be burned and the people murdered. There now lie in ashes near a dozen towns and villages in my district. Four of them were county seats, and two of them the best towns in the district. The poisonings were only arrested by information which came to light before the plan could be carried into execution. The citizens were forced to stand guard for months, so that no man could have passed through the towns between dark and daylight without making himself known. A portion of them paid the penalty of their crimes. Others were driven out of the country. These things had their effect on the public mind. They were the results of abolition teachings; a part of the irrepressible conflict; a part of the legitimate fruits of Republicanism.

The State of the Country

(New Orleans: "True Witness and Sentinel" Office, 1861)

> *James Henley Thornwell (1812–62) was born in Marlborough District, South Carolina. He graduated from South Carolina College (later the University of South Carolina) and began the study of law but instead became a Presbyterian minister. Considered a brilliant preacher and scholar, he took the professorship of logic and belles lettres at South Carolina College in 1836, served as president of the College in 1852, and joined the faculty of the Presbyterian Theological Seminary in Columbia, South Carolina, in 1856. This old-school Presbyterian also served at a number of important churches, held the editorship of the* Southern Quarterly Review *and the* Southern Presbyterian Review, *and published collections of his sermons, including* Arguments of Romanists Discussed and Refuted *(1845)* and Discourses on Truth *(1854). His Thanksgiving Day sermon of November 1860,* The Rights of the South Defended in the Pulpit, *was printed as a pamphlet and distributed widely, as was his article,* Our Dangers and Our Duties. *Thornwell's most important secessionist pamphlet, printed below, was first published in the January 1861* Southern Presbyterian Review.[1] *In it he sought to sum up South Carolina's reasons for secession and to explain why other Lower South states had turned to secession to redress their grievances with the North. Thornwell also stressed the legitimacy, morality, and responsibility of the Southern cause to defend slavery. He predicted that no military power could force the slave states back into the Union. For information about Thornwell's career and ideas, see Benjamin M. Palmer,* The Life and Letters of James Henley Thornwell *(Richmond: Whittet and Shepperson, 1875), and James Oscar Farmer Jr.,* The Metaphysical Confederacy: James Henley Thornwell and the Synthesis of Southern Values *(Macon, Georgia: Mercer University Press, 1986); also valuable is William W. Freehling, "James Henley Thornwell's Mysterious Antislavery Moment,"* Journal of Southern History 57 *(1991): 383–406.*

It is now universally known that, on the twentieth day of last December, the people of South Carolina, in Convention assembled, solemnly annulled the ordinance by which they became members of the Federal Union, entitled the United States of America, and resumed to themselves the exercise of all the powers which they had delegated to the Federal Con-

---

1. It was reprinted in New Orleans and, later in 1861, by Appleton & Co. of New York.

gress. South Carolina has now become a separate and independent State. She takes her place as an equal among the other nations of the earth. This is certainly one of the most grave and important events of modern times. It involves the destiny of a continent, and through that continent, the fortunes of the human race. As it is a matter of the utmost moment that the rest of the world, and especially that the people of the United States, should understand the causes which have brought about this astounding result, we propose, in a short article, and in a candid and dispassionate spirit, to explain them, and to make an appeal, both to the slaveholding and non-slaveholding States, touching their duty in the new and extraordinary aspect which affairs have assumed.

That there was a cause, and an adequate cause, might be presumed from the character of the Convention which passed the Ordinance of Secession, and the perfect unanimity with which it was done. That Convention was not a collection of demagogues and politicians. It was not a conclave of defeated place-hunters, who sought to avenge their disappointment by the ruin of their country. It was a body of sober, grave, and venerable men, selected from every pursuit in life, and distinguished, most of them, in their respective spheres, by every quality which can command confidence and respect. It embraced the wisdom, moderation, and integrity of the bench, the learning and prudence of the bar, and the eloquence and piety of the pulpit. It contained retired planters, scholars, and gentlemen, who had stood aloof from the turmoil and ambition of public life, and were devoting an elegant leisure—*otium cum dignitate*—to the culture of their minds, and to quiet and unobtrusive schemes of Christian philanthropy. There were men in that Convention who were utterly incapable of low and selfish schemes; who, in the calm serenity of their judgments, were as unmoved by the waves of popular passion and excitement, as the everlasting granite by the billows that roll against it. There were men there, who would have listened to no voice but what they believed to be the voice of reason, and would have bowed to no authority but what they believed to be the authority of God. There were men there who would not have been controlled by "uncertain opinion," nor betrayed into "sudden counsels"; men who could act from nothing, in the noble language of Milton, "but from mature wisdom, deliberate virtue, and dear affection to the public good." That Convention, in the character of its members, deserves every syllable of the glowing panegyric which Milton has pronounced upon the immortal Parliament of England, which taught the nations of the earth that resistance to tyrants is obedience to God. Were it not invidious, we might single out names, which, wherever they are known, are regarded as synonymous with purity, probity, magnanimity, and honor. It was a noble body, and all their proceedings were in harmony with their high character. In the midst of intense agitation and excitement, they were calm, cool, collected, and self-possessed. They deliberated without passion, and concluded without rashness. They sat with closed doors, that the tumult of the populace might not invade the sobriety of their minds. If a stranger could have passed from the stirring scenes with which the streets of Charleston were alive, into the calm and quiet sanctuary of this venerable council, he would have been impressed with the awe and veneration which subdued the rude Gaul, when he first beheld in senatorial dignity the Conscript Fathers of Rome. That, in such a body, there was not a single voice against the Ordinance of Secession, that there was not only no dissent, but that the assent was cordial and thorough-going, is a strong presumption that the measure was justified by the clearest right. That such an assembly should have inaugurated and completed a radical revolution in all the external relations of State, in the face of acknowledged dangers, and at the risk of enormous sacrifices, and should have done it gravely, soberly, dispassionately, deliberately, and yet have done it without cause, transcends all the measures of probability. Whatever else may be said of it, it certainly must be admitted that this solemn act of South Carolina was well considered.

In her estimate of the magnitude of the danger, she has been seconded by every other slaveholding State. While we are writing, the telegraphic wires announce what the previous elections had prepared us to expect — that Florida, Alabama, and Mississippi have followed her example. They also have become separate and independent States. Three other States have taken the incipient steps for the consummation of the same result. And the rest of the slaveholding States are hanging by a single thread to the Union — the slender thread of hope — that guarantees may be devised which shall yet secure them to their rights. But even they proclaim, that, without such guarantees, their wrongs are intolerable, and they will not longer endure them. Can any man believe that the secession of four sovereign States, under the most solemn circumstances, the determination of others to follow as soon as the constituted authorities can be called together, and the universal sentiment of all that the Constitution of the United States has been virtually repealed, and that every slaveholding State has just ground for secession — can any man believe that this is a factitious condition of the public mind of the South, produced by brawling politicians and disappointed demagogues, and not the calm, deliberate, profound utterance of a people who feel, in their inmost souls, that they have been deeply and flagrantly wronged? The presumption clearly is, that there is something in the attitude of the Government which portends a danger and demands resistance. There must be a cause for this intense and pervading sense of injustice and of injury.

It has been suggested, by those who know as little of the people of the South as they do of the Constitution of their country, that all this ferment is nothing but the result of a mercenary spirit on the part of the cotton-growing States, fed by Utopian dreams of aggrandizement and wealth, to be realized under the auspices of free trade, in a separate Confederacy of their own. It has been gravely insinuated that they are willing to sell their faith for gold—that they have only made a pretext of recent events to accomplish a foregone scheme of deliberate treachery and fraud. That there is not the slightest ground in anything these States have ever said or done for this extraordinary slander, it is, of course, superfluous to add. The South has, indeed, complained of the unequal administration of the Government. Her best and purest statesmen have openly avowed the opinion, that, in consequence of the partial legislation of Congress, she has borne burdens, and experienced inconveniences, which have retarded her own prosperity, while they have largely contributed to develope the resources of the North. But grievances of this kind, unless greatly exaggerated, never would have led to the dissolution of the Union. They would have been resisted within it, or patiently borne until they could be lawfully redressed. So far from contending for an arbitrary right to dissolve the Union, or the right to dissolve it on merely technical grounds, the South sets so high a value on good faith, that she would never have dissolved it, for slight and temporary wrongs, even though they might involve such a violation, on the part of her confederates, of the terms of the compact, as released her from any further obligation of honor. It is, therefore, preposterous to say, that any dreams, however dazzling, of ambition and avarice, could have induced her to disregard her solemn engagements to her sister States, while they were faithfully fulfilling the conditions of the contract. We know the people of the South; and we can confidently affirm, that if they had been assured that all these golden visions could have been completely realized by setting up for themselves, as long as the Constitution of the United States continued to be sincerely observed, they would have spurned the temptation to purchase national greatness by perfidy. They would have preferred poverty, with honor, to the gain of the whole world by the loss of their integrity.

When it was perceived that the tendency of events was inevitably driving the South to disunion, a condition from which she at first recoiled with horror, then she began to cast about for considerations to reconcile her to her destiny. Then, for the first time, was it maintained, that, instead of being a loser, she might be a gainer by the measure which the course of the Government was forcing upon her. It was alleged that good would spring from evil; that the prospect of independence was brighter and more cheering than her present condition—that she had much to anticipate, and little to dread, from the contemplated change. But these considerations were not invented to *justify* secession—they were only adduced as motives to reconcile the mind to its necessity. Apart from that necessity, they would have had as little weight in determining public opinion, as the small dust of the balance. We do not believe, when the present controversy began, that the advocates of what is called disunion *per se*, men who preferred a Southern Confederacy upon the grounds of its intrinsic superiority to the Constitutional Union of the United States, could have mustered a corporal's guard. The people of the South were loyal to the country, and if the country had been true to them, they would have been as ready to-day to defend its honor with their fortunes and their blood, as when they raised its triumphant flag upon the walls of Mexico.

It has also been asserted, as a ground of dissatisfaction with the present Government, and of desire to organize a separate Government of their own, that the cotton-growing States are intent upon reopening, as a means of fulfilling their magnificent visions of wealth, the African slave-trade. The agitation of this subject at the South has been grievously misunderstood. One extreme generates another. The violence of the Northern abolitionists gave rise to a small party among ourselves, who were determined not to be outdone in extravagance. They wished to show that they could give a Rowland for an Oliver. Had abolitionists never denounced the domestic trade as plunder and robbery, not a whisper would ever have been breathed about disturbing the peace of Africa. The men who were loudest in their denunciations of the Government had, with very few exceptions, no more desire to have the trade reopened than the rest of their countrymen; but they delighted in teasing their enemies. They took special satisfaction in providing hard nuts for abolitionists to crack. There were others, not at all in favor of the trade, who looked upon the law as unconstitutional which declared it to be piracy. But the great mass of the Southern people were content with the law as it stood. They were and are opposed to the trade—not because the traffic in slaves is immoral—that not a man among us believes—but because the traffic with Africa is *not* a traffic in slaves. It is a system of kidnapping and man-stealing, which is as abhorrent to the South as it is to the North; and we venture confidently to predict, that should a Southern Confederacy be formed, the African slave-trade is much more likely to be reopened by the old Government than the new.

The conscience of the North will be less tender when it has no Southern sins to bewail, and idle ships will naturally look to the Government to help them in finding employment.[2]

The real cause of the intense excitement of the South, is not vain dreams of national glory in a separate confederacy, nor the love of the filthy lucre of the African slave-trade; it is the profound conviction that the Constitution, in its relations to slavery, has been virtually repealed; that the Government has assumed a new and dangerous attitude upon this subject; that we have, in short, new terms of union submitted to our acceptance or rejection. Here lies the evil. The election of Lincoln, when properly interpreted, is nothing more nor less than a proposition to the South to consent to a Government, fundamentally different upon the question of slavery, from that which our fathers established. If this point can be made out, secession becomes not only a right, but a bounded duty. Morally, it is only the abrogation of the forms of a contract, when its essential conditions have been abolished. Politically, it is a measure indispensable to the safety, if not to the very existence, of the South. It is needless to say that, in this issue the personal character of Mr, Lincoln is not at all involved. There are no objections to him as a man, or as a citizen of the North. He is probably entitled, in the private relations of life, to all the commendations which his friends have bestowed upon him. We, at least, would be the last to detract from his personal worth, The issue has respect, not to the man, but to the principles upon which he is pledged to administer the Government, and which, we are significantly informed, are to be impressed upon it in all time to come. His election seals the triumph of those principles, and that triumph seals the subversion of the Constitution, in relation to a matter of paramount interest to the South.

This we shall proceed to show, by showing, first, the Constitutional attitude of the Government towards slavery, and then the attitude which, after the inauguration of Mr. Lincoln, it is to assume and maintain for ever:

I. What, now, is its Constitutional attitude? We affirm it to be *one of* ABSOLUTE INDIFFERENCE OR NEUTRALITY, with respect to all questions connected with the moral and political aspects of the subject. In the eye of the Constitution, slaveholding and non-slaveholding stand upon a footing of perfect equality. The slaveholding State and the slaveholding citizen are the same to it as the non-slaveholding. It protects both; it espouses the peculiarities of neither. It does not allow the North to say to the South,

2. Clearly, Thornwell here was making an attempt to defuse the divisive issue among Southern states over reopening the slave trade.

Your institutions are inferior to ours, and should be changed; neither does it allow the South to say to the North, You must accommodate yourselves to us. It says to both, Enjoy your own opinions upon your own soil, so that you do not interfere with the rights of each other. To me there is no difference betwixt you. Formed by parties whose divisive principle was this very subject of slavery, it stands to reason, that the Constitution, without self-condemnation on the part of one or the other, could not have been made the patron of either. From the very nature of the case, its position must be one of complete impartiality. This is what the South means by equality in the Union, that the General Government shall make no difference betwixt its institutions and those of the North; that slaveholding shall be as good to it as non-slaveholding. In other words, the Government is the organ of neither party, but the common agent of both; and, as their common agent, has no right to pronounce an opinion as to the merits of their respective peculiarities. This, we contend, is the attitude fixed by the Constitution. The Government is neither pro nor anti slavery. It is simply neutral. Had it assumed any other attitude upon this subject, it never would have been accepted by the slaveholding States. When Mr. Pinckney could rise up in the Convention and declare, that "if slavery be wrong, it is justified by the example of all the world"; when he could boldly appeal to the unanimous testimony of ancient and modern times—to Greece and Rome, to France, Holland, and England, in vindication of its righteousness, it is not to be presumed that he never would have joined in the construction of a Government which was authorized to pronounce and treat it as an evil! It is not to be presumed that the slaveholding States, unless they seriously aimed at the ultimate extinction of slavery, would have entered into an alliance which was confessedly to be turned against them. That they did not aim at the extinction of slavery, is clear from the pertinacity with which some of them clung to the continuance of the African slave-trade, until foreign supplies should be no longer demanded. When Georgia and South Carolina made it a *sine qua non* for entering the Union, that this traffic should be kept open for a season, to say that these States meditated the abolition of slavery, is grossly paradoxical. It is remarkable, too, that the time fixed for the prohibition of this traffic, was a time within which the Representatives of those States were persuaded that the States themselves, if the question were left to them, would prohibit it. These States conceded to the Government the right to do, as their agent, only what they themselves would do, as sovereign communities, under the same circumstances. No presumption, therefore, of an attitude, on the part of the Constitution, hostile to slavery, can be deduced from the clause touching the African slave-trade.

On the contrary, the presumption is, that, as the trade was kept open for a while—kept open, in fact, as long as the African supply was needed—the slave-holding States never meant to abolish the institution, and never could have consented to set the face of the Government against it. No doubt, the fathers of the Republic were, many of them, not all, opposed to slavery. But they had to frame a Government which should represent, not their personal and private opinions, but the interests of sovereign States. They had to adjust it to the institutions of South Carolina and Georgia, as well as those of New England. And they had the grace given them to impress upon it the only attitude which could conciliate and harmonize all parties—the attitude of perfect indifference.

This, at the same time, is the attitude of justice. We of the South have the same right to our opinions as the people of the North. They appear as true to us as theirs appear to them. We are as honest and sincere in forming and maintaining them. We unite to form a government. Upon what principle shall it be formed? Is it to be asked of us to renounce doctrines which we believe have come down to us from the earliest ages, and have the sanction of the oracles of God? Must we give up what we conscientiously believe to be the truth? The thing is absurd. The Government, in justice, can only say to both parties: I will protect you both, I will be the advocate of neither.

In order to exempt slavery from the operation of this plain principle of justice, it has been contended that the right of property in slaves is the creature of positive statute, and, consequently, of force only within the limits of the jurisdiction of the law; that it is a right not recognized by the Constitution of the United States, and therefore, not to be protected where Congress is the local legislature. These two propositions contain every thing that has any show of reason for the extraordinary revolution which the recent election has consummated in the Government of the United States.

They are both gratuitous:

(1) In the first place, slavery has never, in any country, so far as we know, arisen under the operation of statute law. It is not a municipal institution—it is not the arbitrary creature of the State, it has not sprung from the mere force of legislation. Law defines, modifies and regulates it, as it does every other species of property, but *law* never *created* it. The law found it in existence, and being in existence, the law subjects it to fixed rules. On the contrary, what is local and municipal, is the *abolition* of slavery. The States that are now non-slaveholding, have been made so by positive statues. Slavery exists, of course, in every nation in which it is not prohibited. It arose, in the progress of human events, from the operation of moral causes; it has been grounded by philosophers in moral maxims, it has always been held

to be moral by the vast majority of the race. No age has been without it. From the first dawn of authentic history, until the present period, it has come down to us through all the course of ages. We find it among nomadic tribes, barbarian hordes, and civilized States. Wherever communities have been organized, and any rights of property have been recognized at all, there slavery is seen. If, therefore, there be any property which can be said to be founded in the common consent of the human race, it is the property in slaves. If there be any property that can be called natural, in the sense that it spontaneously springs up in the history of the species, it is the property in slaves. If there be any property which is founded in principles of universal operation, it is the property in slaves. To say of an institution, whose history is thus the history of man, which has always and everywhere existed, that it is a local and municipal relation, is of "all absurdities the motliest, the merest word that every fooled the ear from out the schoolman's jargon." Mankind may have been wrong—that is not the question. The point is, whether the law made slavery—whether it is the police regulation of limited localities, or whether it is a property founded in natural causes, and causes of universal operation. We say nothing as to the moral character of the causes. We insist only upon the fact that slavery is rooted in a common law, wider and pervading than the common law of England— THE UNIVERSAL CUSTOM OF MANKIND.

If therefore, slavery is not municipal, but natural, if it is abolition which is municipal and local, then, upon the avowed doctrines of our opponents, two things follow: 1st. That slavery goes of right, and as a matter of course, into every territory from which it is not excluded by positive statute; and 2nd. That Congress is competent to forbid the Northern States from impressing their local peculiarity of non-slaveholding upon the common soil of the Union. If the Republican argument is good for any thing, it goes the whole length of excluding for ever any additional non-slaveholding States from the Union. What would they think, if the South had taken any such extravagant ground as this? What would they have done, if the South had taken advantage of a numerical majority, to legislate them and their institutions for ever out of the common territory? Would they have *submitted*? Would they have glorified the Union, and yielded to the triumph of slavery? We know that they would not. They would have scorned the crotchet about municipal and local laws which divested them of their dearest rights. Let them give the same measure to others which they expect from others. It is a noble maxim, commended by high authority—do as you would be done by.

The South has neither asked for, nor does she desire, any exclusive benefits. All she demands is, that as South, as slaveholding, she shall be put upon the same footing with the North, as non-slaveholding—that the Government shall not undertake to say, one kind of States is better than the other—that it shall have no preference as to the character, in this respect, of any future States to be added to the Union. Non-slaveholding may be superior to slaveholding, but it is not the place of the Government to say so; much less to assume the right of saying so upon a principle which, properly applied, requires it to say the very reverse.

There is another sense in which municipal is opposed to international, and in this sense, slavery is said to be municipal, because there is no obligation, by the law of nations, on the part of States in which slavery is prohibited, to respect within the limits of their own territory the rights of the foreign slaveholder. This is the doctrine laid down by Judge Story. No nation is bound to accord to a stranger a right of property which it refuses to its own subjects. We can not, therefore, demand from the Governments of France or England, or any other foreign power, whose policy and interests are opposed to slavery, the restoration of our fugitives from bondage. We are willing to concede, for the sake of argument, that the principle in question is an admitted principle of international law, though we are quite persuaded that it is contrary to the whole current of Continental authorities, and is intensely English. We doubt whether, even in England, it can be traced beyond the famous decision of Lord Mansfield, in the case of Somersett.[3] But let us admit the principle. What then? The Constitution of the United States has expressly provided that this principle shall not apply within the limits of Federal jurisdiction. With reference to this country, it has abrogated the law; every State is bound to respect the right of the Southern master to his slave. The Constitution covers the whole territory of the Union, and throughout that territory has taken slavery, under the protection of law. However foreign nations may treat our fugitive slaves, the States of this Confederacy are bound to treat them as property, and to give them back to their lawful owners. How idle, therefore, to plead a principle of international law, which, in reference to the relations of the States of this Union, is formally abolished! Slavery is clearly a part of the municipal law of the United States; and the whole argument from the local character of the institution, falls to the ground. Slaveholding and non-slaveholding are both equally sectional, and both equally national.

(2) As to the allegation that the Constitution no where recognizes the

3. For the lasting importance to the South of the English Somersett case, see David B. Davis, *The Problem of Slavery in the Age of Revolution* (Ithaca, N.Y.: Cornell University Press, 1975), 470–505.

right of property in slaves, that is equally unfounded. We shall say nothing here of the decision of the Supreme Court, though that, one would think, is entitled to some consideration. We shall appeal to the Constitution itself, and if there is force in logic, we shall be able to make it appear that the right is not only recognized, but recognized with a philosophical accuracy and precision that seize only on the essential, and omit the variable and accidental. The subject, in the language of the Constitution, is transferred from the technicalities of law to the higher sphere of abstract and speculative morality. Morally considered, to what class does the slave belong? To the class of persons held to service. The two ideas that he is a person, and as a person, held to service, constitute the generic conception of slavery. How is his obligation to service fundamentally differenced from that of other laborers? By this, as one essential circumstance, that it is independent of the formalities of contract. Add the circumstance that it is for life, and you have a complete conception of the thing. You have the very definition, almost in his own words, which a celebrated English philosopher gives of slavery: "I define slavery," says Dr. Paley, "to be an obligation to labor for the benefit of the master, without the contract or consent of the servant."

Now, is such an obligation recognized in the Constitution of the United States? Are there persons spoken of in it, who are held to service by a claim so sacred that the Government allows them, however anxious they may be to do so, to dissolve it neither by stratagem nor force? If they run away, they must be remanded to those who are entitled to their labor, even if they escape to a territory whose local laws would otherwise protect them. If they appeal to force, the whole power of the Union may be brought to crush them. Can any man say that the Constitution does not here recognize a right to the labor and service of men, of persons which springs from no stipulations of their own, is entirely independent of their own consent, and which can never be annulled by any efforts, whether clandestine or open, on their part? *This is slavery*—it is the very essence and core of the institution. That upon which the right of property terminates in the slave, is his service or labor. It is not his soul, nor his person, nor his moral and intellectual nature—it is his *labor*. This is the thing which is bought and sold in the market, and it is in consequence of the right to regulate, control and direct this, that the person comes under an obligation to obey. The ideas of a right on one side, and duty on the other, show that the slave, in this relation, is truly a person as his master. The Constitution, therefore, does recognize and protect slavery, in every moral and ethical feature of it. The thing which, under that name, has commanded the approbation of mankind, is the very thing, among others analogous to it, included in the third clause of the second section of the fourth chapter of the Constitution. We see no way to getting round this argument. It is idle to say that slaves are not referred to—it is equally idle to say that the right to their labor is not respected and guarded. Let this right be acknowledged in the territories, and we are not disposed to wring changes upon words. Let the Government permit the South to carry her persons held to service, without their consent, into the territories, and let the right to their labor be protected, and there would be no quarrel about slavery. It is unworthy of statesmen, in a matter of this sort, to quibble about legal technicalities. That the law of slaveholding States classes slaves among chattels, and speaks of them as marketable commodities, does not imply that, morally and ethically, they are not persons, nor that the property is in them, rather than in their toil. These same laws treat them in other respects as persons, and speak of their service as obedience or duty. The meaning of chattel is relative, and is to be restricted to the relation which it implies.

We are happy to find that the Supreme Court of the United States has fully confirmed the interpretation which we have given to this clause of the Constitution. In the case of Prigg vs. the Commonwealth of Pennsylvania, it was asserted by every Judge upon the Bench, that the design of the provision was "to secure to the citizens of the slaveholding States the complete right and title of ownership in their slaves, as property, in every State in the Union into which they might escape from the State where they were held in servitude." These are the very words of Mr. Justice Story, in delivering the opinion of the Court. He went on to add: "The full recognition of this right and title was indispensable to the security of this species of property in all the slaveholding States; and, indeed, was so vital to the preservation of the domestic interests and institutions that it cannot be doubted that it constituted a fundamental article without the adoption of which the Union could not have been formed." Again: "We have said that the clause contains a positive and unqualified recognition of the right of the owner in the slave." Chief Justice Taney held: that, "by the national compact,this right of property is recognized as an existing right in every State of the union." Judge Thompson said: the Constitution "affirms, in the most unequivocal manner, the right of the master to the service of his slave, according to the laws of the State under which he is so held." Judge Wayne affirmed that all the Judges concurred "in the declaration that the provision in the Constitution was a compromise between the slaveholding and the non-slaveholding States, to secure to the former fugitive slaves as property." "The paramount authority of this clause in the Constitution," says Judge Daniel, "to guarantee to the owner the right of property in his slave, and the absolute nullity of any State power, directly or indirectly, openly or covertly, aimed to impair that right, or to obstruct its enjoyment, I admit, nay, insist upon, to the fullest extent."

If now, the Constitution recognizes slaves as property, that is, as persons to whose labor and service the master has a right, then, upon what principle shall Congress undertake to abolish this right upon a territory, of which it is the local Legislature? It will not permit the slave to cancel it, because the service is due. Upon what ground can itself interpose between a man and his dues? Congress is as such the agent of the slaveholding as it is of the non-slaveholding States; and, as equally bound to protect both, and to hold the scales of justice even between them, it must guard the property of the one with the same care with which it guards the property of the other.

We have now refuted the postulates upon which the recent revolution in the Government is attempted to be justified. We have shown that slavery is not the creature of local and municipal law, and that the Constitution distinctly recognizes the right of the master to the labor or service of the slave; that is, the right of property in slaves. There is no conceivable pretext, then, for saying that the Government should resist the circulation of this kind of property, more than any other. That question it must leave to the providence of God, and to the natural and moral laws by which its solution is conditioned. All that the Government can do, is to give fair play to both parties, the slaveholding and non-slaveholding States; protect the rights of both on their common soil, and as soon as a sovereign State emerges, to which the soil is henceforward to belong, remit the matter to its absolute discretion. This is justice—this is the impartiality which becomes the agent of a great people, divided by two such great interests.

That the rights of the South, as *slaveholding*—for it is in that relation only that she is politically a different section from the North—and the rights of the North, as *non-slaveholding*, are absolutely equal, is so plain a proposition, that one wonders at the pertinacity with which it has been denied. Here let us expose a sophism whose only force consists in a play upon words. It is alleged that the equality of the sections is not disturbed by the exclusion of slavery from the territories, because the Southern man may take with him all that the Northern man can take. The plain English of which is this: if the Southern man will consent to become *as* a Northern man, and renounce what distinguishes him as a *Southern* man, he may go into the territories. But if he insists upon remaining a *Southern* man, he must stay at home. The geography is only an accident in this matter. The Southern man, politically, is the slaveholder; the Northern man, politically, is the non-slaveholder. The rights of the South are the rights of the

South as slaveholding; the rights of the North are the rights of the North as non-slaveholding. This is what makes the real difference betwixt the two sections. To exclude *slaveholding* is, therefore, to exclude the South. By the free-soil doctrine, therefore, she, as South, is utterly debarred from every foot of the soil, which belongs, of right, as much to her as to her Northern confederates. The Constitution is made to treat her institutions as if they were a scandal and reproach. It becomes the patron of the North, and an enemy, instead of a protector, to her.

That this is the attitude which the Government is henceforward to assume, we shall now proceed to show:[4]

(1.) In the first place, let it be distinctly understood, that we do not charge the great body of the Northern people, who have accomplished the recent revolution, with being abolitionists, in the strict and technical sense. We are willing to concede that they have no design, for the present, to interfere directly with slavery in the slaveholding States. We shall give them credit for an honest purpose, under Mr. Lincoln's administration, to execute, as far as the hostility of the States will let them, the provisions of the fugitive slave law. All this may be admitted, but it does not affect the real issue, nor mitigate the real danger. We know that there are various types of opinion at the North with reference to the moral aspects of slavery, and we have never apprehended that, under the Constitution as it stands, there was any likelihood of an attempt to interfere, by legislation, with our property on our own soil.

(2.) But, in the second place, it must likewise be conceded that the general, almost universal, attitude of the Northern mind is one of hostility to slavery. Those who are not prepared to condemn it as a sin, nor to meddle with it where it is legally maintained, are yet opposed to it, as a natural and political evil, which every good man should desire to see extinguished. They all regard it as a calamity, an affliction, a misfortune. They regard it as an element of weakness, and as a draw-back upon the prosperity and glory of the country. They pity the South, as caught in the folds of a serpent, which is gradually squeezing out her life. And, even when they defend us from the reproach of sin in sustaining the relation, they make so many distinctions between the abstract notion of slavery and the system of our own laws, that their defense would hardly avail to save us, if there were any power

4. Thornwell tried to sum up the divisive issue of territorial expansion. His focus, like that of John C. Calhoun before him, was on the power of the Northern people to use the federal government to stop slave expansion and not on economic and social necessity for slave society.

competent to hang and quarter us. We are sure that we do not misrepresent the general tone of Northern sentiment. It is one of *hostility* to slavery—it is one which, while it might not be willing to break faith, under the present administration, with respect to the express injunctions of the Constitution, is utterly and absolutely opposed to any further extension of the system.

(3.) In the third place, let it be distinctly understood that we have no complaint to make of the opinions of the North, considered simply as their opinions. They have a right, so far as human authority is concerned, to think as they please. The South has never asked them to approve of Slavery, or to change their own institutions and to introduce it among themselves. The South has been willing to accord to them the most perfect and unrestricted right of private judgment.

(4.) But, in the fourth place, what we do complain of, and what we have a right to complain of, is that they should not be content with thinking their own thoughts themselves, but should undertake to make the *Government* think them likewise. We of the South have, also, certain thoughts concerning slavery, and we can not understand upon what principle the thinking of the South is totally excluded, and the thinking of the North made supreme. The Government is as much ours as theirs, and we can not see why, in a matter that vitally concerns ourselves, we shall be allowed to do no effective thinking at all. This is the grievance. The Government is made to take the type of Northern sentiment—it is animated, in its relations to slavery, by the Northern mind, and the South, henceforward, is no longer *of* the Government, but only *under* the Government. The extension of slavery, in obedience to Northern prejudice, is to be forever arrested. Congress is to treat it as an evil, an element of political weakness, and to restrain its influence within the limits which now circumscribe it. All this because the *North thinks* so; while the South, an equal party to the Government, has quite other thoughts. And when we indignantly complain of the absolute suppression of all right to think in and through our own Government, upon a subject that involves our homes and our firesides, we are coolly reminded, that, as long as Congress does not usurp the rights of our Legislatures, and abolish slavery on our own soil, nor harbor our fugitives when they attempt to escape from us, we have reason to be grateful for the indulgence accorded to us. The right to breathe is as much as we should venture to claim. You may exist, says free-soilism, as States, and manage your slaves at home—we will not abrogate your sovereignty. Your runaways we do not want, and we may occasionally send them back to you. But if you think you have a right to be heard at Washington upon this great subject, it is time that your presumption should be rebuked. The North is the thinking power—the soul of the Government. The life of the Government is Northern—not Southern; the type to be impressed upon all future States is Northern—not Southern. The North becomes the United States, and the South a subject province.

Now, we say that this is a state of things not to be borne. A free people can never consent to their own degradation. We say boldly, that the Government has no more right to adopt Northern thoughts on the subject of slavery than those of the South. It has no more right to presume that they are true. It has no right to arbitrate between them. It must treat them both with equal respect, and give them an equal chance. Upon no other footing can the South, with honor, remain in the Union. It is not to be endured for a moment, that fifteen sovereign States, embodying, in proportion to their population, as much intelligence, virtue, public spirit and patriotism, as any other people upon the globe, should be quietly reduced to zero, in a Government which they framed for their own protection! We put the question again to the North: If the tables were turned, and it was your thoughts, your life, your institutions, that the Government was henceforward to discountenance; if non-slaveholding was hereafter to be prohibited in every territory, and the whole policy of the Government shaped by the principle that slavery is a blessing, would you endure it? Would not your blood boil, and would you not call upon your hungry millions to come to the rescue? And yet, this is precisely what you have done to us, and think we ought not to resist. You have made us ciphers, and are utterly amazed that we should claim to be any thing.

But apart from the degradation which it inflicts upon the South, it may be asked, what real injury will result from putting the Government in an attitude of hostility to slavery?

The answer is, in the first place, that it will certainly lead to the extinction of the system. You may destroy the oak as effectually by girdling it as by cutting it down. The North are well assured that if they can circumscribe the area of slavery, if they can surround it with a circle of non-slaveholding States, and prevent it from expanding, nothing more is required to secure its ultimate abolition. "Like the scorpion girt by fire," it will plunge its fangs into its own body, and perish. If, therefore, the South is not prepared to see her institutions surrounded by enemies, and wither and decay under these hostile influences, if she means to cherish and protect them, it is her bounden duty to resist the revolution which threatens them with ruin. The triumph of the principles which Mr. Lincoln is pledged to carry out, is the death-knell of slavery.

In the next place, the state of the Northern mind which has produced this revolution can not be expected to remain content with its present victory. It will hasten to other triumphs. The same spirit which has prevaricated with the express provisions of the Constitution and resorted to expedients to evade the most sacred obligations, will not hesitate for a moment to change the Constitution when it finds itself in possession of the power. It will only be consistency to harmonize the fundamental law of the Government with its chosen policy, the real workings of its life. The same hostility to slavery which a numerical majority has impressed upon the Federal Legislature, it will not scruple to impress upon the Federal Constitution. If the South could be induced to submit to Lincoln, the time, we confidently predict, will come when all grounds of controversy will be removed in relation to fugitive slaves, by expunging the provision under which they are claimed. The principle is at work and enthroned in power, whose inevitable tendency is to secure this result. Let us crush the serpent in the egg.

From these considerations, it is obvious that nothing more nor less is at stake in this controversy than the very life of the South. The real question is, whether she shall be politically annihilated. We are not struggling for fleeting and temporary interests. We are struggling for our very being. And none know better than the Republican party itself, that if we submit to their new type of Government, our fate as slaveholding is for ever sealed. They have already exulted in the prospect of this glorious consummation. They boast that they have laid a mine which must ultimately explode in our utter ruin. They are singing songs of victory in advance, and are confidently anticipating the auspicious hour when they shall have nothing to do but to return to the field and bury the dead.

The sum of what we have said to briefly this: We have shown that the Constitutional attitude of the Government towards slavery is one of absolute neutrality or indifference in relation to the moral and political aspects of the subject. We have shown, in the next place, that it is hereafter to take an attitude of hostility; that it is to represent the opinions and feelings exclusively of the North; that it is to become the Government of one section over another; and that the South, as South, is to sustain no other relation to it but the duty of obedience.

This is a thorough and radical revolution. It makes a new Government— it proposes new and extraordinary terms of union. The old Government is as completely abolished as if the people of the United States had met in Convention and repealed the Constitution. It is frivolous to tell us that the change has been made through the forms of the Constitution. This is to add insult to injury. What signify forms, when the substance is gone? Of what value is the shell, when the kernel is extracted? Rights are things, and not words; and when the things are taken from us, it is no time to be nibbling at phrases. If a witness under oath designedly gives testimony, which, though literally true, conveys a false impression, is he not guilty of perjury? Is not his truth a lie? Temures kept the letter of his promise to the garrison of Sebastia, that if they would surrender, no blood should be shed, but did that save him from the scandal of treachery in burying them alive? No man objects to the legality of the process of Mr. Lincoln's election. The objection is to the legality of that to which he is elected. He has been chosen, not to administer, but to revolutionize, the Government. The very moment he goes into office, the Constitution of the United States, as touching the great question between North and South is dead. The oath which makes him President, makes a new Union. The import of secession is simply the refusal, on the part of the South, to be parties to any such Union. She has not renounced, and if it had been permitted to stand, she never would have renounced, the Constitution which our fathers framed. She would have stood by it for ever. But, as the North have substantially abolished it, and, taking advantage of their numbers, have substituted another in its place, which dooms the South to perdition, surely she has a right to say she will enter into no such conspiracy. The Government to which she consented was a Government under which she might hope to live. The new one presented in its place is one under which she can only die. Under these circumstances, we do not see how any man can question either the righteousness or the necessity of secession. The South is shut up to the duty of rejecting these new terms of Union. No people on earth, without judicial infatuation, can organize a Government to destroy them. It is too much to ask a man to sign his own death-warrant.

II. We wish to say a few words as to the policy of the slaveholding States in the present emergency.

We know it to be the fixed determination of them all not to acquiesce in the principles which have brought Mr. Lincoln into power. Several of them, however, have hesitated—and it is a sign of the scrupulous integrity of the South in maintaining her faith—whether the mere fact of his election, apart from any overt act of the Government, is itself a *casus belli*, and a sufficient reason for extreme measures of resistance. These States have, also, clung to the hope that there would yet be a returning sense of justice at the North, which shall give them satisfactory guarantees for the preservation of their rights, and restore peace without the necessity of schism. We respect the motives which have produced this hesitation. We have no sympathy with any taunting reflections upon the courage, magnanimity, public spirit or patriotism of such a Commonwealth as Virginia.

The mother of Washington is not to be insulted, if, like her great hero, she takes counsel of moderation and prudence. We honor too, the sentiment which makes it hard to give up the Union. It was a painful struggle to ourselves; the most painful struggle of our lives. There were precious memories and hallowed associations, connected with a glorious history, to which the heart cannot bid farewell without a pang. Few men, in all the South, brought themselves to pronounce the word DISUNION, without sadness of heart. Some States have not yet been able to pronounce it. But the tendency of events is irresistible. It is becoming every day clearer, that the people of the North hate slavery more than they love the Union, and they are developing this spirit in a form which must soon bring every slaveholding State within the ranks of secession. The evil day may be put off, but it must come. The country must be divided into two people, and the point which we wish now to press upon the whole South is, the importance of preparing, at once, for this consummation.

The slaveholding interests is one, and it seems to us clear that the slaveholding States ought speedily to be organized under one general Government. United, they are strong enough to maintain themselves against the world. They have the territory, the resources, the population, the public spirit, the institutions, which under a genial and fostering Constitution, would soon enable them to become one of the first people upon the globe. And if the North shall have wisdom to see her true policy, two Governments upon this continent may work out the problem of human liberty more successfully than one. Let the two people maintain the closest alliance for defence against a foreign foe, or, at least, let them be agreed that no European power shall ever set foot on American soil, and that no type of Government but the republican shall ever be tolerated here, and what is to hinder the fullest and freest development of our noble institutions. The separation changes nothing but the external relations of the sections. Such a dismemberment of the Union is not like the revolution of a State, where the internal system of Government is subverted, where laws are suspended, and where anarchy reigns. The country might divide into two great nations tomorrow, without a jostle or a jar; the Government of each State might go on as regularly as before, the law be as supreme, and order as perfect, if the passions of the people could be kept from getting the better of their judgments. It is a great advantage in the form of our Confederacy, that a radical revolution can take place without confusion, and without anarchy. Every State has a perfect internal system at work already, and that undergoes no change, except in adjusting it to its altered external relations. Now, given this system of States, with every element of a perfect Government in full and undisturbed operation, what is there in the circumstances of *one* Confederacy of *divided interests*, that shall secure a freer and safer development than *two Confederacies*, each representing an *undivided* interest? Are not two homogeneous Unions stronger than one that is heterogeneous? Should not the life of a Government be one? We do not see, therefore, that anything will be lost to freedom by the union of the South under a separate Government. She will carry into it every institution that she had before—her State Constitutions, her Legislatures, her Courts of Justice, her halls of learning—every thing that she now possesses. She will put these precious interests under a Government embodying every principle which gave value to the old one, and amply adequate to protect them. What will she lose of real freedom? We confess that we cannot understand the declamation, that with the American Union, American institutions are gone. Each section of the Union will preserve them and cherish them. Every principle that has ever made us glorious, and made our Government a wonder, will abide with us. The sections, separately, will not be as formidable to foreign powers as before. That is all. But each section will be strong enough to protect itself, and both together can save this continent for republicanism for ever.

Indeed, it is likely that both Governments will be purer, in consequence of their mutual rivalry, and the diminution of the extent of their patronage. They will both cherish intensely the American feeling, both maintain the pride of American character, and both try to make their Governments at home what they would desire to have them appear to be abroad.

Once take away all pretext for meddling with one another's peculiar interests, and we do not see but that the magnificent visions of glory, which our imaginations have delighted to picture as the destiny of the Anglo-Saxon race on this North American continent, may yet be fully realized. They can never be, if we continue together, to bite and devour one another.

But, whether it be for weal or woe, the South has no election. She is driven to the wall, and the only question is, will she take care of herself in time. The sooner she can organize a general Government, the better. That will be a centre of unity, and, once combined, we are safe.

We can not close without saying a few words to the people of the North as to the policy which it becomes them to pursue. The whole question of peace or war is in their hands. The South is simply standing on the defensive, and has no notion of abandoning that attitude. Let the Northern people, then, seriously consider, and consider in the fear of God how, under present circumstances, they can best conserve those great interests of freedom, of religion, and of order which are equally dear to us both, and which they can fearfully jeopard. If their counsels incline to peace, the most friendly relations can speedily be restored, and the most favorable treaties entered into. We should feel ourselves the joint possessors of the continent, and should be drawn together by ties which unite no other people. We could, indeed, realize all the advantages of the Union, without any of its inconveniences. The cause of human liberty would not even be retarded, if the North can rise to a level with the exigences of the occasion. If, on the other hand, their thoughts incline to war, we solemnly ask them what they expect to gain? What interest will be promoted? What end, worthy of a great people, will they be able to secure? They may gratify their bad passions, they may try to reek their resentment upon the seceding States, and they may inflict a large amount of injury, disaster and suffering. But what have they gained? Shall a free people be governed by their passions? Suppose they should conquer us, what will they do with us? How will they hold us in subjection? How many garrisons, and how many men, and how much treasure, will it take to keep the South in order as a conquered province, and where are these resources to come from? After they have subdued us, the hardest part of their task will remain. They will have the wolf by the ears.

But, upon what grounds do they hope to conquer us? They know us well — they know our numbers — they know our spirit, and they know the value which we set upon our homes and firesides. We have fought for the glory of the Union, and the world admired us, but it was not such fighting as we shall do for our wives, our children, and our sacred honor. The very women of the South, like the Spartan matrons, will take hold of shield and buckler, and our boys at school will go to the field in all the determination of disciplined valor. Conquered we can never be. It would be madness to attempt it; and after years of blood and slaughter, the parties would be just where they began, except that they would have learned to hate one another with an intensity of hatred equaled only in hell. Freedom would suffer, religion would suffer, learning would suffer, every human interest would suffer, from such a war. But upon whose head would fall the responsibility? There can be but one answer. We solemnly believe that the South will be guiltless before the eyes of the Judge of all the earth. She has stood in her lot, and resisted aggression.

If the North could rise to the dignity of their present calling, this country would present to the world a spectacle of unparalleled grandeur. It would show how deeply the love of liberty and the influence of religion are rooted in our people, when a great empire can be divided without confusion, war, or disorder. Two great people united under one government differ upon a question of vital importance to one. Neither can conscientiously give way. In the magnanimity of their souls, they say, let there be no strife between us, for we are brethren. The land is broad enough for us both. Let us part in peace, let us divide our common inheritance, adjust our common obligations, and, preserving, as a sacred treasure, our common principles, let each set up for himself, and let the Lord bless us both. A course like this, heroic, sublime, glorious, would be something altogether unexampled in the history of the world. It would be the wonder and astonishment of the nations. It would do more to command for American institutions the homage and respect of mankind, than all the armies and fleets of the Republic. It would be a victory more august and imposing than any which can be achieved by the thunder of cannon and the shock of battle.

Peace is the policy of both North and South. Let peace prevail, and nothing really valuable is lost. To save the Union is impossible. The thing for Christian men and patriots to aim at now, is to save the country from war. That will be a scourge and a curse. But the South will emerge from it free as she was before. She is the invaded party, and her institutions are likely to gain strength from the conflict. Can the North, as the invading party, be assured that she will not fall into the hands of a military despot? The whole question is with her, and we calmly await her decision. We prefer peace — but if war must come, we are prepared to meet it with unshaken confidence in the God of battles. We lament the wide-spread mischief it will do, the arrest it will put upon every holy enterprise of the Church, and upon all interests of life; but the South can boldly say to the bleeding, distracted country, *"Shake not thy gory locks at me; Thou canst not say I did it."*

Letter to John S. Littell

(Philadelphia: C. Sherman & Son, 1861)

Richard Keith Call (1791–1862) was born in Prince Georges County, Virginia, and taken to Kentucky as a youth. He received little schooling save for his attendance at an academy in Tennessee, joined the regular U.S. Army, and fought in the Creek War and at the battle of New Orleans in 1815. He received a transfer to the west Florida Territory and soon after left the army to practice law, and in 1825 he settled permanently in Tallahassee, where he ultimately became a successful railroad builder. Call entered public life as territorial delegate to the U.S. Congress, and later served eight years as governor of Florida. When civil war was declared, the Unionist volunteered for the Florida militia only to be rejected for his lack of support for the Florida secession effort. The pamphlet printed in this volume, which was written in the form of a letter to a Northern friend,[1] shows how upset Call was about the inability of the country's leaders to accept the expansion of slavery. He launched into a lengthy account of how slavery had helped to build the nation, how the expansion of slavery would benefit all who wanted to conquer the Western wilderness, and that, once the country was completely settled, slavery would come to an end. Call also believed that the Upper South would never join the Lower South and that the resulting civil war would be disastrous for all of the slaveholding states. For an account of his life see Dorothy Dodd, "The Secession Movement in Florida," Florida Historical Quarterly 12 (July and October 1933): 3–24 and 45–66. The Library of Congress has Call correspondence.

We live in an age of miracles and wonders. Great events are in progress, and I look with amazement and mortification at the developments of every day and hour. We are in the midst of the most extraordinary revolution, and the most stupendous ruin is now in rapid progress that the world has ever known.

A great nation has been dismembered. The bonds of the American Union, the work of Washington, of Franklin, of Madison, and other great sages and statesmen of a glorious age, have been rent and snapped like cobwebs; and the greatest fabric of human government, *without complaint of wrong or injustice*, has been destroyed in a few months—*madly and rashly destroyed*, without reflection, and without loss of life or stain of blood.

Star after star from the once glorious, but now drooping, banner has

1. Call's original letter was dated February 12, 1861, from Lake Jackson, Florida.

[179

fallen, others are waning in their light, and the whole heavens are covered with the gloomy portent of universal destruction. When shall this ruin end? Where is the rock which will stand and throw back the mad destructive waves of revolution, and arrest the fearful, fatal, desolating progress of secession! Through the mist of the tempest, I think I see *that rock* rising in *moral* power and sublimity along the whole southern line of North Carolina, Tennessee, and Arkansas, supported by Missouri, Kentucky, Virginia, Maryland, and Delaware, and above the mad, riotous, and exulting shout of successful secession and triumphant revolution. From that rock I hear a voice, like the voice of God, saying to the raging sea, "thus far shalt thou go and no further, and here shall thy proud waves be stayed." Here I trust, is the rock of safety, standing in the centre of the American Union. The extremities may become cold, and lose their sensibilities, their love for our gallant flag, their pride for our prestige and national glory, won on so many battle-fields, and consummated by so many civil achievements; they may retire to the idolatrous worship of their local and sectional divinities, but the American heart will love and worship the God of our fathers; it will continue to beat in the American bosom, in the centre of the American Union; its warm blood will continue to circulate on both sides of the line of slavery, binding together, in national bonds, the kindred affections of one race in different communities.

Here, I trust in God and in the wisdom and virtue of my countrymen, that there is and that there ever will be an American union, bearing as the emblem of its power and glory, the broad stripes and bright stars, the banner of freedom at home, and the sign and hope of liberty to the world. Here, at least, I hope, a glorious Union of sovereign States may stand forever, to vindicate the success of the representative Republican system, to vindicate the success of the great experiment of popular government, to rebuke despotic power, to disrobe tyranny of its pomp and pride, to rebuke anarchy and riot in the sanctuary of secession; to sustain the cause of law and government, the holy cause of civil and religious liberty; to bless the living, honor the dead, justify the blood of our glorious Revolution, and vindicate the cause in which Hampden, Elliot, and Moore suffered and died; to vindicate the cause in which the hundreds and thousands of victims, through ages and generations, have been sacrificed on the altar of human liberty! May God bless and preserve this remnant of the great American Republic for all these high purposes, and permit it to stand forever as a perpetual monument to the memory and glory of the patriotic men who shall have the wisdom, virtue, and courage to resist local sectional feelings, to resist the progress of a mad, desolating revolution!

Disunion, under certain contingencies, may be justified; it may become an imperative necessity, but it should be the last resort; like the *rite of extreme unction*, it should be reserved for the last, and administered only in the dying hour of the only remaining hope within the Union. Disunion must be fatal!—fatal to the peace, safety, and happiness of both divisions of the country—fatal to the progress of liberty and civilization—fatal to the pride and glory of the American name.

Every enlightened statesman may see, even through the mist of prejudice, that there is not room between the lakes of Canada and the Gulf of Mexico for two great nations of the same race and lineage, the same language and religion, the same pride, ambition, energy, and high courage, to live in peace and good fellowship together. Every one may see, from the map of our country, that there is no desert waste, no mountain bar, dividing the Northern from the Southern States. Every one may see the great rivers, with their outstretched arms, rising in the Northern States, flowing down the rich valleys through the Southern States, to the Gulf of Mexico, proclaiming the unity of a great empire, and indicating the design of the Creator, that this beautiful land should be forever one country, for one great, united, prosperous people. And why should this unity be destroyed? Why should this beautiful land be divided? Why should this one kindred people become two hostile nations, to exhaust in ruinous wars and battles between themselves, those vast resources, those great energies heretofore so successfully united for the unequalled progress of one country, one great and happy people?

There is one disturbing, one dangerous cause,—the angry controversy arising on the institution of AFRICAN slavery, and unless this controversy can be amicably adjusted *there must be a perpetual end of the Union, an everlasting separation of the North from the South.*

The institution of slavery, then, demands the earnest attention and the unprejudiced consideration of every American citizen. It should be viewed as it is, and not as we might wish that it should be. Not as an abstract question of right or wrong, not as a blessing or a curse, but as an existing reality, for good or evil, thrown upon us by inheritance from a past generation and another government, and for which no man of the present day is in any manner the least responsible. It should be considered as it is, an institution interwoven and inseparably connected with our social and *political system*, as a domestic institution of the States, and *a national institution, created by the American people and protected by the Constitution of the United States.* It should be considered as an institution which *cannot be disturbed in its present political* relation to some of the States of the confederacy, *with-*

out great detriment to all, and without, perhaps, *destruction to some one of the parties to this relation*. It should be considered as an institution which *could not now be abolished, even with the consent of all, without fatal consequences to some of the parties holding relations to it. . . .*[2]

This race, so distinctly marked by nature with inferiority, physical, moral, and mental, as forever to forbid amalgamation, and keep it distinct from our own, has become a great class of laboring, civilized people, domesticated with the white race, and dependent on the discipline of that race for the preservation of the civilization it has acquired. It has now become a *nation considerable* in *numbers*, and *justly considerable*, for its usefulness to the whole civilized world. Members of this race form a part of the domestic association of almost every family in the South; and although the relation of master and slave is that of authority on one hand and obedience on the other, there is a mutual dependence, which produces mutual sympathies, mutual kindness, and mutual attachments. The African seems designed by the Creator for a slave. Docile and humble, with a heart full of the kindest sensibilities, generally grateful and affectionate, and with a mind incapable of a higher elevation than that which is required to direct the machinery of his limbs to useful action. He is naturally social, cheerful, and contented; and when he has a good master, which is generally the case, he is much the happiest man. The rapid increase of numbers proves his comforts of life. All his wants are abundantly supplied, and he has no care for to-morrow, either for himself or his posterity. His spirit and pride of character wants the elevation, and his mind wants the capacity, to contemplate slavery as a degradation; and no liberty, no freedom from the control of his master, can exalt him to a higher moral and intellectual condition. You may give him physical liberty, but it will be only the liberty of indulgence in sloth and indolence — the liberty of gratification in animal passions and propensities. No human power can ever liberate his mind. It is enslaved in the despotism of superstition and ignorance, of natural imbecility and inertness. It can never be elevated to the comprehension of the dignity and sublimity of that human liberty which, with all its imperfections and inferiority, approaches nearest to the liberty and power of God. He never can be exalted to that society and regulation of liberty which gives man his high place, his proud dominion on earth. Whether physically bond or free, *mentally* he must ever remain in bondage. He has animal courage as high and as fierce

2. Here Call inserted a lengthy history of African slavery in the American colonies, which he described as "as wonderful as any other portion of our wonderful history."

as the energy of the beast, when driven to desperation; but he is docile and submissive, with a moral timidity arising from his instinctive knowledge of natural inferiority, which makes him ever yield passive obedience to every reasonable will of his master. He looks on his master as a superior being, depends on him for instruction and direction in all things, and looks to him for support and protection. Though naturally indolent and improvident, he works cheerfully for his master (*even without compulsion*) much better than *he does for himself*. He feels himself identified with his master; he is interested in all that belongs to his master. He participates in his master's pride of reputation, fortune, and success. He prides himself on his master's position in society, rejoices with him in prosperity and happiness, and mourns with him, deeply and feelingly, in all his sorrows and afflictions. His heart is filled with the kindest affections, and there are few friendships among men more true and faithful than those of the African slave for a kind master. Those who have seen the unfeigned sorrow of the African nurse, watching over the dying child of her mistress, with anguish little less than the heart-rending affliction of the mother, those who have heard the lamentations, and seen the tears, of the slaves around the grave of the master, can want no higher proof of their fidelity and attachment. And under the civilizing and humane influence of the Christian religion, there are few communities of people of any race or color who would be more shocked and distressed, or who would shudder and shrink with greater horror and dismay from scenes of bloodshed and human suffering, than the African slaves of this country.

With this brief historical sketch of the institution of slavery, and the description I have given of the slave, the relation subsisting between the master and slave, we are prepared to examine the angry controversy which has arisen on this institution, which has already caused seven States to withdraw from the confederacy, and if not soon amicably adjusted, may cause every Southern State to retire with indignant scorn from a Union prostituted of every virtue, and proposed to be continued only for the advantage of one section, the ruin of another, and the violation of the rights of humanity.

The first point arising in this dangerous controversy is from the disregard and violation, by certain Northern States, of the law and the Constitution requiring the rendition of fugitive slaves to their masters. This alone, if continued, must be fatal to the Union. But there is another point, involving still more dangerous consequences. It has been proposed by statesmen of great ability, and a sectional party has come triumphantly into power on the proposition, to *confine slavery forever within its present limits*. This proposition is not the result of hasty and thoughtless determination. It has been long discussed, maturely considered, and deliberately made. And yet

I could hope, for the sake of law and justice, for the sake of humanity, and the civilization of the age, I could hope that the far-sighted statesman by whom this proposition has been made, and that few of the Christian men by whom it has been successfully maintained, have yet fully contemplated, and measured, the stupendous and terrible consequences which must inevitably follow the execution of this fearful design. It is admitted by those sagacious statesmen, and by all other intelligent men, that the government of the United States has no power to abolish slavery in any State of the confederacy; and yet here is a proposition distinctly made, and a President of the United States has been elected on an implied pledge to carry that proposition into execution, *which must destroy slavery in all the States, and may destroy 4,000,000 of slaves and their increase*, or drive the white population beyond those limits. The present population of the slaveholding States is now estimated at 12,000,000 of people; of this number, near 4,000,000 are slaves. When we look back fifty years, and see the number of slaves of that time, and consider the present number, it may not be an extravagant calculation to estimate the slave population within its present limits, at the end of the next half century, at 20,000,000 of people. The natural increase of this prolific race far exceeds the increase of the white race. But its proportion to the white race, within this area, will be augmented by another process. The black race *must remain forever where it is*. The white man, following the native instinct of the Anglo-Saxon, as well as obeying the impulse on necessity, must emigrate as the population becomes more dense, and the means of subsistence more limited, leaving the slaves behind. Thus producing annually a greater increase of one, and a decrease of the other. And this disproportion must continue to augment year after year, in a ratio not now to be calculated, until the black race must so far preponderate, unless destroyed by want and famine, war or pestilence, as to compel their masters to abandon their homes, and leave them to the possession of their famished slaves; who, when relieved from the authority and discipline of their masters, to which alone they are indebted for their elevation as a civilized and Christian people—when the white man shall have retired, and left them to themselves—will follow their native instincts of indolence and sloth—they will fall back to the vices and barbarism from which they have been but partially redeemed, through a succession of generations and the progress of centuries. Here another Africa, with all its loathsome depravity, would be established in the heart of America. The confinement of African slavery to its present limits must either produce this result, or it must be followed by the *destruction of one of the races; they never can live together in social equality*, even if there should be room enough.

This is the proposition of a Christian people, in the nineteenth century of the Christian religion. There is no crime or barbarity of the present day which may not claim some precedence on the records of past ages. Thus this revolting proposition, though unequalled in the number of victims it would sacrifice, and the extent of human suffering it would inflict, may find something approximating to a parallel in the history of heathen nations. The Egyptians murdered the children of the Hebrew women to prevent the increase of numbers, and the heathen people of India smothered their Christian prisoners in the loathsome dungeon of Calcutta; but here is a proposition, deliberately made by a Christian people, under the immediate influence of the Gospel of God, teaching charity and humanity, "peace on earth, good will to men" — a proposition to *confine forever 4,000,000 of unoffending people within a boundary, where, from the natural increase of numbers in a few years, they must perish from famine, pestilence, and war, or drive 8,000,000 of white men into exile to avoid the same calamities.* Can the philanthropist, the Christian, the civilized man, find a place in his heart, or a precept in his religion, for a sentiment which contemplates the misery or destruction of so many millions of the human race? Can the statesman find a place in his mind, or a principle in his philosophy of government to justify a policy, which must produce ruin to so many of his countrymen, and bring desolation to so large a portion of the country? Is the design merciful? Is the intent charitable? Is the institution of slavery so shocking to humanity, so repugnant to the principles of Christianity and civilization, as to justify the *destruction of the slave*, and the ruin of the master, in its abolition? If so, in what new school of humanity has this sublimated refinement of the Christian charities been matured to this heaven-born perfection? In the New England school of morals, religion, and benevolence. In the same New England whose men, ships, and money, were foremost in catching the wild barbarian on the coast of Africa, and bringing the "*merchandise of human flesh, and human souls and bodies,*" to the colonies of Britain. The same New England that peopled America with the African race, would now commit greater barbarity by destroying millions of civilized people. The same New England whose present commercial and manufacturing wealth is founded on the rich inheritance derived from the profit of the African slave trade, and the profitable productions of African slave labor.

But if the confinement of slavery within its present limits should produce consequences less terrible and fatal, if it should be followed only by the *abolition of slavery*; while it would be a *palpable violation of the Constitution of the United States, would it elevate the slave? Would it make him more comfortable? More happy than he is in his present condition?* Would it *provide him with a better home?* Would it give him a more elevated social position? Would it make him more the equal of the white man than he now is? Let these questions be answered by New England men, with a third and fourth generation of liberated Africans among them, where the number is not so great as to crowd the humble place they fill in New England life and society. Let them say what they, with all their charitable sympathy for the African—with all their religious benevolence and humane generosity, have been able to accomplish by an experiment of half a century, in giving elevation, dignity, and social equality to the free African. Let men of Old England answer and say, what liberty has done for the African in Jamaica; let Frenchmen answer for the liberated African in Hayti. Search through the history of all time, and you will search in vain to find *any portion of the African race, from its first appearance on record until the present day, in the aggregate, so elevated, intelligent, enlightened, civilized, comfortable, and happy, as that portion of this degraded race* found as slaves in our country. You will not find it among the barbarian hordes of Africa. You will not find it under the Crescent, in Europe or Asia. You will not find it under the sign of the Cross, of South America. You will not find it in Hayti, Jamaica, or New England. In every country where there is an approach to equality between the races, it is in the degradation of the one, and not the elevation of the other. If then the condition of the African slave would be rendered worse by liberation, why this *mad crusade against African slavery?* The theory of universal human freedom is the mad offspring of delusion and passion, and not the result of enlightened reason. Liberty is the refinement of blessing to enlightened people, capable of its rational enjoyments, while it is the greatest curse which can befall a race incapable of estimating the value of freedom. History is full of proofs to illustrate this truth. History proves that the votaries of freedom of a great nation, in an enlightened age, once in their madness placed the Goddess of Liberty in their adoration above the God of nature, and the night of atheism closed upon these deluded worshippers of a false divinity, until they saw no other light, and they impiously denied the existence of a living God. New England will not go so far in her madness. There is a conservative power of wisdom and virtue among her great and enlightened people, and a moral energy, which, although it has long slumbered, is not yet dead, and it will come forth in dignified authority to rebuke fanaticism, and, with the sceptre of reason, expel the idolatrous worshippers of *negro freedom* from their altars, as Napoleon drove the mad votaries from the worship of their heathen divinity, and restored the worship of the true and living God. But the time has arrived when she must awake and come to the judgment—when she must aid, by her counsel, in deciding the most vital question, and one involving more stupendous considerations than any other that can arise in the relations of mankind. It is time that New England — Old England — Europe — America — and the whole civilized world, should come to the judgment bar, to consider the mission, the relations, the value of the institution of African slavery. It has too long been considered as a mere question of right in the master to property in slaves. It has so been regarded for ages, and the universal judgment of all civilized nations has confirmed and approved the right of the master. That right is now denied. Great and unquestionable as I regard this right, it would sink in my estimation far below its present position, if it did not involve the *high considerations of humanity*, the great *consideration of political and domestic economy*. The race is now too numerous, and it is increasing too rapidly to be confined within its present limits. Though divided into families, and domesticated with white families, it is a *distinct nation of near* 4,000,000 *of people, and constitutes a part of the American* people. The institution of African slavery forms *part of our political system of government*. It is entitled, then, to a higher consideration than the mere right of the master to property in the slave. The institution of slavery must now be considered in its relation to the American people, in its relation to our constitutional government, and in relation to the American Union, whose safety it has placed in jeopardy, and whose ruin it may yet accomplish. Slaves must be considered in their personal relation; they must be considered as both *persons and property*. Slavery never can be confined within its present limits. It is freed from that confinement by the granted freedom of the Constitution of the United States. If it were otherwise, the bonds of the Constitution *are not strong enough*, with all their *reverenced power*, to resist the *energies of the imperative necessity which demands its expansion*. It must expand with the extension of the white race into every region congenial to its nature and possible for its labor. Each has its sphere of action — each its place of usefulness in accomplishing the great design of Providence. The African, in the humble inferiority of his nature, must ever, as he has done, give place to the European race. They commenced their labors together in the wilderness of Massachusetts; and from time to time, as the white man, from the increase of population, has required the place, the labor, and the head of the African, it has been yielded. The African has gone with the pioneer of the forest, over rivers, mountains, hills, and valleys, from State to State, until his arrival at the present boundary. But his destiny is not yet fulfilled, his career of usefulness not yet completed. A vast unmeasured wilderness, to make room again, as he has done before, for the white man, who will want his present place in a few years in many, and in time in most of the present slaveholding States. He must go into new territories, open new cotton, sugar, and tobacco fields. He must drain other swamps, to form new rice-fields, to supply the increasing demands of commerce, and relieve the increasing necessities of nations. The productions of slave labor are carrying commerce into every land, navigation over every sea: civilization and Christianity are going hand in hand with commerce and navigation into every barbarous country. The institution of slavery is doing more in the agency of the world's great progress, more for the improvement and comfort of human life, more for the preaching of the Gospel to heathen nations, more for the fulfillment of prophecy, than any other institution on earth.

This institution cannot be stopped in its career of usefulness to the whole world. *It cannot be confined to its present limits. Dire and uncontrollable necessity will impel the master and the slave to cut their way through every barrier which may be thrown around it, or perish together in the attempt. The consequences of confinement are too terrible to be borne. The attempt to confine the explosion of gunpowder, or stop the eruption of the burning volcano*, would not be more perilous and unavailing. If the institution of African slavery was not already in existence, with its immediate connection with the interest and necessities of all nations, *it could not now be established. I would not bring one other African to this continent.* The principles and prejudices of the whole world are against it. But the entire world has helped to build up the institution, through the progress of centuries. The whole world is deriving advantages from its continuance, and the whole world has not the right to abolish it, if, by doing so, they should destroy (as I have endeavored to prove that they would) 4,000,000 of people, or render their condition far worse than it is, and destruction or ruin to the master. If the institution is beneficial to mankind; if it has elevated a part of the African race to a position in civilization, intelligence, morality, religion, and the comforts of human life, which have never been attained by any other portion of that degraded race; and if the discipline of slavery is essentially necessary to sustain this improved position, and prevent a recession to its original condition of indolence, ignorance, superstition, and depravity—the whole world should unite in sustaining it, and give every encouragement in raising it to a still higher degree of civilization, intelligence, and respectability, and a still higher degree of usefulness to mankind. It may be in the Providence of God that the American Union, which has cheered the whole world with its promises, like the star which stood for a while over the cradle of Bethlehem, may fall and lose its light forever. It may be in his dispensation of human events, that the great American family shall be divided into many nations. But divided or united, the path of destiny must lead the Anglo-

Saxon race to the mastery of this whole continent. And if the whole column should not advance, the division of this race will, with the institution of African slavery, *advance from the banks of the Rio Grande to the line under the sun*, establishing in their march the waymarks of progress, the altars of the reformed religion, the temples of a higher civilization, a purer liberty, and a better system of human government. And when this great work shall be done, as all the institutions of man must perish like man's mortality, here the institution of slavery may end. Here the day of African bondage on this continent may close. Here the slave may be free. And here, under the same burning sun which yet beams on the birthplace of his ancestors, released from the discipline of the master (if the earth shall endure so long), a few succeeding generations of his posterity will find the African in America the same naked, wild barbarian that his forefathers were when landed on the shores of Massachusetts, or the coast of Virginia, vindicating the truth of Scripture, and verifying the eternal curse on the children of Ham. But until this great consummation of destiny, the African slave is entitled to a comfortable home with his master. He is entitled to pure air to breathe, land to work and to live on, with the enjoyment of abundance. Although the government of the United States has no right to liberate the slave by any measure, direct or indirect, no right to interpose between the master and the slave, though the authority of the master must remain despotic, mitigated and softened in its administration by State laws, the progress of civilization, and the charities of the Christian religion, the government is bound by every principle of justice to accord to the slave every right of humanity; thus it can never confine him within limits where he must suffer and perish for the want of bread without the violation of all these sacred obligations. If the extension of slavery into yet unexplored and unpeopled regions, where the climate and soil are congenial to the nature of the slave, and the productions profitable to his labor, be, as every one must know it must be, necessary for his abundant and comfortable subsistence, his life and happiness, I challenge the application of any principle of the Constitution of the United States to prohibit that extension; and I maintain that the denial of the government to the master the right to emigrate with his slave to such region would be as wrongful, arbitrary, unjust, and despotic, as the denial of the master's right himself to emigrate without the slave. African slaves, under the Constitution of the United States, are regarded both as *persons* and *property*. As property, the master has unquestionably the moral and legal right to carry his slave to any territory within the jurisdiction of the United States, and there is no expressed or implied constitutional power to interpose a prohibition. *As persons*, in what letter, of principle, of our free and beneficent Constitution, can the arbitrary, and despotic, power be found to prohibit the emigration of the slave with his master, more than to prohibit the emigration of the master with his apprentice, the ward with the guardian, or the child with the parent? The Constitution of the United States, in all its provisions for those persons and relations, places the apprentice and the slave in the same personal and proprietary condition. It regards the apprentice, during the term of service for which he is bound, on the same footing as the slave for life. The master of the absconding apprentice, and the master of the runaway slave, have the same *right to the rendition of their property*, when found in any State into which the apprentice or slave may escape. If the right of the master to carry his apprentice into any territory of the United States has never been questioned, can any sufficient reason be assigned why the master should not carry his slave into the same territory? The public domain is the property of the nation. The institution of slavery *is a national institution*. History proves that for more than century the young and vigorous energies of our whole nation under the colonial government of Britain were directed to the building up of this institution. History proves that Britain during the past century demanded and received from Spain, as the price of peace and friendship, the exclusive right and monopoly of the African slave-trade. History proves that the New England States were the great reapers of this rich harvest of commerce in African slaves,—in "human flesh," if you prefer. History proves that the foundation of the present wealth and prosperity of Massachusetts, Rhode Island, and Connecticut, was laid in the profitable traffic and in the labor of slaves. History proves that every one of the original thirteen States of this nation were once slave States, and that New York and New England had much more to do in building up the institution of slavery in this country than all the Southern States of the Confederacy. And history proves that, for twenty years after the date of the Constitution, the whole people of the United States, and every State of the Union, either by active participation or by tacit acquiescence, gave encouragement and aid in building up the institution of African slavery. It is, therefore, essentially and emphatically, a national institution, though now only existing in the South. It is as truly national as the custom-house on the import on commerce in the city of Boston. It was created by the nation; the nation has derived wealth and power from its creation; the nation is responsible for it. The Constitution protects it, and the nation is bound to find a comfortable home for these 4,000,000 of the African race, with their masters.

The African is a foreign and inferior race, domesticated with and attached to the American people, doing a great work—a work which must be done—a work not degrading to the proud white man—but a work he cannot do. It is exalting to the natural degradation of the black man. These laborers are numbered in the ratio and represented in the popular branch of the American government. The nation is bound by the charities of the Christian faith, by the principles of benevolence, and the rights of civilization, to administer to the African race born on its soil, cherished in its bosom, enriched by its labor, all the rights of humanity. I do not pretend that African slavery is without its evils and its objections. It has many, very many. But it has not so many, nor are they so great, as the evils which must inevitably fall on both races from the liberation of the slaves by the process of confinement to present limits. By turning loose an inferior race—amounting to one out of three in a whole population—a nation of near 4,000,000 of people—without a country, without homes, to wander as vagabonds, without social position in the land of their masters, without the care of these to make them labor for their daily bread and necessities, and without restraint of their vices, can any one imagine a greater calamity to befall master and slave? And in what way have either master or man deserved such a visitation of calamity at the hands of Northern men, who brought the African to our common country, and who sold their slaves to the South as soon as they could procure white labor cheaper than that of the black man? Every State has a right to exclude slavery, or abolish slavery, within the limits of its own jurisdiction. But no State has a right to disregard its nationality; no State has a right to *secede* from the moral and legal *national* obligations to sustain the institution of African slavery where it is, or where it may be lawfully established. I have opposed secession persistently, vehemently. I have thrown myself in the breach to oppose it. In resisting it I have stood almost alone, while others gave way to its angry surges which dashed around. I dared to oppose it, because I thought secession, whether in the majority or the minority, whether supported by one man, or by millions of men, wrong, eminently wrong, and that the approval of multitudes can never make it right. If it has a principle in the philosophy of human government, it is a *principle of destruction*. The secession of a Southern State from the Union is not more disloyal to the government, not more revolutionary, than the treachery, insubordination, and hostile resistance, of a Northern State to the obligations of the Constitution. They are both violations of the public law—both defiant of the public authority—with this difference in favor of the Southern State, that she is not the aggressor, that she has not stricken the first blow. She is resenting an insult, avenging a wrong. True, not where resentment is merited, not where revenge is due. She strikes not the offender, but in her madness she strikes her country, and wounds herself. At a single dash she breaks the bonds of the Union, she braves all dangers, defies all power, denies herself all advantages, and proudly disdains all protection from the Union. A proud spirit, wounded by wrongs, excited by passion, led by bold, ambitious leaders, and hurried on with the *pitiful taunt of "submissionist,"* indiscriminately thrown upon all who have the courage and firmness to resist the *mad impulse* of secession, however determined they may be to resist every aggression.

The offending Northern States act with no passionate precipitation. She deliberately meditates and coolly consummates a violation of the Constitution. While she withdraws her allegiance to the government, by denying the authority of its judicial, and legislative, power in special cases, while she withholds her allegiance to some of the bonds of the Constitution, she sings anthems of praise and glory to the Union she has violated, and claims all the blessings and advantages of the government to which she renders only a partial fealty, a selfish allegiance. It is thus that the two extremities are madly rending the vitals of our once great and glorious country. It is thus the American Union, once the pride of every American heart, once the admiration and wonder of the whole civilized world, has been disrupted and destroyed. It is thus the public peace has been broken, and we stand on the verge of calamitous, desolating, ruinous, civil war. But may we not hope, sir, that some propitiating power may interpose to save us, and avert this dire and fearful calamity? May we not hope that the doomsday of the great American Union has not yet dawned? I cannot believe that our nation is yet so mad as to spurn, and impiously reject, the blessings which a beneficent Providence has sown broadcast over a whole land, and given indiscriminately to a whole people. I have ever regarded our Constitutional Union as the greatest structure of human government, and I have cherished for it and for our whole country the deepest devotion. I have considered the union of the North and the South indispensable to the peace and happiness of both sections — almost as essential to each other as hands and feet to the human body. While I have shed bitter tears over the present ruin, I have been cheered with the hope that the North, reanimated with love and duty to our whole country, would return with renewed allegiance to the Constitution, that she would award cheerfully every legitimate right and privilege to the South, and that our once glorious Union might be reconstructed more permanently, and more happily, than before. But we are now approaching the culminating point in our national fortunes. The "Ides of March" is at hand; then, for the first time, a sectional party will take possession of our government. The fate of the nation may be decided by the policy that party may inaugurate. The application of any coercive measure to drive back a seceded State, *will be fatal to the last remaining hope of the Union*. Although I deny the right of secession, I acknowledge the right of revolution, and hold to the principles enunciated in our Declaration of Independence. And if it be the will of the majority of the people of the seceded States to form an independent government, they *have the right, and it can be only a question of power. No coercive measures can reunite them with the North*. It is forbidden by the genius of our free institutions, and any attempt at coercion must unite every Southern State and every Southern man in the most determined and energetic resistance. I was opposed to the seizure of the fortifications, and other property, of the government in the South, but *they can never be restored to the government until every constitutional right of the South shall have been fully acknowledged by the North*. If it should be the determination of Mr. Lincoln and the party which has brought him into power, *to confine slavery to its present limits, the day of battle need not be deferred*, and, when it comes, I trust in God that every Southern man will be ready and willing to die rather than yield to a proposition so unjust, so abhorrent and so dishonorable.

I rejoice at the noble and patriotic stand taken by the conservative Southern States, in resisting the impulse of secession, not because I am disposed to submit to wrong and injustice, not because I am willing to preserve the Union longer than it continues to be the Union of the Constitution, but because I hope they will do, what I had hoped the whole South would have done. Because I hope they *will with one voice demand of the North a full and perfect recognition of every constitutional right and privilege of the South, and if this just demand should not be complied with*, then with my long-cherished devotion to the Union our fathers, I shall be reconciled to *see it end forever!* The North and South can never live in peace together except on terms of perfect social and political equality, therefore a separation, with war, and all its attendant calamities, will be far better than a discontented unity, *with the confinement of slavery to its present limits*. This I shall regard not only as the greatest indignity and insult to the South, but the greatest calamity which could be inflicted, and rather than bear this insult, and endure this calamity, I prefer that the last Southern man should fall, on the last battle-field of the terrible war, in which we may soon be engaged.

But I trust that Mr. Lincoln may not be unmindful of his official oath, that he will not disregard the obligations of the Constitution, that he will feel the high responsibilities of his position,—a responsibility more sublime than that of the Roman senate in the last days of the republic, higher and more stupendous than the responsibility of the Roman general, on the fatal battle-field of Pharsalia. The American destiny is, under a directing Providence, in his hands! The peace, the safety, the life of a great nation, the happiness of 30,000,000 people—the hope, anxiety, and expectation of the world—depend on his wisdom, virtue, firmness, and patriotism, for a wise and peaceable adjustment of our national differences. He may save, or he may consummate the ruin of this country! If he should adhere to the false theory of government on which he has advanced to power, if he should attempt to put that theory into practice, if he should attempt the recapture of the fortifications, before the just demands of the South shall have been conceded, ALL IS LOST FOREVER! If he, and the sectional party he leads, should recede from the hostile position they have assumed to the Constitution, and the people of the South, all may yet be well. I trust, in that event, that there would be conservative men enough, both North and South, men who remember the past happiness and prosperity of the people, the past fame and glory of our country, to reconstruct our glorious Union, with greater stability, and restore peace and tranquility to our now divided and unhappy nation. Oh! that I had the genius to lead, the power to reach, and win the hearts of my countrymen, in every latitude, in every place, how earnestly I would plead the cause of my unhappy country! In the name of the living and the dead, in the name of unborn millions of our posterity, how fervently I would invoke the union of all hearts and minds—to re-construct and preserve for all time the Union of our fathers! How gladly I would hail the returning sign of peace, the gallant flag—no missing star—no rent in the stripes of the banner, which has waved so proudly, over the destinies of our once united, great, and glorious country! And if the death of *one man* could atone for the improprieties of a whole nation, if the blood of one man could redeem the lost American glory, how freely mine should flow, how cheerfully would I hail the death that should bring regenerated life, peace, and safety to our once again united, happy country.[3]

3. Call concluded: "My only wish is, if I can, to be serviceable to our unhappy country, and aid in restoring it once more to Union, peace, and happiness. . . . Any attempts at coercion must be fatal to all hopes of reunion."

ROBERT H. SMITH

An Address to the Citizens of Alabama, on the Constitution and Laws of the Confederate States of America, . . . at Temperance Hall, on the 30th of March, 1861

(Mobile: Mobile Daily Register Print, 1861)[1]

Robert Hardy Smith (1813–78) was born in North Carolina, attended the U.S. Military Academy, taught school, and later practiced medicine before settling in 1835 in Mobile, Alabama, to practice law. He held office in the state legislature and became known as an excellent parliamentarian. At first Smith opposed the secession movement in Alabama, but he accepted election to the Provisional Confederate States Congress, where he assisted in perfecting the style and the substance of the Confederate Constitution. During the Civil War he served as a colonel in the Alabama infantry but had to resign because of poor health. The pamphlet included in this volume was given as a speech ostensibly to explain the contents of the new Constitution to the people of the Lower South, but it really served to inform the Upper South of the moderate behavior of the new Confederacy by describing the similarities between the Confederate Constitution and the Federal Constitution. Smith also appeared to threaten the Upper South with refusal to allow the sale of slaves in the new Confederacy. For biographical information see Jon L. Wakelyn, Biographical Dictionary of the Confederacy *(Westport, Connecticut: Greenwood Press, 1977). Marshall L. DeRosa,* The Confederate Constitution of 1861 *(Columbia: University of Missouri Press, 1991), has useful information on Smith's life.*

The Congress of which I am a member, and whose labors have been eventful in our history, has, after a session of six weeks, taken a recess until the second Monday in May next: and in view of the momentous questions with which it has had to deal and of the consequences which hang upon its work, it seems to me proper on returning home to address the citizens of our Commercial Metropolis, and the people of Alabama generally who may be here, upon the present condition and future prospects of our political affairs. I have, therefore, invited your attendance this evening to lay before you, so far as an observance of the secrecy of our proceedings

1. Delivered at Temperence Hall on March 30, 1861, and published immediately by request of citizens of Mobile.

will admit, the course and action of the Congress of the Confederate States of America and to express my views of the destiny of our New Republic. I shall seek to discharge the task plainly and simply for my object is not to entertain you with a speech, but to converse with you as a neighbor.

Our ordinance of secession invited the People of the Southern States to meet the People of the State of Alabama at Montgomery on the 4th day of February, "for the purpose of consulting with each other as to the most effectual mode of securing concerted and harmonious action in whatever measures may be deemed most desirable for our common peace and security." And the resolution, under which we were elected, authorized us to meet such deputies as might be appointed from the other slaveholding States, which should secede from the Federal Union, for the purpose of "framing a Provisional Government upon the principles of the Constitution of the United States, and also to prepare and consider upon a plan for the creation and establishment of a Permanent Government for the seceding States upon the same principles, which shall be submitted to Conventions of such seceding States for adoption or rejection."

We met and consulted and framed a Provisional Government, by adopting the Constitution and enacting the laws to which you are now obedient, and we have submitted a plan for the creation and establishment of a Permanent Government of the seceded States. I am gratified to know that our State Convention has accepted this Constitution by an almost unanimous vote and the act meets, so far as I have ascertained, the approbation of our people.

The first question, which necessarily arrested the attention of the Convention was what powers should it exercise, in view of the authority conferred and the condition and wants of the constituency represented. We assembled as the Deputies of six separate States for the purpose of securing concerted and harmonious action in such measures as might be deemed most desirable for our common peace and security; and to this end we were instructed, as I have said, to frame a Provisional Government upon the principles of the Constitution of the United States.

Each State had seceded with the expectation of speedily forming a close bond of union with her sympathizing sisters, and the great object of the Convention was to bind together the broken fragments of a separated, but homogeneous people, and thus "establish justice, insure domestic tranquillity, provide for the common defence, promote the general welfare, and secure the blessings of liberty to ourselves, and our posterity."

The long strife with the non-slaveholding States had ended in a disruption of our relations with the Government. The Constitution of our

Fathers had been long and persistently abused to our injury, until a hostile party was coming into power, whose rule of action was the almost single idea of embittered hate towards our people and our institutions, unmindful of the Constitutional guaranties which were intended as checks against popular majorities. It's elected President looked to his advent to power with the narrow vision of a sectional partisan and heard in the complaints and saw in the resistance of a free people nothing but the clamor of rebels, who were to be punished. It is impossible to doubt that it was Mr. Lincoln's policy, under the name of enforcing the laws, to retake the forts, to collect the revenue of the United States in our Ports and to reduce the seceded States to obedience to the behests of his party. His purpose therefore was war upon, and subjugation of our people. I need not tell you that this state of things demanded prompt and united resistance and that the position assumed by the seceded States was to be maintained at any and every hazard. Each State had for herself put on the armor of war, but the cause was a common one, and the cardinal object of assembling a Congress was to meet and provide for a common exigency and the required Provisional Government could only be framed, so as to respond to the high purposes aimed at, by the exercise of legislative powers. Indeed the letter of our authority would not have been fulfilled, had we simply made a Provisional Constitution without the enactment of laws; for by stopping at the creation of the fundamental law, we should have performed but one important part in framing a Government.

The necessities of the occasion demanded prompt and efficient military organization under the direction of one power the collection of revenues at a few seaports for defraying the expenses of the common cause the enactment and administration of laws emanating from an acknowledged head empowered to speak, within the sphere of its authority, in the name of the whole the creation of a Government which would command obedience at home and acknowledgment and respect abroad, and which, by the promptitude, efficiency and wisdom of its action, might avert the calamities of war, or, failing in this high hope, successfully maintain, through the last appeal of nations, the rights of these States.

For myself, I never doubted but the warrant of our authority, the expectations of the public and the necessities of the occasion, demanded that the Convention should adopt and put in motion the Government of the Confederate States, by enacting as a Congress such laws as the exigency required. In my opinion, we are this day indebted to such a course for the pacific policy now beginning to prevail at Washington for a change from threatening war to promised peace for that revival of confidence which business to-day exhibits in your streets, and for that cementing together of public opinion so happily illustrated in the councils of our State in the adoption of a permanent Constitution; and what is more and least disputable, to it we are indebted for the power of this Confederacy to maintain by arms the position we have taken.

Fellow-citizens, you have but to trace with your memories a little more than one short month, to know what prospects, what hopes, what realities have been created. Division, doubt and uncertainty have been succeeded by unanimity, confidence and stability. Revolution has been accomplished without anarchy; and, whether our independence is to be received and treated as a fact by other nations or is yet to be baptized in blood, we feel assured that our nationality is a successful and an irrevocable deed. You have but to read the speeches of Mr. Lincoln on his journey to Washington, in contrast with the present tone of the Administration, to realize the effect of our conduct upon our enemies. You have but to compare the speeches of the President of these Confederate States with those of the President of the United States to feel proud of the contrast between the statesman and the narrow-minded and ignorant partisan. For the truth of which latter assertion, if proof be wanted, I would refer you to the editorials of the National Intelligencer, supposed to represent the views of the Premier of the United States, refusing even to credit the accuracy of the reports of speeches made by Mr. Lincoln on his journey to Washington.

We met on the fourth of February to create a Government, and to give to it such solidity and strength as would challenge the confidence of our public and the respect of the world. To be effectually done it had to spring into strength in one short month and to spread, as if by a magic touch, confidence to the pursuits of our people. I need not pursue this part of my subject. The act and its results are before you, and for one I stand ready to answer at the bar of present opinion and to abide by the judgment of posterity as to the patriotism and wisdom which caused the Convention of the Confederate States to resolve itself into a Legislative Congress.

We deliberated and acted with closed doors, but the results of our labors are before the world, for our laws were promulgated as they were approved by the President. If they are wise it matters not what discussion caused their adoption; if unwise nothing can or should redeem them from censure. I do not deny nor even doubt the importance of open discussion in a free Government, but there are occasions when every Power must deliberate with closed doors, and, in our case, all circumstances combined to render this not only proper but necessary. We had much to do in a short time and the matter was of the gravest importance; for we had a nation to form, and peace and war hung trembling in the balance. The Convention that in time of peace passed the Constitution of the United States had given us its high example of the necessity of secret sessions. Calm, unbiased deliberations, unrestrained even by the pre-expressed opinions of the members themselves; as well as freedom from all motive or hope of individual eclat were promoted by closed doors; but apart from these considerations, it was of the highest importance that our actions should not be anticipated and misrepresented through the appliances of news mongers and sensation telegrams. The matters of legislation with which we had to deal were of a high and often confidential character and required celerity of action. Such are always, more or less, the nature of Governmental affairs appertaining to Foreign relations. Much too had to be done in a short time and every one is aware of the facility imparted to deliberation and action by retired, quiet and calm labor. To the fact that Congress sat on all important business in secret session is mainly attributable the unusual amount of work performed; and it affords me pleasure to know, that seldom have men labored for the public weal more assiduously, or brought to the discharge of their duties a higher sense of obligation than my associates in the Congress of the Confederate States.[2]

The provisional Constitution has been before the country since the 8th day of February last, and its adaptation to the expectation and wants of the people seems to be generally conceded. It secures every cardinal principle of American liberty indeed, adds additional safeguards to its preservation. Save that the legislation of Congress is made during the brief existence of the provisional Government to devolve upon a single body, and that the President and Vice President were chosen by Congress (changes which the urgent necessity of the occasion demanded) we have followed with almost literal fidelity the Constitution of the United States, and departed from its text only so far as experience had clearly proven that additional checks were required for the preservation of the Nation's interest. Of this character is the power given the President to arrest corrupt or illegitimate expenditures, by vetoing particular clauses in an appropriation bill, and at the same time approving other parts of the bill. There is hardly a more flagrant abuse of it's power, by the Congress of the United States than the habitual practice of loading bills, which are necessary for Governmental operations with reprehensible, not to say venal dispositions of the public

2. For reaction to the Confederate convention's secret proceedings see Charles Lee, *The Confederate Constitutions* (Chapel Hill: University of North Carolina Press, 1963).

money, and which only obtain favor by a system of combinations among members interested in similar abuses upon the treasury.

Bills necessary for the support of the Government are loaded with items of the most exceptionable character, and are thrown upon the President at the close of the session, for his sanction, as the only alternative for keeping the Government in motion. Even however under this salutary check, the evil might be but mitigated, not cured, in the case of a weak or highly partisan President, who would feel that the responsibility of such legislation rested but lightly on him, so long as the unrestrained power and duty of originating appropriations depended upon a corrupt or pliant Congress— hence the Convention of Confederate States wisely determined that the Executive was the proper department to know and call for the moneys necessary for the support of Government, and that here the responsibility should rest. Therefore the Provisional Constitution prohibits Congress from appropriating money "from the treasury unless it be asked for by the President or some one of the heads of the Departments, except for the purpose of paying its own expenses and contingencies." This provision proceeds upon the idea that the chief Executive head of the country and his Cabinet should understand the pecuniary wants of the Confederacy, and should be answerable for an economical administration of public affairs, and at the same time should be enabled and required to call for whatever sums may be wanted to accomplish the purposes of Government. . . .[3]

The denial of extra compensation to public contractors, agents or servants, and the limitation upon the power of Congress to determine on claims against Government, and the establishment of Courts for their adjudication, doubly commend themselves for, while they interpose effective barriers to heedless or corrupt legislation, they offer to the honest bidder fair competition, and to the public creditor an impartial tribunal, better fitted for the investigation and adjudication of his rights than a mere political body can be.

The want of facility of communication between the Executive and Legislature, has, it is believed, been a serious impediment to the easy and harmonious working of Government. Experience has shown that our Fathers, by refusing the Executive the right to be heard through his constitutional advisers on the floor of the Legislature, had interposed barriers to that free intercourse between the two departments which was essential to the wise and healthy action of each. Hence, by the Provisional Constitution, members of Congress may fill Executive places, while by the Per-

3. Smith went on to quote congressional appropriation powers.

manent one, the old prohibition is retained that "No person, holding any office under the Confederate States, shall be a member of either House during his continuance in office," subject however to the qualification that "Congress may, by law, grant to the principal officer in each of the Executive Departments a seat upon the floor of either House, with the privilege of discussing any measures appertaining to his department." It will be at once perceived that the provision, respecting the appropriation of money upon estimates from the Executive, and that giving Congress power to admit the Ministry to seats on its floor, are but modified derivations from the British Constitution. In England, the rule is absolute that no money can be appropriated by Parliament, unless asked for by the Crown, and the principal ministerial officers must be members of Parliament, and are required, upon being called to office, to resign their seats in the House of Commons, and to return to the body by reelection. The ministry bring their Budget before Parliament, and retire from office when their measures fail to receive its approbation. The King declares war and makes peace. He too possesses the unqualified power of making treaties and of appointing to office; yet the control of Government resides in Parliament, because of the power in the House of Commons to withhold supplies, and by a vote of censure or of rejection of ministerial measures, to change the actual Executive heads of the Realm. As the measures passed are those of the Crown; and as its policy must always be attuned to the wishes of Parliament, it follows that the Executive department will never fail to ask for all proper appropriations, and it has necessarily resulted that the veto power has fallen into disuse in England; for the Crown would employ it, if at all, against measures, originated or proposed or assented to by its Ministers before and as part of the Legislature. The effective veto power in England really resides in Parliament and is absolute, and hence we truly say that the Government of Great Britain is a Parliamentary one. While these principles may be said to be the modern sheet-anchors of English liberty, and to commend themselves to us as wise and long-tried safeguards of freedom, deserving the high eulogiums of her jurists, orators, statesmen and historians, it will readily occur to the student of American institutions, that they could not be safely transferred, in their full proportions, to the soil of permanent American legislation; for with us Congress declares war, and the President appoints to office and makes treaties, only by and with the advice and consent of the Senate; and his advisers are not, like those of the Crown, subject to removal at the will of the Legislature, nor are they, like the British Ministry, the responsible administrators of Government. So harmoniously adjusted are the parts of the English Constitution, that each seems necessary to the symmetry of the whole, but it is apparent that with us the President might refuse to ask for appropriations to execute measures passed by Congress, which failed to meet his approbation, and that to give to the chief officer of the country, who was not amenable to Congress, and whose tenure of place and freedom of action were in no wise controlled by it, the right, through his Cabinet, fully to participate in legislation, and the power not only of absolute veto in advance, but that of preventing even full discussion of the wants of Government by refusing to call for appropriations, would be creating a power unknown to the British Constitution and dangerous to public liberty.

By refusing to a mere majority of Congress unlimited control over the treasury, and by requiring the yeas and nays to be taken whenever two-thirds assume to vote away money not asked for by the Executive; by placing upon the administration the duty and responsibility of calling for appropriations by virtually excluding congress from passing upon claims against the Government; by prohibiting extra compensation to employees by enabling the Executive to be heard on the floor of Congress, and by giving the President the power to veto objectionable items in appropriation bills, we have, I trust, greatly purified our Government, and, at the same time, placed its different parts in nearer and more harmonious relations.

Proceeding upon the idea that a just economy in the administration of government is due to those who are taxed to support it, and that the authority to raise more money than the public exigency demands invites abuse, and taught by the history of the legislation of the United States, that too much money is corrupting to public morals, the Convention, by the provisional Constitution, restrained Congress from laying and collecting taxes, duties, imposts and excises, except for discharging the debts and carrying on the Government; and lest, in after times, the ingenuity of construction might enlarge the provision and turn loose again the pent up evil, the permanent Constitution emphatically forbids the Legislature from granting bounties from the treasury, or promoting or fostering any branch of industry. Holding steadily in view the principle that the great object of the Federal Government is to perform national functions and not to aggrandize or depress sectional, or local, or individual interests, and adhering to and enforcing the doctrine that a people should be left to pursue and develop their individual thrift without direct aids or drawbacks from Government, and that internal improvements are best judged of, and more wisely and economically directed by the localities desiring them, even when they legitimately come within the scope of Federal action, and knowing that, as the regulation of commerce was one of the chief objects of creating the Government, and that under this power lurked danger of sectional legislation and lavish expenditure, the Constitution denies to Congress the right to make appropriations for any internal improvement, even though intended to facilitate commerce, except for the purpose furnishing lights, beacons, buoys and other aids to navigation upon the coasts, and the improvement of harbors and the removing of obstructions in river navigation; and the cost and expenses of even these objects must be paid by duties levied on the navigation facilitated. And in order that each State may the better attain such objects for itself, the exclusive power of Congress over commerce is subject to the qualification, that any State may accomplish the work within her borders by a duty on the sea-going tonnage, participating in the trade of the harbor or river improved provided that such impositions shall not conflict with treaties of the Confederacy, and that any surplus so raised shall be paid into the Federal treasury. Thus, are not only fruitful sources of discord cut off, by abolishing the hot-house system of imparting artificial heat and growth to chosen localities, at the expense of others, through bounties, navigation and tariff and internal improvement laws, but great facilities are offered to each and every State to secure, on its own judgment and at its own risk of unduly burdening its trade, the improvement of its waters at the expense of the sea-going vessels using them; and whether the work be undertaken by the State or Federal Government, the burden falls substantially on the immediate beneficiary.

We may congratulate ourselves that henceforth the Federal Government will know no favorite State or section; that prosperity however widely, profusely or partially scattered, is to be the legitimate results of legitimate causes, and that agriculture, commerce and manufactures will no longer breed jealousy and discontent, but will, hand in hand, each advance the prosperity and harmony of the whole.

Were we here to pause and point our people to the past, tracing the abuses of Government and all the ills of discord, which partial and hostile legislation engendered in the public mind, until, long before our dissolution, we had become an alienated and almost belligerent people, we should find that in the construction of a Government for the Confederate States, the lessons of experience have not been overlooked, and that whatever of contention the future may bring forth, from the necessary conflicts of opinion and interest, new checks and balances have been added to the old Constitution, and hopes of long continued, fraternal feelings, indulged by our Fathers, have again revived.

We come here to-night to indulge in no Utopian idea, that we have attained perfection in Government, or that we have, by the clearness of language, left no room for evasion or perversion or usurpation of power; but we may, I think, congratulate ourselves that grave errors have been corrected, and additional hopes given for the preservation of American liberty.

When we see that while Government is restrained as to the objects to which money is to be applied, and that the appropriation of it is put under material checks that the patronage of the Executive is almost cut off by the tenure of good behavior, attached to the vast number of offices which before were the mere spoils of a victorious party, and by the ineligibility of the President to a second term, we are prepared to realize the good which has bowed from a movement, the necessity for which we must all admit, however that necessity may be deplored. And while we may spend a sigh of regret over the disappointments of the past, and linger in memory around the things that were, we gather fresh hopes from the present, and find in our new Constitution a firmer foundation for that faith which we have hitherto had in the capacity of man to work out a high destiny under the genial influence of Republican institutions.

Prominent among the evils of the old Government, felt and acknowledged by all, was the mode of electing the President, the tenure of his office, and his reeligibility. The chief officer of the nation had come to be the appointee of a mere self-constituted and irresponsible Convention, and the measures of Government had received direction in advance, not so much from the wisdom and for the good of the people as for the triumph of party. As a consequence, each four years heralded the advent of a politician, sometimes thrown upon the surface by accidental causes and reflecting the latest heretical dogma of a section, rather than addressing himself to the good of the whole country. The Executive of the United States had come to be too dependent upon the party that elected him, and too independent of the wishes and interests of the country at large. The framers of the Constitution of the United States did not intend that the Executive should be the direct representative of the democratic principle, but they interposed between the elector and the elected a feeble barrier which proved a mere form without substance. Each election for Chief Magistrate inaugurated doctrines which were the mere watchwords of party, dictated to the people by self-constituted power, and caught up as the rallying cry of a campaign and carried into elections for the State and Federal offices, until the different branches of Government became more or less demoralized until appointees to office degenerated into mere partisans, and the halls of Congress, from being places for statesmen, were fast becoming arenas of strife. The system of platforms and caucus nominations was fast changing the Government from its representative character to one much worse than that of a pure democracy,—to a mere oligarchy, and that not of intelligence and virtue, but of low ambition. All was coming to be done in the name of the people—nothing by them, save to follow in the train of self-appointed dictators.

I regret to say that the chief defect of the Constitution of the Confederate States is, in my opinion, the retention of the old mode of electing the President. The task of reformation would, however, have been nice and difficult, and I doubt if you can, by interposing machinery of any kind between the elector and the elected, prevent the candidate from standing directly before and being in fact chosen immediately by the people, so long as they retain the right to vote for the office; a right which cannot in our Government be elsewhere lodged without materially altering its form and essence. While, then, the evil exists, I am inclined to think it may be one inherent in institutions whose corner stone rests on the popular will; and to hope that the change in the tenure of office, the deprivation of its patronage, the ineligibility of the incumbent and the additional obligations imposed on the Executive in regard to the public expenditures will greatly mitigate, if not remove, the ills with which the United States have been and are so sorely afflicted from Presidential elections. Should, however, experience prove that the present mode of election ought to be abandoned, a greater facility is afforded for its attainment by allowing three States to call a convention of all to consider proposed amendments to the fundamental law, which, if assented to by a majority of this body, shall be effectual, on being ratified by two-thirds of the States through their several Legislatures or Conventions, as the one or the other mode of final action shall be determined by the general body.

The restrictions thrown around amendments to the organic law by the Constitution of the United States proved to be a practical negation of the power to alter the instrument. Discontent, however loud or well founded, was sure to receive no heed in advance from two-thirds of both Houses of Congress, or from two-thirds of the Legislatures of the several States and, without a concurrence of such, no body could be assembled even to consider the complaints of members of the Union. Hence, restlessness when once created, could not be allayed, and a wound once inflicted on the body of a State never healed, but festered into a chronic and incurable complaint. The substituted provision imparts a wholesome flexibility to our Constitution and, at the same time, assures us against an assembling of the States for light or transient causes, or hopeless purposes, and the consultative body, when convened, will be confined to action on propositions put forth by three States.

Robert H. Smith [205

Among other felicitous provisions of the permanent Constitution may be mentioned that requiring the electors in each State to be citizens of the Confederate States and prohibiting any person of foreign birth, not a citizen of the Confederate States, from voting for any office, civil or political, State or Federal. As the right of voting was not correlative to or dependent upon that of citizenship, under the government of the United States, and as the institutions we were about to establish were for our own citizens, it was wisely determined that none but such should exercise the highest political right ever given to a people. Nor is there in the provision any of the spirit of hostility to or proscription of foreigners; for Congress is empowered to pass uniform laws of naturalization, and the simple rule, above indicated, is, that whatever probation is necessary to fit a man for the rank of citizen is essential to his wisely exercising *the high privilege of voter*. Wishing to see no proscription of any, but desiring that our land may remain the asylum of all freemen, yet I hope and believe that Congress while giving facility to naturalization, will place such safeguards around its attainment, that it will be felt to be a high boon to be admitted to participation in the control of this Republic. It may be worthy of remark in this connection that the Constitution of the United States confers on Congress the power "to establish an uniform *rule* of naturalization" and "uniform *laws* on the subject of bankruptcies" and, it has been insisted, with much plausibility, derived from history and from the language used, that the naturalization clause was designed only to give the Congress of the United States power to prescribe an uniform rule, to be observed by *each State* in making citizens, and not power to make citizens of the Federal Government. From this proposition has been drawn the deduction that there are no citizens of the United States, but that the people are citizens of the several States owing allegiance to the United States only through the several States. The convention of the Confederate States, after mature deliberation, adopted the judicial decisions and the practice of Congress on the question, and hence changed the expression—"*rule*" to "*laws* of naturalization." It will also be observed that the power to pass laws on the subject of bankruptcies finds the important qualification that "no law of Congress shall discharge any debt contracted before the passage of the same."

A new policy is to be inaugurated in regard to postal affairs; for the permanent Constitution declares that the expenses of the postoffice department, shall after the 1st day of March, 1863, be paid out of its own revenues. Without entering upon the mooted question whether the correspondent should pay for the transmission of his own letters or whether cheap postage should be purchased at the expense of the whole people, the clause in question recommends itself to me for the secondary benefits it will bring; for it is manifest that the much abused franking privilege is thus cut up and that our mails will not be loaded with the carriage, nor our treasury burdened with the printing of political trash, tending more to mislead than to enlighten the public mind. I am pleased to say that our postal act is in conformity with these views.

The question of negro slavery has been the apple of discord in the government of the United States since its foundation. The strife has now and then lulled, but has not ceased. All observing men must have felt, for at least ten years, that this fanatical agitation was the death knell of the Union. A triumphant party, that repudiated the constitution and set up a law higher even than that of the Bible, came into power on a single idea — hostility to our people and our rights. We have long borne with the evil and endured reproach, until our national character has been greatly injured, and our enemies have read, in our forbearance, a want of courage to defend our rights. The scales have at last fallen from their eyes, and they begin to survey with surprise and regret the deed they have done. But the die is irrevocably cast. *Henceforth and forever* we are separate nations. The Confederate States are a nation; to be maintained in peace if it may be, but to be maintained. . . .[4]

The right of transit and sojourn with our slaves in any State of the Confederacy is secured, and slaves escaping or lawfully carried from one State or Territory to another, shall not be discharged from service or labor by any law or regulation therein, but shall be delivered up on claim of the party to whom they belong; and the power to acquire new territory and legislate for the inhabitants thereof, is subject to the qualification that, "the institution of negro slavery, as it now exists in the Confederate States, shall be recognized and protected by Congress and by the territorial government; and the inhabitants of the several Confederate States and Territories shall have the right to take to such Territory any slave lawfully held by them in any of the States or Territories of the Confederate States." Thus, by language too plain to be misunderstood, is the question of our right in the Territories settled — and upon the principle that what is acquired from the common means of the whole is held in trust equally for each and every part, and that property under the Constitution must remain such under the Acts of Congress.

So much for this question of strife; but there was another point of view

4. Smith digressed here to mention that slavery was an ancient institution of labor.

from which our institution was to be regarded and treated; one solely concerning ourselves. I mean, of course, the African slave trade.

Had we been sitting as Legislators for Dahomey, the richest boon we could have conferred upon its savage people would have been to send them into American bondage; but called on to act as Legislators of the Confederate States, the question, required, in my opinion, a different solution. I cannot now pursue the argument at any length; but whether regarded as an economical question, or one of mere political policy, or looked at in the light of duty to our own civilized negroes, the propriety of writing in the Constitution a prohibition against the trade, is to my mind clear. That it was demanded by the instructions of the Convention of Alabama we know from its ordinances, and that it was required by public opinion I am fully satisfied. It is not strange that ardent minds, aroused by libellous assaults upon our institution, should, now and then, be driven so far into the extreme of opposition as to desire the re-opening of the trade; but the charge that any considerable portion of our people entertained such views is but one of the many unfounded imputations of our enemies; and now that the public mind is left to think of the subject, free from irritation, I believe there will shortly be entire unanimity upon it.

Slavery as it now exists in North America, is not that of seventy years ago. The latter was the slavery of the African trade, throwing among us the most bestial and untutored savages. At this our fathers revolted, and hence, admitted the evil of slavery itself; while we rightly justify and defend it, because that of today is a civilized and christianized domestic institution. The wild savage from Africa was almost a mere beast; his American descendant is a civilized appendage to the family relation. Therefore it is, that we have rightly come to defend slavery, and to contrast the condition of our laborers favorably with that of the operative classes in other parts of the world. If it be said that it was founded in wrong, and therefore cannot be right, the ready answer to England and to New England is (the argument being admitted for convenience) that the money their people obtained from the sale of African negroes to our forefathers was obtained by wrong, and it and its proceeds should be given up; that the tenures to estates in England are held under the title of plunder from an invaded and overrun people, and that New England holds its lands by but a little better origin; that most, if not all of the rights of modern civilization have sprung from wrongs protected by a far shorter statute of limitation than the slave trade, which is coeval with history.

Let the negro philanthropist come to the confessional and make restoration for all the rights which he holds from a wrong, and we will then listen to him; but till then let him be silent and abashed.

As an economical question the fact is before us that about four hundred thousand Africans have been imported into the United States. From these have sprung about four millions of improved, civilized, hardy and happy laborers.

Cuba, on the other hand, has relied upon Africa for recruits, and a fresh supply is constantly necessary to keep up the population of her slaves.

We have dissolved the late Union chiefly because of the negro quarrel. Now, is there any man who wishes to reproduce that strife among ourselves? and yet does not he, who wished the slave trade left for the action of Congress, see that he proposed to open a Pandora's box among us and to cause our political arena again to resound with this discussion. Had we left the question unsettled, we should, in my opinion, have sown broadcast the seeds of discord and death in our Constitution. I congratulate the country that the strife has been put to rest forever, and that American slavery is to stand before the world as it is, and on its own merits.

We have now placed our domestic institution, and secured its rights unmistakably, in the Constitution; we have sought by no euphony to hide its name — we have called our negroes "slaves," and we have recognized and protected them as persons and our rights to them as property. We have further declared that "Congress shall also have power to prohibit the introduction of slaves from any State not a member of, or Territory not belonging to, this Confederacy."

I trust it may not be necessary to exercise this power, because I hope to see the Southern States of the United States joined in Government with us; but the power was essential, and, as a legislator, I shall he ready to exercise it to absolute prohibition whenever I shall be driven to adopt the conclusion that these States have chosen to remain a fringe upon the skirts of New England abolition. I shall then think the day has come to force them to keep their blacks or to seek other outlets for them than this Confederacy.[5]

"Other States may be admitted into this Confederacy by a vote of two-thirds of the whole House of Representatives, and two-thirds of the Senate, the Senate voting by States."

This provision secures us as amply against the admission of undesirable

5. For Upper South reaction to the issue of the sale of slaves to the Lower South see William W. Freehling, "The Editorial Revolution, Virginia, and the Coming of the Civil War: A Review Essay," *Civil War History* 16 (1970): 64-72.

associates as language can; for the Constitution itself may be amended by two-thirds of the States, and three States can call a Convention to consider proposed alterations. It is therefore morally certain that whenever any feature of it becomes obnoxious to two-thirds of the States, it will and ought to be altered or abolished.

But I justify the Catholicism of the above provision on higher ground, and throwing aside the feelings which the irritation of the moment create, and looking to the future with full confidence that our domestic policy will justify itself and long outlive the puny assaults of maddened fanaticism, led on by ambitious politicians, I earnestly hope that not only will the kindred States join us, but abide in confidence that some of the great Northwestern States, watered by the Mississippi, will be drawn by the strong current of that mighty river and by the laws of trade, to swell the number and power of this Confederation and that we shall receive them on such terms of their organic law as we ourselves may prescribe; and in doing so, grasp the power of empire on this continent and announce to the startled North that it has reached its western limit, and must spread, if spread it can, towards the frozen sea. If in adopting these views I may seem to have listened to the whispers of fancy, I beg to call your attention to the prosaic fact that sentiment in nations never long rules master of interest. Who thinks that our late sister Southern States, or even Indiana and Illinois, will pay millions per year as a tribute for joining in hozannas to the Union. As sure as "blood is thicker than water"—as sure as Virginia is the mother of States— as sure as she is the parent of the doctrines of 1798 and 1799; and as sure as North Carolina's young men have become Alabama's sons, so sure will the Southern States of the United States blend their destiny with ours. And as sure as the Mississippi flows towards the Gulf, and bears on its bosom the great commerce of the West—and as sure as we are consumers of Western products and our tariff will be lower than that of the United States, so sure will the trouble be, not to have the West with us, but to keep it from us. The only escape from this is by their Government's adopting our system of low duties, or by New York's cutting loose from New England and spreading its gates of commerce wide to free trade.

Fellow-citizens, I have thus gone briefly through the material amendments we have made upon the Constitution of the United States, except that I have not noticed the few, and not vital changes in the judiciary system. Suffice it to say, to an unprofessional audience, that, save the withholding from the Federal Courts jurisdiction of suits between citizens of different States of the Confederacy, the judicial power of this Government is the same as that of the United States, and that the Congress have enacted a judiciary act chiefly modelled on that of the old Government. One important and wholesome provision in regard to the judiciary I ought to mention. It is that "any judicial or other federal officer, resident and acting solely within the limits of any State, may be impeached by a vote of two-thirds of both branches of the Legislature thereof."

The Senate of the Confederate States have the sole power to try such and all other impeachments. The provision noticed applies only to the Federal officer, acting solely within the limits of a State, whose conduct could not, therefore, be expected to fall under the observation of the nation at large. The entire freedom of the inferior judiciary of the United States from State influence, and virtually from that of the general government, served to render the provision necessary. It is hardly possible that it will be perverted to injustice, or can be abused to the serious detriment of the officer, for the State authority goes no farther than impeaching. It does not extend to trying the officer. It is but the inquest of the grand jury which is given to the State.

Georgia and Louisiana have responded to Alabama in adopting the Constitution of the Confederate States, and, while we write, the joyful news comes dancing over the wires that Texas and Mississippi have accepted and thus, by the assent of the required number, formed a permanent federal body. Soon will South Carolina complete the circle of the stars, and then the seceded States will form one united sisterhood.

The new charter of our rights has been spread before the world, and not only has censure been struck dumb, but the conservative press of the North is swelling a chorus to the loud anthems of our people.

We have organized the departments of Government, and, with one voice, have called to the head of it a statesman and soldier renowned alike in peace and war—in the councils of the nation and on the field of battle and he has summoned into his cabinet men of national renown and established capacity and honor.

We have placed, in the next highest office, him who stood second to none among his Peers in the Congress of the United States. We have raised and put into the field a national army of ten thousand men, officered by the flower of the soldiery of the old Government, and our several States have raised the best spirits of the land, who stand ready to throw themselves into the front of the battle. So rapidly and effectively have our military operations gone forward that Fort Sumter is about to be surrendered, and already are we told that, on sober second thought of the authorities at Washington,

"*Grim-visaged war hath smooth'd his wrinkled front.*"

In my opinion, we shall have no war. We shall have none because we are ready to meet and maintain the stand we have taken, and because we are right, and the soldiery of the United States know we are, and will not fight against us.

We are organizing a navy sufficient for coast defences, and shall be ready to keep our ports open; and should a blockade be attempted, Europe will see that it must be close and effectual to be regarded and when the little navy of the United States shall be persuaded to fight our people, or to attempt to blockade our ports, we will license the privateer to prey upon the unprotected commerce of the North. Our Mr. Lincoln, we are told, has at last ascertained that he has no power to collect revenues, otherwise than at the custom-houses and through the officers of custom and the courts of the country; nor power to blockade the ports, or to attempt it; and descending from his big words he has drivelled down to the puling and imbecile head of a fanatical party, and is reaping a rich harvest of abuse from his radical Republican journals while Mr. Seward is no doubt enjoying over again his day dream, by standing in imagination on the shores of the Northern Lakes and contemplating the spread of Northmen over frozen lands.

We have originated and will soon put in motion an effective postal service; have established courts of justice, and learned and honest judges have been appointed to administer the law; we have sent our diplomats to Europe with the Constitution in one hand and a low tariff in the other; carrying the news that the surrender of Fort Sumter is a "military necessity"; and the intelligence of these material facts will follow fast upon the tidings that the Morrill tariff has become the law of the United States.

Who thinks that Europe will not gladly acknowledge our advent into the family of nations? Surely none who know the charm of trade or the influence of interest.

We have made the Mississippi a free highway of commerce and have offered, and are ready to adjust and settle "between the States forming this confederacy and their late confederates of the United States, everything pertaining to the common property, common liability and common obligations of that Union, upon the principles of right, justice, equity and good faith."

Our revolution has hardly made so great a pressure on the pursuits of our people as is often experienced from derangements resulting from ordinary causes and already has trade, ever sensitive to danger, resumed its wonted confidence and thrift. Our fields have not had a furrow less plowed and our women and children have not lost the sleep of a single night from the realization of Northern predictions of troubles among our slaves. Fed, clothed, worked and treated as usual, this happy and careless people have gone to their daily labors, as willingly and contentedly as before.

With exports of about two hundred and sixty millions per annum, of that staple upon which five millions of England's people subsist, and without which the New England dweller in palaces would descend to the hut of his pilgrim fathers, who dreams that this people have not the means to uphold their Government or that it cannot raise money to meet its frugal expenses?

Our custom houses are not only springing into renewed activity, but, unless the North soon changes its policy, its own imports will flow into our cities and pay their duties into the coffers of these Confederate States. The loan now sought by our Treasury will be taken, and I trust only by our own people; taken because it is a good and safe investment, and because it is meet that we should come forward with the alacrity of the French to the support of the Government, and because in upholding it we uphold not only our political rights but our direct material interests.

We are now a nation, and with nationality will come development of commerce, of manufactures of arts. The public mind will receive a new impetus. We shall learn to make much of what we use, and to spend our money among our own people. Before, we bought and we sold, but we went from home to sell and to buy. Our simplest importations and much of our exportations were carried on by New York; our exchange went there. In short, the North reaped the profits of our labor and upon it grew rich and defiant. But the picture is reversed and henceforth the south will stand out in the full proportions of her nationality and her power.

It would be a pleasing and useful task to examine and contrast the different bases on which free institutions rest at the North and at the South, and an easy one to prove, that, while our system of labor may admit equal political rights for all freemen, society at the North rests on a foundation, which produces that conflict among voters necessarily arising between capital and the labor which furnishes only subsistence, as the life long reward of toil. But this is a fruitful theme and cannot be here discussed. Let the North ponder over and consider the question, for her social fabric rests on a volcano.

Having taken our political destinies into our own hands, let us not, in the moment of exultation, forget the duties that devolve upon us, and let us remember that, however wise and beneficent may be the working of the General Government, it is to State action we must mainly look for that advancement which shall secure high civilization; for the enactment and enforcement of laws, which shall give security to life, liberty and property;

for that intellectual and moral culture which shall enable us wisely to govern men and guide the State. Let us prize, as we ought, the broad freedom we enjoy, and to obtain which Europe has in vain been convulsed again and again with bloody revolution, and let us, in the elevation of our legislative bodies, prove to the world that Wisdom is the Goddess of Liberty.

PART III. *The Upper South*

The Border States: Their Power and Duty in the Present Disordered Condition of the Country

(Philadelphia: J. B. Lippincott & Co., 1861)

> *John Pendleton Kennedy (1793–1870) was born in Baltimore, Maryland, attended Sinclair's Academy there, graduated in the Baltimore College class of 1812, and after service in the War of 1812 began the practice of law. His active public career began in the Maryland state legislature, advanced to a term in the U.S. Congress, and concluded as secretary of the Navy in 1852. Kennedy also became an important man of letters and published the first plantation novel,* Swallow Barn *(1832), as well as* Rob of the Bowl *(1838), and a biography,* Memoirs of the Life of William Wirt *(1842). An avowed Unionist, he supported the Federal cause throughout the Civil War. Kennedy's contribution to this volume, published on December 17, 1860, attempted to reveal South Carolina as a fanatical state, hardly representative of the slave states as a whole. He claimed that the decline of slavery and the rise of urban, factory life in slave Border states indicated that they had common interests. Kennedy concluded that the "Border States have their own welfare to protect, their injuries to redress," and united they could negotiate with Northern radicals. The finest study of his fiction and public life remains Charles C. Bohner,* John Pendleton Kennedy *(Baltimore: Johns Hopkins University Press, 1961). Also see Thomas B. Alexander's, "The Civil War as Institutional Fulfillment,"* Journal of Southern History *47 (February 1981): 3–32, for his analysis of the Lower South's reception of Kennedy's pamphlet.*

Whatever may be the right of secession, it is about to become a practical fact. South Carolina has announced her purpose, as far as it is in her power, to dissolve the Union. Other States belonging to that series which has lately assumed the designation of the Cotton States—as expressive of a peculiar affinity in interest and policy—are likely to follow her example. Alabama, which is, in some sense, the offspring and pupil of Carolina, has shown herself already too eager to precipitate herself into revolution to leave us any hope that she will hesitate to array herself on the side of her teacher. Perhaps we may still find some encouragement to a better augury, in the good sense and prudence of Georgia and the other States which have not been wholly possessed and fevered by that extraordinary contagion of frenzy which Carolina has spread through the lowlands of the South. But I confess my fears. The signs are against it. The chances are—for this event is not under the control of the sober judgment and wise estimate by which all matters of State should be directed—the chances are that passion will rule the hour, and that the revolution will move onward, swayed by the same rash impulses as those in which it originated.

We of the Border States, therefore, cannot too soon take counsel together, touching our own interest and duty in the new condition of affairs which is about to be forced upon us. The question that now concerns us is—What position are we to assume in the beginning of the strife; where are we to place ourselves at the end of it?

Is it not very obvious that Virginia, Kentucky, Tennessee, Missouri, North Carolina, and Maryland cannot, with any respect for their own dignity, with any regard for their own welfare, or with any security for their own peace, suffer themselves to be dragged into that track of revolution and civil war, of wild experiment and visionary project into which Carolina is endeavoring to force them? These States are quite able to determine for themselves what griefs they suffer and what redress they require: they want no officious counselor nor patronizing friend to tell them what it becomes them to do, either for the maintenance of their own honor or the promotion of their own advantage; they can hear with quiet scorn the taunt that they "have placed the Union above the rights and institutions of the South"—and hold at what it deserves the offensive rebuke "that no Southern State intent on vindicating her rights and preserving her institutions would go into conference with them."[1]

Every substantial hope of a successful issue out of the afflictions of the country, produced equally by the wickedness of Northern fanaticism, and the intemperate zeal of secession, depends upon the calm and earnest wisdom of the Border States. That they will be true to the duties of the crisis, no one who had studied their character can for a moment doubt.

However the lowland States may now slight their counsels and disparage their patriotism, it is a most weighty and significant truth, for the consideration of the leaders of the projected revolution, that the Border States are at this time the most authentic representatives of the conservative power of the Union. Their various and equal relations to the North, the South, and the West, their social organization for the support of every interest connected with good government and permanent peace, their internal strength, and above all, their healthful tone of opinion toward the

1. See the Charleston *Mercury*, November 19, 1860.

preservation of constitutional right and resistance against wrong, point them out as the safest and best arbiters in the present difficulties of the country. Whatever there is of real vigor in the slaveholding communities, exists in *them* and is derived in greatest degree, by others, from *their* sympathy and alliance. Without them, we may affirm, that no confederacy of Slave States, at all worthy of respect and consideration as an independent power, can possibly be formed.

The attempt, whenever made, will speedily prove itself to be a most unhappy failure.

The Border States have a better right to claim a hearing, just now, than any other member of the Union. Indeed, until *they* have spoken, it would almost seem to savor of an unbecoming officiousness on the part of any other State to put itself in the van to raise an outcry of wrong or to dictate the measure of remedy.

While these States have always manifested a just and becoming sensibility to their rights, connected with the employment of slave labor, and have shared in the common indignation of the South against the malignant hostility of certain sections of the Northern people; while they have been the chief and almost only sufferers from the inroads of organized abolitionists, who have stealthily abstracted their slaves in numbers whose value may be reckoned at little less than a million of dollars a year; while, indeed, it may be said, that these States are the only portions of the slaveholding region which have any direct, immediate or definite interest, worthy of special consideration, in the vexed questions touching the present or the future of slavery in the United States—that is to say, in the question of emigration to the territories, the rendition of fugitives, and the organization of new States—they have, nevertheless, shown themselves in all contingencies, the confident and considerate assertors of their rights in the mode ordained by the Constitution, and at all times the determined friends of the union. They have never yet felt an aggression which they did not believe more effectively to be repelled by the due exercise of the power of the government, than by retreat before the aggressor and resort to a covert revolution that seeks to legalize its action by taking the name of secession.

They certainly cannot be expected now, with the painful conviction which passing events are creating in their minds—that the Union itself is the chief grievance which stirs the hostility of those who are most active in raising a banner of revolt, and that the assaults upon the property of slaveholders, of which they, the Border States, have so much cause to complain, are but the pretext to cover a concealed design of portentous mischief— they cannot be expected now, with such a conviction, to renounce the wisdom of their accustomed trust in the law, and allow themselves to be persuaded or beguiled into a desertion at once of the Constitution which they have always respected, or of the Union which they have always revered. Their course is too plainly marked out to them by the incidents of the day to admit of any such fatal aberration as that. They are not blind to the fact that the present crisis has been forced upon the country with a haste that allowed no halt, chiefly because its contrivers feared the sound of that voice from the Border States, which they knew would speak peace to the troubled waves in strife, and would reach the heart of hosts of loyal citizens in the very bosom of the commotion,—citizens, alas! now bereft of their loyalty by the force of the tempest of revolution that has swept over them.

If thus Carolina and her comrades are lost—all is not lost. There is space for arbitrament still left which may at least secure an opportunity for mediation, and I would hope an eventual settlement that may, perhaps, include even those who are at present the most resolute in their recusancy. Carolina now repeats defiantly that all chance of her return is gone forever. I would fain believe that affairs may be conducted into such a channel as to awaken in her a better view of her own future.

It is very important that the country should consider the true character of the danger that threatens it. The public mind is sadly at fault upon this point. There has been a singular concurrence of accident and design to lead even sensible and observant men off from the perception of the real causes of this disturbance; and a not less singular exhibition of practiced skill in the address with which the popular masses in the region of the commotion have been enlisted in an enterprise of the scope and consequences of which they had neither the leisure to examine nor the temper to comprehend.

The public for the most part believe that the impending revolution grows out of the organization of the Republican party, and that the recent election presented the culminating point at which that organization could no longer be endured with safety to the Southern States.

Unfortunate as that election is, not only in its results, but in all the stages of its progress from the day of the Chicago Convention down to that of its consummation—unfortunate for the tranquility of the country, and for the predominance it has given to certain men and certain political sects—it is not less unfortunate for the opportunity it has afforded to the accomplishment of designs long nourished, which have been held in suspense only to await a juncture favorable to their success.

The graver and more thoughtful portions of the community have recognized with no little pain, the steady growth in some sections of the South, for many years past, of a disposition in the leaders of Southern opinion to undervalue both the strength and the beneficence of the Union. It belongs to the school of doctrine of which South Carolina is the head, to imbue the people with the idea that the State Sovereignty has the first claim to the allegiance of the citizen, and that no more is due to the National Sovereignty than may be found not incompatible with this superior duty; that to support the State, right or wrong, in whatever demand it may make in conflict with the Federal authority, is the natural and most proper exhibition of a becoming State pride.

This school has also been the source of certain theories touching the structure and aims of our government, which, although founded, as we conceive, on mistaken views both of the facts of its history and of the necessary conditions upon which alone any government of a population so extensive as ours is practicable, could not but lead in time to angry dissension and inveterate sectional prejudice.

Conspicuous among these theories are two which have taken a deep hold upon the Southern mind. To their influence we may trace no small amount of the discontent which has weakened the attachment of some of the Southern States to the Union; and which has also led to the large acceptance they have given to the efficacy and lawfulness of that extreme measure which Carolina now proposes as the proper remedy for the evils which threaten her in common with all other slaveholding States.

The first of these theories asserts that the Federal Government was constructed on the basis of an equilibrium of power between the Free and Slave States, which equilibrium was designed to be forever preserved in all the vicissitudes of the future. The failure to preserve it is consequently regarded as a violation of a fundamental compromise.

The second is that which affirms all import duties to be an exclusive tax upon the Planting States, by virtue of which they are burdened with the charge of the entire support of Government.

I might add to these, that other theory from the same school, and equally questionable, which conceives the ever-present and effective remedy for all real or fancied griefs to exist in the doctrine of a lawful right of secession.

Without stopping to debate the soundness of these several tenets, I refer to them as presenting the real germs of the discontent which has been smouldering at the heart of Carolina for years, and as suggesting the true explanation of that phenomenon which puzzles the whole nation at this day, the activity, namely, and apparent supererogatory zeal with which Carolina has first, and before all her sister States of the South, flung herself into the arena to vindicate them by revolution and destruction of the Union.

These teachings have been long silently undermining her attachment to the Federal Government, and have at last wholly obliterated in her that sentiment of reverence for the Union which our forefathers inculcated, with a religious earnestness, as the foundation of American Nationality.

It is a fact of common observation that the present generation of public men in Carolina have been educated in ominous familiarity with the thought of disunion. It has been the toy of their childhood, the weapon of their age of active life. It has gathered edge and strength in a long and petulant quarrel with the National Government. It has, at last, taken visible shape in the instant, defiant act of secession.

Carolina frankly avows the Union to be an obstruction to her prosperity. That is not the sentiment alone of to-day. It has, for years past, been her earnest conviction that the Federal Government, administered on the principles most accordant with the wishes of a large number of the States, is not compatible with her welfare. She, therefore, thinks she has right to retire from the compact and assume the position of an independent nation.

She, moreover, thinks that it is altogether consistent with her duty to her sister States with whom she has had no ground of quarrel, to propagate her own discontent among such of them as she may deem useful to her project, and by persuasion, solicitation, and convention, to lure them out of the Union into alliance with herself.

The short compend of these claims is expressed in the postulate—a right, at her pleasure, to dissolve the Union.

Every one has heard and read how pertinaciously she has argued this right in every forum open to her service.

Persuading herself that she has this right, to be used whenever she thinks proper, she deduces from it, quite logically, the right to meditate over every problem of possible contingencies which might, in the evolution of events, be turned to her advantage. As for instance, whether she would not thrive better if certain prohibitions of the Constitution were removed? Would it be to her benefit to make Charleston a free port?—to make a new Confederacy within the territory of the Union?—to open and reestablish the African slave-trade?—a hundred such questions which she may deem fit to consider and determine while she remains a member of the Confederacy— and the objects of which, if she cannot accomplish them in the Union, she thinks it unreasonable to be denied the privilege of accomplishing by secession from the Union.

I would not willingly misrepresent Carolina—much less speak in derogation of her really high and admirable qualities of character. There is no community of the same size, I believe, in the world that has produced a larger share of distinguished men. There is no society in the United States more worthy of esteem for its refinement, its just and honorable sentiment, and its genial virtues.

The men of Carolina are distinguished by the best qualities of attractive manhood. They are brave, intelligent and frank. They speak what they think, and they mean what they say. They are the last people in this Union we should desire to part with—notwithstanding their strange insulation of opinion, their exclusive philosophies, and, what they must pardon us for thinking, their political sophisms!

In these sundry meditations of theirs, they have long since struck upon one or more of the conclusions which I have hinted above—the opinion, namely, that they would do better in a Southern Confederacy than in the Union made by their forefathers. And having come to that conclusion, they have wrought themselves to the sober—or rather, let me say, the vehement conclusion that they are the most oppressed people of Christendom. . . .[2]

Extravagant as this declamation may appear to a calm reader, capable of estimating, at their true value, the happy certainties that belong to the present and the future of a State in the American Union, and the dreadful uncertainties that impend over separation, even in its most hopeful reckoning, it nevertheless expresses the views and expectations of that portion, at least, of the community in which it is uttered, who have been allowed "to instruct the Southern mind and fire the Southern heart" for the momentous struggle which is now inaugurated in South Carolina. In that aspect it is worthy of special notice at this time.

It demonstrates what I have already intimated, that the secession movement is not the suddenly inspired project of the present day; that it does not grow out of the events of the recent canvass and election, nor even primarily out of that agitation of slavery, which constitutes the flagrant cause of disturbance in the Border States.

If we analyze this paper we shall see that the aggressions of the Northern States upon the peaceful employment of Southern labor, is scarcely referred to at all: that the real and predominant grievance complained of is found in the old question of taxation. The support of the government by imports, regulated to the revenue standard, is presented as an abuse tenfold

2. Kennedy discussed and quoted from John Townsend, the Charleston radical and leader of the abortive secession movement of 1848–52 who wrote "South Carolina, Her Present Attitude and Future Action," in *The Southern Quarterly Review* 4 (October 1851): 273–98.

more oppressive than all the tyranny that led to the revolution of seventy-six. The State of South Carolina and her few uncomplaining sisters are represented as groaning under the intolerable burden of paying the *whole revenue* of the Federal Government and getting nothing in return. This is a repetition of the grief of 1832, when the country was mystified with that most inscrutable of all revelations, "the forty bale theory"—and which so far prevailed in the philosophy of the National Councils, as finally to secure the triumph of what is claimed to be the free trade adjustment of 1846,— which adjustment, it seems now, is no more satisfactory than the protective system it displaced.[3]

It is also worthy of note, that the rabid abolitionism of England, of which so much has been said of late in the way of denunciation, and which, in fact, is quite as mischievous to Southern peace as the fanaticism it encourages in New England, is regarded not only as harmless, but even as not standing in the way of a most cordial alliance with Great Britain. The reviewer actually apologizes for this little indiscretion in the expected ally, and treats it with a temper of good sense which might be commendably adopted in regard to the same transgression at home—"can they interfere with our institutions? No. They can but make us angry."

We have a further exposition of the policy of disunion, in the imagination of a Southern Confederacy composed of Jamaica, and other British West India Islands, and Demerara—or, I suppose, the reviewer meant British Guiana on the South American continent—to which may now be added, as a more recent development of the grandeur of the contemplated republic, the conception of similar accretions embracing Cuba, San Domingo, Mexico, and perhaps Central America. This Confederacy, if we mistake not the significance of many ill-suppressed hints from indiscreet friends, is to be rendered still more magnificent and bountiful of blessings, still more attractive to the contemplation of mankind by the aid of a productive commerce in African slaves, which seems to be not the least winning feature in the project.

These are the fervid dreams of the contrivers of disunion. For such fantasies as these, our great Republic, the matured product of so much thought and suffering, is to be rent asunder, just at the era when we fondly imagined it to have risen to that height in the estimation of mankind which gave it an assured position among the proudest empires of history. For such im-

3. See the first pamphlet in this volume for information on the Nullification controversy.

practicable conceits as these, it is to be resolved into discordant fragments whose perpetual jars may illustrate the saddest moral of blighted hopes the world has ever known!

We might bear this melancholy lot with submissive patience, as the chastisement of offended Heaven, if we could believe there was any cause to give it the semblance of an unavoidable affliction: if, indeed, it did not spring from the merest wantonness of a temper engendered by too much prosperity—or ingratitude to God for blessings too profusely bestowed to be valued.

There is something in the time and in the pretext chosen for this great work of mischief that peculiarly provokes remark. The pretext is the general agitation of the Southern mind by the Northern triumph over slavery. What quarrel there is that grows out of this, is, as we have affirmed, the just and proper quarrel of the Border States. That quarrel does not necessarily, and most probably would not, lead to a breach of the Union. Firm remonstrance and wise counsel, aided by that strong attachment to the government, which, both North and South, lives in the heart of millions of conservative men may bring a truce,—which, indeed, is already begun,— auspicious to reflection and the settlement of all these differences. It is no difficult matter in this breathing space, when considerate citizens are brought face to face with honest purpose of peace, to frame an adjustment in which future repose and sufficient pledge against the renewal of strife may be obtained.

It is just at such a time as this—in the interval when reason, judgment, and fraternal affection are beginning to infuse a benignant influence over the disturbed mind of the country—that the master-spirits of the new Confederacy rush to the verge of the gulf and drive their maddened partisans to the dreadful leap that makes recall impossible. They pursue their course without a moment's pause, neither looking back, nor taking breath; deaf to all entreaty of friends, and blind to all sights but the visions that rise in the distant prospect. There they behold their Arcadia, with its phantoms of untold wealth, its free ports, its untaxed commerce, its illimitable cotton fields, its flattering alliances, its swarms of reinforcement from the shores of Africa. To reach this promised land, the only condition of the enterprise is to press forward with fiery haste and outrun the speed of the peace-makers.

In 1851, Carolina pursued her scheme of secession as resolutely as she does at this day, and only failed through the prudence of those who refused to accompany her. Her purpose was as ripe then, her hopes as high, as now.

Yet, at that epoch there was no fear of a Republican President. There was then no question of intervention or non-intervention, no debate of equal rights in the territories, no Kansas, no John Brown. In the absence of all these, she had nothing but California and the Compromise to disturb her repose. Yet her sufferings, as she declared, were too intolerable to be borne. Let her speak for herself. It was the Union she could not endure. "Welcome as summer showers to the sun-parched earth"—(was the wail of her Quarterly of that time)—"welcome as heaven's free air to the heart-sick tenant of a dungeon, would come to us the voice of freedom, the word, the deed which would tend to burst our bonds, and in earnest faith contribute to the disruption of this proud fabric (once beautiful, but now rotten to the core) which, under the name of Union, threatens to crush us beneath its unholy power."[4]

But I leave this topic to recur to the question,—What is the proper duty of the Border States, looking to the contingencies of this unhappy strife?

Obviously they cannot, in the present circumstances, cast their lot with Carolina. They cannot adopt either her passion or her policy. They can go into no confederation of the lowland States, organized on the principles and motives which they have so much reason to fear now direct and stimulate the ambition of Carolina. Then let them say so at once.

Let them say to her and to those who may unite their fortunes with hers, that, deeply deploring a separation which they would make every just or generous sacrifice to avert,—a separation that is forced upon them by a profound conviction that it is the only expedient left open to them to guard against still greater evils—they must submit to it as the inevitable destiny of their position.

The Border States have their own welfare to protect, their own injuries to redress. They believe that both of these may be accomplished within the Union. They have no issue with any section of the Union, but that which springs from the hostility engendered in the minds, and manifested in the public action, of certain portions of the Free States. They have no hopes or fears which may not be encouraged or quieted by the lawful and orderly administration of the constitutional powers of the Federal Government. They regard that government as the wisest scheme that can be devised for the rule of this nation. They can never abandon it until experience shall convince them that it is no longer capable to resist its perversion by faction, or to protect the rights of every State and citizen.

4. Reference again to the Townsend article in the October 1851 issue of *Southern Quarterly Review*.

That experience they have not yet had.

They acknowledge that in the resolution of the Union into fragments, which may be the possible result of the present disturbances, a contingency may be presented to them in which they will be compelled to choose their own lot.

Their first and greatest desire is to avert that contingency and to restore peace and universal concord among the whole sisterhood of States.

Supposing these to be the sentiments of the Border States, which, from every authentic indication, I cannot doubt, I venture to suggest for their consideration, —

The expediency, as a preliminary measure, of holding, at an early day, an informal Conference to be conducted by one or more distinguished citizens from each of the border States, and from such of the other southern States as may be opposed to secession in the present state of affairs — these to be selected by the Executive of each State — for the purpose of determining on a course of joint action to be recommended to the adoption of the whole number.

To such a conference I would submit the following propositions: —

1. The propriety of making an earnest appeal to the seceding States to retrace their steps and await the result of the measures proposed for the establishment of general harmony: with a declaration that if this appeal be unsuccessful, they, the Border States, will be compelled to decline entering into a Southern Confederacy as now proposed by South Carolina and her allies in secession.

2. That if the secession of South Carolina be followed by that of Alabama or any other State, and a serious breach of the Union be thus established, it will then be incumbent on the Border States and the other Southern States concurring with them, to take measures for their own security, by demanding from the free States a revisal of all topics of complaint between them and the Slave States, and the adoption of such stipulations on both sides as shall be satisfactory to each for the determination and protection of Southern rights, and for the restoration of harmony.

These stipulations would, of course, become the subject of a negotiation with the Free States: a negotiation which should be conducted in a frank and conciliatory spirit, through such agencies as the parties may arrange.

I think it would be just to both parties, and would be likely to meet the general approval of the country, to direct these stipulations to the following points: —

The re-establishment of the Missouri line and its extension to the

Pacific, as an easy, practicable mode of settling the territorial question on a basis with which the people are familiar.

The adjustment of the question of the rendition of fugitive slaves:

By such modifications of the provisions of the act of Congress on that subject, as shall remove every reasonable objection to it, compatible with its efficient adaptation to its purpose: and by an agreement on the part of the Free States, to execute it in good faith, and to repeal all laws heretofore passed with a view to its obstruction:

This, coupled with an engagement, in case any State should find itself unable, by reason of the repugnance of the people to the execution of the law, to deliver up the fugitive—then, to be allowed and required, by way of alternative, to make a just indemnity to the owner, under such regulations as may be devised.

The settlement of the question in regard to the admission of New States on the foundation at present adopted, of leaving each territory to form a State Constitution in accordance with its own wishes.

Finally, a pledge to be given by the free States to exert their influence, as far as possible, to discourage discussions of slavery in a tone offensive to the interests of the slaveholding States; and to endeavor to procure legislative enactments against preparations for assault on the peace of these States, either by individuals or organized bodies.

If there be any of the provisions proposed in these stipulations which may require an amendment of the Constitution—an agreement should be made to propose and support it.

3. If these stipulations can be obtained—then the Border States and concurring States of the South, which have not seceded, shall retain their present position in the Union.

But in the adverse event of these stipulations, or satisfactory equivalents for them, being refused, the Border States and their allies of the South who may be disposed to act with them, will be forced to consider the Union impracticable, and to organize a separate Confederacy of the Border States, with the association of such of the Southern and Free States as may be willing to accede to the proposed conditions.

4. When this programme of action, or such substitute for is as the Conference may devise, shall be adopted, it should be submitted, through the respective Executives of the States represented in the Conference, to the people of each, to be acted upon in a General Convention of those States, called by the direction and appointment of their several Legislatures.

5. That pending the whole course of this proceeding, the Border states and those concurring with them shall engage to prevent, by all the means

in their power, any attempt on the part of the Federal Government or of any State or States to coerce the seceding States by armed force into submission.

It may be a proper subject for such a Conference, as I have proposed, to consider whether it would not be useful, in any event—even in that of the single secession of South Carolina, before any other State shall have followed her—to offer the Border States as mediators in the present unhappy differences, and to endeavor to procure, for the benefit of all, the stipulations I have described above, or some other pacific arrangement of the same character and object.

If the Border States can be brought into combination in the manner pointed out by those propositions, it is easy to perceive that they must immediately become the masters of the position from which the whole national controversy is most likely to be controlled. They will not only hold the general peace in their hands, by their authority to persuade an abstinence from all attempts at coercion; but they will also be regarded and respected on all sides, as the natural and appropriate medium through which the settlement of all differences is eventually to be obtained.

By taking the ground, at the earliest moment, that they cannot unite in the scheme of the Southern Confederacy, and that, if separation should, at last, after all efforts to avert it, be imposed upon them by an inexorable necessity from which there is no escape, they will be compelled to construct a Confederacy of their own, in which they may be able to associate with themselves, perhaps, the whole body of the Middle and Western States. If they, the Border States, shall firmly and dispassionately take this ground, such a determination cannot but suggest to the seceding States the gravest motive to pause in their meditated career, and to await an opportunity for further conference and debate. It will then be for these States to inquire with more deliberation than they have yet given to the subject, what will be the strength and capacity for self-support of a Confederacy unsustained by the power and resource of such communities as those which decline the alliance. When that question comes to be seriously discussed by them it will present many new and momentous considerations which have not yet been canvassed.

The popular notion of a united South is but an impracticable fancy. A united South is a more uncertain problem than even the support of the present Union under the difficulties that now surround it.

I think it will appear to any careful explorer of the subject, that if the fifteen States south of Mason and Dixon's line were to enter into a confederacy among themselves, such an organization would speedily prove itself to be more productive of dissension than the present union has been during the last twenty years.

The policy prefigured by the seceding States is in many points wholly repugnant to the views and interests of the Border States.

These latter could never be reconciled to be made accomplices in the disgrace and guilt of a restoration of the slave-trade, they would never undertake to face the indignation of Christendom which would arise upon its revival—much less would they agree to involve themselves in the expense and burden of the wars that it would inevitably provoke.

The Border States would scarcely less endure the commercial system, so often and conspicuously insisted on by Carolina and her comrades in secession, by which free ports are demanded and the consequent necessity of a public revenue resting upon direct taxation.

They could not be persuaded into that expansive policy of annexation and conquest which has dazzled the imagination of the South and tormented the ambition of its people, in persistent forays upon neighboring States and perpetual schemes of acquisition.

The Border States exhibit within their area a representation of almost every interest and pursuit in the Union. They are thriving and vigorous communities, with most prolific resources for every species of industry. Their agriculture furnishes an abundant supply of the sustenance of life, with a large surplus for external commerce. The region occupied by these States embraces also a wide area adapted to the culture of hemp and flax, tobacco and cotton. It abounds in mineral wealth, in water power, in pasturage, in cattle, sheep, horses,—in all the elements of the most diversified manufacturing industry. Its healthful climate, its robust population, and its cheap means of livelihood are singularly favorable to the growth and prosperity of the mechanic arts, the multiplication of villages, and the gradual increase of thrifty and industrious workmen in every department of handicraft—invariably the best indications of the progress of a State to wealth and power.

Beginning at the Cities of Baltimore, Richmond and Norfolk on the Atlantic, and extending over a broad domain studded with flourishing inland towns, it ends at the City of St. Louis on the Missouri, presenting throughout the series every facility for a wide and profitable commerce, already furnished with railroads, canals, and navigable rivers.

Here are all the elements necessary to the organization of the polity of a first-class power. In extent of territory, in resource, in population, it may take rank among the master States which, in any new combinations of the fragments of our once happy Union, broken by the madness of faction, may hereafter be gathered from the wreck.

In the worst event that may happen, therefore, greatly as every old-fashioned lover of the Union may deplore the necessity for such a work, here are the ready materials for the construction of a new nation able to protect the welfare of its people, secure their peaceful pursuit of happiness, and furnish a safe refuge to all who may flee to it to escape the disorders and distractions of the time.

It is a sad speculation which forces us to the computation of the resources of any section of our present Union, with a view to the exhibition of its capacity for independent existence; but when the vision of a united South is conjured up to our contemplation, as a possible or impending reality, we are compelled to face and question it.

I have therefore looked at the character of the Border States, to show how incompatible their interests are likely to prove with the policy which is deemed essential to other sections of the South. It must be apparent from even this brief examination, that communities of such different pursuits, and marked by such variant conditions, would scarcely find, in political alliance with the projected Southern Confederacy, that harmony of interests which is essential to the prosperity of both.

The four or five States now reputed to be most likely to enter into compact with Carolina may be described as chiefly representing one vast cotton field. The whole region embraced by them is, in all physical quality, if we except Georgia, thoroughly homogeneous. Its business is planting. It has no mechanic art and but few manufactures. Its rural inhabitants are divided between numerous proprietors of the soil and their slaves—the proprietors, in great degree, migratory, the slaves stationary—thus necessarily creating, in many locations, a great preponderance of slave population. Its productions are singularly valuable as one of the most indispensable wants of mankind, and readily exchangeable into money. This exchange is made through an active factorage that has built up prosperous cities and created a large commerce. So far as this commerce is concerned with the planting region, it is reduced into a simple system of transactions in the great staple of the country—a commerce without variety of resource, and too dependent upon the accidents of a single product and the vicissitudes of season, to support a costly mercantile marine, and which is therefore compelled to seek its transportation from foreign and friendly sources. Such a commerce, we must perceive, is peculiarly exposed, not only to damage, but utter overthrow by the occurrence of war. In its overthrow, the whole resource of the country is destroyed. This is the common and inevitable weakness of all merely agricultural countries.

If Louisiana, shaken from her balance by the fervor of the moment, could be persuaded to join this Confederacy, she would contribute, it is true, not only another resource in her product of sugar, but a great commercial mart of commanding importance in the trade of the world. It might nevertheless be questioned whether even so valuable an acquisition as this would, in the end, turn out to be a permanent accession of strength. The prosperity of the City of New Orleans is so essentially united with the fortunes of the West—in fact, so entirely dependent upon them—as to suggest many possibilities of collision, both on the part of the city and State, with the policy of the government to whose control they would have surrendered themselves. Indeed, with the obvious motives for hesitation, which must occur to the intelligent judgment of Louisiana, against the wisdom of entering into the proposed Confederacy, it is scarcely to be presumed that she may be seduced, even by the passionate solicitations of her present anger against Northern aggression, into a measure, in its best aspect, so doubtful; in its apparent probabilities, so rash.

She cannot slight the consideration that the adverse possession of a great seat of trade at the mouth of the Mississippi may furnish in the future, as it has done in the past, a fruitful source of quarrel between the power that holds it and the numerous commonwealths upon the banks of the river and its tributaries, which now claim its free and uninterrupted use, together with its depots, at all times and in all contingencies; that there is no form of agreement or treaty which can afford complete and invariable protection to this enjoyment; none that would probably be regarded as an adequate equivalent for the surrender of the right which has been acquired by purchase out of the common treasure, for the benefit of these claimants.

Will not these reflections suggest a pregnant inquiry whether the defence of this mart by a confederacy foreign to the claimants may not prove a charge too costly to be compensated even by the unquestionably great advantages of such a possession? Does it presignify no danger that, in the vexatious emergencies of future years, there may be provoked a new motive in Louisiana, for *secession* from a confederacy that is to be built upon a full recognition of that doctrine? In view of these possibilities and many others that experience may bring to light, may we not assume that Louisiana will prudently weigh the question of her own permanent peace and prosperity before she takes the step to which she is now invited? Will it not be equally well for the new Confederacy to deliberate upon the point whether such a possession may not be as much a source of weakness as of strength?

Looking back to the elements—with that notable exception to which I have already adverted—which are expected to compose this Confederacy; to its people and pursuits, and the peculiar character of a large portion of its population; to its deficiency in mechanic art; its defective supply of the staff of life; to the influence of its climate; to its entire destitution of the means to build and man ships, and to many other disabilities which will occur in any review of its resources, we cannot but think that this fancied New Atlantis, which has so possessed the imagination of its votaries, will, upon trial, prove itself to be the most defenseless, and, in a significant sense, the weakest of independent nations.

It may have some hope of rising above this condition by the accession of the State of Georgia. If that vigorous commonwealth, in an hour of blindness to its own happy destiny in this Union, should fall into the fatal error of joining in this alliance, it will be, as every one must admit, a constituent of real strength in the Confederacy. Georgia would then arise to the unenviable supremacy of being the only solid and trusty support of the whole fabric. She has already, under the auspices of a Union which has conferred nothing but blessings upon her, advanced beyond all her compeers of the South, to the position of a truly powerful and commanding commonwealth. Surely, before she takes this fatal step, she will meditate over the prosperity of her admirable effort in the establishment of manufactures, her multiplying towns and villages, her fertile and healthy uplands, her rapid growth in peaceful arts, and her thousand capabilities of ever-varied industry, and anxiously and coolly weigh the question, whether she should put all these in jeopardy by submitting them to the domination of such a policy as the new Confederacy will offer her. But if, in full view of these admonitions, she chooses to be led into the first movement toward this combination, may we not hope that in a calmer moment than the present she will retrace her steps, and once more place her better destiny under the guardianship of the Stars and Stripes—the only symbol worthy of her fortunes and her hopes?

Georgia has not yet left us. Let us trust to the clear judgment and earnest patriotism of her hosts of friends to the Union, and to the eloquent and manly counsel of her sons, that she will move with more deliberate pace, and in company with more temperate comrades, along the path of conciliation and trial, before she ventures to lend a hand to the demolition of the government under which she has grown to her present stature. And if that day of destruction must ever come, let her be found among the ruins, with kindred congenial to her own nature, employed in the task of gathering the fragments of our broken Union together for reconstruction and renewal of its ancient harmony.

Texas is looked to as a component of the new Confederacy. Her lot, if dissolution be a settled fact, and a general *sauve qui peut* should compel her to decide upon her whereabout, I presume, would be once more to raise her banner of the Lone Star. She is a young nation, quite able to take care of herself. She exists as a portion of the American Union by a simple resolution of Congress. A dissolution repeals that act and remits her to her original position. She becomes again a detached and independent power; and, in that event, may wisely judge it to be her true policy to accept the position and maintain it. We have yet no proof that she has so soon become weary of the Union which, but a few years gone by, she so eagerly sought, and which has, in that short interval, heaped almost fabulous treasures into her lap. On the contrary, what proof we have presents her in the attitude of a hopeful friend of peace. We pray that she may prove steadfast to the admonitions of the wise and true-hearted hero whom she has honored with the highest gifts she has had to bestow!

This is a brief survey of the materials which, in the sad event of the disruption of our Confederacy, many suppose may be moulded into a united South. It exhibits two divisions of the present slaveholding States—separate, not hostile—but divided from each other by nature and incompatible conditions, impossible to be brought into harmonious alliance under any system of political organization founded upon the basis of what are deemed the essential and peculiar interests of either.

I have endeavored to demonstrate my conviction that with whatever caution or friendly spirit of compromise they might begin the experiment of Confederation, they would infallibly lapse into antagonisms through the collision of which their association would soon be reduced to a mere political form, as impotent to hold them together as our present Union is likely to prove under the doctrines which one of the divisions I have mentioned above has already proclaimed and adopted as the indispensable condition of its alliance.

Among many topics of discussion which would arise in the course of that experiment, there is one which would certainly loom into fearful proportions as a source of constantly increasing discontent. It is exemplified in our present history, and would find even more acrimonious revival in the progress of the supposed new alliance.

The tendency of nearly all—perhaps I might say of the whole—of the

Border States, in considerable portions or sections of each, must be under any form of organization—whether in the present Union or out of it; whether pursuing their own welfare united with the whole South, or in a Confederacy of their own—toward the increase of free labor by immigration and settlement, and to a correlative gradual diminution of slave labor. That process is marked out for them in the future, as it has been in the past, by the irresistible law of their nature. It is an onward force which derives its vigor from the stimulus of interest, and is both the issue and the exponent of the prosperity of the community itself. In the grain-growing portions of these States, this process will be more rapid; but, even in the planting portions, though slower and perhaps for a time imperceptible, its influences will be felt. As population increases and the competition of labor becomes more intense, these States must expect a continuance of the same partial and progressive mastery of free over slave labor which is now visible in many local divisions of their own area, and which has been slowly and steadily converting slave into free States from the date of the Revolution down to the present time. Maryland, portions of Virginia, Kentucky, and Missouri are moving onward to the final condition—remote but certain— of free labor communities. That movement may be greatly accelerated by extrinsic forces. The enhancement of the value of slaves draws this labor from a less productive to a more productive region—from the wheat to the cotton field. The depreciation of the value has, to some extent, a similar effect. By impoverishing the owner, it compels a necessity to sell, and the purchaser is most likely to be the agent or factor of the cotton planter. In either case the gradual decrease of slavery in the farming region—I use this designation in opposition to the planting—is the constant result. The establishment of the slave-trade would not be without its effect in the same direction. It would create disgust in many against slavery itself, and thus lead to emancipation. These contingencies are entitled to consideration as causes which, in the lapse of time, may operate more or less actively upon the interests, habits, and sentiments of the Border States to produce not only a sharp diversity of views and policy, but also dissension and conflict between them and other sections of the South. They would grow to be reckoned as unfriendly to the South, or, in the current phrase of our day, "unsound" on the question of Southern institutions. They would thus be regarded with a growing dislike, and, in the end, put to the ban of extreme Southern opinion, under the odious and comprehensive appellation of abolitionists. . . . [5]

5. Kennedy was citing a letter of Thomas Jefferson to John Taylor written in

It is proper for me to say here that the propositions I have submitted as the foundation of a settlement, to be urged by the Border States, are but selections from the many suggestions which have in various forms been lately thrown before the public. I have selected these, not only because I think them altogether just, in view of the rational demands which both North and South are entitled to make upon each other, but also because they seem to have met a larger concurrence from the conservative portions of the people, on both sides, than any others that have been brought into discussion. A temperate debate of these propositions and their recommendation by the authority of a grave and influential convention of eminent citizens representing the moderate conservative opinion and the most important interests of the country—which I do not doubt greatly preponderate in both sections, and are quite able to outweigh and overmaster all the leaders and followers of the ultraisms of both—would, it strikes me, command, at once, the assent of the most authoritative mass of citizens, and gradually bring into submission, if not concurrence, the whole disturbing force which now distracts the public peace.

The advantage which the Border States hold in this controversy is very manifest. As I have said before, they are the masters of the position and may control the events of the future. It is in their power to isolate those portions of the Union which are most violent and reckless in driving the country to extremes, and thus give them occasion to perceive that they are to find no support out of the circle of their own impetuous allies. They have, also, the power to give, even to these, a strong assurance that every fair and just complaint they are entitled to make shall be redressed by satisfactory arrangements which they, the Border States, will demand, and will most assuredly procure. The North will listen to their demands and meet them in honorable conference, with a temper of conciliation which it would be hopeless to expect from a conference representing the more excited and exacting portions of the South. We have proof of this temper furnished every day in the Northern journals. The abolitionists proper, the firebrands of the North, have lost their influence and would have no share in any movement toward a settlement. The truth is, that by far the greater number of the people of the Free States are awakened to a new perception of the danger which has been produced by the violent assaults of the North upon the South, in which they themselves have more or less participated without dreaming of the bitter injuries they were inflicting upon the

---

1798 about the bickering among states and the early threats of secession as examples of ongoing divisions within the country.

public peace and integrity of the Union. They have listened to evil counselors and have been led away by the inflammatory philosophies of their own ambitious leaders. They see this now, although they have not seen it before; and in this awakening of their minds to the reality of the crisis, they are ready and willing to make every proper concession for the restoration of present tranquility and for protection against future disturbance. They are thus fortunately able and well inclined to drop, henceforth and forever, this offensive and detestable agitation of slavery, which they now perceive to be a real and dangerous grievance.

Our purpose should be to negotiate with this class of men. It can be only effectually done by the Border States. A General Convention of all the States would, inevitably, produce more bickering and confusion in the present state of affairs. Even a General Convention, as has been proposed, of all the Southern States, with a view to their own course of proceeding, would be attended with the same difficulties. It would run the risk of being converted into a theatre of angry debate upon extreme propositions, and would be as likely, as the Charleston Convention in May, to be broken up by the secession of discontented members who could not get all they asked. A Convention of the Border States would have no difficulty of this kind. They would be harmonious, just and reasonable in their views, and firm in meeting the real evils of the time, by offering and demanding a full and adequate remedy for them.

This would be their position in the first efforts toward peace and permanent security. If they succeed in obtaining a just settlement, the seceding States could not resist the necessity of acquiescing in such a settlement, and of returning to the Union. As they calmed down into a cooler mood, and brought their unclouded judgment to a consideration of the case, they would cordially approve and support the settlement, and the whole country would thus receive an incalculable benefit from the present commotion. It would be a great and happy purification of the *morale* of the country, and we should all rejoice that the crisis has been turned to such good account.

But if this service, proffered by the Border States, should unhappily fail to produce these results, in this first stage of the process of pacification, they would still occupy a ground not less important and beneficial in the second and more remote phase of the quarrel.

Supposing a disintegration of the Union, notwithstanding all efforts to prevent it, be forced upon us by the obstinacy and impracticability of parties on each side—the case would still be far from hopeless. The Border States, in that event, would form, in self-defense, a Confederacy of their own, which would serve as a center of reinforcement for the reconstruction of the Union. The attraction of interest and good brotherhood would instantly become effective to draw to this nucleus, one by one, every State in the Confederacy. A beneficent power of gravitation would work with irresistible energy in bringing back the dislocated fragments. New York, New Jersey, and Pennsylvania would be among the first to fall in. Illinois, Indiana, Ohio, perhaps all the Western States, would be unable to resist the tendency toward this center, and would come into cohesion with an utter abjuration of all those fancies and follies which have been engendered by the slavery question. And when it was seen that North and South could thus unite on a basis perfectly free from the disturbance of these old questions, the more moderate of the seceding States—Georgia especially, if she be one of them—would come to the acknowledgement that their true interests directed them to the same reunion. Last of all, the most ultra States of the secession movement would obey the same law of attraction, and, once more, after a lapse of weary trial and profitable experience, we should see the Union reconstructed by the healthful agency of the Border States.

Those who have carefully noted the progress of political opinion for more than thirty years past, and marked the tendency of its teaching, toward the adoption of certain distinctive theories of government having reference to supposed geographical interests, have been able to predict the certainty of a convulsion that, sooner or later, would present an inevitable necessity for a reconstruction, or, at least, a reconsideration and explicit determination, of the principles upon which the Union is to be preserved.

The present ferment is but the verification of this prediction.

If wisely handled, as I have shown, it may be productive of inestimable good. If allowed to solve its problem under the guidance of the fierce instincts and rash counsels of those who have first assumed its direction, it will become the source of an "Iliad of woes"—not to the present generation alone, but to many generations hereafter.

The time and the occasion, therefore, demand the most free and full examination of the causes, open and concealed, which are shaking the loyalty of the people and turning men's thoughts toward disunion.

I have endeavored in these pages to demonstrate that there are other and more secret discontents in our condition than those which grow out of the slavery question.

While we painfully perceive and feel that the action of the Northern States on that question, and, still more, the wicked fanaticism of individuals and sects in preaching hostility to the peace of the South, have kindled in the mind of the whole population of this division of the United States a profound and just indignation against this wanton spirit of aggression which, if not arrested, we have long been conscious, would surely lead to a rupture of the Union,—it is also a matter of deep concern that we should apprehend and notice the fact that there are other disturbing forces operating upon sections of the South—perhaps in some degree owing their vitality to the alienation produced by the slavery agitation, but now apart from it and looking to other subjects,—which have grown to be seriously hostile to the harmony of our united system of government. My aim has been to bring these into view, as well as the more pervading topic of discontent, in order that, in the attempt to restore peace and confidence, which is practicable through the settlement of the slavery dispute, we may not be misled by the clamor of those to whom such a settlement would be but the frustration of a cherished design. The dissatisfaction of this class of agitators must be left to the cure of time. There is no mode of treating it but to let it alone, consigning it to the good sense and right reason which it has to encounter at home.

It will, doubtless, be received as a bold assertion, when I say that the slavery question, as one for political cognizance in the United States, presents the most futile subject for legislation or administrative policy, perhaps, within the whole range of measures consigned to the notice of government.

It cannot be controverted that the whole power of the Federal government is inadequate to change the condition of a single slave within any State of the Union. Nor can any combination of party, with all the aids which the apparatus of government may afford, with all the temper of proscription and intolerance that fanatical zeal may beget, with all the concurrence of sectional State legislation, ever be able to make a successful invasion of the rights of the smallest of the Slave States. Such an attempt would meet the instant resistance not only of the whole circle of those States, but with the resistance of three-fourths of the people of the whole country. That parties and individuals may threaten irrepressible conflicts and undying hostility, is true. But, as to acting upon such threats, the Constitution renders them as powerless as children.

And in regard to slavery in the territories—although there may be ground on which the Government may claim to control it, I affirm that, as a practicable policy, no exercise of that power, in the present actual condition of the domain possessed by the nation, can either force the establishment of slavery into a territory ungenial to it, nor keep it out of one adapted to its employment. I mean, that there is no motive of interest to take slavery, as a permanent thing, to a region where it is unproductive; nor any motive, either political or philanthropic, to forbid its transfer to the region where it is essential to the interests of production. At this time we have no territory in which there is any possibility of raising the question, but if we should obtain one in a planting region, it would be settled from the population of the slaveholding States without notable opposition from any section of the Union.

The agitation of slavery, therefore, notwithstanding its engrossment of the country and the odious prominence it has assumed, is, after all, but a parade of idle and mischievous debate. It lives upon the incessant ministration of stimulants supplied by small declaimers in quest of notoriety. It is, in the present generation, a moral epidemic which has seized upon the whole districts, like St. Anthony's Dance in the fourteenth century. The fancy of getting up "a great abomination," in order to turn it to account as a topic of popular preaching, is as old as the first consecrated cobbler. Nor is it at all a new thing to set up a popular sin to be extirpated by law. Many quack politicians have been wasting their energies for years, upon the abortive attempt to legislate peaceable families into the disuse of spirituous liquors, by bringing alcohol into platforms and making parties upon it: but alcohol has gained the day and the Maine Liquor Law has become a dead letter. The world laughs at this prodigality of ineffectual zeal. May we not learn to treat with quiet scorn the more malignant but still impotent ebullitions of the sanctimonious vanity of New England?

In truth, slavery has not, in itself—I mean African slavery as now existing in the United States—the condition for any vehemently honest indignation against it; nor, on the other side, for any vehemently honest affection for it. It is simply a very appropriate and necessary agent in the interests of civilization, where it is; and would be, generally, a very wretched thing where it is not. The wrath that is stirred against it, and the patriarchal beauty that is claimed for it, are both the offspring of excited imaginations. African slavery, in this country, at least, is for the most part, a clear gain to the savage it has civilized. Whatever it may be to others, it has been a blessing to *him*. It is also clearly a blessing to Massachusetts, and to England, France, Germany. But, it is a very doubtful blessing to the master who has charged himself with the solicitude of supporting, employing, and caring for the slave; it is, at best, but a mixed and greatly diluted blessing to him. Strange, that those who enjoy the unmixed blessing of sharing the profits of slavery, should be the rancorous conspirators against the peace of him who takes all its burdens and hazards upon himself!

The true solution of all this extravagance is, that the importance given to the questions evolved by the slavery excitement, is the mere artifice of politicians. Our slavery would have slept quiet under the surface of society, until the day of its appointed term, if it had not been found serviceable as a figure for the arena of politics. Unfortunately, it is a topic of singular capability for either a discourse in the pulpit or a speech upon the stump; the most fruitful for exaggeration, the most sensitive for alarm. It has proved to be a "drawing" theme for sensation parsons in pursuit of popularity; for sensation politicians in pursuit of the Senate; for speculative editors who are anxious to increase their subscription lists by means of pious politics and cheap philanthropy. It has shown itself capable of converting atrabilious tradesmen into governors, legislators, and judges; and of lifting up innumerable apprentices, journeymen, colporteurs and pedagogues to the elevation of shining lights in the Conventicle. It has fired the soul of many a cross-road orator of the "sunny South" with indignant and eloquent wrath against universal Yankeedom; and given birth to scores of conventions and thousands of resolutions, to expound the Constitution on the theory that its authors did not know what they were about.

Then, again, it has furnished to strong-minded women, who have declared their independence of the petticoat, an occasion for an equally heroic abnegation of the prejudice of color, and so to bring both pantaloons and amalgamation into their bill of rights.

It has over and over again supplied a conclave of crazy fanatics, in the orgies of their anniversaries, with an opportunity to denounce the Union as a covenant of hell, and the Bible and the Constitution as a double curse to mankind. It has, on the other hand, wrought the remarkable effect of diverting hot-headed young politicians from their newspapers to the study of the Scriptures, to find texts in the Pentateuch and the Epistles of Paul, to convict the whole North of the iniquity of blaspheming the "divine institution."

It has done all this and a thousand times as much, but it has never yet succeeded in establishing a single point for which it has professed to contend, nor accomplished a single result at which slavery would not have sooner arrived, if left to the silent evolution of its own destiny; always excepting, from this denial of its doings, that solitary achievement—in which its success has been perfect—the opening of a Pandora box of murder, rapine, implacable hatred and revenge.

It has made and defeated Presidents, cabinets, and diplomatists, has got up wars and annexations, built and destroyed platforms; but it has been utterly impotent to arrest the steady increase of slave labor, or its transfer to whatever region it has been found profitable to remove it. So far from promoting lawful emancipation, or checking either the growth or productiveness of slavery, it has wholly arrested the first, and has witnessed the augmentation of the value of the slave and the profits of his work a hundredfold since the agitation began.

These are the chief triumphs, and these the failures of a slavery agitation of thirty years, conducted by men claiming to be intellectual, conscientious, and stricken with a conviction that it is the great and paramount duty of the age to reform, what they have wrought themselves to believe, the damming sin of a nation. For this clergymen who think they have "a mission," spouters who think themselves orators, and politicians who think themselves statesmen, have gone on laboring all these thirty years, in the same ceaseless and fruitless routine of sermons, philippics, conventions, and discourses; vexing the heart of the South with vulgar vituperation and insult, and ruffling the temper of Congress with silly petitions to do impossible things, showered, in endless profusion of repetition, from the kitchens and primary schools and factories of New England.

So far as the agitation kept within the limits of this phase of its career, it was comparatively harmless. It could only provoke, but could not sting. In the language of the reviewer I have quoted above: "It could but make us angry." The South, indeed, are to blame for their loss of temper under this provocation; as that really afforded the assailants the only gratification they had. It would have been wiser to treat it as more self-possessed nations are accustomed to treat the extravagancies of fanatacism; as we ourselves, indeed, now treat Mormonism, or free love, or the nonsense of Fourierism.

But the agitation in the last few years has become venomous. It has directed its activity toward disunion and destruction of the government. Finding that the pretence of conscientious regard for law, and action within the pale of the statutes cramped its benevolent designs, it changed its tactics and entered into a more congenial career — devoting its energy to a plot for illegal and even treasonable disturbance, by enlisting companies and providing facilities for stealthy abduction of slaves, by provoking servile insurrection, and by armed incursions against the peace of communities within the slaveholding region; while, at the same time, it solicited and won the co-operation of many States to this organized plan of felony, so far as to obtain from them the passage of laws to nullify the provision of the Constitution and the statutes of the National Legislature for the recovery of the fugitives which might escape or be abducted from the South.

This is the second and now existing phase of the agitation. Could any sensible man in the North suppose, that a union of our States was at all possible, if this system of assault and disturbance were recognized and sustained by any respectable or authoritative opinion in the Free States? Could any one imagine, that if such a system of annoyance should receive the sanction of legislative bodies, of conventions representing a predominant power in any State, of religious communities, of parsons holding a grade above an insane fanatic, of professors of colleges, lawyers, merchants or gentlemen of any weight in society—in short, of any portion of Northern society that might be regarded as the exponent of the common opinion of the community—and not inevitably and inexorably force upon the whole South, not only the desire, but the duty to retire from a compact of union with all such States as fostered such an agitation? Between independent nations, such provocations would be the instant and just cause of war, and no nation, with the power to protect its own peace and honor, would hesitate to vindicate itself in that way.

This later scheme of aggression presents the first earnest and effective movement toward disunion, which has been made outside of the seceding States. The Free States which have encouraged, or co-operated in, this scheme, may claim whatever credit there is, in being the first to set the ball of disunion in motion. The Border States, though the chief sufferers from these attacks, have been loyal to the Constitution and Union, when these agitators have been recreant.

When the Republican party was organized in the bosom of this agitation, and abstract and useless speculations, touching the control of slavery by the Federal Government, were brought into the political field by both parties, to heighten and embitter the feud between the two sections; when all the prestige and power of organized political forces predominant in the popular vote of the Union, were enlisted in battle array against the South; when a President and Vice-President, contrary to all previous usage, were selected from the same section to represent it; and when this new embodiment was heralded to the country, with proclamation that its purpose was the administration of the Government toward the enforcement of the theory of an irrepressible conflict with slavery, until every vestige of it should be banished from the Republic; and that the aid of a higher law than the Constitution should be sought for the ratification of the act,—was there not enough to propagate a wide and fearful alarm throughout the whole South for the safety, not only of its property, but of its very existence?

The systematic abduction of slaves, through organized Northern agencies, is already sequestering not much less than a million of Southern wealth every year. The final consummation of this movement to the destruction of slavery, would be the sequestration of one or two thousand millions of that wealth. It would be to turn several States back into a jungle for wild beasts. It would be to paralyze the industry and subtract one-half from the comforts of Europe and America. Is it at all wonderful that now, when that party has succeeded and has elected its President, that the alarm of the South should be increased, and that the Southern States should feel that a crisis had been forced upon them which is to determine whether we can have a Union in peace — or peace without a Union?

These are the true sources of alarm to the South, and these the questions which the people there earnestly believe they have to solve.

If it were really true that the whole North were united in this scheme of aggression, then, indeed, the case would be hopeless. Hundreds of thousands in the South — the great majority of the people — believe this to be so. But, it is not true. Happily, it is not true. The belief is the delusion by which the Southern mind has been cruelly abused: abused by credulous and ardent politicians; by selfish demagogues; by a prejudiced, and, sometimes, by a wicked press; by the politicians of party, who hope to find in the wreck of society something serviceable to the reconstruction of their power. No, it is not true that these are the purposes of any portion of the Free States, worthy of a moments consideration as a force to influence the current of government. Three-fourths — I might say nine-tenths — of the people of the Free States are as guiltless of any imagining against the rights of the South, or its peaceful enjoyment of its own pursuits, as the people of the South themselves. Any one acquainted with the real opinion of the North will say, that the masses in those States are profoundly unconscious of the tendency of the doctrines of which they have heard so much, toward any serious assault upon the South. Their prurient tastes have been fed to plethora, with the stories of the barbarism of slavery; and, naturally enough, they believe that it is a very bad thing; but as to meddling with it, further than going to hear a lecture upon it by the Rev. Mr. Pepperpot, and to feast upon his spiced flummery, they have not the least wish or purpose. As to dissolving the Union for it! — they open their eyes to an incredulous stare, and won't, even now, believe that there is a man in the United States so insane as to dream of such a thing.

To the conception of all this mass, constituting the whole real power of the Free States, the Republican party and the Republican President are but the regular successors to the administration of the government which, in their belief, is to be conducted in the old fashion of attending to the business of the country, to the preservation of the Union, and to giving as much content as possible to every section and every interest in the country.

They are quite ready — I speak now of the people, and not the politicians; the latter have already proved themselves to be Incapables, and the matter will have to be taken out of their hands — these masses are now quite ready to make any arrangements, constitutional or conventional, which may be found necessary for peace. They will come to any reasonable agreement upon intervention or non-intervention, squatter or non-squatter sovereignty, protection or non-protection of slavery in the territories, — without the attempt to unriddle these jargons, — that may be found requisite for the restoration of good temper and good will among the States. *They will do anything to save the Union on principles adapted to make it perpetual.* It will not be three months before that will be the whole creed of the Republican party. Let the South be assured of this.

The first day of conciliation lies on the side of that party. Let the North dismiss its obstinacy and its silence, and come, with its customary shrewdness, to doing the right thing. Get slavery out of that gigantic and tenacious conscience of theirs, which is such a voracious absorbent of other people's sins, and fill its place with Christian charity, and love of its neighbor, and other forgotten virtues, and we shall then find some returning sunshine. But let the Free States everywhere, and the sober, reflective, and honest men in them, understand, that *the old Union is an impossibility unless the agitation of slavery is brought to an end.*

There is nothing in the election of Mr. Lincoln which may now be regarded as an obstacle to this pacification. With whatever apprehension many may have allowed themselves to anticipate, from the election, the inauguration of a policy which would be one of continual exasperation, it is very evident, now that the election is over and the views of the new President are becoming known through the best accredited organs of the party he represents, that there is no reason to fear his administration will not be conducted with a salutary and becoming respect for the rights and interests of every portion of the country. Indeed, from the date of the nomination of Mr. Lincoln, the presages of political events have all been favorable to a better hope of the future, than we might gather from the pernicious zeal and intemperate proclamation of those who assumed to be the leading champions and most authentic expounders of the principles of his party.

His nomination was both a surprise and a disappointment to what may be termed the most demonstrative portion of the Republican party. He was selected as the more eligible candidate, in the belief that he would attract support from States and large masses of the people who were not willing to adopt the extreme views upon which his rival for the nomination was put forward. And in the eventual trial he was elected, in great part, by a vote representing rather an opposition to the democratic, than a concurrence with the distinctive and exceptionable principles of the Republican party. In other words, Mr. Lincoln was both nominated and elected by what may be called the moderate, conservative division of the Republican party. And it is now claimed for him—and apparently with his own approbation—that he stands before the people of the United States unembarrassed by the extreme pretensions which were set up for the party in the canvass; and that he will enter into office not only with the determination, but with the desire to render his administration one of impartial justice to the South.

There is at least a good omen in this, and the strongest motive for an appeal to the South to wait for more explicit demonstration of the policy of the coming administration.

If the seceding States, in their zeal for a separate confederacy, are not willing to wait for this demonstration, it will be justly regarded by the world as a confession that the revolution in which they have embarked has only been promoted, but not originated, by the event upon which they have heretofore placed its justification.

If *they* are not willing to wait, the Border States will not be shaken from their resolves to wait and avail themselves of every favorable incident that may be turned to the account of peaceful adjustment.

Upon the new President will then devolve the responsibility of bringing the influence of the government, and the weight of his own admonition and example, to the duty of defining and determining (if that be not successfully done by his friends before his inauguration) the pledges which his party are disposed to give for the permanent establishment of friendly relations between the two sections of the Union. We have no reason to doubt that Mr. Lincoln's influence to this end will be propitious to peace. It will then be seen, that in the position assumed by the Border States—in their firmness, justice, and dignified bearing throughout this controversy—they will have become the authoritative and controlling power to devise and establish the foundations of a secure and durable settlement, with every provision for the preservation of Southern rights which the seceding States themselves could reasonably demand.

Discourse Delivered on the Day of
National Humiliation, January 4, 1861,
at Lexington, Kentucky

(Baltimore: John W. Woods, 1861)

> *Robert Jefferson Breckinridge (1800–1871) was born in Lexington, Kentucky,*
> *into a prominent family. (His father was a U.S. senator and Jefferson's attor-*
> *ney general.) He was educated at Jefferson College in Kentucky and Yale College*
> *in Connecticut, and he graduated from Union College in New York. For a time*
> *he practiced law and then held office in the Kentucky state legislature before em-*
> *barking on a career as a Presbyterian minister. Breckinridge had a church in*
> *Baltimore, became president of Jefferson College in Pennsylvania, held the pas-*
> *torate of the prestigious First Presbyterian Church in Lexington, Kentucky, and*
> *taught at the Danville Theological Seminary. An excellent preacher and gifted*
> *writer, this old-school theologian employed his skills to argue against immigra-*
> *tion, support prohibition, work for a reformed public school system, and advocate*
> *the general emancipation of slavery. Among Breckinridge's most important works*
> *were the books* Hints on Slavery *(1843) and* The Knowledge of God *(1858),*
> *and the articles "Our Country: Its Perils and Deliverance" (1861) and "The State*
> *of the Country" (1861). Throughout the Civil War he edited the* Danville Quar-
> terly Review, *a Unionist magazine.*[1] *The pamphlet in this volume began with a*
> *religious argument against secession in general, then focused on secession in South*
> *Carolina. Breckinridge rejected what he called a geographical division based on the*
> *slave line and discussed the merits of a central states confederacy. For information*
> *about Breckinridge's life see Edward Arthur Moore,* Earlier Life of Robert J.
> Breckinridge *(Ph.D. diss., University of Chicago, 1932), and Victor B. Howard,*
> *"Robert J. Breckinridge and the Slave Controversy in Kentucky,"* Filson Club
> Historical Quarterly *53 (October 1979): 328–43.*

It is in circumstances, my friends, of terrible solemnity, that this
great nation presents herself in an attitude of humiliation before the Lord
God of Hosts; in circumstances of great solemnity, that she stands before the bar of all surrounding nations, under that universal public opinion
which gives fame or stamps with infamy; and hardly less solemn than both,

---

1. This pamphlet was reprinted along with two others by Breckinridge in the
June 1861 issue of the *Danville Quarterly Review*.

is her attitude at the bar of distant ages and especially our own posterity that awful tribunal whose decrees can be reversed only by the decree of God. It is the first of these three aspects, either passing by in silence or touching very slightly the other two, that I am to consider before you now. And what I shall chiefly attempt to show is, that our duties can never be made subordinate to our passions without involving us in ruin, and that our rights can never be set above our interests without destroying both.

In taking this direction, let us bear in mind that the proclamation of the Chief Magistrate of the Republic which calls us to this service, asserts, in the first place, that ruin is impending over our national institutions; and asserts, in the second place, that so far as appears to him no human resources remain that are adequate to save them; and, in the third place, that the whole nation, according to his judgment, ought to prostrate itself before God and cry to him for deliverance. —Upon this I have to say, in the great name of God, and by the authority of Jesus Christ, the Saviour of the world, these two things: *First*, that national judgments never come except by reason of national sins; nor are they ever turned aside except upon condition of repentance for the sins which produced them; and, *Secondly*, that repentance for sin, as it is the absolute and universal, so it is the infallible condition of divine pardon and acceptance, not only in the case of individuals, but more obviously still and more immediately in the case of nations, since nations, as such, have no existence in a future life. Wherefore, if we are in the way of fearful evils, we are also in the way of clear duty, and therein we may hope for assured deliverance in the degree, first, that every one will go before another in earnest endeavors to rectify in himself all that is abominable to God; and, secondly, that every one will evince towards others the forbearance which he desires that God should extend towards him. Wherefore, also, we may boldly say that the remedy from God to us need not be expected to manifest itself by means of political parties, or by means of combinations of political leaders, or by means of new political compacts, or by means of additional legal enactments, or by means of more explicitly constitutional provisions; but that it must come from God to us, and be made manifest through a profound movement in the source of all power in free governments, namely, first, in the hearts of individuals, men turning from their sins, their follies, and their madness; and, secondly, in the uprising of an irresistible impulse thus created, which over the length and breadth of the land shall array itself in the power of God, against every endeavor to bring upon us the evils which we are imploring God to avert.

The first and greatest of these evils that we beseech God to avert, and that we should strive with all our might to prevent, is the annihilation of the nation itself, by tearing it into fragments. Men may talk of rights perpetually and outrageously violated—they may talk of injuries that are obliged to be redressed—they may talk about guarantees without which they can submit to no further peace-and there is doubtless much that has force and much more that is captivating to ardent minds in such expositions of our sad condition. For what problem half so terrible was ever agitated upon which it was not easy to advance much on every side of it? I will not consume the short time allowed to me in examining such views. What I assert, in answer to them all is, that we have overwhelming duties and incalculable interests which dictate a special line of conduct, the chief aim of which should be the preservation of the American Union, and therein of the American nation.

To be more explicit, it seems to me that there are inestimable blessings connected with the preservation of our National Union; and that there are intolerable evils involved in its destruction. For the blessings: there is the blessing of peace amongst ourselves, there is the blessing of freedom to ourselves and to our posterity, there is the blessing of internal prosperity secured by that peace, and freedom, never before excelled, if attained, by any people; there is the blessing of national independence secured by our invincible strength, against all the powers of the earth combined; there is the blessing of our glorious example to all nations and to all ages; there is the blessing of irresistible power to do good to all peoples, and to prevent evil over the face of the whole earth: there is the blessing of an unfettered Gospel and an open Bible and a divine Saviour, more and more manifested in our whole national life as that life deepens and spreads, subduing and possessing the widest and the noblest inheritance ever given to any people, and overflowing and fructifying all peoples besides. It is the problem sought to be solved from the beginning of time, and, to say, the least, the nearest approximation made to its solution, namely, the complete possession of freedom united with irresistible national force, and all directed to the glory of God and to the good of man. And this is that glorious estate now declared to be in fearful peril, and which we are called upon to beseech God to preserve unto us.

On the other hand, the evils of rending this nation. Which of the blessings that I have enumerated—and I have enumerated only those that appeared to me to be the most obvious—which of these is there—peace, freedom, prosperity, independence, the glory of our example, the power to do good and to prevent evil, the opportunity to give permanent efficiency all over this continent, and in a certain degree all over this earth to the Gospel of God; which of these blessings is there that may not be utterly lost to vast portions of the nation; — which of them that may not be jeoparded over this whole continent; which of them is there that may not depart forevermore from us and our posterity in the attempt to destroy our oneness as a people, and in the results of that unparalleled self-destruction? Besides all this, how obvious and how terrible are the evils over and above, which the very attempt begets, and which our after progress must necessarily make permanent if that attempt succeeds. First, we have already incurred the perils of universal bankruptcy before the first act is achieved by one of the least important of the thirty-three States. Secondly, we have already seen constitutional government both in its essence and in its form, trampled under foot by the convention of that State; and all the powers of sovereignty itself, both ordinary and extraordinary, assumed by it in such a manner that life, liberty and property have no more security in South Carolina than anywhere under Heaven where absolute despotism or absolute anarchy prevails, except in the personal characters of the gentlemen who hold the power. Thirdly, we have already seen that small community preparing to treat with foreign nations, and if need be introduce foreign armies into this country; headlong in the career in which she disdains all counsel, scorns all consultation and all entreaty, and treats all ties, all recollections, all existing engagements and obligations as if her ordinance of secession had not only denationalized that community, but had extinguished all its past existence. Fourthly, we see the glorious flag of this Union torn down and a colonial flag floating in its place; yea, we see that community thrown into paroxysms of rage, and the Cabinet at Washington thrown into confusion because in the harbor of Charleston our national flag instead of being still further dishonored, yet floats over a single tower! What then did they expect, who sent to the harbor of Charleston, to occupy the national fortress there, the son of a companion of Washington, a hero whose veins are full of revolutionary blood, and whose body is covered with honorable scars won in the service of his country? Why did they send that Kentucky hero there if they did not intend the place they put into his hands to be kept, to the last extremity?[2] But I need not enlarge upon this terrible aspect of what is coming to us all if the Union is destroyed. These are but the beginnings of sorrows. The men and the parties who initiate the reign of lawless passion, rarely escape destruction amid the storms they create, but are unable to control. Law comes from the depth of eternity, and in its sublime sway is the *nexus* of the universe. Institutions *grow*; they are not

2. Breckinridge referred to Major Robert Anderson, the Union commander at Fort Sumter who would distinguish himself during the Civil War.

made. Desolated empires are never restored. All history furnishes no such example. If we desire to perish, all we have to do is to leap into this vortex of disunion. If we have any just conception of the solemnity of this day, let us beseech God that our country shall not be torn to pieces; and under the power of these solemnities let us quit ourselves like men in order to avert that most horrible of all national calamities.

Let us consider, in the next place, those rights, as they are called, by means of which, and in their extreme exercise, all the calamities that threaten us are to be brought upon us at any moment; nay are to be so brought upon us that our destruction shall be perfectly regular, perfectly legal, perfectly constitutional! In which case a system like ours—a system the most enduring of all others, whether we consider the history of the past or the laws which enter, into its composition—a system the hardest of all others to be deranged, and the easiest of all to be readjusted when deranged; such a system is alleged to have a secret in it, designed expressly to kill it, at the option of the smallest fragment of it. I allude to the claim of the right of Nullification and the claim of the right of Secession as being Constitutional rights; and I desire to explain myself briefly in regard to them.

Secession is a proceeding which begins by tearing to pieces the whole fabric of government, both social and political. It begins by rendering all redress of all possible evils utterly impossible under the system that exists, for its very object is to destroy its existence. It begins by provoking war, and rendering its occurrence apparently inevitable, and its termination well-nigh impossible. Its very design is not to reform the administration of existing laws, not to obtain their repeal or modification, but to annihilate the institutions of the country, and to make many nations out of one. If it is the constitutional right of any State to do this, then we have no National Government, and never had any. Then, also, it is perfectly idle to speak of new Constitutions, since the new Constitutions can have no more force than the Constitution already despised and disobeyed. Then, also, the possibility is ended—ended in the very theory of the case, and illustrated in the utter failure of its practice—of uniting republican freedom with national strength in any country, or under any form of government. But according to my belief, and according to the universal belief of the American people but a little while ago, no such right, legal or constitutional, as that of secession, does or can exist under any form of government, and least of all under such institutions as ours. . . . [3]

3. The Kentucky minister here drew on Jefferson's thoughts on state rights to argue for the right of Nullification and reject the right of secession.

Now the pretext of founding the right of secession upon the right to change or abolish the government, which is constitutionally secured to the people of the nation and the States, seems to me, and I say it with all the respect due to others, to be both immoral and absurd. Absurd, since they who claim to exercise it are, according to the very statement of the case, but an insignificant minority of those in whom the real right resides. It is a right vested by God, and recognized by our constitutions as residing in the greater part of those who are citizens under the constitution, which they change or abolish. But what, in the name of God, and all the possible and all the imaginable arrogance of South Carolina, could lead her to believe that she is a major part of all the people that profess allegiance to the Constitution of the United States? And it is immoral, because it is trifling with the sacred rights of others, with the most solemn obligations on our own part, and the most vital interests of all concerned. And it is both immoral and absurd in one, because, as a political pretext, its use in this manner invalidates and renders perilous and odious the grandest contribution of modern times to the science of government, and therein to the peace of society, the security of liberty, and the progress of civilization; namely, the giving constitutional validity to this natural right of men to change or to abolish the government under which they live, by voting, when the major part see fit to do so. It is trifling with this great natural right, legalized in all our American constitutions, fatally caricaturing and recklessly converting it into the most terrible engine of organized legal destruction. More than that; it is impossible, in the very nature of the case, and in the very nature of government, that any such legal power, or any such constitutional right, could exist; because its existence pre-supposes law to have changed its nature; to have become mere advice; and pre-supposes government to have changed its nature, and ceasing to be a permanent ordinance of God, to become a temporary instrument of evil in the hands of factions, as they successively arise. Above all places under heaven, no such right of destruction can exist under our American constitutions, since it is they that have devised this very remedy of voting instead of fighting; they that have made this natural right a constitutional right; they that have done it for the preservation and not for the ruin of society. And it has preserved, for more than seventy years, the noblest form of human society, in constant security, and it could, if justly exercised, preserve it forever.

But let us go a little deeper still. It can not be denied that the right of self-preservation, both in men and States, is a supreme right. In private persons, it is a right regulated by law, in all communities that have laws. Among nations, there is no common supreme authority, and it must be regulated in their intercourse with each other by the discretion of each; and arms are the final appeal. In our system of government, there is ample provision made. In all disputes between any State and foreign nation, the General Government will protect and redress the State. In disputes between two States, the Supreme Court is the constitutional arbiter. It is only in disputes that may arise between the General Government and a particular State that any serious difference of opinion as to the remedy has manifested itself in this country; and on that subject it is the less necessary that I add any thing to what has been said when speaking of nullification, as the grounds of our existing difficulties are not between disaffected State and the General Government chiefly, if at all; but they are difficulties rather founded on opposite states of public opinion touching the institution of negro slavery, in the Northern and in the Southern States.

It may be confidently asserted that if the power of nullification, or the power of secession, or both of them, were perfectly constitutional rights, neither of them should be, under any circumstances, wantonly exercised. Nor should either of them, most especially the right of secession, ever be exercised except under extreme necessity. But if these powers, or either of them, is a mere usurpation, founded on no right whatever, then no State may resort to rebellion or revolution without, in the first place, such a necessary cause as may not be otherwise maintained; or, in the second place, without such a prospect of success as justifies the evil of rebellion or revolution, or else such intolerable evils as justify the most desperate attempts. Now it is my profound conviction that nothing has occurred, that nothing exists, which justifies that revolution which has occurred in South Carolina, and which seems to be impending in other Southern States. Beyond all doubt, nothing has occurred of this description, connected with any other interest or topic, except that of negro slavery; and connected with that, my deep assurance is, that the just and necessary cause of the slave States, may be otherwise maintained than by secession, revolution, or rebellion; nay, that it may be incomparably better maintained otherwise; nay, that it can not be maintained in that way at all, and that the attempt to do so will be fatal as regards the avowed object, and pregnant with incalculable evils besides.

In such discussions as these, the nature of the institution of slavery is perfectly immaterial. So long as the Union of the States survives, the constitutional guaranty and the federal power, which have proved adequate for more than seventy years, are that much added to whatever other force States or sections may possess to protect their rights. Nor is there, in the nature of the case, any reason why States with slaves and States without slaves, should not abide together in peace, as portions of the same great nation, as they have done from the beginning. The unhallowed passions of men; the fanaticism of the times; the mutual injuries and insults which portions of the people have inflicted on each other; the cruel use which political parties have made of unnatural and transient popular excitements; and, I must add, the unjust, offensive, and unconstitutional enactments by various State Legislatures at the North; the repeal of the Missouri Compromise by Congress; the attempt of the Supreme Court to settle political principles deemed to be of vast importance by all parties, in the Dred Scott case, which principles were not in the case at all; the subsequent conduct of the Federal Government and of the people in Kansas; the total overthrow of the Whig and American parties, the division and defeat of the Democratic party, and the triumph of the Republican party; the ordinance of secession of South Carolina; the agitation pervading the whole nation, especially the greater part of the Southern States; and to crown all, and if possible to make all desperate, the amazing conduct of the President of the United States amidst these great disorders: this is the sad outline of this slavery agitation, the posture of which for a moment is thus exhibited, no one knowing how soon new and fatal steps may hurry us still further. What I assert in the face of so much that is painful and full of peril, and what I confidently rely will be the verdict of posterity, is that all this, terrible as it is, affords no justification for the secession of any single State of the Union —none for the disruption of the American Union. They who make the attempt, will find in it no remedy for the evils from which they flee. They who goad others to this fatal step, will find that they have themselves erred exceedingly. They who have had the lead in both acts of madness, have no hope for good from coming ages, half so great, as that they may be utterly forgotten. Posterity will receive with scorn every plea that can be made for thirty millions of free people, professing to be Christian, in extenuation of the unparalleled folly of their self-destruction, by reason that they could not deal successfully with three or four millions of African slaves, scattered amongst them. Oh! everlasting infamy, that the children of Washington did not know how to be free! Oh! degradation still deeper, that children of God did not know how to be just and to forbear with one another!

It is said, however, it is now too late.—The evil is already done. South Carolina has already gone. Florida, it is most likely went yesterday, or will go today, even while we are pleading with one another and with God to put a better mind in her. Soon, it may be possible within the present month, all the Cotton States will go. We, it is added, by reason of being a slave State, must also go. Our destiny, they say, our interests, our duty, our all, is bound up with theirs, and we must go together. If this be your mind, distinctly made up, then the whole services of this day are a national mockery of God; a national attempt to make our passionate impulses assume the dignity of divine suggestions, and thus seduce the Ruler of the Universe into complicity with our sins and follies, through which all our miseries are inflicted upon us. Let it be admitted that a certain number of States, and that considerable, will attempt to form a Southern Confederacy, or to form as many new sovereignties as there are seceding States. Let it be assumed that either of these results is achieved, and that either by way of peace or by war. Let all be admitted.—What then? Thirteen States by their delegates formed the present Constitution, more than seventy years ago. By the terms of the Constitution itself, it was to be enforced when any *nine* of these thirteen States adopted it—whether by convention of their people or otherwise is immaterial to the present matter. Thirteen States made the Constitution by their delegates. A clause is inserted in it that it shall go into effect when any nine of the thirteen States adopt it, let any four refuse as they might. If they had refused, what would have happened would have been, that these four States, born States, and born United States, by the Declaration of Independence, by the war of the Revolution, by the peace with Great Britain, and by the articles of confederation, would, by a common agreement among the whole thirteen, have refused to go further or to make any stronger national government; while the other nine would have gone further and made that stronger national government. But such was the desire of all parties that there should be no separation of the States at all, that the whole thirteen unanimously adopted the new Constitution, putting a clause into it that it should not go into effect unless a majority so great as nine to four would sign it. I say if a minority of States had not adopted the new Constitution, it would have occurred, that they would have passed by common consent into a new condition, and for the first time have become separate sovereign States. As you well know, none of them refused permanently. What I make this statement for, is to show that, taking that principle as just and permanent, as clearly laid down in the Constitution, it requires at least eleven States out of the existing thirty-three States to destroy, or affect in the slightest degree, the question as to whether or not the remaining States are the United States of America, under the same Constitution. Twenty-two States, according to that principle, left after eleven had seceded, would be as really the United States of America under that Federal Constitution, as they were before, according to the fundamental principle involved in the original mode of giving validity to the Constitution. Kentucky would still be as really one of these United States of America, as she was at first when, as a district of Virginia, who was one of the nine adopting States, she became, as such district, a part thereof. And by consequence, a secession of less than eleven States, can in no event, and upon no hypothesis, even so much as embarrass Kentucky in determining for herself, what her duty, her honor, and her safety require her to do.

This fact is so perfectly obvious, that I presume if the six New England States were to revolt, and to establish a new confederacy, there is not a man in the State of Kentucky who would be led thereby to suppose, that our relations with the Union and the Constitution were in the slightest degree affected; or that we were on that account under the slightest obligation to revolt also. It may sound harsh, but I am very much inclined to think that there are many thousands of men in Kentucky who might be apt to suppose that the secession of the New England States would be a capital reason why nobody else should secede. It is the principle however, which I am attempting to explain.

The answer to this view, I am aware is, that we are a slave State, and that our relations are therefore necessarily different with respect to other slave States, as compared with the free States, or with the nation at large. The reply to which is various: First. The Institution of Slavery, as it exists in this country, represents a threefold, and very distinct aspect. First, the aspect of it in those States whose great staples are rice, sugar and cotton, commonly and well enough expressed by calling them the Cotton States. Then the aspect of it presented by those States in portions of which these staples are raised, and in other portions of which they are not; which we may well enough call the mixed portion of the slave States. And then its aspect in those slave States which are not producers of those great staples, in the midst of which, and out of which these great commotions come. What I assert is, that the relation of slavery to the community, and the relation of the community by reason of slavery to the General Government and the world, is widely different in all three of these classes of States. The relation of slavery to the community, to the government and to our future, in Missouri, in Kentucky, in Virginia, in Maryland, in Delaware, is evidently different from the relation of slavery in all these respects in Louisiana, in South Carolina and in all the other Cotton States. In the meantime also, the relation is different from both of those, wherein it exists in what I have called the mixed States; in Arkansas, part of which is a farming country and a part of which is thoroughly planting; in Tennessee, part cotton, and the eastern part a mountainous farming country; in Texas and North Carolina, where similar facts exist; and perhaps in some other States. What I desire is that you get the idea I have of the matter; that while it is true that all the slave States have certain ties and sympathies between them which are real, and ought not to be broken; yet, on the other hand, it is extremely easy to carry this idea to a fatal and a false extent, and to ruin ourselves forever under the illusion begotten thereby. In Kentucky, the institution of slavery exists about in the proportion of one slave to four white people, and the gap between the two races is widening at every census. In South Carolina there are about five slaves to three white persons, and the increment is on the slave side. In the Cotton States, I know of no way in which the institution of slavery can be dealt with at all, except by keeping the relation as it stands, as an integral portion of the body politic, unmanageable except in the present relation of the negro to the white man; and, in this posture, it is the duty of the nation to protect and defend the Cotton States. In regard to Kentucky, the institution of slavery is in such a position that the people can do with it whatever they may see fit, both now, and at any future period, without being obliged, by reason of it, to resort to any desperate expedient, in any direction.

The state of things I have sketched necessarily produces a general resemblance, indeed, because slavery is general—but, at the same time innumerable diversities, responsive to the very condition of slavery, of its prospects, and of its influence in the body politic, in the different slave States. And you never committed a greater folly than you will commit if, disregarding these things, you allow this single consideration—that you are a slave State—to swallow up every other consideration, and control your whole action in this great crisis. We in Kentucky are tolerant of opinion. Inform yourselves of what is passing, of an opposite character, throughout South Carolina: and reflect on the change that must pass on you, before you would be prepared to tear down the most venerable institutions, to insult the proudest emblems of your country's glory, and to treat constitutions and laws as if they were play-things for children; before you are prepared to descend from your present noble posture, and surrender yourself to the guidance and dictation of such counsels and such statesmen as rule this disunion movement. Nothing seems to me more obvious, and nothing is more important to be pressed on your attention at this moment, than that the non-cotton States stand in a position radically different in all respects from the position in which the Cotton States stand, both with regard to the institution of slavery, and with regard to the balance of the nation. The result is that all these States, the Cotton States, and the mixed States, and the non-cotton slave States, and the free States, may enjoy peace and may enjoy prosperity under a common government, and in a common Union, as they have done from the beginning; where the rights of all, and the interest of all may be respected and protected, and yet where the interests of every portion must be regulated by some general consideration of the interests which are common to every body. On the other hand, in a confederacy where cotton is the great idea and end, it is utterly impossible for the mixed, much more for the non-cotton States, to protector adequately any of their rights, except the right of slavery, to carry out any of their purposes except purposes connected with slavery, to inaugurate any system of policy or even to be free, otherwise than as they servilely follow the lead, and bow to the rule of the Cotton States. The very instant you enter a confederacy in which all is regulated and created by the supreme interest of cotton, every thing precious and distinctive of you, is jeoparded! Do you want the slave trade re-opened? Do you want free trade and direct taxation? Do you want some millions more of African cannibals thrown amongst you broadcast throughout the whole slave States? Do you want to begin a war which shall end when you have taken possession of the whole Southern part of this continent down to the isthmus of Darien? If your design is to accept the principles, purposes and policy, which are openly avowed in the interest of secession, and which you see exhibited on a small scale, but in their essence, in South Carolina; if that is your notion of regulated freedom and the perfect security of life and property; if that is your understanding of high national prosperity, where the great idea is more negroes, more cotton, direct taxes, free imports from all nations, and the conquest of all outlaying land that will bring cotton; then, undoubtedly, Kentucky is no longer what she has been, and her new career, beginning with secession, leads her far away from her strength and her renown.

The second suggestion I have to make to you is, that if the slave line is made the line of division, all the slave States seceding from the Union, and all the free States standing unitedly by the Union; what I assert in that case is, that the possibility of the perpetuity of negro slavery in any border State terminates at once. In our affected zeal for slavery, we will have taken the most effectual means of extinguishing it; and that in the most disastrous of all possible ways. On the contrary, if this Union is to be saved, it is by the cordial sympathy of the border States on one side and on the other side of the slave line that it must be saved. We have nothing to hope from the extreme States on either side; nothing from the passionate violence of the extreme South — nothing from the turbulent fanaticism of the extreme North. It is along that slave line — and in the spirit of mutual confidence, and the sense of a common interest of the people on the north and on the south of that line, that the nation must seek the instruments of its safety.

It is Ohio, Indiana, Illinois, Pennsylvania, New Jersey, on the one side; and Maryland, Delaware, Virginia, Kentucky, Missouri—God send that I might add with confidence Tennessee and North Carolina—on the other side; these are the States that are competent to save this Union. Nothing, therefore, can be more suicidal, than for the border slave States to adopt any line of conduct which can justly deprive them of the sympathy and confidence of the border free States—now largely possessed by them. And nothing is more certain than that a patriotic devotion to the Union, and a willingness to do all that honorable men should do, or moderate men ask, in order to preserve it—is as strongly prevalent at this moment, among the people of the border free States, as amongst those of the border slave States. The great central States I have enumerated—must necessarily control the fate both of the nation and of the continent—whenever they act in concert; and the fate, both of the nation and the continent, is utterly inscrutable after the division of them on the slave line—except that we know that when Samson is shorn of his strength, the enemies of Israel and of God will make the land desolate. Fronting on the Atlantic Ocean through many degrees of latitude, running back across the continent so as to include an area larger than all Western Europe, and finer than any of equal extent upon the globe, embracing a population inferior to none on earth, and sufficiently numerous at present to constitute a great nation; it is this immense power, free, to a great extent, from the opposite and intractable fanaticisms of the extreme States on both side of it, that is charged with the preservation of our national institutions, and with them our national power and glory. There are two aspects of the case thus put—in either of which success by peaceful means, is impossible; first, if these great central States fail to apprehend this part of the great mission committed to them; secondly, if the Cotton States, following the example of South Carolina—or the Northern States adhering to extreme purposes in the opposite direction—by either means render all peaceful adjustment impossible.

But even in that case, the mission of these great States is not ended. If under the curse of God, and the madness of the extreme Northern and Southern States, the preservation of the Union should be impossible; then it belongs to this immense central power, to re-construct the nation, upon the slave line as its central idea; and thus perpetuate our institutions, our principles, and our hopes, with an unchanged nationality. For even they who act in the mere interests of slavery, ought to see, that after the secession of the Cotton States, the border slave States are obliged, even for the sake of slavery, to be destroyed, or to adhere to the Union as long as any Union exists; and that if the Union were utterly destroyed, its reconstruction upon the slave line, is the solitary condition on which slavery can exist in security anywhere, or can exist at all in any border State.

I have considered three possible solutions of the existing state of things: The preservation of the Union as it is; the probable secession of the cotton slave States, and the effect thereof upon the Union, and upon the course Kentucky ought to take; the total destruction of the Union, and its reconstruction upon the slave line. I have considered the whole matter, from the point of view understood to be taken by the President of the United States; namely: that he judges there is no power in the General Government to prevent, by force, its own dissolution by means of the secession of the States; and I have done this, because however ruinous or absurd any one may suppose the views of the President to be, it is nevertheless under their sway that the first acts of our impending revolutions are progressing. Under the same helpless aspect of the General Government, there remain two more possible solutions of the posture and duty of Kentucky, and other States similarly situated. The first of these is, that in the progress of events, it may well become the border slave States to unite themselves into a separate confederacy; the second is, that it may well become Kentucky, under various contingencies, to assume a separate sovereign position, and act by herself. Having clearly stated my own conclusions, I will only say that the first of these two results is not one to be sought as desirable in itself, but only as an alternative to be preferred to more dangerous arrangements. For my unalterable conviction is, that the slave line is the only permanent and secure basis of a confederacy for the slave States, and especially for the border slave States, and that the union of free and slave States, in the same confederacy, is the indispensable condition of the peaceful and secure existence of slavery. As to the possible isolation of Kentucky, this also, it seems to me, is not a result to be sought. If it should occur as the alternative to evils still greater, Kentucky ought to embrace it with calmness and dignity, and, awaiting the progress of events, show by her wisdom, her courage, her moderation, her invincible rectitude, both to this age and to all that are to come, how fully she understood in the midst of a gainsaying and backsliding generation, that no people ever performed anything glorious who did not trust God, who did not love their country, and who were not faithful to their oaths.

It seems to me, therefore, that the immediate duty of Kentucky may be clearly stated in a very few words.

First. To stand by the Constitution and the Union of the country, to the last extremity.

Second. To prevent, as for the moment the impending and immediate danger, all attempts to seduce her, all attempts to terrify her, into the taking of any step inconsistent with her own constitution and laws—any step disregardful of the constitution and laws of the United States, any step which can possible compromise her position, or draw her on otherwise than by her own free choice deliberately expressed at the polls, according to her existing laws and constitution, whereby she will choose her own destiny.

Third. To settle in her heart that the rending of this Union on the slave line is, for her, whatever it may be for others, the most fatal issue that the times can have; and that doing this in such a way as to subject her to the dominion of the Cotton States for all time to come, is the very worst form of that most fatal issue.[4]

4. The sermon ended with a prayer: "Great then, is our consolation, as we tremble for our country, to be confident in our Lord!"

ROBERT M. T. HUNTER

Speech . . . on the Resolution Proposing to Retrocede the Forts . . . Delivered in the Senate of the United States, January 11, 1861

(Washington: Lemuel Towers, 1861)

Robert Mercer Taliaferro Hunter (1809–87) was born in Virginia. He was edu-
cated at the University of Virginia and attended the prestigious Winchester School
of Law. He served in the state house and the state senate, the U.S. House of Rep-
resentatives, where he rose to Speaker in 1839, and the U.S. Senate for fourteen
years until his resignation in late March, 1861. A delegate to the Confederate
Provisional Congress, he held office in the Confederate States Senate, where he
supported President Davis throughout the Civil War. After the war he practiced
law. In the pamphlet included in this volume, Hunter was responding to the dan-
gers over federal protection of Fort Sumter. He believed that unless the controversy
were resolved civil war would ensue and any hope to reunite the Union would for-
ever be lost. Hunter also analyzed the problems of excessive powers of the federal
government; he argued against presidential patronage and political corruption,
believed the party system evil, and advocated a dual presidency based on slave and
free state alignments. For information about his career see Henry H. Simms, Life
of Robert M. T. Hunter *(Richmond, Virginia: Dietz Press, 1935), and James*
Scanlon, "Life of Robert M. T. Hunter" (Ph.D. diss., University of Virginia,
1969). Charles Ambler, ed., Correspondence of Robert M. T. Hunter, 1826–
1876, 2 vols. *(Washington: American Historical Association, 1918), reveals the*
subtle game Hunter played as a secessionist living in the Border state of Virginia.

I have not sought to speak hitherto on the momentous question of
the day, because I did not believe that any good would be accomplished by
speaking. The disease seemed to me to be too deeply seated that none but
the most radical remedies would suffice; and I had no hope that the public
mind of the North was in a condition to receive any such proposition. I do
not know that it is even now prepared to weigh carefully such a suggestion;
but surely none can longer doubt the imminence of the extremity of the
danger. All must see that the bonds which have hitherto bound together
the members of this Confederacy are parting like flax before the fire of
popular passion. Our political fabric is reeling and tottering in the storm;
so that, if it were not based on the solid foundation of State organization,

there would be every reason to expect its entire destruction. Before the end of this month, it is almost certain that six or seven of the States will have seceded from this Union. It is therefore now no more a question of saving or preserving the old Union. We cannot recall the past; we cannot restore the dead; but the hope and the trust of those who desire a Union, are that we may be able to reconstruct a new Government and a new Union, which perhaps may be more permanent and efficient than the old. I know, sir, that there are difficulties in the way; but I put my trust in the good sense and in the instincts of empire, which have heretofore characterized the American people, to accomplish that great work. If we would do it, we must not sit idly, bewailing the condition of public affairs; but in the heroic spirit of the mariner who is cast away on a distant shore, see if we cannot find materials to build another ship, in which we may once more take the sea, and rejoin our kindred and friends. To do this, we must face and acknowledge the true evil of the day. To-day we must deal wisely with the mighty present, that we may be ready for perhaps the still more eventful future which will be on us to-morrow. New ideas, like new forces, have entered into our system; they are demanding the legitimate expression of their power, or they threaten to rend and destroy it in their wild and irregular play. There are now portions of this Union in which population already begins to press on the means of subsistence. In all of the States there is a desire—in some of them a necessity—for further expansion. It is that which has led to the warfare between the two social systems which have been brought together in our Constitution; a war waged with a bitterness and asperity that has reduced us to the sad pass in which we now find ourselves.

This Constitution was designed to unite two social systems, upon terms of equality and fairness, different in their character, but not necessarily hostile. Indeed, the very differences in these systems, it would seem, ought to have formed causes of union and mutual attraction, instead of giving rise to the "irrepressible conflict" which it, is said, some law of nature has declared between them. What the one wanted, the other could supply. If the carrying States did not make their provisions, the provision-growing States, on the other hand, had not the ships in which to transport their surplus productions. If the manufacturing States did not raise the raw material, the planting States, on the other hand, did not have the manufactories to convert that material into useful and necessary fabrics. Thus, what the one wanted, the other could supply. The very difference of products would seem to have afforded the means for forming a perfect system of industry, which should have been stronger by the mutual dependence and support of the parts. Unfortunately, however, as those who represented the non-slaveholding system of society grew into power, they commenced a warfare upon the other system which was associated with it under the Constitution. It was commenced in 1820, when it was declared that the social system of the South was founded upon sin, was anti-republican in its character, and deserved to be repressed and suppressed by the General Government wherever it had exclusive jurisdiction. The claim was made, that so far as the Territories of the United States were concerned, they were to be given up to the exclusive expansion of one of these systems at the expense of the other. Unhappily, in the first contest, the weaker system was overpowered; a law passed which did put it under the ban of the Empire; which did exclude the South from a large portion of the domain of the United States.

After that sprang up a party, at first not so large as it now is, which commenced a regular warfare upon the system of slavery in the South; upon the social system of the States which tolerated the institution of slavery. They commenced a system of agitation through the press, the pulpit, and the common halls of legislation, whose object it was to wound the self-respect of the slaveholder, and to make him odious in the eyes of the rest of the world. They denied that there could be any property in slaves—the very foundation of the social system of the South—and, as a consequence, they maintained that this government was bound to prevent its extension, and to abolish and suppress it whenever it had exclusive jurisdiction. They sought, by petition, to put an end to the slave trade between the States, that the institution might be pent up, and made dangerous and unprofitable.

In process of time, they either evaded or they denied the constitutional obligation to return fugitive slaves; and at last it was proclaimed here in these Halls that there was a law higher than the Constitution, which nullified its obligation and its provisions. Practicing upon this preaching, the majority of the non-slaveholding States, as was shown by my friend from Georgia in his able argument on this subject; passed personal liberty bills, the practical effect of which was to nullify the fugitive slave law, which was passed in pursuance of the Constitution of the United States.[1]

It is but a year since there was an armed invasion of my State for the purpose of creating servile insurrection; and yet not a State—and it is with the States alone that effectual remedies can be applied—has interfered, to make any such combinations penal in time to come. We have heard it pronounced, sir, by a distinguished leader of that party, that there was to be an "irrepressible conflict" between the two social systems, until one or

1. Robert Toombs of Georgia, *Speech in the United States Senate*, January 7, 1861 (Washington, D.C.: Lemuel Towers, 1861).

the other was destroyed. A president has been nominated and elected by a sectional majority, who was known to have avowed and to entertain such opinions; and a party has come into power, with full possession of this Government, which has elected a President and a standard-bearer who has made such declarations in regard to the rights of the South.

Is it surprising, then, that the southern States should say: "it is not safe for us to remain longer in a Government which may be directed as an instrument of hostility against us; it is not safe for us to remain longer under the rule of a government whose President may misuse his patronage for the very purpose of stirring up civil strife among us, and also for the purpose of creating civil war in our midst?" For it is known that a large portion—and that was but a year ago—of the Republican leaders and members of the House of Representatives indorsed and recommended a book which proposed the extinction of slavery by such means. Under such circumstances, I ask, is it surprising that the southern States should say: "it is unsafe for us to remain under a Government which, instead of protecting us, may be directed against us, as an instrument of attack, unless we can be protected by some new constitutional guarantees, which will save our social system from such a warfare as this!"

The southern people number now some thirteen million, and cover between eight hundred thousand and nine hundred thousand square miles of territory. They have within themselves all the capacity of empire. It is to be supposed that when they are threatened in the common Government with an attack upon their social system, upon which their very being depends, they will not withdraw from that Government—unless they can be secured within the Union—for the purpose of establishing another, which they know can and will protect them? Why, sir, what people is it that can stand a constant warfare upon their social system, waged for the purpose of dwarfing and suppressing and destroying it? The social system of a people is its moral being; and the Government which would dwarf or suppress it is like the parent who would consign his child to vice or ignorance. I know of instances in which nations have thriven under bad laws; I know of instances in which nations have prospered when their allegiance was transferred by force from one country to another; I know of none which survived the sudden and total prostration of its social system. To destroy that is to reduce them to anarchy, which is the death of a nation or a people.

I say, therefore, sir, that the South is bound to take this course unless it can get some guarantees which will protect it in the Union, some constitutional guarantees which will serve that end; and I now ask, what should be the nature of the guarantees that would effectually prevent the social system from such assaults as these? I say, they must be guarantees of a kind that will stop up all the avenues through which they have threatened to assail the social system of the South. There must be constitutional amendments which shall provide: first, that Congress shall have no power to abolish slavery in the States, in the District of Columbia, in the dock yards, forts, and arsenals of the United States; second, that it shall not abolish, tax, or obstruct the slave trade between the States; third, that it shall be the duty of each of the States to suppress combinations within their jurisdiction for armed invasions of another; fourth, that States shall be admitted with or without slavery, according to the election of the people; fifth, that it shall be the duty of the States to restore fugitive slaves when within their borders, or to pay the value of the same; sixth, that fugitives from justice shall be deemed to be those who have offended against the laws of a State with its jurisdiction, and who have escaped therefrom; seventh, that Congress shall recognize and protect as property whatever is held to be such by the laws or prescriptions of any States within the Territories, dock-yards, forts, and arsenals of the United States, and wherever the United States has exclusive jurisdiction; with the following exceptions: First, it may leave the subject of slavery or involuntary servitude to the people of the Territories when a law shall be passed to that effect with the usual sanction, and also with the assent of a majority of the Senators from the slaveholding States, and a majority of the Senators from the non-slaveholding States. That exception is designed to provide for the case where we might annex a Territory almost fully peopled, and whose people ought to have the right of self-government, and yet might not be ready to be admitted as a State into the Union.

The next exception is, that "Congress may divide the Territories to the effect that slavery or involuntary servitude shall be prohibited in one portion of the territory, and recognized and protected in another; provided the law has the sanction of a majority from each of the sections as aforesaid," and that exception is designed to provide for the case where an unpeopled Territory is annexed, and it is a fair subject of division between the two sections.

Such are the guarantees of principle, which, it seems to me, ought to be established by amendments to the Constitution; but I do not believe that these guarantees alone would protect the social system of the South from attack, and perhaps overthrow, from the superior power of the North. I believe that, in addition to these guarantees of principle, there ought to be guarantees of power; because if you do not adopt these, the South would still be subjected to the danger of an improper use of the patronage of the

Executive, who might apply it for the purpose of stirring up civil strife and dissension among them. The southern States might, too, notwithstanding these provision, find themselves in a position in which the stronger party had constructed them away, and asserted, perhaps that there was some higher law, which nullified and destroyed them. To make the South secure, then, some power ought to be given it to protect its rights in the Union—some veto power in the system, which would enable it to prevent it from ever being perverted to attack and destruction.

And here if the Senate will bear with me, I will proceed to suggest such remedies in this regard as I think ought to be applied, premising that I do not mean, by any means, to say that I suppose I am suggesting the only means on which a settlement may be made. I know there are others—others on which I would agree to settle the differences—but I am suggesting the means on which I think the best and the most permanent settlement can be made; and I do not believe that any permanent peace can be secured, unless we provide some guarantees of power, as well as of principle.

In regard to this guarantee of power, in the first place, I would resort to the dual executive, as proposed by Mr. Calhoun, not in the shape in which he recommended it, but in another form, which, I think, is not obnoxious to the objection that may be fairly taken against his plan.[2] I would provide that each section should elect a President, to be called a first and a second President; the first to serve for four years as President, the next to succeed him at the end of four years, and to govern for four other years, and afterwards to be ineligible. I would provide that, during the term of service of the first President, the second should be President of the Senate, with a casting vote in case of a tie; and that no treaty should be valid which did not have the signature of both Presidents, and the assent of two-thirds of the Senate; that no law should be valid, which did not have the assent of a majority of the Senators of the section from which he came; that no person should be appointed to a local office in the section from which the second President, or in the event of his veto, the assent of a majority of the Senators from the section from which he came.

And if I had the power, I would change the mode of electing these Presidents. I would provide that each State should be divided into presidential electoral districts; that each district should elect one man, and that these representatives from the whole United States should meet in one cham-

2. Hunter took his idea of a dual presidency and many other political-structural views from John C. Calhoun, *Disquisition on Government* (Charleston: Press of Walker and James, 1851).

ber, and that the two men who, after a certain number of ballots, received the highest number of votes should be submitted as the candidates to the people, and he should be declared as President who received a majority of the districts—the districts each voting singly. I would do this to destroy the opportunities which are given under our present system of nomination to the formation of corrupt combinations for purpose of plunder and patronage. I would substitute this, instead of the national conventions, which have already done so much harm in our system.

I would also diminish the temptation to such corrupt combinations for spoils and patronage, by the fact that the President, after the first election, would be elected four years before he commenced his service as President, and in the mean time he would be training as a second President at the head of the Senate, and exercising the veto power. The fact that he was elected four years beforehand would do much to prevent such combinations; but, further than this, the effect of such a division of the Executive power would be to destroy, to a great extent, the miserable system of rotation in office, which exists at present, and to make merit the test of the fitness for office and a guarantee for permanence in place; for, as the second President would probably keep those in office during his term of President whom he had protected by his veto power before, if they were worthy of the place, the effect would be at least, if this system were introduced, that the rotation principles would be applied, if at all, not once in four years, but once in eight years.

But this plan would have another good effect. It would save us from most of those agitations attending a presidential election which now disturb the country, which unsettle public affairs, and which are doing so much to demoralize and corrupt the people. The election would take place once in four years, but in one section at a time; it would take place in each section alternately, and but once in eight years; and in this way we should escape those disturbances which are now dividing and destroying us.

I do not believe that under this system the objection would apply which has been urged against the common dual executive. I have no idea that it would get up two parties, each concentrated around the different Presidents; because the second President would exercise his veto power only for the protection of his section, and would not wish to offend the other section, whose good will would be valuable to him hereafter; nor would he wish to impair and injure the influences of the office to which he was to succeed after his predecessor had passed through his term of service. The rule between them would be the rule of justice; and the probability is, that whenever there was a dispute, it would be apt to end in adopting that course which either was just, or which seemed to be just, to both sections.

Neither would operate to retard or delay the operation of the Government to too great an extent. In time of war, the operation would be quick enough. In time of peace, the delay would only occur where there was a dispute between the sections; and there the movements of Government ought to be slow until some measure found for conciliating and adjusting the difficulty.

But I will go further. I believe, putting out of consideration these sectional questions, that the working of the present executive system of our Government will destroy it in the end, and lead either to disunion or despotism, if some amendment be not made. I believe it will do so because the working of our executive system is now such as to beget and bring up a party whose existence and foundation depend upon spoils and plunder. I have often heard Mr. Calhoun say that most of the conflicts in every Government would be found at least to result in the contest between two parties, which he denominated the tax-consuming and the tax-paying parties. The tax-consuming party, he said, was that which fed upon the revenues of the Government, the spoils of office, the benefits of unequal and class legislation; the tax-paying party was that which made the contributions of the Government by which it was supported, and expected nothing in return but the general benefits of its protection and legislation; and he said, and said wisely, in my opinion, that whenever this tax-consuming party, as he called it, got possession of the Government, the people must decline, and the Government must either go to pieces or assume another and different form.

Now I say that the working of our present exclusive system is such as to produce a party of that description in the country, and give it the power of ruling its affairs. Place the predominant power in this Government in such hands, and I say one of two things must certainly happen: the Union will go to pieces in the collision which such a state of things would occasion, or else the Government would eventuate in a despotism.

The check which I propose would not only remedy this evil, by giving a sectional check where a sectional check is necessary, but it would do more; it would do much to purify the general legislation of the country, and do much to elevate the tone of public morals and manners throughout the land. I believe that this single change would do more to give us a permanent Union, a just and efficient Government, than any other that could be made.

But that is not the only check which, in a reconstruction of this Government and Union, ought, in my opinion, to be introduced. It is well known that some of the most important objects of this Constitution and Union are left simply to the discretion of the States; that there is a large class of rights, and important rights, for which there are no remedies, or next to no remedies. Those provisions which are designed to secure free trade and free intercourse between the citizens of the States can all of them be nullified or set aside by State legislation. The States can pass laws so to obstruct this free intercourse that the constitutional privilege may amount to nothing; and if this Union had endured, and these contests had continued, we should have seen laws passed in a spirit of retaliation by the States which would have broken up free trade between them. They could have taxed the commodities of the obnoxious States after the package was broken, under the decision of the Supreme Court itself. They could make it penal in their citizens to use the ships of another State, if it was obnoxious to them; and in many other ways they could, by their legislation, destroy some of the most important objects of the Constitution.

I believe, myself, that it was intended, by the framers of that instrument, that the State should have been mainly instrumental in restoring fugitives from labor, or, to speak more plainly, fugitive slaves. We know that it is in their power, not only to refrain from discharging this duty, but actually to obstruct and impede the Government of the United States in its effort to execute the law. There are certain rights for which there are no remedies. It is provided, for instance, that no State shall maintain an army; and yet, if it does, so there is no remedy to prevent it.

Now I propose, in order to secure the proper enforcement of these rights for which, as I say, there are no adequate remedies, that the Supreme Court should also be adjusted. It should consist of ten judges—five from each section—the Chief Justice to be one of the five. I would allow any State to cite another state before this tribunal to charge it with having failed to perform its constitutional obligations; and if the court decided a State thus cited to be in default, then I would provide, if it did not repair the wrong it had done, that any State might deny to its citizens within its jurisdiction the privileges of citizens in all the States; that it might tax its commerce and the property of its people until it ceased to be in default. Thus, I would provide a remedy without bringing the General Government into collision with the States, and without bringing the Supreme Court into collision with them. Whenever international stipulations in regard to the duties imposed on the States, as laid down in the Constitution, are violated, I would remedy the wrong by international remedies. I would give a State the right, in such cases, after the adjudication of the courts, to deny to the offending State the performance of the mutual obligations which had been created for its benefit. In this way I believe that these wrongs might be remedied without producing collision in the system. A self-executing process would thus provide a remedy for the wrong, without a jar to the machinery of Government.

In order to make this check efficient, it should be provided that the judges of the Supreme Court in each section should be appointed by the President from that section, and this is the only original appointing power which I would give to the second President.

I have presented this scheme as one which, in my opinion, would adjust the differences between the two social systems, and which would protect each from the assault of the other. If this were done, so that we were made mutually safe, I, for one, would be willing to regulate the right of secession, which I hold to be a right not given in the Constitution, but resulting from the nature of the compact. I would provide that before a State secede, it should summon a convention of the States in the section to which it belonged, and submit to them a statement of its grievances and wrongs. Should a majority of the States in such a convention decide the complaint to be well founded, then the State ought to be permitted to secede in peace. For, whenever a majority of States in an entire section shall declare that good cause for secession exists, then who can dispute that it ought to take place? Should they say, however, that no good cause existed, then the moral force of such a decision, on the part of confederates of those who are bound to the complaining State by identical and homogenous interests, would prevent it from prosecuting the claim any further. I believe that the system thus adjusted would give us a permanent Union, an efficient, a useful, and just Government. I think our Government would then rank among the most permanent of human institutions. It is my honest opinion that, with a Government thus balanced, and with such capacities for empire as our people possess, we should build up a political system whose power and stability and beneficial influences would be unparalleled in all the history of the past.

I know it may be said that such a distribution of power does not accord with the principle of distributing power according to numbers; but I say that if that be the true principle at all, it applies only to States which have a single government; it does not apply to confederacies; and if it were left to me to amend this Constitution, I would stamp upon this Government a character still more distinctly federative than that which it now bears. I say, then, that the distribution of power which I propose would be entirely just upon the federative principle. Nor would my proposition be at all more inconsistent with the principle of distributing power according to numbers than the arrangement of the present Federal Constitution. Nothing in my scheme is more unequal than the provision which gives the six New England States twelve senators while New York has only two, although the population of that state is as great, and I believe greater, than all of the New England states together. There is nothing in the scheme now proposed inconsistent with the federative principle; and if the slaveholding and the non-slaveholding States had been standing apart for a dozen years in different confederacies, and there was a proposition to unite those confederacies in one, no man would think it extreme, or be surprised, if each of the confederacies insisted upon such powers and such guarantees as would enable it to defend its own social system and to secure quality, together with the opportunity for expansion according to the peculiar law of its development.

But as I said before, I do not mean to declare that this is the only scheme upon which I will settle. I say I believe it to afford the best basis of settlement which has yet been devised. There are other schemes upon which I would settle. I would settle upon something which would give only a truce, provided it promised to be a long truce, and then trust to public opinion and the progress of truth to remedy future evils when they might arise. But I would prefer, when we do settle, after this turmoil and confusion, that we should do so upon some principle which promises us a permanent adjustment, a constant and continuing peace, a safe, and efficient, and a stable Government.

I have founded my suggestions upon the fact, which I take to be an accomplished fact, that some of the States of this Union have already withdrawn, and that the old Union has been dissolved, and has gone. I believe there is no way of obtaining a Union except through a reconstruction, because I utterly repudiate and deny that it can be done through a system of coercion, which some have proposed. I say, if you were to attempt coercion, and by conquest to restore the Union, it would not be the Union of our fathers, but a different one. I maintain it would be a Union constructed in entire opposition to the true American spirit and American principles; a Union of a number of subjugated provinces with others who governed them and wielded the whole power of the Confederacy.

But I maintain that coercion, if it were possible, is not right; and that if it were right, it is not possible. I think it can be shown that it is neither right nor possible. I believe that it can be proved that the only effect of an attempt at coercion would be to destroy the chances of a reconstruction of the Union, or, in other words, to defeat all the hopes that are left to the friends of a Union in the country. I say that if it were possible, it is not right. I believe it is not right, because I believe in the right of secession in the States. It is not my purpose to repeat the argument which has been so much better made by my friend, the distinguished Senator from Louisiana. I do not mean to argue that question; I merely say that, to my mind, it lies in a nutshell.[3] If it be true that our Constitution is a compact, as history demonstrates, between the States as parties; and if it be true, as Mr. Madison has demonstrated, that there is no common arbiter in disputes between these parties; and if it be true, as Mr. Webster has said, that a bargain broken on one side is broken on all sides, then it results inevitably that it is for the State to say whether the bargain has been broken, and to act accordingly. I do not say that this right of secession is laid down in the Constitution. It results from the nature of the compact. When two nations enter into a treaty of mutual obligations, and one fails to fulfill its part, the other may cancel it; not from any stipulation in the treaty, but from the nature of the compact. It is the very remedy for the very wrong; and, indeed, it is the only remedy for the wrong.

But I care not what you will call it; call it revolution, if you choose; let this be the name you give it; I still say I think I can show you from the Constitution that you have no right to interfere with it. If it be revolution, it is organized revolution; it is a revolution conducted by an organized body; and so acknowledged to be in the Constitution itself. If it be revolution, it is a revolution managed by the government which the Constitution acknowledges to be a legal government—I mean the government of the State. How, then, could this Government pretend to treat as a rebel him who obeys a government that it acknowledges to be legitimate? Especially, how can it interfere to treat him as such when he has acted under a warrant from the very power from which this Government derives its authority? How does this Government derive its authority to administer its functions within the State of Virginia? It derives it from the assent of the people of the State of Virginia, given in the convention which represented them in their sovereign capacity. How does the State government derive its authority? From the very same source; and in any dispute between the two, as to authority, it is for the source of authority to both to say whom the citizens shall obey. This Government rests and has its being in the assent of the people of the different States; and without it the Constitution has clearly created a Government which cannot exist or be administered within a State. Then, if it be true that this Constitution created a Federal Government which cannot be administered within its limits without the assent of the people of the States, it would follow that the Constitution has declared, by implication, that the only authority of that Government

3. See Judah P. Benjamin's pamphlet in this volume.

rests upon the assent of the people of the State, and that when this is withdrawn, it has no longer any rightful jurisdiction within it. Is it, then, true that this Government is so constructed by the Constitution that it cannot execute its functions within the State without the assent of the State, or against its will and authority? If so, then the Constitution clearly implies that the authority of the General Government is gone within the limits of a State when the people of that State have withdrawn their assent to its jurisdiction—a conclusion which is in entire accordance with the principles of free governments as laid down by the fathers of the Constitution.

I proceed then to make good my proposition, that this Federal Government cannot be carried on within the limits and jurisdiction of a State, without the assent, the aid, and the sympathy of its people. In the first place, it depends on the Legislatures of the different States to elect numbers of this body. If a majority of the States, although they might represent a small minority of the people, were to refuse to send Senators here, our Government is gone; you have lost one of the most important arms of the system; you have no longer a Senate.

But in order to carry out the functions of this Government you must administer its judicial powers. Can you administer the judicial powers of this Government within a State if that State withdraws its assent and is determined to resist that administration? Can you do it by any means given you under the Constitution? Suppose a State repeals the penalties for false imprisonment as against those officers; suppose it should say it has reason to fear that the officers of the general Government would be appointed under influences which would be utterly destructive to its domestic peace and social system, and that they must give bonds for good behavior, with sureties to be found in the States itself: if a State were to undertake to obstruct the course of Federal justice in that way, where would the remedy be found within the constitutional power of this Government! Would it undertake to pass a code of municipal legislation in order to protect the persons, and property, and effect of its officers? Could it say that its officers should not be answerable to the jurisdiction of the State for offenses against the laws of the State when they were within its jurisdiction? Certainly they could not do that, consistently within the Constitution. When it comes to such a pass as that, they would have the same right to enact and execute a municipal code for all people of the States, that they would have to make one for that portion of the people who constituted the mass of the Federal officers.

But that is not all. To obtain the right of exclusive legislation within dock-yards, forts, arsenals, and other needful buildings, Congress must have, first, the consent of the States. That must be given under the Constitution. Suppose a State refuses its consent. Where would be your courthouses, your forts, your custom-houses? Where would you have the *loqus in quo*, from which to administer the functions and the power of this General Government everywhere, if they were to refuse to give you this assent, you would be under State jurisdiction; and thus it would be in the power of the State constantly to thwart, obstruct, and prevent the administration of the Federal justice, or the administration of Federal power, within her limits and jurisdiction.

So, too, it is in the power of the States, if they choose, if they undertake to withdraw their assent from this Constitution, to defeat these great ends of the Union, which I have before described, as designed to insure free intercourse and free trade between the citizens of the several States. Thus it will be found, when you come to examine the matter, that this Federal Government cannot exercise its most important and its essential functions within the limits of a State if the people of that State refuse to assent to its power, and choose to obstruct it by means which they have under the Constitution of the United States. If this be so, what is the result to be derived from that fact? The result is, that the framer of the Constitution supposed that this Federal Government would only be an authorized Government within a State so long as it had the assent of the people of that State; and that when the people of that State withdrew their assent, it was not the authorized Government; and therefore they provided no means for enforcing its powers and for exercising its jurisdiction. Is not that the inevitable conclusion, from the facts to which I have just alluded? The only mode in which you could protect the administration of the Federal affairs and the Federal jurisdiction within the State, would be to set aside the State government by force, and to reduce it to a territorial condition; and then what would be the result? You first coerce a State because it secedes from thirty-two other members of this Confederacy; and you turn around and secede yourselves from it by reducing it from the condition of a State to the position of a Territory!

But I say that if coercion were right, it is impossible. I say that no man can doubt that if it be attempted against one of the seceding States, all the slaveholding States will rally to the aid of their sister; and the idea that you can coerce eight, or ten, or fourteen, or fifteen States of this Confederacy when standing in a solid body, is preposterous. I acknowledge that you may make a civil war which will produce immense disasters in both sections of the country; I acknowledge that you can inflict immeasurable evils and great calamities upon both the contending sections; but as to supposing that either one could subdue the other so as to place it under its yoke, and impose its laws upon it, I do not entertain the idea for an instant.

How would this war of coercion be waged? It would take $100,000,000 yearly, for you cannot wage it with less than a hundred thousand men, and where would you get this sum? Not from imports; for what would the imports of the northern portion of the Confederacy be when you took from them all that comes in return for the exports of the South? You would have to sustain the war by loans and direct taxation; and is it to be supposed that the people would bear such burdens in such a cause as that? I believe they might submit to any just and necessary taxation in the defence of their own legal and necessary rights; but would they submit to such a scheme of taxation for the purpose of enforcing their yoke upon other people — for the purpose of depriving those other people of the right of self-government? Whose would be the commerce that would be preyed upon? Not the southern commerce. That would go in foreign bottoms. The commerce to be prayed upon by privateers would be the commerce of the other section of the Confederacy. If it came to a question of plunder, which of the sections would afford the greatest temptation to plunder? Where are the cities, villages, the concentrated wealth of community to be found in the greatest number and quantity? Those are the objects which tempt the capacity of a soldiery. You could steal our negroes. Your own people would not allow you to take them and set them free among them, to enter into competition with them for labor and for wages. How would you carry on such a war? Where would you find the means? You would not continue the attempt for more than six months before you would find it impossible, and you would abandon it.

I say, therefore, that it is not possible by any such means, to coerce the southern people into submission. I know there is a talk of attaining all the valuable purposes of a Union, by a simple blockade of the coast; that is, by a blockade which should collect the customs and do nothing more. Where would the ships come from to blockade the whole southern coast? And how could they effect their purpose under this Constitution, unless, indeed, they intend to violate it? Where would be their judges, their inspectors, their appraisers, their collectors? Where would they exercise their functions? On shipboard? That would be impossible. Would you transfer the cargo of the ship to another port of a collection district in another State, which had not seceded? Why the charge would not be wanted there. How in regard to the commerce of the South during that period? You can lay no duty upon exports. They would forbid their people, under penalties, to send their commodities by any but foreign bottoms; they might forbid the people, by penalties, from consuming any good which they did not manufacture themselves, or import from abroad; and thus you would loose your most valuable customers in the carrying trade, and the most profitable consumers of your manufactures.

And what would you get in return? Would the customs that you thus collected pay the expenses of the blockade? Would they pay half the expenses of the blockade? It is manifest they would not. The blockade, to be effectual would have to be a blockade of war, in which you prevented vessels from going either out or in; and it is to be supposed that foreign nations would allow this? It is to be presumed that Great Britain, which has millions of human beings whose very existence depends upon cotton, that the great interests of civilization would allow this grand material of human industry to be thus shut up and denied to them? It is not to be supposed for a moment. There are other powers which would prevent such a blockade, in addition to the resistance which might be expected from the section that it was attempted thus to coerce.

I say, then, that it is idle to think of coercion. You may, if you choose, if such be your feeling, inflict evils by waging civil war; but will you inflict more on others than you will receive in return? Will you be benefited by the operation when you come to sum up its results and effects? I think not. But suppose you could succeed—I put the question to you now—suppose you had succeeded according to your utmost wishes; suppose you had conquered the South; that you had subjugated the entire section; that you had reduced those States to the condition of dependent provinces, how then would you exercise your power? Would you apply your doctrine, that there can be no property in slaves? In that community of eight or nine million white men and four million slaves, would you turn them loose together, and set the slaves free? Would you repeat the experiment of the British West Indies—of the Island of the bush, the white man being gradually reduced to the level of the negro, and the negro remitted and restored to his primitive condition of barbarism? Would the great interests of civilization and humanity permit such a result? Would your own interests, your manufacturers, your shipowners, agree to it? It is not to be supposed that such a thing would be permitted; and what then would be the result? You would have to maintain the social system; you would have to recognize property in slaves; and what would follow from that? If you recognize property in slaves, you must cause fugitive slaves to be restored. If you recognize a property that is under the jurisdiction of your Government, you must protect it; and if you do protect it, you must punish persons who attempt to make raids upon it, and to incite servile insurrections. And if you once commit yourselves to the duty of protecting it throughout all these conquered States, you would find that if followed, as a necessary consequence, that you must protect it whenever you had the exclusive jurisdiction. What, then, would become of your dogma of excluding it from the Territories? What would be the effect of such an experiment? You pen them up until there comes to be a surplus population in the old States; you pen up the negroes, and say the negro shall not move, but the white man may. What is the effect of that? The white man does move when the wages of labor are low; the negro remains and gains the preponderance in population until you give him the best part of the continent, and remove the white man to the worst. Could such an absurdity as this be tolerated? No; not after it was made manifest.

Then, if you would be forced to all these things, if you succeeded according to your wishes, and conquered and subdued us, after a bloody and harassing civil war, why not do it beforehand, when it would save the Union? Why not do it now, when it would avert all these calamities? Why not avail yourself of the present opportunity, when you may do so without the dreadful inconsistency which will be charge upon you, when you may be forced to do these very things after you have carried on this cruel and harassing and distressing system of civil war?

I say, then, that it is impossible to coerce the southern States, if you were to attempt to do so. If you had the constitutional right to do so, it would be impossible. Why create a civil war wantonly, without purpose, without use or benefit to any one? If this be so, why not adopt the proposition in my resolution—why not cede back the forts to those States that claim to have seceded, and to have withdrawn from this Confederacy? What do you want with the forts in the harbor of Charleston? If you do not mean to coerce her, you ought not to have them. The whole thing lies in a nutshell; because, if you do mean to use them for the purpose of coercion, you light up the flames of civil war, and there is no telling when those flames will be extinguished; if you do attempt to use them for the purpose of coercion, you destroy the chances of the construction of another Union, which I still hope and trust may take place, and which may prove to us a more permanent bond of alliance and fraternity than that one which is passing away from us.

I say, too, that you have no right, when you come to weigh the question of right, to hold on to these forts. You could not have obtained them without the consent of the Legislature of the State; that is the provision of the Constitution. Upon what consideration was that consent given? Not for pecuniary considerations. It was given upon the consideration that they were to be used for the defence of the State, but are proposed to be used for offensive purposes against her. The consideration, therefore, in my opinion, has failed; and in justice and equity, you ought to restore them.

But if there were no moral obligations upon you to do so, I maintain that consideration of policy ought to prompt you to do it. In no other way can you prevent the commencement of civil war. They say they have seceded; they say they are out of this Union. I believe myself that they are. You maintain a different opinion; but certain it is, that while you might give them up without inconsistency, so far as your opinions are concerned, they could not yield them without absolute inconsistency, so far as their pretensions are to be considered. If they are an independent people, they are bound to take them, if they have the power to do so, when they believe they are in the possession of a foreign Government. But how is it with you? What inconsistency do you manifest, provided it be policy to do so, when you withdraw from them? You do not admit the doctrine of secession. In the form in which the resolution is proposed, you are not called upon to admit it. You may support the resolution upon the ground of policy; for, under the resolution, a State which did not intend to secede might apply for a retrocession of the forts, and the retrocession might be given in some cases from motives of policy, and without the least violation of the Constitution. Suppose the city of New York had said to us, at a time when the public defenses were going up at a rate which did not satisfy her, because they were too slow, "retrocede to us the jurisdiction; it is essential to us to have the forts; we will construct them rapidly; pass a law allowing the State to maintain troops, and we will man them and keep them." It is obvious that there might be circumstances under which it would be politic for New York to make such a demand, and there might be circumstances under which it would be just and proper to grant it. I say, therefore, you do nothing inconsistent with your opinions against secession, when you agree to return these forts; and there is nothing impolitic in such a concession, unless you desire to use them for purposes of coercion.

I maintain that every consideration of policy should induce us to remove that bone of contention, that cause of strife between us; and I am especially anxious for it, because I believe that if we had civil war, we lose all hopes of reconstructing this Union. I desire myself to see it reconstructed on principles of fairness, equality, and justice, between the sections. I believe that if a drop of blood is once shed, if you do not destroy the chances of it, you postpone it to a very distant day; and, for one, I do not desire to see this. I presume that we shall soon see nearly all the southern States out of the Union. I think it probable that they will unite first and form a union of the South for the sake of the South; and having done so, I hope and trust and believe that they will call a southern convention for the purpose of proposing a recommendation and readjustment on proper terms; and if the nonslaveholding States at the same time shall assemble in convention and exchange propositions, I hope and trust that some settlement may be had, some reconstruction to make this Union more permanent and this Government more valuable than ever it has been to us in the past. Secession does not necessarily destroy the Union, or rather the hope of reunion; it may turn out to be the necessary path to reconstruction. The secession of the Roman people to the Sacred Mount did not destroy Rome. One the contrary, it led to a reconstruction and liberty of the people. The Roman Government became more permanent and powerful than before, and the Roman people benefited by the change. But if it should turn out that in this exchange of propositions it was impossible to accommodate the difference, still it might result in the establishment of some league, not merely commercial, but political, holding us together by a looser bond than any which has bound us heretofore, and we might thus still secure many of the benefits of this Government and this Union, while we left each section free to follow the law of its own genius, and to develop itself according to the promptings of its own nature.

I say, therefore, that, so far as I can weigh the question, it is no more a question of Union, but one of reunion. To produce reunion, it is essential that the southern States should be allowed to take that position, which it is obvious they are going to take, in peace. You must give, too, all the time you can, and offer all the opportunities you may, to those who desire to make an effort for the reconstruction of this Confederacy. I say I am one of those; for while I believe that the South owes it to itself first to secure its own position, to provide for its own protection, to unite in such strength as will enable it to defend itself against all goers and comers, I also believe that the interests of mankind, our own interests, and the interests of our confederates, would then require that we should reconstruct the old Union if we can, or rather construct a new Union on terms of equality and of justice.

But, will this be possible if we enter into a course of civil war? If brother begins to shed the blood of brother, and people become irritated and excited at the sight of blood, will it be possible to reunite us again? And I ask if Republicans are willing, if they mean to insist, to add civil war to the long catalogue of enormities for which they are to be held responsible hereafter? Is it not enough that they have marched into power over the ruins of the Constitution, and that they have seized this Government at the expense of the Union? Will they be contented with nothing less now than civil war, and such a strife, according to their own account of it, as is unparalleled in the history of modern and civilized warfare? It is said that this fratricidal contest is to be attended with the horrors and atrocities at which even the men of Wallenstein, his "whiskered pandours and fierce hussars," would stand aghast and pale.

I would ask if they are, indeed, willing to let loose the dogs of war, hot from hell, to ravin through this land; if they desire that "one spirit of the first-born Cain" shall reign in every American bosom, to prepare the hearts and minds of men for blood, and to stir up fratricidal strife throughout this once happy country? What excuse, when they have returned from such a war of devastation and ruin, will they be able to give to their own consciences? How will they account with humanity for its best hopes, which they have destroyed; for having crushed out and extinguished the highest capacities for usefulness, progress, and development which were ever bestowed on man? What judgement will posterity pronounce upon them when it comes to sit in judgement on the deeds occasioned by such unhallowed ambition? Will it not say, "You found peace, and you established war; you found an empire of the United States, and you have rent and scattered it into separate and hostile fragments?"

And, more awful still, what account will they render at the bar of Heaven, when, from many a burning homestead and many a bloody battlefield, spectral hosts shall appear to accuse them there; when the last wail of suffering childhood shall rise from the very depths of the grave to make its feeble plaint against them, and the tears of woman, helpless woman, shall plead against them for her wounded honor in the voiceless woe of her ineffable despair? How will they account for it before man and God, before earth and Heaven, if they close with blood this great American experiment which was inaugurated by Providence in the wilderness to insure peace on earth and good will to man; an experiment which was maintained and conducted by our fathers, not only by their blood, but with their most pious care? How will they hide themselves from the accusation, when one universal voice of misery and despair shall be heard throughout the land?

I say to them that it will be no compensation or excuse for such sins that they have succeeded in enabling themselves to waive a barren scepter over a mutilated empire, and exhausted and suffering land! Why is it that these threats are made? Is it done for the purpose of preventing the southern States from seceding? Never have been taken more ill-judged steps to secure an end. They but precipitate and hasten what they wish to prevent. Such threats of coercion as these only serve to make the southern States precipitate themselves into the arms of each other, that they may stand together in a common cause, and unite their strength to make a common defence. I say, for my own State, that she has not yet commissioned me to speak; she is taking counsel at home as to her future action; but this I do feel authorized to declare: she loves peace, and she desires to avoid war; but she will not be deterred for asserting her rights by threats of coercion of from any fear of consequences. Once before in her past history, in the sacred name of honor, liberty, and equality, she staked her destiny on the war of the Revolution, when "the cause of Boston was the cause of all"; and for the same high considerations, I know that she will imperil all again, if she believes it to be her duty to do so. And if the day shall ever come when she can neither defend her honor nor assert her rights because the hand of power wields its bloody sword before her, she will feel that it would be better for her name and fame to perish with them.

Republican Senators, why are these threats of coercion sent to the southern States, who are seeking to do no evil to others, but merely to protect and defend themselves? Do they go out with any purpose of attacking your rights? Do they secede with the wish to injure or disturb you in any manner? Are they not going out simply for the purpose of exercising that first law of nature and of nations, the right of self-government, because they believe they are not safe under your rule? Are they not willing to meet all the responsibilities which they may have incurred while they were carrying on a joint government with you? Why, then, do you claim to pursue them with fire and with sword; why do you deny to them that right which belongs to every organized people? When we were asserting that right against the Government of Great Britain, we claimed and we received the sympathies of the whole civilized world. When the Spanish provinces rebelled against the mother country, we were quick to express our sympathy and regard for their cause. When Greece, distant Greece, asserted her independence, we were among the first to express our sympathy for her. Now, the right which we are free to offer, and the sympathy which we gladly extend to foreigners and to aliens, are refused to our own brethren; and you say that, if they attempt to exercise them, you will pursue them to the death.

Is it to be supposed that any Anglo-Saxon people, people of our own blood and race, would submit to such demands? Is there any free people who are worthy of liberty, who would not say that sooner than yield to such demands as these we bid you to wrap in flames our dwellings, and float our land in blood? I believe if they attempt to coerce the southern people in this regard, they will meet not only with the detestation of mankind, but with such resistance as has never been shown before in the world, except, perhaps, in the history of Holland, whose people fought behind the dikes, and flooded their lands with the waves of the sea, preferring death in any and every form rather than submission to such oppression and tyranny.

But, I do not wish to pursue this line of argument. I do not desire to engage in any discussion which so much stirs the blood as the supposition that such rights as these are to be denied to any portion of my countrymen. I choose rather to stand in the character in which I appear this day. I stand here to plea for peace; not that my State, in my opinion, has any reason to fear war more than another, but because it is the interest of all to preserve the peace. In the sacred names of humanity and of Christian civilization; in the names of thirty million of human souls, men, women, and children, whose lives, whose honor, and whose happiness depend upon the events of such a civil war as that with which we are threatened; in the name of the great American experiment, which, as I said before, was founded by Providence in the wilderness, and which, I insist, has not yet failed. I appeal to the American people to prevent the effusion of blood. It is said the very scent of blood stirs up the animal passion of man. Give us time for the play of reason. Let us see, after the southern States have secured themselves by some united action, if we cannot bring together once more our scattered divisions; if we cannot close upon broken ranks; if we cannot find some place of conciliation, some common ground upon which we all may rally once more; and when the columns come mustering in from the distant North and the farthest South, from the rising and from the setting sun, to take their parts in that grand review, the shout of their war-cry shall shake the air until it brings down the very birds in their flight as it ascends to the heavens to proclaim to the world that we are untied once more, brothers in war, and brothers in peace, ready to take our wonted place in the front line of the mighty march of human progress, and able and willing to play for the mastery in that game of nations where the prizes are power and empire, and where victory may crown our name with eternal fame and deathless renown. . . .

THOMAS L. CLINGMAN

Speech on the State of the Union, Delivered in the Senate of the United States, February 4, 1861

(Washington: L. Towers, 1861)

> *Thomas Lanier Clingman (1812–97) was born in North Carolina, attended private schools, graduated from the University of North Carolina, and studied law. He served in the North Carolina House and Senate, entered the U.S. House of Representatives, became a U.S. senator in 1858, and resigned from Congress on March 28, 1861. Clingman joined the North Carolina secession convention and helped to achieve secession. During the Civil War he held rank as brigadier general but was wounded seriously and forced to retire from military service. After the war he practiced law. In the pamphlet below Clingman offered the North a number of compromises, but he warned that the Southern states would resist any attempt at coercion to liberate slaves. He spoke specifically to Border state fears of the federal government's financial activities. Clingman also maintained that the Southern states would prevail in a civil war and gave as reasons the certainty of England's recognition of the Confederacy, covert Northern support for slavery, and a Northern people determined to resist any war taxes. There is no good study of Clingman's life, though Thomas Jeffrey is at work on one. For a view of just how Clingman tried to persuade his constituents to support the Lower South see John C. Inscoe,* Mountain Masters, Slavery, and the Sectional Crisis in North Carolina *(Knoxville: University of Tennessee Press, 1989), 177–256. See also Thomas L. Clingman,* Selections from the Speeches and Writings of Hon. Thomas L. Clingman *(Raleigh: J. Nichols, 1877).*

After the very interesting occurrence which has just taken place, it is difficult for me to address the Senate as I would wish to do. It is not my purpose, to-day, to attempt anything like an elaborate speech upon the questions that have been so much debated. The whole country so thoroughly understands them, that that is now unnecessary. I shall rather direct my remarks to some of the practical questions which are daily presented, for the phase of things is constantly changing, and new issues are continually coming up. The message of the President is commendable in its spirit and temper, whatever gentlemen may think of its specific recommendations.[1]

1. Clingman made reference to President Buchanan's support for the Washington Peace Conference.

I have, myself, regularly voted with the honorable Senator from Kentucky (Mr. Crittenden) for his proposition to compromise existing difficulties; and I shall continue to vote for any measure that may improve the existing status, whether it, in my judgment, be all that the South is entitled to ask or not, leaving to my constituents and other Southern States the right to determine how far it satisfies them. But I have felt all the time, that unless some movement came from the other side of the chamber, or was at least taken up by them, any effort on our part would be futile. Even though every Democratic member should vote for a proposition, and that should chance to make a majority, yet we could not here pass a proposition for any amendment to the Constitution by the necessary two-thirds vote, nor carry any proposition through the House of Representatives, much less cause its adoption by the free States.

The whole country looked to the speech of the honorable Senator from New York (Mr. Seward) made some two weeks since, in the hope that it might present a basis for adjustment. Though that speech was conciliatory in its tone, in its practical recommendations it failed to meet, I am sorry to say, the anticipations of the people of the South. I understood him only to say, in substance, that he was willing, in the first place, to provide that slavery never should be interfered with in the States, a point about which no great anxiety is felt at this time; next, that he was willing that that provision of the Constitution which relates to the return of fugitive slaves should be made a permanent and irrepealable one; (that is a provision which heretofore has been, in fact, very inefficient.) But, upon the great question of the territories, I understood him to say that he would be disposed to vote for the proposition of the honorable Senator from Minnesota provided there were a repeal of the existing organic laws, if it were not that the proposition of that Senator, making arrangements for the future division of the States, was, in his judgment, unconstitutional; and if that division did not take place, the mischief would be greater than that under which we now labor.

In other words—and I do not wish to do injustice to the Senator from New York—I understood him to state three formidable objections to that proposition. First, requiring the repeal of the organic laws, by which I presume, he meant that the New Mexican slave code should be repealed; and even if this were done, there stood a constitutional objection which he cannot get over, and if it were modified so as to provide that these States are to be permanent, then he holds they will be so vast that they will bring greater mischief on the country than it is already laboring under. Upon other points, I do the Senator the justice to say that he eulogized the Union handsomely, and showed that it might be productive of great mischief to

dissolve it; and he also declared that, after this eccentric secession movement had come to an end, one, two or three years hence, he would be disposed to see a convention called to amend the Constitution. It struck me
that the position of the honorable Senator on the present crisis was like that
of a man who, when a city was on fire and the flames were spreading far and
wide, instead of advising means to stop the fire immediately, should enter
into an elaborate speech upon the inexpediency and mischief of having a
city burnt, and suggests that when the heat and fury of the conflagration
had come to an end, it might be well to have an assemblage of the people
and see if there could not be made some provision to prevent similar evils.[2]

The honorable Senator from New York, in one of his speeches last fall
in the Northwest, said that the government of the United States had been,
in 1820, diverted from its former course, and thrown into a wrong direction; in other words, that, for forty years past, it was moving upon an improper track, and that its course was now to be essentially changed. Well,
during that time our government has been administered by Monroe and
John Quincy Adams, by Jackson and Van Buren, by Harrison and Tyler,
by Polk and Taylor, and by Fillmore, Pearce and Buchanan. During these
forty years, therefore, administered in that way, the honorable Senator and
those who act with him hold that the government has been wrong, and they
now propose to reverse its action. Wrong in what respect? Why, in admitting, by the act of 1820, that the Southern States were entitled to go with
their property into a portion of the public territory. The whole purpose,
as I understand it, and as the people of the South understand it, of this
Republican movement is to produce a new condition of things. They say,
in effect, "you of the South are not to have the influence or the privileges
of the government that you heretofore had." It cannot be pretended that,
during this period, we have had an undue power over the administration,
for the presidential office has been fairly divided between the sections; and
for the last twelve years, during which the sectional troubles have been aggravated, it has been entirely in the hands of Northern men. I say that the
whole purport of the movement, as understood at the South, is this: "Your
institutions are not equal to ours, and you must accept an inferior position
under the government." I am free to say even if they menaced us with no
practical wrong, in my judgment, such a policy would justify resistance;

2. Seward replied to Clingman: ". . . I could wait in order to have a proper
consultation whether any of the States have such grievances as required relief by
amendments of the Constitution."

for I know of no nations, no community, that ever consented to accept an inferior position, without, in the end, being ruined.

But the practical measures which these gentlemen propose are, in my judgement, in the highest degree dangerous. Look over the Southern country, and ask yourself what would be the greatest injury that could be done to it? It would not be the establishment of a monarchy, or a military despotism, because we know that monarchies and military despotisms often afford a high degree of security and civil liberty to those subject to them. The greatest possible injury would be to liberate the slaves, and leave them as free negroes in those communities. It is sometimes said that they are worth $4,000,000,000 in money. This, I suppose, is true; but that is only a portion of the pecuniary loss, if we are deprived of them. In the North, for example, if the horses and working cattle were removed, in addition to this loss, other property, such as vehicles and working utensils, the lands themselves would be rendered valueless to a great extent; and so, in fact, if you were to liberate the slaves of the South, so great would be the loss that financial ruin would be inevitable. And yet, this is not the greatest evil. It is that social destruction of society by infusing into it a large free negro population that is most dreaded. Northern gentlemen may realize the evil, perhaps, by considering this case, which I put to them. The negroes of the South are, in most of the States, worth more than the lands. Suppose there was a proposition now to abolish the land titles through the free States, that, if adopted, would produce immense mischief; but, in addition, suppose there were to be transferred to those States a free negro population, equal to half their own, or, as they have eighteen million of people, turn loose among them a population equal to nine million free blacks, and that accompanied with the destruction of the land titles and abolition of the landed property; would not the people of those States at once rise in rebellion against such measures?

The British newspapers seem to be at a loss to account for the excitement and revolution prevailing in this country. It is very natural that they should not understand it, because they draw their ideas altogether from opinions expressed in the North, which are unjust to our section, and partly, also, from the condition of things prevailing in Europe. There, revolutions do not occur, except from extreme physical suffering. The consequence was, that Great Britain, before our revolution, could not understand that our people would make a revolution upon what Mr. Webster declared was a mere preamble—a mere assertion of the right of Great Britain to tax us; and they never did realize, until the war had actually begun, that we would fight merely to escape a contemptible tea-tax of three cents a pound. So, seeing that the United States is one of the most prosperous countries on the earth, they do not seem to realize the idea that we should go to war upon a mere question of right, before actual suffering had begun. Now, our slave property exceeds the national debt of England in value. How long could a ministry stand that was for abolition of that national debt? Remember, too, that the population of the British Isles is three times as great as ours; and it would have to be increased three-fold to make the losses there proportionately as great as those the abolition of slavery would inflict upon us.

In England they are very hostile to a Catholic monarch. If there were a Catholic monarch on the throne, it might produce a revolution. But suppose England were united with a country like France, greater in population; and that that country had the power to impose a Catholic monarch on England against the wish and feeling of the entire body of the people in the British Isles; and that it was known that monarch favored the abolition of the national debt; does any man doubt that the British Isles would be in a blaze of revolution? And yet, that is not as strong a case as that which is now presented to the South.

I am told, however, by gentlemen, with a great deal of seeming plausibility, that this is a condition of things that cannot be carried out; that, though Mr. Lincoln may have said that the war must never cease until slavery is abolished, and that he hoped during his lifetime to see this result produced, yet, under the existing Constitution, he will not be able to effect it; and we are told that we ought to wait, at least, for overt acts. Now when an honorable Senator tells me, for example, that he stands upon the Georgia platform, and that he is ready to resist its violation, I give him credit for the utmost sincerity; but I tell you as a Kentuckian, as one who represents a conservative and border State, I do not believe, if we submitted now to this election, that those overt acts would be resisted.[3] Take, for example, the Fugitive Slave Law. If it were repealed twelve months hence, it might be said that this law violated grossly Northern sentiment; that it was very inefficient; that we did not recover more slaves under it than we did under the old law; that we would be simply thrown back to where we were in 1850; that the border States, being those most interested, ought to be the first to move, and no resistance would in fact be made.

Secondly. Suppose the Wilmot proviso, or the exclusion of slavery from

3. Clingman was referring to Senator John J. Crittenden of Kentucky rather than himself, as the passage seems to imply.

the Territories, was adopted: It would be said, that this was what had been often done; it had been repeatedly passed, and even sanctioned by Southern men, and that in fact slavery never would go into the Territories; that this right was a mere abstraction, and the question would be asked, "Will you dissolve the glorious Union for a mere abstraction?" I do not think there would be resistance by the Southern people after they had been demoralized by submission to Lincoln.

Thirdly. Suppose slavery were abolished in this district, it would doubtless be done with compensation to the owners. The people of the North would not object, of course, to paying a small amount for that purpose, and those who are favorable to a high tariff might be very willing to make that expenditure. Even now the leading Republican journals are discussing the propriety of buying all the slaves in Maryland, in your State, and in Missouri and Delaware, and thereby making them free. This proposition finds favor. If, therefore, slavery in this district were abolished in that way, it would be said, "what right has South Carolina or North Carolina, or any other State to object?" While these things were going on, you would see a division to some extent created in the South. There are, in all communities, discontented elements; there are everywhere men who are ready for a change and ripe for revolution. So powerful is this element in most countries in the world, the people have to be kept down by force. There is, perhaps, not a country in Europe where there would not be a revolution every ten years if it were not for the arms and power of the government. But when a government undertakes to foment revolution, it is omnipotent; and I have no doubt that, with all the patronage and all the power which a Republican President could bring to his aid, with a free post-office distribution of abolition pamphlets, you would see a powerful division in portions of the South. In the meantime, the forts and arsenals could all be well occupied and strengthened, and all the public arms removed from the Southern States. Last winter, before these difficulties happened, when Mr. Floyd made an order directing the removal of arms from the Northern to the Southern States, though he removed less than half of them, he was vehemently denounced for it.[4] You are too well read in history not to remember that Carthage was destroyed because she permitted the Romans, under a promise of good treatment, to remove all her public arms; and if the South, in that condition, with additional armaments in all the forts, with some division among our people, and threatened with negro insurrection, and deprived of all share in the public arms, were then to resist

4. John B. Floyd of Virginia served as President Buchanan's secretary of war.

more serious aggressions, we should fight under great disadvantages and, perhaps, if not subdued, have a long and bloody struggle before us.

I say, therefore, to the honorable Senator from Kentucky, in all sincerity, that, in my judgment, the issue which his State and mine have to determine is, whether there shall be a manly resistance now, or whether our States shall become free negro communities. It is my deliberate judgment that, if this issue had met with no resistance, the latter alternative would have been the result. But, six States have resisted, and are out of the Union, and the seventh, Texas, has probably gone out during the past week. There are causes in operation which will inevitably, too, if they are not arrested, drive out other slave States. In North Carolina, in Kentucky, and in Virginia, for example, a large number of the people now are waiting to see if there can be any proper adjustment. If it fails—if some such scheme as the honorable Senator from Kentucky has offered, is not adopted, a large and powerful body of conservative men will at once go to the side of the secessionists. Even if that does not carry out those States, there is one other contingency, urgent and pressing, which will do it. Your State has determined, by an almost unanimous vote of her Legislature—and so has Virginia—that any attempt to coerce the seceding States should be resisted by force. True, gentlemen say they are not for coercion, but they are for enforcing the laws and collecting the revenue. I will not enter into an argument to prove to any Senator that this is coercion. If I were met on the highway by a man, with a pistol in hand, and he should say that he had no right to rob me, but that he meant to take my money, and would use force to accomplish his purpose, I should not enter into an argument with that man to convince him that this was robbery. So, when honorable Senators tell me that they are for enforcing the laws, I will not argue that this is coercion. All that Great Britain even demanded in the Revolution was, that the colonies should obey the acts of Parliament, and pay such taxes as she imposed; and there was no day, during that long struggle, when, if George Washington and his compatriots had agreed to pay the taxes and obey the acts of Parliament, that the British armies would not have been withdrawn.

This is the only sort of coercion that is ever used among civilized nations. Great Britain, France, Russia, or any other civilized country does not send out the armies to shoot down peaceable, obedient men. All they require is, that the laws should be obeyed and the taxes paid. This idea of sending armies to kill people who are obedient prevails only among savages. It is done in Africa, where one negro community turns out and destroys another. It was the mode of enforcement used among the aborigines of this country, when one Indian tribe went out and destroyed another. Therefore, when honorable Senators tell me that they are not for coercion, but they are for enforcing the laws, I understand them as simply saying that they are civilized men, and mean to resort to that process which prevails in civilized nations, and not among savages.

They suppose that they will be able to have a little war; and I have been astonished, in conversing even with Senators, to say nothing of the newspapers, to find that the idea prevailed that you could have a small war, confined to the blockading of a few ports, and that it would stop there. At an early day of this session, my attention was called to a plan, coming from a distinguished source, in which the opinion was maintained that there were not at that time, in several of the planting States, provisions enough to support the people for two months; and that certainly, with all they could get, by June they would be starved out and brought to terms of submission by a simple blockading of their ports. I was astonished that such an idea should have been entertained in the quarter from which it came. Why, sir, everybody familiar with the South knows that those States have ample means of living until the next crop is produced.

If you could enforce a strict blockade, there is no country on the earth that it would injure so little as the South. All that is made in the United States can be produced there in the greatest abundance, as far as agriculture is concerned, and we might manufacture everything on earth that is needed; and if the whole cotton crop were detained at home, it would not, in a material degree, affect our ultimate prosperity. I say that, if the $200,000,000 worth of cotton which is annually sent from the slave States, were kept here, or never produced, we might still be one of the most prosperous countries on earth; but how would it be with Europe and the North? Can they do without cotton?

It was said, boastingly, at an early state of the session, that King Cotton was dethroned. There never was a time when that monarch seemed to be, in fact, so powerful. When this panic began, and all other kinds of property fell, cotton rose rapidly. The monarch had but to wave his scepter and the bankers of Europe opened their coffers and sent a stream of gold across the Atlantic in ships such as old Neptune never saw when his trident ruled the Mediterranean. Neptune's power was limited to the sea. Alexander claimed to have conquered the world; but his dominions were confined to Asia and the territories on the shores of the Bosphorous. Julius Caesar, a still mightier monarch, ruled only on the eastern continent. King Cotton governs two hemispheres, and dominates on land and sea, and the kings of the east and the merchant princes of the west obey his bidding. Most fortunate was it for New York and the North that his power was unbroken; for when the panic was progressing everywhere, and the banks were failing, and traders were being ruined, and New York itself was staggering and likely to go down with the mercantile interest of that section, producing wide-spread misery, it was this stream of gold which came from Europe that upheld the New York banks, and enabled them to sustain the merchants and prevented a scene of ruin such as we have not hitherto seen. Suppose New York had lost that gold; suppose the cotton which her ships were engaged in carrying had gone out in foreign vessels directly to Europe—above all, suppose it were kept at home, and that neither the North nor England could obtain it; you would see such a commercial revulsion, such a panic, such a pressure, as has not been known in a century. Things would indeed look as if Chaos had returned to assert his ancient dominion over the world. I find a short extract in one of the British papers, the *London Chronicle*, of January 18, which comes to me in the newspapers this morning, that illustrates the view that they are now taking in England of this danger:

"The question is, in fact, little short of life and death. Ruin to merchants and mill-owners, and starvation to the rest of the population, hang immediately in the balance. One year's failure of the American crop, or postponement of the American supply, would produce calamities worse than any war or famine within modern experience."

That is the statement of a British organ, not at all friendly to us and our institutions. The southern coast is too extensive to be actually blockaded by the greatest naval Power on earth; and do you think Great Britain and France would regard a mere paper blockade? You know they would not; they could not afford to do it; and it would never be effective if attempted. Again, as was said by the Senator from Louisiana this morning, the whole ocean would swarm with privateers, and the Northern shipowners would find themselves deprived of our freights, and also liable to capture on the high seas. But, I ask, does anybody for one moment suppose that the war would stop there? Does anybody suppose for one moment that the people of the South would sit down quietly and be cooped up in that way? No, sir. They would march until they found an enemy on land; and with two thousand miles of frontier, stretching from the Atlantic to the extreme West, does anybody really suppose they would not find vulnerable points? I ask gentlemen what is to prevent an attack upon this capital? This city could be destroyed by an army that did not cross the Potomac. A shell could be thrown from Virginia into this very Senate Chamber. I do not say this by way of menace; but to let gentlemen see that there is no difficulty in finding points of collision; and lest I should be supposed to insinuate that there is on foot a plan to attack this capital, I wish to disclaim emphatically all purpose of any design to interfere with it as far as I know or believe. This capital is not of the smallest consequence in a military point of view. It was said by a great commander that, as to fortified places and cities, he would leave them to the end of the war; for they were the prizes which fall to the conqueror. This is eminently true of this District. It is obliged to follow the fate of the territory around it. Though the whole South were anxious that a northern government should be kept here, if Maryland and Virginia, or Virginia alone should leave the Union, we all know that the North would not find it to be to its interest to keep a capital either surrounded by foreign territory or on its border. I should regret deeply any struggle for a place like this, which is of no value in a military point of view, and which would impel the country into civil war; but I am free to say, that if a war begins down in the South, it is as likely to come up here as to any other point that I know of. It cannot be confined to Charleston harbor; it cannot be confined to Pensacola; but when it begins there, it will find its way perhaps to this very city.

Gentlemen will see that, with these two thousand miles of frontier, it is practicable to have war, and it would certainly occur, a regular old-fashioned war, if the present line of policy be continued. There can be no doubt about it. It is so clear to any gentleman who reflects, that I do not think it necessary to enlarge upon it. But it is sometimes said that, if a war begins, the North, being the more powerful of the two sections, will certainly be able to overrun the South. There are a million and a half of men in the slaveholding States capable of bearing arms; and it is generally supposed that a country can maintain permanently in the field one-sixth of its able-bodied men. That calculation would afford two hundred and fifty thousand men for a fighting force. You must recollect, however, that among our four million slaves there are at least two million laborers. This circumstance would largely increase the force we could keep in the field. I have no doubt that a million of men at home, with all the slaves, would carry on our industrial occupations, while we might have at least four or five hundred thousand men capable of being kept in the field. Such a force would certainly require an immense sum of money to maintain it; but a community struggling for existence will not count the cost of armaments.

How will it be in the North? You ought to have a larger force than this to enable you to carry on war abroad. Suppose it is no larger: how are you to keep in the field a body of four hundred thousand or five hundred thousand men? At the outset, I grant that your bankers might come forward, and enable you to begin the war on credit; but all wars of any length cannot be maintained in that way. The exports of the free States are generally less than one hundred millions; and your imports can be no greater, without draining you of specie. Any tariff you can impose will give no more money than you will want to support your Government in time of peace. I put this matter to gentlemen seriously, because it is well enough to look at these things now; for in a few weeks we may have them upon us as actual realities. I ask Senators to exercise no greater foresight than any farmer manifests when, in the spring of the year, he provides for the coming autumn and winter. These issues may be upon us in a few weeks.

Now, do you believe that you can get your people to consent to support an enormous system of taxation for the mere purpose of subjugating us? From the very nature of your population, your industrial occupations must suffer more than ours. A large portion of your people are engaged in commerce, and others in manufactures; and they depend partly upon us for freights, and partly, also, for markets. Deprived of these you must have a large, idle, discontented, and suffering class. There is, besides, a still greater difficulty to be encountered before you. A large portion of your people believe that you are wrong in this movement.

I say, then, that one of three contingencies is inevitably before you: either a settlement of these difficulties such as is satisfactory and arrest the movement; or a recognition of a peaceable separation; or thirdly, war. No human ingenuity can find any other result. The best course, undoubtedly, would be to adjust things now, if possible, on a satisfactory and permanent basis. The next best is a peaceable recognition of the independence of the seceding states; and the worst of all, but inevitable, if neither of the others be taken, is war. I tell gentlemen, if they sit still war will make itself; it will come of its own accord. Look now at the condition of the forts in the South. They were originally built, mainly to protect those States in which they are situated, as a portion of the Union, but there were some additional reasons for their erection. When States secede, the government is entitled to be paid for its property, undoubtedly; but the States have a moral and political right to occupy, and they will hold those fortifications in the end. I may say, in relation to the manner in which they came to be taken, something by way of explanation. On the last day of December, there were orders issued from the War Department, for the purpose of sending troops South. It is true, that late in the evening, perhaps as late as eleven o'clock, these orders were countermanded; but in the meantime, telegraphic despatches were sent to the South, and a number of forts were taken. In my own State, on the day following, the 1st of January, we were advised there was a similar movement on foot, and a dispatch went down which prevented it, by giving assurances that the orders had been counter-manded. Not long afterwards, however, the sending down of the Star of the West occurred, other reports of hostile movements went abroad, and our own people occupied some of the forts in North Carolina; but they were informed again that there was no purpose on the part of the government to reinforce them, and they were abandoned.

I mention this in order that Senators may understand the *animus* of our people. They do not want to interfere with the government property; they do not mean to interfere with its rights while it may be disposed to do them justice; but they do not intend that these forts shall be used for their oppression. Of what use is Fort Sumter to the government of the United States unless it be to vex and harass Charleston? If things remain as they are now, with the understanding that these places are to be held by the government, or retaken, of course you will have war; it is obliged to come on. And this question presents itself to honorable Senators: had you rather have this war; or do you prefer doing something to avoid it? If you let things remain as they are, until Mr. Lincoln comes into power, with the well understood purpose of holding the forts in the South, to compel those States to pay taxes to, and obey the laws of, what is now a foreign government, you leave them no alternative but to take those forts by force. I repeat, if under these circumstances you stand still, all the world will know that you mean to have war.

I am sorry to see, Mr. President, that many on the other side, instead of meeting these questions as I think they ought to do, are laboring under strange delusions. When Senators—I refer particularly to the Senator from Mississippi (Mr. Davis), who has left, and the Senator from Virginia (Mr. Hunter)—spoke of the evils of war, and deprecated them, it was trumpeted far and wide through the North that the South was afraid of the result, and was begging for peace. There never was a greater mistake. I have yet to see the first Southern man who believes that his section could be conquered; but in speaking of the evils of war, these gentlemen show that they have counted the cost of the enterprise, and are willing to hazard all its consequences.

But another and still greater delusion under which I think Republicans are laboring is, that a Southern Confederacy would not be recognized by the great Powers of the earth. Do they not know that it is a well-settled principle to recognize *de facto* governments? Oh, yes; but they suppose that the humanity of Great Britain will prevent her recognizing a slave-holding community. Let us look a little to the acts of that government. Its humanity did not prevent its waging war with China to compel the Chinese to take opium for the benefit of her India colonists. She is just now concluding a war with China; and one of the very objects—if the newspapers are to be relied on—to be effected, is the right to take coolies from China, and transport them to the British Colonies. Remember, that China had earnestly resisted the seizure of her people by British agents, and done all in her power to suppress this trade in the bodies of her subjects. . . . [5]

But it is supposed that Great Britain has such a sympathy and friendship for the North, and that there is such a feeling upon this slavery question, that she would not recognize a revolting slaveholding Southern Confederacy. Great Britain and Portugal had been on the most friendly terms for a century. Little Portugal was a *protege* of Great Britain, and Great Britain took many a fight on her hands for her sake. She loved her like an orphan child; but her love for Portugal did not prevent her recognizing Brazil, when that country revolted and established its independence. England and Brazil (the greatest slaveholding country in the world except our own) are now on terms of the closest friendship. . . . [6]

I beg, gentlemen not to be deluded by all they see in the English papers. There is, no doubt, a great deal of ignorance in England about this country. I read the other day, and have read it again and again in the English papers, that the plantations at the South were all mortgaged to the North; and that the negroes and lands were, in fact, owned by the North, and if it were not that the North supplied the means, no cotton could be made. Any opinion of British papers founded on such delusions as these is not worth much to any body. But I do say there is now a great deal of intelligence among the well informed in England in relation to our country. and they evidently understand things far better now than they did formerly. . . . [7]

Another mistake which I think gentlemen make is this: they suppose this movement at the South may be the mere result of the efforts of designing politicians; and that the break up at Charleston has caused it. No one was more averse than myself to seeing this separation of the Democratic party; and I thank the honorable Senator from Ohio for his efforts on that occasion, and those of all others, to prevent it. But, so far from its contributing

5. What followed here were short comments on the Chinese coolie trade.

6. Clingman cited the English diplomat and political leader Robert Peel on the problems of emancipation in the West Indies.

7. The London *Times* of January 18, 1861, stated: ". . . if a Southern federation be formed . . . there can be no hope of keeping the border slave States." Clingman went on to discuss why he believed England would either remain neutral or recognize a Southern Confederacy.

to this secession movement, it has been the main obstacle in its way. The great body of the people of the South do not hate the North, I think, as has been said by some Senators. I know it is not true in North Carolina. There is a very great distrust of the dominant majority of the North, and an apprehension of mischief; but the great body of our people would far prefer a union with the North upon honorable terms. While this is true, however, it is equally well known that the division of the Democratic party has retarded the action of the South in defence of its honor and its rights.

I say, to you, that but for this division of the party, if we had however, been beaten, the whole South would have gone out just as South Carolina has done—I mean without division. It was that party division and the discussion growing out of it, and the charges and crimination and recrimination of Union and disunion in the canvass, that were the great obstacles in the way. But our people are gradually getting over those prejudices; and they see that the Republicans of the North intended to beat us, whether we were united or not; and the very men who most regretted the divisions of the party are gradually falling into the movement. They see we will be ruined by submission to the election of Mr. Lincoln. The Republicans meant to beat us, whether we were united or not, and the injury from their rule is the same either way; and it is not for them to say that we fought the battle unskillfully. I admit we did fight unskillfully; but everybody in the South was against them. We say that their domination is just as mischievous to us as if we had been well united. Another fact presents itself, that they have a clear, large, overwhelming majority in the northern States; enough to give them the control of the Government; and it is a knowledge of this fact that is driving our people forward, and they will gradually come up to one line of action. History reproduces itself; human nature is the same; and it might have been said in our struggle with Great Britain that the colonies were divided. They did not defend themselves well. Gates, by his rashness, incurred the defeat at Camden. There were dissentions in the colonies, and even many tories among them; but that was no excuse for Great Britain. She intended to subdue them, whether they were united or not, and the injury of her domination would have been the same in either event.

Again: it is said, very plausibly, I admit, that we ought not to abandon our Northern friends, our allies. That identical remark might have been made, and was, in substance, made during our Revolution, for there were Chatham and Burke and others whom our colonies had to abandon. Lord Chatham never justified, but always condemned, the secession of the colonies; but that secession or revolution vindicated him and Burke and Fox. And, if we were now to submit, where would our Northern allies be?

Trampled under foot by a resistless anti-slavery party. It would be said: "Your Southern friends are gasconading braggarts; ready to submit to us like whipped spaniels." They would be trodden down and annihilated; but by our resisting we vindicate the Senator from Ohio as a patriot, a sagacious statesman, and a just man. We vindicate the Senator from Illinois; the Senators from Indiana; the Senator from Oregon; the Senators from Pennsylvania and New Jersey; and last though not least, the generous Senator from Minnesota. They will stand in after times as men who had the sagacity to see the right, and the courage to defend it.

Again: we are told that having gone into the contest, we are bound to submit to the result, just as a gambler who plays a game must pay the stakes he loses. Why on this principle, if the Republicans were to nominate a free negro, I suppose we ought to let him be elected without opposition, for if we run a candidate against him, we would be bound to submit to him if elected, and therefore ought to let him go in without opposition. If we had not attempted to defeat Lincoln, in fact, by running a rival candidate, we might have been obliged to submit, and ought to have been, and would have been, justly held responsible. We, however, did our duty to the country by making an honest effort to defeat him, though possibly we may not have conducted the contest skillfully. I maintain that no party in the South is justly chargeable with Lincoln's election, as, in spite of their resistance, he obtained a large majority over all opposition in States enough in the North to elect him.

I will say in candor also to Senators, that there are three measures now passing which will add very much to the secession movement in the South. I allude, first, to the Pacific railroad bill, by which we have undertaken, as far as this Senate can undertake anything, to build three railroads, at a cost of $120,000,000. Now some of our people deny your right to make improvements. Those who admit the right, doubt very much whether you ought to go to the expense of making a single railroad across a thousand miles of desert and uninhabited country; and this proposition for building three railroads, under these circumstances, and incurring a debt, perhaps to be increased to two or three hundred millions (for the best informed men say it cannot fall below $300,000,000), will drive many of the most sagacious and reflective men of the South, men of philosophical minds, to acquiesce in dissolution.

Again, here is this tariff bill, likely to be adopted, which passed the House by a large vote, containing most iniquitous provisions for the benefit of particular classes; and then there is another measure which, with due respect to those who endorse it, to my mind, is the most indefensible of all propositions hitherto advocated—I mean the homestead bill. The idea of giving up the public property by wholesale at any time to men, many of whom are the least meritorious of the community, is wholly indefensible, in my judgment; but now, with a bankrupt Treasury, borrowing money at the rate of fifty or sixty million a year, the policy of giving up these public lands in a body, to any one who chooses to take them, shocks the whole community.

Recollect that, with the sum already authorized to be borrowed at this session, the bills from the House now before us, and which it is understood are sure to be passed here, make a sum total of $70,000,000. This does not include the $121,000,000 for the Pacific railroads, and, in addition, we are to have this most oppressive tariff bill to tax the country outrageously, while the pending homestead bill gives the public property to the "landless."

Our people are coming to the conclusion that this government has become so vast that it is an impracticable one. I am not sure of this. I think, large as the country is, that the government might be well administered, but for the anti-slavery excitement. When a family is divided into two sections, who are warring against each other, of course household duties must be neglected. We have had a struggle for the last ten years; the North pressing, and the South struggling for its honor and safety against the movement; and such measures are its results. In fact they are directly traceable to that hostility of Northern anti-slavery men. The people of the Northwest do not want high protective tariffs—by no means; and many Republicans do not want them; and yet you find the Republicans in a body, in the House and on this floor, coming up and voting for a most enormous tariff. Why? It is to secure the support of the tariff-men of Pennsylvania and elsewhere.

Again, New England does not like this homestead bill. At any rate, when I came here fifteen years ago, I found the men from New England were in favor of holding on to the public lands, and so far from wishing to encourage settlement in the West, they used to object strenuously to opening that territory to take off their laborers from them. They wished to retain them at home and thus keep down the price of wages. Now you find the solid vote of New England, I believe, for the homestead bill to tempt their people to go away. Why is this? They want to satisfy the West; and you find the northwestern Republicans going for this high protective tariff to secure the votes of Pennsylvania and the East. The anti-slavery men form the great nucleus of the party, and they spread out their arms in all directions and gather in allies.

Now, I am free to say if, when this homestead bill was up, I could substitute for it a proposition giving the lands absolutely to the new States in which they lie, I would prefer it. It is a less evil to the government. If they choose to give them out to the landless, let them do it. I would in that way, if I could, cut them loose from this combination. In the same way, if you present to me a well-guarded Pacific railroad bill for a single track, I will vote it through, if it is on the cheapest and best line; but if you ask me to tax my people outrageously to benefit a few manufacturing capitalists, I will not do it. What I desire, then, is this: we should, even if this Government is to endure, dissolve this combination. Remember, the South has no share in this copartnership. The Northeast is to get the tariff; the Northwest the Pacific railroad and the homestead bill; and the Republicans, or Abolitionists are to get anti-slavery. These are the parties to the combination. The sagacious men of the South see the danger; and sooner than submit to be cheated and plundered in this mode, with the prospect in the future of the abolition of slavery and the utter destruction of their section, they are coming resolutely into the struggle. Nor will they pause now unless full justice be done them on this slavery question. The Legislature of my own State, as well as that of Virginia has planted itself firmly on the basis of the Crittenden propositions, with certain additions, and they will not be satisfied with less.

I am astonished that the North hesitates to take the proposition of the honorable Senator from Kentucky. What is it? Why, of the existing territory, it gives the South about one-fifth and the North four-fifths. We are entitled to have two-fifths according to population. They say it is carrying out the platform on which Mr. Breckinridge was nominated; I allude to the presidential candidate. All that is a mistake. By that platform, as they understand it, slavery was to be protected in all the Territories; and the people of the South honestly believe that it ought to be so, and that, according to the true intent of the Constitution, it is protected; and the opinions of the Supreme Court sustain this view. Now, instead of carrying it out, that proposition proposes to give the North four-fifths of the territory, and only one-fifth to the South. Why, a man who claims a tract of land, and offers, as a compromise, to give up four-fifths of it, would not obtain his claim, certainly. It seems to me, therefore, the Republicans ought not hesitate one moment, but ought at once to have taken it.

They say, however, that their platform requires that they shall have the whole of the territory, and exclude us altogether. I submit to honorable Senators as just men (for I know that in the ordinary transactions of life they are just men) that there is not a Senator on that side of the Chamber that does not know that the South has contributed its money fairly with the North; that in every war we have turned out more than our proposition of men; and I ask them if it is just that our people should altogether be excluded from those acquisitions which we jointly made?

But some of them object to that provision which applies it to future Territories. They say we will take Mexico, Central America, &c. Why, if none of the States had seceded, the North would have a majority now of eight Senators on this floor. With all the States represented in the other branch, she had fifty-seven majority, and under the incoming apportionment will have over sixty. They know that no territory can be ever acquired without a large support from them; and the new States of the Northwest coming in will very soon swell still more their majorities. It is idle, therefore, for these gentlemen to try to convince any one that they are afraid of acquisitions against their wishes. So, I apprehend that they want to keep this question open. I fear they want to have materials to electioneer at home; and put down those men who are just enough to recognize our right. I fear that they want to keep it an open question, by which they can crush out such Northern Democrats as my friend from Ohio. If not, why object to settling the whole territorial question for all time to come?

Again, why not agree that slavery shall be protected in the District of Columbia, the forts and arsenals in the slave States, and to the slave trade between the States? They can do that without interfering with any Northern interest. If they do that—if they place this entire question where it cannot be reached, you may, perhaps, end this agitation; otherwise it cannot be ended; and, for the sake of our Northern friends, I think we ought now to take a stand and leave the Union at once, unless a complete adjustment can be made.

Ten years ago I became apprehensive that we should have a dissolution of the Union between these States. Up to that time I had not thought it possible. I think there was a great error committed then. I have always regretted that Mr. Clay and Mr. Webster, patriotic as they were, did not seem to appreciate the magnitude of the question, and did not place that settlement on its proper ground. If that Missouri line had been run through, as was demanded by the South (and if they had gone for it, it could have been done), possibly we should have had peace. Nay, more: after it was determined that we should try non-intervention, I earnestly endeavored to induce them to repeal the Missouri restriction, and let non-intervention apply to Kansas and all the territory north of the line of 36°30'. If they had done that at that time, we should have avoided the excitement and discussion growing out of the application of the principle to Kansas, and possibly we might have had peace. But ever since then, looking to the future, I have had apprehensions; and in examining the map of America I have often been brought to the conclusion that it seemed as if Providence had marked out on it two great empires—one lying on the Mississippi and around the Gulf of Mexico; the other upon the basin of the St. Lawrence. We know that natural boundaries control very much the form of nations. A great and powerful force sometimes carries a nationality over boundaries; but nature conquers in the end. Italy has extended itself into France and Spain; and France and Spain have each extended themselves into Italy; but the Alps and the Pyrennees still stand as the boundaries of those empires.

Now, there are States which lie partly upon the waters of the Mississippi, and partly upon the St. Lawrence. Which empire they will go with, if this division occurs, is a matter of speculation. Whether they will be divided, I know not; but it would seem that political feeling is now tending to such a division. The section nearest the St. Lawrence is anti-slavery strongly, while in the southern borders of those States there are opposite sentiments. It would seem as if the political, and the social feelings of the Northern and Southern sections of the Union were drifting in the direction of the flow of these immense rivers, and that future nationalities were to have their forms determined by these natural divisions.

We have had thirteen Presidents of the United States elected by the people. I mean Mr. Buchanan is the thirteenth man thus chosen who has presided over all the States. At the time the Confederacy was formed, was it written in the book of fate that it should endure until there had been a man elected for each of those States? Senators on the other side of this Chamber will determine that question.

The honorable Senator from New York spoke with regret of a division of the Union when the dome of this capital was almost completed. The tower of Babel was not finished when the nations of antiquity were divided. There was a providential purpose in that movement—to humble the pride of man, and extend humanity over the eastern continent. Whether there is such a purpose now, by dividing this Union, to send two streams of civilization over America, or whether this unfinished tower is to stand as a monument of human folly and dissention upon a continent strewn far and wide with the immense ruins of a gigantic political and social fabric, time alone can disclose. If evil should happen, the finger of history will fix the responsibility on those who commenced and carried out this anti-slavery revolution. When Julius Caesar looked over the field of Pharsalia, and saw it strewn with the bodies of his slain countrymen, he exclaimed, "They would have it so." Posterity will say of those who persist in this warfare, "You would have these results."

The most impressive ceremony which I have witnessed in this Chamber was on the occasion when a number of Senators from the seceding States took leave of us. It reminded me of the funeral ceremonies when a Senator has died, but was far more impressive, because the annunciation of the death of a State of this Confederacy is more momentous than that of its representative. I use the term, because there is an analogy between the cases. When a Senator dies, his spirit goes from one state of existence to another; it may be a brighter and a better one. When those States no longer live to this Government, they pass into a new Confederacy. The Israelites, with wailing and lamentation, deplored the loss of one of their tribes. When recently the annunciation of the departure of a single State was made here, it was met with strange levity on the other side of the Chamber. How will it be when the ten tribes have gone, when fifteen States have departed? In those States were born and nourished such slaveholders as Washington and Jefferson and Madison and Henry and Marshall and Jackson and Clay and Calhoun. They are filled at this day with such slaveholders and "poor whites," as our non-slave owners are stigmatized by abolition speakers, as formerly went up with George Washington to defend Massachusetts and New York and Pennsylvania and the Jerseys, and, at a later day, stood upon the Canada line with Forsyth and Scott and Harrison and Johnson. When pressed by a formidable foe, the North did not refuse the aid of these southern "barbarians." If it has now grown to be so great that it regards a further association with them an encumbrance or a disgrace, then for the sake of past recollections, why not let them go in peace?

The Senator from New York said on one occasion, not long since, that, in this dispute between the North and the South, it was a matter of conscience with the North, while with the South it only a matter of interest; and therefore the South ought to yield. By this mode, the conscience of the North can be relieved without subjecting the South to financial bankruptcy, political degradation and social ruin. The anti-slavery current can then run its course unchecked and untrammeled. It has already demanded, at Boston, the removal of the statue of Daniel Webster because he was willing to compromise with the South. How long will it be until it reaches that stage when it will require that the statues of such slaveholders as Washington and Jackson shall be thrown into the Potomac, the monument of the former razed to the ground, and the very name of this city changed to one in harmony with the anti-slavery feeling? Hereafter, if the North should meet adverse fortune, and again change its views, then there might be a reunion and reconstruction of the government. Twice did the Plebians secede, and twice did the haughty Patricians make such terms of conciliation as rendered Rome the foremost empire upon earth.

If the States were now divided into two confederacies, and their interests required a union, I do not know why it might not occur. But war places an impassable gulf between them. A Roman ambassador, addressing those to whom he was sent, said: "I carry in my bosom peace and war; which will you have?" Reversing his declaration, I say to Senators on the other side of this Chamber, "You carry in your bosoms, for the country, peace or war; which do you mean to give it?" If you say war, then our people will meet you, and struggle with you all along the lines, and wherever else you come; and they will defend their honor and the safety of their wives and children, with the same spirit and resolution which was exhibited at Sullivan's Island and at King's Mountain, at Yorktown and at New Orleans, and over the many battle-fields of Mexico. I have no doubt that the South will make a triumphal defence if assailed; but sooner than submit to disgrace and degradation, she would, if fall she must, rather go down like the strong man of the Bible, carrying with her the main pillars of the edifice, the edifice itself, and the lords of the Philistines, into one common ruin.[8]

8. The pamphlet printed three days after Clingman's speech contained appendixes that included extracts from the London *Post* and the London *Economist*. Clingman was attempting to show North Carolinians that the Confederacy did not plan to reopen the African slave trade.

ANDREW JOHNSON

Speech ... On the State of the Union, Delivered in the Senate of the United States, February 5 & 6, 1861

(Washington: Congressional Globe Office, 1861)

Andrew Johnson (1808–75) was born into poverty in North Carolina. In 1826 he moved to Greeneville in mountainous eastern Tennessee and educated himself. He entered the Tennessee House and later the Tennessee Senate, and in 1843 he gained election to the U.S. House of Representatives, then served in the U.S. Senate. A Unionist, Johnson remained in the Senate when the Civil War started and supported the Lincoln administration as military governor of Tennessee. He became vice president of the United States in 1864. When Lincoln was assassinated he assumed the presidency, only to feud with the Republican Party and be impeached in 1868. His vigorous repudiation of Lower South secession in this pamphlet reveals his passion and his devotion to the Union. He argued forcefully for unity among Upper South and Border states, attempted to divide the Lower South with accusations that a radical antidemocratic plot to achieve secession was afoot, and vowed that no army would invade his beloved Tennessee. His life has been studied by Eric McKitrick in Andrew Johnson and Reconstruction *(Chicago: University of Chicago Press, 1969); also see Hans Trefousse,* Andrew Johnson *(New York: W. W. Norton, 1989). The University of Tennessee Press is publishing his papers.*

On the 19th of December, I made a speech in the Senate, with reference to the present crisis, which I believed my duty to my State and to myself required. In making that speech, my intention—and I think I succeeded in it—was to place myself upon the principles of the Constitution and the doctrines inculcated by Washington, Jefferson, Madison, Monroe, and Jackson. Having examined the positions of those distinguished fathers of the Republic, and compared them with the Constitution, I came to the conclusion that they were right; and upon them I planted myself, and made the speech to which I have referred, in vindication of the Union and the Constitution, and against the doctrine of nullification or secession, which I look upon as a great political heresy. As far back as 1833, when I was a young man, before I made my advent into public life, when the controversy arose between the Federal Government and the State of South Carolina, and it became necessary for Andrew Jackson, then President of the United

States, to issue his proclamation, exhorting that people to obey the law and comply with the requirements of the Constitution, I planted myself upon the principles then announced by him, which I advocated on the 19th of December last. I believed that the positions taken then by General Jackson, and those who came to his support, were the true doctrines of the Constitution, and the only doctrines upon which this Government could be preserved. I have been uniformly, from that period to the present time, opposed to the doctrine of secession, or of nullification, which is somewhat of a hermaphrodite, but approximates to the doctrine of secession. I repeat, that I then viewed it as a heresy and as an element which, if maintained, would result in the destruction of this Government. I maintain the same position to-day. I then opposed the doctrine of secession as a political heresy, which, if sanctioned and sustained as a fundamental principle of this government, will result in its overthrow and destruction; for, as we have seen already, a few of the States are crumbling and falling off.

But, since I made that speech on the 19th of December, I have been the peculiar object of attack. I have been denounced, because I happened to be the first man south of Mason and Dixon's line who entered a protest or made an argument in the Senate against this political heresy. From what I saw here on the evening when I concluded my speech—although some may have thought that it intimidated and discouraged me—I was inspired with confidence; I felt that I had struck treason a blow. I thought then, and I know now, that men who were engaged in treason felt the blows that I dealt out on that occasion. As I have been made the peculiar object of attack, not only in the Senate, but out of the Senate, my object on this occasion is to meet some of these attacks, and to say some things in addition to what I then said against this movement. . . .[1]

I never do things by halves. I am against this doctrine entirely. I commenced making war upon it—a war for the Constitution and the Union—and I intend to sink or swim upon it. In the remarks that I made on the 19th of December, I discussed at some length the alleged right of secession. I repudiated the whole doctrine. I introduced authorities to show its unsoundness, and made deductions from those authorities which have not been answered to this day; but by innuendo and indirection, without reference to the person who used the authorities, attempts have been made to answer the speech. Let those who can, answer the speech, answer the authorities, answer the conclusions which have been deduced from them. I was more

1. Johnson disputed Louisiana claims over who controlled the Mississippi. (I have dropped many of his quotes from other speeches and pamphlets.)

than gratified, shortly afterwards, when one of the distinguished Senators from Virginia delivered a speech upon this floor, which it was apparent to all had been studied closely; which had been digested thoroughly; which, in the language of another, had been conned and set down in a note-book, and got by rote; not only the sentences constructed, but the language measured. In the plan which he proposed as one upon which the Government can be continued and administered, in his judgment, he brought his mind seemingly, irresistibly, to the conclusion that this doctrine of secession was a heresy. What does he say in that able, that methodical, that well-digested speech? he goes over the whole ground. He has been reasoning on it; he has been examining the principle of secession; he has gone to the conclusion to which it leads; and he is seemingly involuntarily, but irresistibly forced to admit that it will not do to acknowledge this doctrine of secession. . . .[2]

I quoted the Old Dominion extensively before. I took the foundation of this doctrine and traced it along step by step, and showed that there was no such notion tolerated by the fathers of the Republic as the right of secession. Now, who comes up to my relief? When the States are seceding, the distinguished Senator from Virginia says, in so many words, that he admits the error, and the force of the principle that a State ought not to be permitted to go out of the Confederacy without the consent of the remaining members. He says, however, that the right to secede results from the nature of the compact. I have read Mr. Jefferson, and I am as much inclined to rely on the former distinguished men of the State of Virginia as I am on the latter. In the old Articles of Confederation, when the revenue required for the support of the Federal Government was apportioned among the States, and each State had to raise its portion, the great difficulty was, that there was no means by which the States could be compelled to contribute their amount; there was no means of forcing the State to compliance. . . .[3]

I have stated that it was under the old Articles of Confederation, when there was no power to compel a State even to contribute her proportion of the revenues; but in that view of the case, Mr. Jefferson said that the injured party had a right to enforce compliance with the compact from the offending State, and that this was a right deducible from the laws of nature. The present Constitution was afterwards formed; and to avoid this difficulty in

2. Johnson quoted Robert M. T. Hunter's January 11, 1861, speech. See Hunter's pamphlet in this volume to understand how Johnson misunderstood the Virginian's views on secession.

3. Like so many of the authors of the pamphlets in this volume, Johnson was capable of using Jefferson's words to make his own case.

raising revenue, the power was conferred upon the Congress of the United States "to lay and collect taxes, duties, imposts, and excises," and the Constitution created a direct relation between the citizen and the Federal Government in that matter, and to that extent that relation is just as direct and complete between the Federal Government and the citizen as is the relation between the State and the citizen in other matters. Hence we find that, by an amendment to the Constitution of the United States, the citizen cannot even make a State a party to a suit, and bring her into the Federal courts. They wanted to avoid the difficulty of coercing a State, and the Constitution conferred on the Federal government the power to operate directly upon the citizen, instead of operating on the States. It being the right of the Government to enforce obedience from the citizen in those matters of which it has jurisdiction, the question comes up as to the exercise of this right. It may not always be expedient. It must depend upon discretion, as was eloquently said by the Senator from Kentucky on one occasion. It is a matter of discretion, even as Mr. Jefferson laid it down before this provision existed in the Constitution, before the Government had power to collect its revenue as it now has. I know that when, on a former occasion, I undertook to show, as I thought I did show, clearly and distinctly, the difference between the existence and the exercise of this power, words were put into my mouth that I did not utter, and positions answered which I had never assumed. It was said that I took the bold ground of coercing a State. I expressly disclaimed it. I stated, in my speech, that, by the Constitution, we could not put a State into court; but I said there were certain relations created by the Constitution between the Federal Government and the citizen, and that we could enforce those laws against the citizen. I took up the fugitive slave law; I took up the post office system; and I might have taken up the power to coin money and to punish counterfeiters, or the power to pass laws to punish mail robbers. I showed that under these we had power, not to punish a State, but to punish individuals as violators of the law. Who will deny it; who can deny it, that acknowledges the existence of the Government? This point, I think, was settled in the decision of the Supreme Court in the case of Ableman *vs.* Booth. When the decision of the Supreme Court is in our favor, we are very much for it; but sometimes we are not so well reconciled to it when it is against us. . . .

When the fugitive slave law was executed in the city of Boston, by the aid of military force, was that understood to be coercing a State, or was it simply understood to be an enforcement of the law upon those who, it was assumed, had violated it? In this same decision the Supreme Court declared that the fugitive slave law, in all its details, is constitutional, and therefore should be enforced. Who is prepared to say that the decision of the court shall not be carried out? Who is prepared to say that the fugitive slave law shall not be enforced? Do you coerce a State when you simply enforce the law? If one man robs the mail and you seek to arrest him, and he resists, and you employ force, do you call that coercion? If a man counterfeits your coin, and is arrested and convicted, and punishment is resisted, cannot you execute the law? It is true that sometimes so many may become infected with disobedience, outrages and violations of law may be participated in by so many, that they get beyond the control of the ordinary operations of law; the disaffection may swell to such proportions as to be too great for the Government to control; and then it becomes a matter of discretion, not a matter of constitutional right. . . .[4]

I subscribe most heartily to the sentiment presented by the Richmond Enquirer of November 1, 1814. Then it was declared by that high authority that the Union was to be saved; that those persons who were putting themselves in opposition to the law were traitors, and that their treason should be punished as such. Now, sir, what is treason? The Constitution of the United States defines it, and narrows it down to a very small compass. The Constitution declares that "treason against the United States shall consist only in levying war against them, or in adhering to their enemies, giving them aid and comfort." Who are levying war upon the United States? Who are adhering to the enemies of the United States, giving them aid and comfort? Does it require a man to take the lantern of Diogenes, and make a diligent search to find those who have been engaged in levying war against the United States? Will it require any very great research or observation to discover the adherents of those who are making war against the United States, and giving them aid and comfort? If there are any such in the United States they ought to be punished according to law and the Constitution. [Applause in the galleries, which was suppressed by the Presiding Officer.] Mr. Ritchie, speaking for the Old Dominion, used language that was unmistakable: "The treason springing out of the hot-bed of the Hartford convention should [be][5] punished." It was all right to talk about treason *then*; it was all right to punish traitors in *that* direction. For myself, I care not whether treason be committed north or south; he that is guilty of treason deserves a traitor's fate.

But, when we come to examine the views of some of those who have been engaged in this work, we find that the foundation of their desire to

4. Quotes from Virginians in opposition to secession followed.

5. Editor's addition.

break up this Government dates beyond, and goes very far back of, any recent agitation of the slavery question. There are some men who want to break up this Government anyhow; who want a separation of the Union. There are some who have got tired of a government *by the people.* They fear the people. Take the State of South Carolina. Although she has had Senators on this floor who have acted a portion of the time with the Democratic party, and sometimes with no party, there is, in that State, an ancient and a fixed opposition to a government by the people. They have an early prejudice against this thing called democracy—a government of the people. They entertained the idea of secession at a very early day; it is no new idea with them; it has not arisen out of the slavery question and its recent agitation. Even to this good day, the people, the freemen of South Carolina, have never been permitted to vote for President and Vice President of the United States. They have never enjoyed that great luxury of freemen, of having a voice in the selection of their Chief Magistrate. . . . [6]

It will be seen, from these two documents, what the early notions of the people of South Carolina were. There never was, and I doubt very much whether, with a large portion of them, there ever will be, any ideas of the people governing themselves. They had, at that early day, a great aversion to a *government by the people.* It was repudiated; and in the document which has just been read, signed by two hundred and ten citizens of Charleston, they proposed to pass back under the British Government. This carries out the previous proposition to remain with Great Britain by treaty stipulation, and not go through the revolutionary struggles with the colonies with whom they had formed a confederation.

Again: in 1833, under the pretense of resistance to the operation of our revenue system and to a protective tariff, they endeavored to break up the Government. They were overruled then. Their pride was wounded by that failure; and their determination was fixed, whenever it was in their power, to break up this Government and go out of the Union. This feeling, I have no doubt, has existed there from that period to the present time. When we turn to the debates which recently took place in the South Carolina convention, we find that Mr. Maxey Gregg, Mr. Rhett, and others, said that their reason for going out of the Union now dates as far back as forty years; some of them said thirty years, and some twenty. Mr. Gregg said, in the South Carolina convention, on the 21st of December last:

6. Johnson quoted a letter of May 12, 1779, from William Moultrie, *Memoirs of the American Revolution* (1802), to reveal South Carolina as promonarchy. Senator Louis Wigfall of Texas challenged Johnson's claims.

"If we undertake to set forth all the causes, do we not dishonor the memory of all the statesmen of South Carolina, now departed, who commenced forty years ago a war against the tariff and against internal improvements, saying nothing of the United States Bank, and other measures, which may now be regarded as obsolete?"

Mr. Rhett, on the 24th of December, said:

"The secession of South Carolina is not an event of a day. It is not anything produced by Mr. Lincoln's election, or by the non-execution of the fugitive slave law. It has been a matter which has been gathering head for thirty years."

Hence we see that there is a design with some to break up this Government without reference to the slavery question; and the slavery question is by them made a pretense for destroying this Union. They have at length passed their ordinance of secession; they assume to be out of the Union; they declare that they are no longer a member of the Confederacy. Now what are the other States called upon to do? Are the other States called upon to make South Carolina an exemplar? Are those slave States who believe that freemen should govern and that freemen can take care of slave property, to be "precipitated into a revolution" by following the example of South Carolina? Will they do it? What protection, what security will Tennessee, will Kentucky, will Virginia, will Maryland, or any other State, receive from South Carolina by following her example? What protection can she give them? On the contrary, she indulges in a threat towards them —a threat that if they do not imitate her example and come into a new confederacy upon her terms, they are to be put under the ban, and their slave property to be subjected to restraint and restriction. What protection can South Carolina give Tennessee? Any? None upon the face of the earth.

Some of the men who are engaged in the work of disruption and dissolution, want Tennessee and Kentucky and Virginia to furnish them with men and money in the event of their becoming engaged in a war for the conquest of Mexico. The Tennesseeans and Kentuckians and Virginians are very desirable when their men and their money are wanted; but what protection does South Carolina give Tennessee? If negro property is endangered in Tennessee, *we* have to defend it and take care of it—not South Carolina, that has been an apple of discord in this Confederacy from my earliest recollection down to the present time, complaining of everything, satisfied with nothing. I do not intend to be invidious, but I have sometimes thought that it would be a comfort if Massachusetts and South Carolina could be chained together as the Siamese twins, separated from the continent, and taken out to some remote and secluded part of the ocean, and there fast anchored, to be washed by the waves, and to be cooled by the winds; and after they had been kept there a sufficient length of time, the people of the United States might entertain the proposition of taking them back. They have been a source of dissatisfaction pretty much ever since they entered the Union; and some experiment of this sort, I think, would operate beneficially upon them; but as they are here, we must try to do the best we can with them. . . .[7]

Let us look at the contest through which we are passing, and consider what South Carolina, and the other States who have undertaken to secede from the Confederacy, have gained. What is the great difficulty which has existed in the public mind? We know that, practically, the territorial question is settled. Then what is the cause for breaking up this great Union of States? Has the Union or the Constitution encroached upon the rights of South Carolina or any other State? Has this glorious Union, that was inaugurated by the adoption of the Constitution, which was framed by the patriots and sages of the Revolution, harmed South Carolina or any other State? No; it has offended none; it has protected all. What is the difficulty? We have some bad men in the South—the truth I will speak—and we have some bad men in the North, who want to dissolve this Union in order to gratify their unhallowed ambition. And what do we find here upon this floor and upon the floor of the other House of Congress? Words of crimination and recrimination are heard. Bad men North say provoking things in reference to the institutions of the South, and bad men and bad tempered men of the South say provoking and insulting things in return; and so goes on a war of crimination and recrimination in reference to the two sections of the country, and the institutions peculiar to each. They become enraged and insulted, and then they are denunciatory of each other, and what is the result? The Abolitionists, and those who entertain their sentiments, abuse men of the South, and men of the South abuse them in return. They do not fight each other; but they both become offended and enraged. One is dissatisfied with the other; one is insulted by the other; and then, to seek revenge, to gratify themselves, they both agree to make war upon the Union that never offended or injured either. Is this right? What has this Union done? Why should these contending parties make war upon it because they have insulted and aggrieved each other? This glorious Union,

7. Johnson then attacked Senator Joseph Lane of Oregon for supporting territorial compromise.

that was spoken into existence by the fathers of the country, must be made war upon to gratify these animosities. Shall we, because we have said bitter things of each other which have been offensive, turn upon the government, and seek its destruction, and entail all the disastrous consequences upon commerce, upon agriculture, upon the industrial pursuits of the country, that must result from the breaking up of a great Government like this? What is to be gained out of the Union that we cannot get in it? Anything? I have been zealously contending for—and intend to continue to contend for—every right, even to the ninth part of a hair, that I feel the State which I have the honor in part to represent is entitled to. I do not intend to demand anything but that which is right; and I will remark, in this connection, that there is a spirit in the country which, if it does not exist to a very great extent in this Hall, does exist in the great mass of the people North and South, to do what is right; and if the question could be taken away from the Congress of the United States, and referred to the great mass of the intelligent voting population of the United States, they would settle it without the slightest difficulty, and bid defiance to secessionists and disunionists.

I have an abiding confidence in the people; and if it were so arranged today that the great mass of the American people could be assembled in an amphitheater capacious enough to contain them all, and the propositions which have been presented here to preserve this Union, could be reduced to a tangible shape, and submitted to them; politicians being left out of view, the question being submitted to the great mass of the people, it being their interest to do right, they being lovers of their country, having to pay all, having to produce all, having to provide all, there would be but one single response, "Do that which will give satisfaction, ample and complete, to the various and conflicting sections of this glorious Republic."

But, sir, how are we situated? There are politicians here, and throughout the land, some of whom want to break up the Union, to promote their own personal aggrandizement; some on the other hand, desire the Union destroyed that slavery may be extinguished. Then let me appeal to every patriot in the land, in view of this state of things, to come forward and take the Government out of the hands of the Goths and Vandals, wrest it from the Philistines, save the country, and hand it down to our children as it has been handed down to us.

I have already asked what is to be gained by the breaking up of this Confederacy. An appeal is made to the border slaveholding States to unite in what is commonly styled the Gulf confederacy. If there is to be a division of this Republic, I would rather see the line run anywhere than between the slaveholding and the non-slaveholding States, and the division made on account of a hostility, on the one hand, to the institution of slavery, and a preference for it, on the other; *for whenever that line is drawn, it is the line of civil war; it is the line at which the overthrow of slavery begins; the line from which it commences to recede*. Let me ask the border States, if that state of things should occur, who is to protect them in the enjoyment of their slave property? Will South Carolina, that has gone madly out, protect them? Will Mississippi and Alabama and Louisiana, still further down towards the Gulf? Will they come to our rescue, and protect us? Shall we partake of their phrenzy, adopt the mistaken policy into which they have fallen, and begin the work of the destruction of the institution in which we are equally interested with them? I have already said that I believe the dissolution of this Union will be the commencement of the overthrow and destruction of the institution of slavery. In a northern confederacy, or in a southern confederacy, or in a middle confederacy, the border slaveholding States will have to take care of that particular species of property by their own strength, and by whatever influence they may exert in the organization in which they may be placed. The Gulf States cannot, they will not, protect us. We shall have to protect ourselves, and perchance to protect them. As I remarked yesterday, my own opinion is, that the great desire to embrace the border States, as they are called, in this particular and exclusive southern confederacy, which it is proposed to get up, is not that they want us there as a matter of interest; so that if they are involved in war, in making acquisitions of territory still further south, or war growing out of any other cause, they may have a *corps de reserve*, they may have a power behind, that can furnish them men and money-men that have the hearts and the souls to fight and meet an enemy, come from what quarter he may.

What have we to gain by that? The fact that two taken from four leaves but two remaining, is not clearer to my mind than it is that the dissolution of the Union is the beginning of the destruction of slavery; and that if a division be accomplished, as some desire, directly between the slaveholding and the non-slaveholding States, the work will be commenced most effectually. Upon this point, I propose to read a short extract from South Carolina herself. Mr. Boyce, late a member of the other House, a distinguished man, a man of talent, and I believe a good man, and who, I have no doubt, in his heart this day regrets most deeply and sincerely the course which South Carolina has taken, said, in 1851, when the same issue was presented:

"Secession, separate nationality, with all its burdens, is no remedy. It is no redress for the past; it is no security for the future. It is only a magnificent sacrifice to the present, without in any wise gaining in the future. . . . For the various reasons I have stated, I object in as strong terms as I can, to the secession of South Carolina. Such is the intensity of my conviction on this subject, that if secession should take place—of which I have no idea, for I cannot believe in the existence of such a stupendous madness—I shall consider the institution of slavery as doomed, and that the great god, in our blindness, has made us the instruments of its destruction."

He said then, that if South Carolina, in her madness (but he did not believe she could), should determine upon secession, he would look upon it that the great god had doomed the institution of slavery. This is the opinion of one of the most distinguished and, I conscientiously believe, best men of South Carolina.

But, sir, I pass on from the paragraph of the speech of the honorable Senator from Oregon to which I have referred; and as there seems to have been a sort of arrangement—at least it appears so to my mind—to make and keep up an attack on me, because I agreed with Mr. Boyce of South Carolina in this respect; because I agreed with many distinguished men; and because I advance the doctrines of the fathers who formed the Republic, I shall take up these Senators in the order in which I was attacked. Without being egotistical, without being vain, when I feel that I have got truth on my side, when I feel that I am standing on principle, when I know that I have got facts and arguments that cannot be answered, I never inquire as to the difference of ability or experience between myself and those with whom I have to contend.[8]

The next Senator in order that made an attack upon me on account of my previous speech was the distinguished Senator from Mississippi, who took occasion to do so in making his valedictory address to the Senate after his State had passed her ordinance of secession. It has been the case not only with that Senator, but with others, that an attempt has been made by innuendo, by indirection, by some side remark, to convey the impression that a certain man has a tendency or bearing towards Black Republicanism or Abolitionism. Sometimes gentlemen who cannot establish such a charge, are yet willing to make it, not directly, but by innuendo; to create a false impression on the public mind— *"Willing to wound, but yet afraid to strike."* If the charge can be successfully made, why not make it directly, instead of conveying it by innuendo? The Senator from Mississippi did not attempt to

8. Johnson here attacked another detractor in the Senate, Judah P. Benjamin. See Benjamin's pamphlet in this volume.

reply to my speech, did not answer my arguments, did not meet my authorities, did not controvert my facts; but after reaching a certain point in his own argument, he disposes of all that I had said in these very few words. . . .[9]

Is that the way for a Senator, a distinguished Senator, an Ajax of his peculiar sect—for when we come to examine this doctrine of secession, it is only broad enough to found a sect upon; it is not comprehensive enough, it has not scope enough, to found a great national party on—to notice the arguments of others? The Senator from Mississippi would not argue the right of secession. I say, that if any government be organized hereafter, in which this principle of secession is recognized, it will result in its destruction and overthrow. But the Senator says that the Senator from Ohio, and "his ally from Tennessee," regard secession as no right at all; and by that statement the whole argument is answered. What is the idea here? Let us talk plainly, though courteously and respectfully. What was the idea which this remark was calculated, if not intended, to convey? I am free to say, that I think it was intended as well as calculated, to convey the impression that the Senator from Tennessee was an ally of Mr. Wade, of Ohio, who was a Republican, and the whole speech of the Senator from Tennessee, the authorities, the facts, and the arguments, are all upturned by that single allusion. Thank God, there is too much good sense and intelligence in this country, to put down any man by an innuendo or side remark like that. But, sir, so far as the people whom I have the honor in part to represent are concerned, I stand above innuendoes of that kind. They have known me from my boyhood up. They understand my doctrines and my principles, in private and in public life. They have tried me in every position in which it was in their power to place a public servant, and they, today, will not say that ANDREW JOHNSON ever deceived or betrayed them. In a public life of twenty-five years, they have never deserted or betrayed me; and God willing, I will never desert or betray them. The great mass of the people of Tennessee know that I am for them; they know that I have advocated those great principles and doctrines upon which the perpetuity of this Government depends; they know that I have periled my all, pecuniarily and physically, in vindication of their rights and their interests. Little innuendoes, thrown off in snarling moods, fall harmless at my feet.

It was said that I was the *ally* of the Senator from Ohio. I turn to the doings of the committee of thirteen to show who were *allies* there. I do not inquire what a man's antecedents have been when there is a great struggle to preserve the existence of the Government; but my first inquiry is, are

9. See the pamphlet of Jefferson Davis in this volume.

you for preserving this Government; are you for maintaining the Constitution upon which it rests. If Senator Wade, or Senator anybody else, is willing to come up to this great work, either by amending the Constitution of the United States, or passing laws that will preserve and perpetuate this great Union, I am his ally and he is mine; and I say to every Senator; to every member of the House of representatives; to every man that loves his country throughout the length and breadth of this great Confederacy, if you are for preserving this Union on its great and fundamental principles, I am your ally, without reference to your antecedents, or to what may take place hereafter. I say to all such men, come forward, and like gallant knights, let us lock our shields and make common cause for this glorious people. If I were to indulge in a similar kind of innuendo, by way of repartee, where would the Senator from Mississippi find himself? In the committee of thirteen, a resolution was introduced by the distinguished Senator from New York—who, I must say, since this question has sprung up, has given every indication of a desire for reconciliation and for compromise, and of a disposition to preserve the Government, that a man occupying his position could do—to the effect. . . . [10]

That was a proposition which was calculated, to a very great extent, to allay the apprehensions and the fears that have been entertained in the South in reference to the institution of slavery. Why do I say so? We know what the argument has been before the southern mind. It has been: first, that the northern anti-slavery party wanted to abolish slavery in the District of Columbia, as an entering wedge; next, to exclude it from the Territories, following up the attack upon slavery; but these points were looked upon as of minor importance; they were looked upon as outposts, as the prelude to an interference with the institution of slavery in the States? Such is the real question, and such it will remain, the territorial question being substantially settled. What does Mr. Seward, who has acquired so much notoriety by his "irrepressible conflict," say? He comes here and proposes an amendment to the Constitution, which puts an estoppel upon his "irrepressible conflict" doctrine. He is willing to make it *perpetual*, so that the institution cannot be interfered with in the States by any future amendment of the Constitution. That is Mr. Seward's measure. Upon the adoption of that resolution, I believe every member of the committee voted for it, save two. The Senator from Mississippi voted for it; Mr. Seward voted for it; and Mr. Wade, of Ohio, voted for it. Whose ally is he? Here we find Wade and Seward and Davis, and the whole committee, with the excep-

10. Johnson quoted William H. Seward on compromise.

Andrew Johnson   [317

tion of two, in favor of amending the Constitution so that the institution of slavery cannot be interfered with in the States, making that provision irrepealable by any number of States that may come into the Confederacy. Who were "allies" then?

Recurring to what I said yesterday, there are two parties in this country that want to break up the Government. Who are they? The nullifiers proper of the South, the secessionists, or disunionists—for I use them all as synonymous terms. There is a portion of them who, *per se*, desire the disruption of the Government for purposes of their own aggrandizement. I do not charge upon them that they want to break up the Government for the purpose of their own aggrandizement. I do not charge upon them that they want to break up the Government for the purpose of affecting slavery; yet I charge that the breaking up of the Government would have that effect; the result would be the same. Who else is for breaking up this Government? I refer to some bad men in the North. There is a set of men there who are called Abolitionists, and they want to break up the Government. They are disunionists; they are secessionists; they are nullifiers. The Abolitionists and the distinguished Senator from Mississippi and his party both stand in the same attitude, to attain the same end, a dissolution of this Union; the one party believing that it will result in the overthrow of the institution of slavery. Who are the disunionists of the North? Who are the "allies" of the distinguished Senator from Mississippi? . . .[11]

He looks upon disunion as the beginning of the destruction and overthrow of the institution of slavery. Then, when we come to a talk about "allies," whose allies are these gentlemen? Whose allies are the Abolitionists of the North, if they are not the allies of the secessionists and disunionists of the South? Are they not all laboring and toiling to accomplish the same great end, the overthrow of this great nation of ours? Their object is the same. They are both employing, to some extent, the same means. Here is Wendell Phillips; here is Garrison; here is the anti-slavery society of Massachusetts; and all, in the very same point of view, the allies of the distinguished Senator from Mississippi and his coadjutors; all in favor of disrupting and breaking down this Union, with the view of destroying the institution of slavery itself. "Allies laboring to destroy the Government!" Who else are laboring to destroy it but the disunionists and secessionists of the South, and Garrison and Phillips, and the long list that might be enumerated at the North? Here they stand, presenting an unbroken front, to destroy this glorious Union, which was made by our fathers.

11. Johnson called the abolitionists counterparts of Jefferson Davis.

I have alluded to this subject of "allies" in order to show who is engaged in this unholy and nefarious work of breaking up this Union. We find first the run-mad Abolitionists of the North. They are secessionists; they are for disunion; they are for dissolution. When we turn to the South we see the red-hot disunionists and secessionists engaged in the same work. I think it comes with a very bad grace from them to talk about the "allies" of others who are trying to save the Union and preserve the Constitution.

I went back yesterday and showed that South Carolina had held this doctrine of secession at a very early day, a very short time after she entered into the Articles of Confederation, and after she had entered the Union by which and through which the independence of the country was achieved. What else do we find at a very early day? Go to Massachusetts during the war of 1812, and the Hartford convention, and there you will find men engaged in this treasonable and unhallowed work. Even in 1845, Massachusetts, in manifesting her great opposition to the annexation of Texas to the United States, passed a resolution resolving herself out of the Union. She seceded; she went off her own act, because Texas was admitted into the Union. Thus we find South Carolina and Massachusetts taking the lead in this secession movement. We find the Abolitionists proper of the North shaking the right hand of fellowship with the disunionists of the South in this work of breaking up the Union; and yet we hear intimations here that Senators from the south who are not secessionists are Black Republican allies! If I were compelled to choose either—I would not wish to be compelled to make a choice—but if I were compelled to be either, having the privilege of choosing, I would rather be a black Republican than a red one. I think the one is much more tolerable than the other. If red republicanism is ever to make its way into this country, it is making its way in this disunion and secession movement that is now going on; for we see that right along with the sentiment of secession the reign of terror prevails. Everything is carried away by it, while the conservative men of the country are waiting for the excited tempest to pass. It is now sweeping over the country. Everything is carried by usurpation, and a reign of terror follows along in its wake.

I am charged with being "an ally" of the Senator from Ohio! I, who, from my earliest infancy, or from the time I first comprehended principle, down to the present time, have always stood battling for the same great principles that I contend for now! My people know me; they have tried me; and your little innuendoes and your little indirections will not alarm them, even if your infuriated seceding southern men dare to intimate that I am an ally of Mr. Wade. The Senator charges me with being "an ally";

while he and the leaders of Abolitionism are uniting all their energies to break up this glorious Union. I an ally! Thank God, I am not in alliance with Giddings, with Phillips, with Garrison, and the long list of those who are engaged in the work of destruction, and in violating the Constitution of the United States.

So much in regard to the argument about allies. I am every man's ally when he acts upon principle. I have laid down, as the cardinal point in my political creed, that, in all questions that involve principle, especially where there was doubt, I would pursue principle; and in the pursuit of a great principle I never could reach a wrong conclusion. If, in the pursuit of principle, in trying to reach a correct conclusion, I find myself by the side of another man who is pursuing the same principle, or acting upon the same line of policy, I extend to him my assistance, and I ask his in return.

I took occasion, in my former remarks, to call the attention of the Senate, and of my constituents to the extent that I have the honor to represent them, to the kind of government that was likely to be formed by the seceding States, and the country they might acquire after they did secede. In relation to this, the Senator from Mississippi said. . . .[12]

He went on to state that that idea was suggested in some paper, he could not exactly tell how; but it was not by the editor, and it did not amount to much. I did not refer to a single paper; but I made various extracts from newspapers and speeches, simply as surface indications, as symptoms of what lay below, and what was intended to be the result. I referred to the Charleston Mercury; I referred to other papers; I referred to the speeches of distinguished men, some of them leaders in this movement. Is it not apparent, now, that unless the public mind is aroused, unless the people are put on the alert, there is a design to establish a government upon the principles of a close corporation? Can anyone that has the least sagacity be so unobservant as not to see what is going on in the South? It is apparent to all. They seem to unite in setting out with the proposition that the new confederacy shall exclude every State which is not slaveholding, for the reason that those States which are interested in slaves should have the exclusive control and management of them. Here is a great family of States, some free and some slave, occupying, in one sense, the same relation to each other that individuals in the community do to one another. The proposition is started to form a government of States exclusively interested in slaves. That excludes all the free States. Is the argument good? Has not slavery been secure heretofore in the Union with the non-slaveholding States; and

12. Johnson quoted Davis and Senator Alfred Iverson of Georgia.

will not our geographical and physical position be just the same after the present Union is dissolved? Where does the argument carry us? We must have a confederacy now composed of slave States exclusively. When we have excluded the free States, and we come to make a new government, does not the same argument apply that we must have a government to be controlled and administered by that description of persons among us who are exclusively interested in slaves? If you cannot trust a free State in the confederacy, can you trust a non-slaveholder in a slaveholding State to control the question of slavery? Where does your argument carry you? We see where they are drifting; and, as a faithful sentinel upon the watch-tower, I try to notify the people and sound the tocsin of alarm. If this idea be not carried out, it will be because the public feeling, the public opinion, is aroused against it.

I alluded yesterday to the fact that the freemen of the State of South Carolina have not been permitted to vote for a President since it was a State. There is a great terror and dread of the capacity of the people to govern themselves. In South Carolina, when the ordinance was passed to withdraw from the Union, did the convention trust the people to pass their judgment upon it? Were they consulted? Did they indorse it? Have they passed their judgment upon it to this day? Taking the language of Mr. Boyce as an index of their feeling, I have no more doubt than I have of my existence that if this reign of terror subsides, and the hearts of the people of South Carolina can be gotten at, it will be found that a majority of them disapprove and repudiate what has been done there. What do we find in the State of Georgia? There the proposition was moved to submit the ordinance to the people; and were the people consulted? The vote was 138 to 116, I think. It shows a great division. Did they submit it to the people? Oh, no. I know something of the people of the State of Georgia, and I believe this day, if that seceding ordinance could be submitted to the voting population of Georgia, and the question be fully canvassed and fairly understood, they would repudiate and put it down. Go to Florida: were the people consulted there? Not at all. Look to Alabama; look to the arguments made there in the convention. It was said, our power is ample; we must consummate this thing, and not let the people pass upon it. Louisiana refused to refer the matter to the people. The people have not been consulted. A reign of terror has been instituted. States have been called upon to make large appropriation of money to buy arms and munitions of war; for what end? The idea has been "we can, almost with the speed of lightening, run States out of the Union without consulting the people; and then, if they dare resist, we have got an army, we have got the money to awe them into submission." These gentlemen are very fearful of coercion, exceedingly alarmed at the word "coerce"; but when you attempt to interpose and stop *their* career, they do not know of any other term but coercion. Look at the dispatch which Governor Pickens sent to Mississippi. . . . [13]

South Carolina has a military establishment, with officers appointed, and the taxes necessary to support them now are grinding her people to the dust; but she expects in a very short time to transfer that military establishment, with her officers, to the southern confederacy that is to be established; and I suppose the great object in getting the leader appointed at once is that they may be able by military force to awe the people into submission. Have we not seen that nine regiments have been authorized to be raised in Mississippi, and a distinguished Senator, who occupied a seat on this floor a short time since, made the major general? No doubt, when the scheme is consummated and carried out, when the military organization is complete, if the people offer to resist, they will be subdued and awed, or driven into submission at the point of the bayonet. Some of these gentry are very much afraid of the people.

A proposition was even started in my own State, to raise sixteen regiments; for what? With whom are we at war? Is anybody attacking us? No. Do we want to coerce anybody? No. What do we want with sixteen regiments? And it was proposed to appropriate $250,000 to sustain them. There is a wonderful alarm at the idea of coercing the seceding States; great dread in reference to the power of this Federal government to secure obedience to its laws, and especially in reference to the power of this Federal Government to secure obedience to its laws, and especially in reference to making war upon one of the States; but the public property can be taken, your flag can be fired upon, your ships driven out of port, your gallant officer, with a few men, penned up in a little fort to subsist as best they may. So far as the officer to whom I have just alluded is concerned, I will give utterance to the feelings of my heart when I express my profound approbation of his conduct. He was put there to defend the flag of his country. He was there not as an intruder. He was there in possession of the property owned by the United States, not to menace, not to insult, not to violate rights, but simply to defend the flag and honor of his country, and take care of the public property; and because he retired from a position where he could have been captured, where the American flag could have been struck and made to trail in the dust, and the Palmetto banner substituted, because he,

13. Johnson quoted from a letter Pickens had written to Governor A. Burt Jackson on January 19, 1861, asking Jackson to come to a Lower South convention.

obeying the impulses of a gallant and brave heart, took choice of another position; acting upon principles of humanity, not injuring others, but seeking to protect his own command from being sacrificed and destroyed, he is condemned and repudiated, and his action is sought to be converted into a menace of war. Has it come to this, that the Government of the United States cannot even take care of its own property, that your vessels must be fired upon, that your flag must be struck, and still you are alarmed at coercion: and because a gallant officer has taken possession of a fort where he cannot very well be coerced, a terrible cry is raised, and war is to be made?

I was speaking of the proposition brought forward in my own State to raise sixteen regiments. As far back as the battle of King's mountain, and in every war in which the rights of the people have been invaded, Tennessee, God bless her, has stood by that glorious flag, which was carried by Washington and followed by the gallant patriots and soldiers of the Revolution, even as the blood trickled from their feet as they passed over the ice and snow; and under that flag, not only at home, but abroad, her sons have acquired honor and distinction, in connection with citizens of the other States of the Union. She is not yet prepared to band with outlaws, and make war upon that flag under which she has won laurels. Whom are we going to fight? Who is invading Tennessee? Conventions are got up; a reign of terror is inaugurated; and if, by the influence of a subsidized and mendacious press, an ordinance taking the State out of the Confederacy can be extorted, those who make such propositions expect to have our army ready, to have their bands equipped, to have their praetorian divisions; then they will tell the people that they must carry the ordinance into effect, and join a southern confederacy, whether they will or not; they shall be lashed on to the car of South Carolina, who entertains no respect for them, but threatens their institution of slavery unless they comply with her terms. Will Tennessee take such a position as that? I cannot believe it; I never will believe it; and if an ordinance of secession should be passed by that State under these circumstances, and an attempt should be made to force the people out of the Union, as has been done in some other States, without first having submitted that ordinance to the people for their ratification or rejection, I tell the Senate and the American people that there are many in Tennessee whose dead bodies will have to be trampled over before it can be consummated. [Applause in the galleries.]

There is no one in the United States who is more willing to do justice to the distinguished Senator from Mississippi than myself; and when I consider his early education; when I look at his gallant services, finding him first in the military school of the United States, educated by his Government, taught the science of war at the expense of his country—taught to love the principles of the Constitution; afterwards entering its service, fighting beneath the stars and stripes to which he has so handsomely alluded, winning laurels that are green and imperishable, and bearing upon his person scars that are honorable; some of which have been won at home; others of which have been won in a foreign clime, and upon other fields— I would be the last man to pluck a feather from his cap or a single gem from the chaplet that encircles his brow. But when I consider his early associations; when I remember that he was nurtured by this Government, I cannot understand how he can be willing to hail another banner, and turn from that of his country, under which he as won laurels and received honors. This is a matter of taste, however; but it seems to me that, if I could not unsheath my sword in vindication of the flag of my country, its glorious stars and stripes, I would return the sword to its scabbard; I would never sheathe it in the bosom of my mother; never! never! . . . [14]

I intend to stand by that flag, and by the Union of which it is the emblem. I agree with Mr. A. H. Stephens, of Georgia, "that this Government of our fathers, with all its defects, comes nearer the objects of all good governments than any other on the face of the earth."

I have made allusions to the various Senators who have attacked me, in vindication of myself. I have been attacked on all hands by some five or six, and may be attacked again. All I ask is, that, in making these attacks, they meet my positions, answer my arguments, refute my facts. I care not for the number that may have attacked me; I care not how many may come hereafter. Feeling that I am in the right, that argument, that fact, that truth are on my side, I place them all at defiance. Come one, come all; for I feel, in the late words of the great dramatic poet:

> "Thrice is he armed that hath his quarrel just; And he but naked, though locked up in steel, Whose conscience with [treason] is corrupted." [15]

I have been told, and I have heard it repeated, that this Union is gone. It has been said in this Chamber that it is in the cold sweat of death; that, in fact, it is really dead, and merely lying in state waiting for the funeral obsequies to be performed. If this be so, and the war that has been made upon me in consequence of advocating the Constitution and the Union is to result in my overthrow and in my destruction; and that flag, that glorious

14. Again to attack Jefferson Davis, Johnson quoted from a speech given by Joel Poinsett in 1830 that revealed that there was Unionist support in South Carolina.

15. Shakespeare, *Henry VI*, part 2, act 3, scene 2, line 358.

flag, the emblem of the Union, which was borne by Washington through a seven years' struggle, shall be struck from the Capitol and trailed in the dust—when this Union is interred, I want no more honorable winding sheet than that brave old flag, and no more glorious grave than to be interred in the tomb of the Union. For it I have stood; for it I will continue to stand; I care not whence the blows come; and some will find, before this contest is over, that while there are blows to be given, there will be blows to receive; and that, while others can thrust, there are some who can parry. God preserve my country from the desolation that is threatening her, from treason and traitors!

> *"Is there not some chosen curse, Some hidden thunder in the stores of heaven, Red with uncommon wrath, to blast the man Who owes his greatness to his country's ruin?"*[16]

In conclusion, I make an appeal to the conservative men of all parties. You see the posture of public affairs; you see the condition of the country; you see along the line of battle the various points of conflict; you see the struggle which the Union men have to maintain in many of the States. You ought to know and feel what is necessary to sustain those who, in their hearts, desire the preservation of this Union of States. Will you sit with stoic indifference, and see those who are willing to stand by the Constitution and uphold the pillars of the Government driven away by the raging surges that are now sweeping over some portions of the country? As conservative men, as patriots, as men who desire the preservation of this great, this good, this unparalleled government, I ask you to save the country; or let the propositions be submitted to the people, that the heart of the nation may respond to them. I have an abiding confidence in the intelligence, the patriotism and the integrity of the great mass of the people; and I feel in my own heart that, if this subject could be got before them, they would settle the question, and the Union of these States would be preserved. [Applause in the galleries.]

16. Joseph Addison, *Cato*, act 1, scene 1.

State or Province? Bond or Free?

(Little Rock: Self Published, 1861)

> *Albert Pike (1809–91) was born in Boston, Massachusetts, attended an academy in Framingham, taught school, and wrote poetry. He moved to the West in 1831, settling in Pope County, Arkansas, where he again took up teaching. Then, in addition to editing a Whig party newspaper, he practiced law. Later, he became reporter of the Arkansas Supreme Court and served in the Mexican War. During the Civil War Pike helped to negotiate treaties with Indians in Western territories and fought as a brigadier general in the Confederate army. But when he quarreled with superiors, he had to resign from the army. After the war he traveled, for a time practiced law in Memphis, Tennessee, and moved to Washington, D.C. Widely published, he wrote* Prose Sketches and Poems *(1854), and* Hymns to the Gods *(1872). Perhaps his best talents were in legal theory, which he displayed in the pamphlet below. After returning from trying to convince Kentuckians to join the Confederacy, on March 4, 1861, the day of Lincoln's inaugural speech, he published his warning to Arkansas to join the Lower South and assist in the formation of the Confederate government. In a foreword to his pamphlet Pike stated: "I address these pages to the people of Arkansas; and I offer no apology for doing so, because it needs done." He insisted that if the Border states joined with the Lower South, the combined effort could avoid civil war. See James M. Woods,* Rebellion and Realignment: Arkansas' Road to Secession *(Fayetteville: University of Arkansas Press, 1987), and Walter L. Brown, "Albert Pike, 1809–1891," (Ph.D. diss., University of Texas, 1955). There are Pike papers at the Masonic Temple, Washington, D.C.*

Appeals to the *non*sense of the people sometimes prove effectual; and the tendency in all political controversies is to limit and narrow questions, and to present them in a practical and empirical manner; because abstract principles, even when fundamental, do not appeal to most men with a thousandth part the force of considerations of present economy, policy or expediency. You must *crystallize* an abstraction into a *fact* that oppresses, before you can arouse a people by it. It is well when a great crisis occurs, that compels the discussion of the first principles of the Government; and when great Constitutional propositions are debated, without appeal to lower or meaner considerations. Then the debate is lifted above the low flat level of ignominious and angry disputation, and we breathe the thin clear atmosphere that wraps the mountain tops where Truth and Reason sit enthroned. . . .[1]

This, which is now in progress in our country, is clearly a Revolution. It has marched with swift steps. The Southern States are rapidly retiring from the Union, and preparing to seek peace and safety in a new confederacy. We can now look back and see that the current of events has been incessantly drifting us towards this consummation for forty years, little as most of our Statesmen believed or even expected it. The Northern States look on, amazed, incredulous, almost distrusting their own senses, busily conjecturing what can be the cause of this movement. They assign for it this or the other reason—that power is passing away from the South, and therefore it is for revolution; that the slave oligarchy are indignant because they cannot have protection for their chattels in the common territory. It is a mere temporary ebullition, many think, that will soon pass away, and the waters be calm and still again. The Union is too strong in the affections of the people to be permanently dissolved: a little wholesome chastisement of the refractory States will soon bring them back into the national fold: a few ambitious politicians have led the South astray, taken it by surprise, and obtained only unreal majorities for secession, while the mass of the people were in favor of the Union; it is a rebellion of the slavery propagandists; but still the mob has taken everything into its own hands; and there is a genuine Reign of Terror.

All this is the merest babble. Revolutions that shatter empires are not improvised, under the spur of a causeless excitement, by a few schemers or malcontents. Habit is a stronger bond of union than affection, and its influence can only be destroyed by the operation of sufficient causes, acting for a long time. It is *continual* dropping only, that wears away the stone. The present movement is a general, and for the most part spontaneous, uprising of the People; and he is a very shallow pretender to statesmanship who supposes it to be the ebullition of a mere temporary fit of passion. We all act very much from instinct; and peoples do so no less than individuals. They are often unconscious of the true springs of their action; and it is well when they possess that unerring instinct that warns them of the approach of an unseen danger. The symptoms of a disease are not the disease

1. Pike referred to the classic work of Alexis De Tocqueville, *The Old Regime and the French Revolution*, trans. John Bonner (New York: Harper and Brothers, 1856). For Pike and others the thought of violent revolution or even of secessionists being called revolutionary required careful use of historical precedence.

itself; the chill is only a consequence of the internal and organic malady. The Border States do not appreciate the questions involved in this controversy; but reproach those further South that they have lost no fugitives, and yet secede because the North refuses to comply with its obligations to return them. The question of southern rights in the Territories, too, they say, is an abstraction, because we have now no longer any Territory into which Slavery can go. This is, in the truest sense, to mistake the mere symptoms for the disease. . . . [2]

Mr. Seward, who is ambitious to wear the honors of philosophic statesmanship, and thinks to attain them by antitheses and paradoxes, pronounced, a year since, that there was an "irrepressible conflict" begun between the North and the South. It was true; but it was not true in the sense in which he applied it. The real controversy between them is as old as the Constitution itself. For it is a radical difference as to the very nature of the Government; and it arrayed against each other the first parties formed in the Republic. The Southern States hold, as Jefferson and Madison and all the Anti-Federal party held, that the General Government is the result of a compact between the States; a compact *made* by the States, amendable by the States only, and dissolvable by the States whenever it fails to answer the purposes for which they created it. The earliest symbol of the Union — a chain, composed of thirteen circular links, each perfect in symmetry and complete in its separate identity—well expressed the true nature of that union, and the Southern States'–rights doctrine. The Northern States, on the contrary, hold that there is no such compact; that the *whole* people of *all* the States, as an aggregate and unit, made the Constitution; and that there is no right of secession retained by a State; from which, by our American common law, it results as an inevitable corollary, that whenever the majority of voters of the whole Union choose to exercise the power, notwithstanding the mode provided by the Constitution or its amendment, they may call a Convention, not of the States, nor in each State, but of the whole People of all; and, the majority being there represented, may set aside the present Constitution of the United States, and make a new one, making, if they please, of the whole Union a single State, and of the States mere Counties.

If seven men agree to go into business together, and make a contract to that effect, and three of them hold that it is an ordinary partnership they have established, while the other four hold that it is a corporation—if such were the different understandings of the parties in framing the contract—

2. Comments on the territorial issue were deleted here.

perhaps on the principle that there is no contract unless the wills of the contracting parties agree, there would be *no* contract between them at all. It clearly could not be a mere partnership for part, and a corporation for part, of them.

If the difference were even only one of interpretation, it would continually reappear in the various transactions of the parties; and it is very evident that, being so radical and fundamental a disagreement, it would in a little time render continuance of the connection impossible.

That is, precisely the case with the Union which is now being dissolved. There is a difference as wide and substantial between this Government, as its nature is understood by the fifteen Slaveholding States, and the same Government, as its nature is understood by the nineteen Non-Slaveholding States, as there is between Constitutional Monarchy in England and Imperial Absolutism in France.

We should not consent to remain a day in such a Government as Mr. Webster confirmed the North in holding this to be. We do not believe that a centralized and consolidated government, built on the theory that the people of all these States were massed into one in order to make it, can have perpetuity or even continuance. To us the value and only recommendation of the Government are that it is the result of a compact between the States, that no individual action, but only State action, is constitutionally felt in the General Government, and that the States remain as they were when they achieved their independence, "FREE, SOVEREIGN, EQUAL, AND INDEPENDENT STATES."

This radical difference of opinion, as to the very *nature*, and of course as to the *powers*, of the General Government, could not help but continually develop itself in legislation as well as in the creeds of parties. Upon it, as I have said, the first parties in the Republic were formed; and parties degenerated into factions when other and pettier questions pushed it to one side. *It is a difference of opinion that cannot be reconciled;—and the Northern people are nearly two to our one.*

While they hold that this is simply a government of popular minorities, and degrade the States to the rank of Parishes or Counties, they have become too strong for us, outnumber us in people and States, receive a hundred thousand emigrants per annum, have open space wherein to make six or seven new States, and announce it as their ultimatum that we shall not expand southwardly or southwestwardly, but slavery shall be prohibited in all territory hereafter acquired.

He who reflects on all this, cannot well fail to see that separation was but a question of time. Sooner or later the North and South could not help but divide, unless the powers of Government here placed and kept in the hands of the wisest Statesmen of each. If they were habitually intrusted to second-rate men, disintegration was inevitable. How much more so, if possible, when the pulpit in the North assumed the powers of legislation, and stirred a practical question that jeopardized the safety of every home in the South, aroused its pride, and touched its honor? It became as easy to destroy the Union as the crazed incendiary found it to burn the Temple of Diana at Ephesus.

The party which calls itself Republican has at length succeeded to power. In the controversies that have finally resulted in the election of its obscure candidate to the Presidency, the questions chiefly discussed have been those provoked by the feeling in the North against Slavery and particularly that of the rights of the Southern States and their citizens in the common territory.

If it was then important, it is now still more important to understand the real issue between the North and the South, and the reach and extent of the principles involved. For now we are about to sever the bonds that have for seventy-three years held us together and to create and set on foot a new government for ourselves; and it is especially essential that the ground of separation should not be misunderstood by any considerable portion of our own people, that a mere corollary should not he mistaken for the essential principle involved, and that a part of our people and some of our States should not imagine that there is no more vital principle or broader question at issue, than the interests of slave-owners and the right of emigration into uninviting and inhospitable territories.

Abstract theories of government rarely enlist the passions of the people. They operate chiefly on the minds of Statesmen. But when these theories, applied to and developed in facts, become palpable realities, then the popular heart is moved by them, and they beget revolutions.

I, for one, have not deplored the agitation of the question of slavery. For in its discussion have been all the time involved the very essential nature and terms of the compact under which our national system exists. The questions to which Slavery has given rise could not have remained unsettled, nor been ignored; and the real issues are far graver than that of the right of Southern citizen to emigrate to a Territory with his slaves.

The theory of the North, that the People of *all* the States, as *one* People, made the Government, has become a living reality in practice. The doctrine of the North as to the Territories is but an application of it; and if the Southern States, from Delaware to Texas, do not mean to abandon their Constitutional faith, admit that there is no union of *the States* and submit to the worst of absolutisms, that of a foreign majority, they must stand shoulder to shoulder, one firm unbroken phalanx, in this great emergency, and prove to the world, that they are strong, wise, and patriotic enough to form and maintain a constitution and Government for themselves.

This issue concerns little Delaware as much as it does Louisiana, if not more; and Kentucky and Virginia as much as it does Alabama and Georgia. And it concerns the man who owns no slaves quite as much as the man who owns them, as I think can be demonstrated; and this is what I wish to show. . . .[3]

If the States did not compose this Union, and were not the members of it, then, called by whatever name, they were mere municipalities, and their crown and robes of sovereignty the mere tinselled trappings of the theatre. It was then folly to prate of State rights and State pride. The old Commonwealths, in whose bosom it was deemed an honor and good fortune to be born, had laid aside their greatness and their glory, and could no longer demand allegiance of their sons, nor extend to them protection. If they were so emasculated and reduced in circumstances, so far below their original high estate, as to be mere images and counterfeits of States, then there was little hope for the perpetuity of our institutions, and little in them for other nations to admire for us to boast of. And it is because the South finds it impossible longer to resist this wretched and degrading doctrine *in* the Union, that it is now seeking safety *out* of it, and on the point of creating a new government, that shall repose on the solid foundation of the equality, independence, and sovereignty of the States. On which side shall Arkansas stand in this great controversy?

If the Union could have continued, as it ought to have done, and would have done, if men had been wise, we should insensibly have become more and more one nation. Our common flag would have made us so. Time and habit would inevitably have consolidated us, and the antagonisms of race would have died out, or combined in harmonious action. Every war we engaged in would have made the feeling of *oneness* more and more irresistible. None, I think, ever served under that flag, who did not for the time feel, with a conviction more potent than all the arguments and logic of statesmen could produce, that we were one nation, in name, fame, and destiny; who did not feel that our national motto, *E Pluribus Unum* — ONE, made

3. What followed was an elaborate historical analysis of the right of secession, which by 1860 was well worn. For full development of the right of secession see Carpenter, *The South as a Conscious Minority* (New York: New York University Press, 1930).

up of many—was a true definition of the nature of our Government—the *manifold* welded into the *one*—oneness grown out of the manifold.

There was no necessity for any irrepressible conflict between the sections. There was no necessity for hatred, jealousies, and wrong-doing. We have been unnecessarily set against each other, by fanatical folly and unprincipled ambition in the North, and passion and rashness in the South. The harm is done. The silver chain of Union is broken; and the restoration of harmony is now as impossible as it is between husband and wife, when, estranged by their own tempers or evil counsellors, their domestic dissensions have been paraded in court, null divorce granted, not alone from bed and board, but from the bonds of matrimony. That they could and ought to have lived together in peace, makes the sentence none the less irrevocable, the separation none the less eternal. But if we had not been estranged, argument and logic would soon have become powerless against the *feeling* that we were one Nation and one People: and it would have become necessary for all men, whatever their theoretical opinions, to make up their minds, and reconcile themselves to it the best way they could, that, as the years glided past us, the Union continuing, we should regard ourselves more and more as one nation, whatever might be the true meaning of the Constitution and this consequence would have been the inevitable result of circumstances, and a mere act of forced obedience to the great laws of God, which constitute what we call human nature.

It is an inflexible legal principle, that whenever a fiction is interposed, it is always done in order to give effect to *rights*, to protect valuable interests, and to attain the very heart of what is just about the matter. The fiction cannot be made an instrument of evil, nor an invader of rights. It cannot be used for the purpose of eluding the intention of the parties; but it is always an instrument and an organism by which to reach the substance and essential reality of things. You incorporate certain persons into a bank: the fiction that there is a legal being, the bank, separate and distinct from each corporator, when substantially it is but a limited partnership, is invented and used for their protection, to carry out their intention, to make their action effectual, and not to annihilate the substantial relations and essential equities that exist between them.

Thus, whenever the United States became, in any mode whatever, by purchase or conquest, the owner of land, that land was in substance the land of the several States. Its legal capacity to act as an individual, the fiction of its identity separate from the States, would be used to give effect to, and make fully available, all the rights of the States and the people of each State, in and upon that common property. They *could not* be used to annul or render ineffectual those rights. Whenever the effectuation of those rights demanded it, the *fiction* would vanish, and the States be regarded as the *real* owners of the lands, the Lords Proprietary.

When a portion of country thus became the common property of the States, it was held in trust for them by the United States; in the same sense, somewhat inaccurate, in which the property of a corporation is said in the law to be held in trust by it for the corporators. The meaning is, that *in law* it is *its* property, but *in reality* it is theirs; that, so far as it is necessary, in order to carry out their intentions and subserve their interests, the law will *use* the legal fiction, and *regard* it as *its* property; but when justice and convenience require the fiction to disappear, it will regard it, as it *really* is, as *theirs*.

Now, besides their real ownership of the land, the States had great political and social interests in the territories, considering them as nascent or embryotic States. Each State had the right to demand that they should be opened as wide to its own citizens, as to those of any other State or number of States; and the *Southern* States, that *they* should have a *fair* chance in the peaceful struggle for additional political weight and power in this confederacy. The duty of each to its own citizens also gave it a right to insist that they should not be directly or indirectly excluded from the common territory. It had necessarily the right to demand that they should be there protected in the enjoyment and possession of whatever they carried thither, that was the property by its laws. And, if the Constitution really warranted the Northern States in Congress, or the people of a Territory, in denying the South these equal rights in the common territory, then it was the duty of the Southern States at once to withdraw from a Union in which they never were equals.

Short-sighted men imagined it was we, who, insisting in 1860 on these rights of the South, brought upon the Country the dangers of Disunion; but a truer wisdom taught us, that only in the principle we proclaimed was safety, and that we were the truest Defenders of the Constitution and the Union. Whether present victory or defeat awaited us, was of little moment. Truth would still march onward in serene majesty, whether we stood or went down in the shock of the battle. The South would at last rally to the flag of the equality of the States and the protection of all constitutional and legal rights, when the passions and angers of the contest should have passed away; and its States would stand with linked shields, in one compact and solid phalanx, demanding in the calm tones of conscious power the maintenance of the Constitution as the condition of the continuance of the Union.

Albert Pike   [333

They have demanded that, if indeed some of them have not conde-
scended to beg for it. What is the result? The Republicans in Congress
refuse Concession and threaten Coercion. They accept no propositions
of Compromise. The personal-liberty laws of many Northern States, that
make it an infamous crime in a master to reclaim and recover his slave,
legally, under the laws of the United States, still remain unrepealed. Although the Supreme Court solemnly decided, if it decided nothing else,
in the Dred Scott Case, that a negro cannot be a citizen of the United
States, fifteen thousand of them voted in Ohio for Lincoln. The whole
North with one voice declares that there shall be no more slave territory;
and its most powerful States tender arms, men, and money to the General
Government, wherewith to subjugate the South. What was it the right and
duty of the Southern States to do, when it thus became evident that folly
and fanaticism, rapacity and lust for power and office taking the Northern men captive, have rendered it impossible for them longer to remain
in the Union as the equals of the Northern States, or without abandoning
the cardinal tenets of their political faith, unless new and ample guarantees can be obtained? and what mode of procedure offered a rational hope
of the obtaining of such guarantees?

It is the deliberate opinion of at least seven of the Southern States, that
withdrawal from the Union is the course most proper to be adopted, the
only remedy of efficacy sufficient to cure the disease and bring the North to
its senses, if indeed any remedy can effect that. In those States and others,
the only question has been, not as to the right or propriety of secession,
but as to the expediency and policy of separate secession, as compared with
separation by the conjoint action of all or several of the Southern States. It
is evident that the right of all or several to secede, must depend upon the
right of *each* to do so. For the right, if it exists at all, flows from this, that the
States are the parties to the compact, and a gross violation of it by the majority of the States, to the injury of any one, gives that one, and each one so
injured, the right, at its option, of regarding it as at an end and rescinded.
The right must needs be the individual right of each State. Certainly it
is qualified by the interests of the other States that have not violated the
compact, as almost all rights are, in societies of States or individuals. But
still, each State having the right to secede, must determine for itself as to
the propriety or expediency of the act; and that right has already been exercised by six States, and will in a few days be exercised by one more.

This right of secession is strenuously denied by the Northern States,
and even by a respectable number of persons in the South; but as a right

to be exercised only in an extreme case, of grave violation of the Constitution, when there is no other sufficient remedy, it seems to me that in the very nature of things it *could* not have been parted with by the States; and that its exercise is neither treason or rebellion.

The right to secede flows necessarily from the fact that the States *made* the Constitution. If one party to a compact violates it, the other may at his option treat it as rescinded; or, as WEBSTER once said: "A bargain broken on one side is broken on all sides."

James II, of England, procured all the Twelve Judges of the Realm to decide, when the question had been purposely raised, and was in issue, that he had the power to dispense with the prohibitions of an Act of Parliament, and remove the disabilities imposed by it. It is not impossible that some future President and Congress may find a majority of the Judges of the Supreme Court, as pliant to work *their* will. If it were to be procured to sustain the Constitutionality of an Act of Congress abolishing Slavery in certain States, would there still be no right to secede on the part of those States? If, acting upon the notion that one people made the Constitution, Congress should call a Convention of Delegates from all the States, and, the South refusing to sit there, the Convention, representing the popular majority, should proceed to change the Constitution, and annul important rights of the South, would there still be no right to secede? The States are equally as much bound by any amendments to the Constitution regularly made, as by the original articles. If the North were to multiply its States until it had three-fourths of all, and then change the basis of representation in the Senate, fixing it according to the population of each State, and so depriving every Southern State of that whereof the Constitution expressly declares no State shall ever be deprived, "its equal suffrage in the Senate," all other remedies failing, would there no right to secede? The new Senate is the sole judge of the elections and qualifications of its members. It admits, for example, ten from New York, and decides that Delaware is entitled to but one. There is no remedy for this *in* the Union, no appeal to the Courts; Power is lawless, and majorities unreasoning. Is there still no right to secede?

Absolutely to deny the right of Secession, is to say that the constitutional rights of the Southern States may be denied, and they continually insulted and outraged; that all remedies in Congress, in the Courts, and elsewhere may fail them that the other States may violate the Constitution at every point, and yet that they may hold the Southern States in the bonds of obedience to it; and that the latter will yet have no right to throw off this intolerable yoke, and escape from this humiliating serfdom, by saying that "a bargain broken on one side is broken on all sides," and that they withdraw from a union that no longer deserves that name.

Admit the right in the extremist case, and you concede the whole principle. Then it only becomes a question of the sufficiency of the cause. I admit that the cause must be grave to be sufficient. I admit that the remedy is a severe and extreme one, fit to be used only in the last resort, and when all others have failed; and I am now satisfied that no *other* remedy could cure the disease under which the body politic now labors, if indeed that of Secession has that virtue. No remedy less sharp and decisive could have brought the North to its senses. Indeed, it still seems to be far from sane. I am now satisfied that even Secession, even the formation of a Southern Union, will not cure the Northern people of their fanatical delirium, unless it bring upon them such ruin as nations have rarely experienced, and experiencing lived.

That the South has, and has long had, ample cause for separation, few men, at the South, will be disposed to deny. We need not fear, on that point, to demand the judgment of an impartial world. For that our rights have long been jeopardized and denied, and the Constitution shamelessly violated by the Northern States, it is in vain for any one to endeavor to dispute.

The provision of the Constitution that guarantees the return of fugitive slaves, is virtually annulled. It costs as much to reclaim a slave as he is worth, and exposes the owner, in many of the Northern States, to be harassed by suits civil and criminal, that make his remedy worthless to him. For this deliberate, shameless violation of the compact, persisted in and become habitual, the South has the present right to dissolve the Union. A State that so nullifies a part of the Constitution, loses all right to any of its benefits; and the Southern States might well have insisted that Connecticut, Vermont, Massachusetts, Wisconsin, and other of the Northern States should be expelled with ignominy from the Union, as the condition of their own continuance in it.

A person who speaks for Massachusetts in the Senate has lately arraigned the Southern States as "the Barbary States of the Union," before the bar of the world, and impeached the courage, the honor, and the decency of all their people, in stilted Ciceronian sentences, steeped with gall and bitterness, and reeking with malignant falsehood. No one should have replied a word. And when his State formally, and with the intention of branding the insult in upon the South, endorsed his harangue and made it her own, either *her* Senators should have been expelled, or those of all the Southern States ought, in strict justice to their constituents, to have withdrawn from that desecrated and dishonored chamber. If they had done so, the whole South would have leaped up with one great cry of joy and applause, and have made the act their own.

It is common enough to hear it said that the right of secession is a *revolutionary* right. That is mere nonsense. Revolution is the means of compelling an acknowledgment of rights denied. The *rights* so denied are not revolutionary, though there is a right to resort to revolution, if they cannot be otherwise enforced. The former right must exist before the latter can arise. There can be no right to deny a right. The exercise of other rights than secession might produce revolution; but it would be a solecism to call them "revolutionary" rights—a solecism only explainable by the incurable propensity of men to use words that mean nothing. Such is the right, in the Senate or House, to be exercised in extreme cases, of refusing to vote supplies, in consequence of unconstitutional conduct on the part of the Executive or the other branch of Congress. The exercise of this right might produce revolution and destroy the government; but it could be none the less a perfect right, and the revolution the consequence, not of its exercise, but of the unconstitutional act which made it necessary.

So the exercise of the President's power of vetoing an act of Congress might produce revolution but nevertheless these and all other such rights and powers are great *conservative* ones, intended to exist, and to be resorted to when extreme measures only will arrest an evil otherwise incurable and deadly. The right to secede is a power in reserve, acting as a restraint upon majorities of the States that might otherwise encroach upon and at last annul the rights of the minorities under the constitution. The *existence* of such a right, though never exercised, is beyond calculation conservative. Deny it, deny that if the Supreme Court persists in holding an unconstitutional act to be constitutional, a State, injured by such decision, may, as a last resort, when all others fail, withdraw from the Union, and you annihilate one of the most important checks of the system.

At any rate, the question of the right of secession is receiving a practical solution. South Carolina, Florida, Alabama, Mississippi, Georgia, and Louisiana have already, by formal ordinance adopted in convention, withdrawn from the Union, and become each a foreign country to us, if it is possible for a State to do so by her own solemn act; and in a week or two more, Texas will have in like manner severed the bonds of union, and resumed her independence.

There may be different opinions as to the necessity, wisdom, policy and expediency of this measure. I, for one, did not believe that the necessity of resorting to this extreme remedy was as yet upon us. I thought we ought not to despair, so long as there was hope of a returning sense of justice in the Northern States. I doubted whether secession would prove a remedy for any of our evils, or give any additional security to our rights; and above all, I was enthusiastically attached to the Union, under whose flag I had fought. Disunion seemed to me equivalent to downfall, disaster and ruin, whereby we should become a mock and a by-word all over the earth.

And I thought, that, when separation should become inevitable, the Southern States ought not to secede separately, but that they should act in concert, meet in convention, decree the separation, construct and set on foot a new government, and thus, being strong to repel attack, make it insanity on the part of the Northern States to attempt to dragoon them into submission.

That was my individual opinion. Perhaps Arkansas thought so. But the other Cotton States did not think so; and they have acted for themselves. Can they ever return into the Union? Is any compromise possible, with which they and we ought to be satisfied? And how can such a compromise be effected? These are the only questions that now concern *them*. The rest are obsolete; and these equally concern *us*; for the inexorable decrees of destiny will compel us to unite with them. Events, as is usual in Revolutions, have outrun us. What was possible yesterday is not possible today. What is possible to-day, will be impossible tomorrow. The Republican leaders have made compromise for the present impracticable. The concessions that would at first have saved Charles the First of England, and Louis the Sixteenth of France, their thrones and heads, withheld too long, were counted as nothing, when granted; and such is the effect of delay in our case.

No concessions would now satisfy, and none *ought* now to satisfy the South, but such as would amount to a surrender of the distinctive principles by which the Republican party coheres, because none other or less would give the South peace and security. That party would have to agree that in the view of the Constitution, slaves are property; that Slavery might exist and should be legalized and *protected*, in territory hereafter to be acquired to the Southwest and that negroes and mulattoes cannot be citizens of the United States, nor vote at general elections in the States. They would have to repeal their laws that make it a crime in a master to reclaim his slave, that menace him with the penitentiary, and are meant to rob him of his property and, instead, they would have to agree to deliver that property up in good faith.

For that party to make these concessions would simply be to commit suicide; and therefore it is idle to expect from the North, so long as it rules there, a single concession of any value. They will not be made, if ever, until the *People*, impoverished and distressed, if not invaded by universal ruin and general bankruptcy, with starvation in the cities and destitution in the fields, shall have learned no longer to intermeddle with what in nowise concerns them. Then proper concessions may be made, by the general consent of the people; and if so made, the settlement will be permanent. But if made sooner, under the influence of a temporary terror, or by the management of politicians, the immediate result could not fail to be, as indeed it would most probably be in any event, after whatever solemn settlement, that, as soon as the danger of disunion was over for the time, as soon as the seceding States had returned into the Union, an agitation would commence in the North, stirring it to its profoundest depths. The compromise would be denounced from every pulpit and rostrum and in every canvass, as a league with hell and a covenant with the Devil. Those who made it would be politically slaughtered and after such convulsions as the country has never felt, the whole work would be undone, and the Southern States be forced again to secede, when secession would have become a farce.

It is certain that none of these concessions can be had at present and events will not wait until they can be obtained. Perhaps a compromise might be brought about, if we had breathing time. It would require a year or two, at least. Except so far as they tend to prove to the South that it is impossible now to obtain any guarantees from the North, thus urging upon the Border States prompt and vigorous action, all the propositions, plans, and projects for a compromise are not worth the paper they have been written on.

We were often enough told in 1860 that the territorial question was a mere abstraction, since we had no territory as to which the matter was not actually settled. Strange! how much men are like bats in the daylight.

The Northern States are now nineteen to our fifteen-counting Delaware as one of ourselves. They outnumber us, in white population, nearly two to one. They increase, principally by foreign emigration, in a much larger ratio than we do. They have a great country yet to be peopled, sufficient to make six or seven States. British America will, in all probability, desire to become, at no distant day, a part of the Union, if it continues; and a simple act of congress will admit it. The North announces it to be its fixed determination, that there shall be no more slave territory; and, therefore, we must either acquire no more from Mexico, or, if we do, we must consent to see it made into Free States. We may fight for and help to pay for more territory; but we must do so for the benefit of the Pharisees among the States, alone. How long would it be, under that system, before the union of North and South would be like that between England and Ireland; which, obtained by bribery, has been always maintained by force?

It is strange that statesmen do not see that here is the great question between the sections. To expand is the destiny and necessity of every young and growing nation. It is a law of its being. You cannot repeal it; and if you oppose it, it will crush you. By the law of growth and by natural right, the Southwest is as much *ours*, as the Northwest is the heritage of the Northern States. This law is more imperative with us, because another law is superadded, by which slavery gradually drifts off to the southward, seeking more profitable fields of labor.

Now the North says to us: "We will expand indefinitely to the Northwest, and make new States there, as Europe pours upon our shores her Teutonic and Celtic multitudes. Our political power in the Confederacy shall increase daily, in a continually accelerated ratio; if we acquire territory to the Southwest, we will fill that likewise with our Vandalic hordes, until our States number three-fourths of the whole. In the mean time, you shall remain as you are. You shall not expand to the Southwest; and we will also force slavery to recoil and disappear from the Border States."[4]

On THIS *point they will make no concession.* The Compromise hardly dare to ask them to do it. Do not deceive yourselves, Virginia and Kentucky with vain hopes! There will be no concession on *this* point.

We have *four* millions of slaves. How many years will elapse before we have ten millions? These—all—are to be henceforward confined to the present Southern States. No doubt it will be well enough so, during *our* lifetime; *but how will it be with our children?* Are we ready, in order to purchase quiet and peace for ourselves, to bequeath such a curse and calamity to *them*, as the perpetual confinement of slavery within its present limits would be? Shall we, to avoid a present danger, and that we may be permitted to fold our hands and sleep in our dishonor, devise to them that accursed legacy of a superabundant, swarming negro population, denied outlet, until their labor, like that of white men elsewhere, is not worth their food and clothing, and hunger and discontent light the torches of servile insurrection, and Earth and Heaven shudder at the hideous atrocities and horrors that follow? I, for one, will not consent to it. Better even Treason against an unrighteous Government, than Treason against our own children!

Here is the *true* and *great* issue; and it concerns *every* man and every woman in the South. We cannot sign the bond which the North insolently

4. Pike here revealed a streak of nativist, anti-immigrant fears and showed the differences, as he saw them, between the Northern and Southern people.

demands, to this effect, that because we are "the Barbary States" of the Union, and "Slavery is the sum-total of all villanies," therefore we shall not seek to expand and grow. For it is both our right and a necessity to grow and plant new States. It is God's law and the attempt to stay its operation has already shivered the Union as one shivers a vessel of fragile glass.

Devotion to the Union was for a long time an almost idolatrous sentiment with nearly the whole South and secession seemed the sum of all horrors and disasters. But we are at last compelled to look separation in the face. Most dangers seem greater at a distance, than when we grapple with them. Secession, at hand, and in part consummated, does not seem to the South one-tenth so terrible, as when it frowned upon us while yet in the future. The act once accomplished, or become inevitable, men begin to find more and more reasons whereby to justify it; to prove its necessity and its expediency; to show that a much longer continuance of the Union was impossible; and that the evils of separation were chiefly imaginary, or at any rate vastly exaggerated. They begin to think and say, that disunion does not necessarily involve civil war, which can settle nothing and effect nothing, at least in the direction of reconciliation. At any rate, they say, it will produce neither anarchy nor disturbance in the South; since it is the American nature to establish order and maintain some sort of free government, even under the most adverse circumstances that in a little while the Southern States will hold a Convention, adopt the present Constitution with a few necessary amendments, and set a national Government on foot, which all will at once respect and obey.

They begin even to say, that as the North entertains views of the nature of the Government, radically and essentially different from those which have always been the political religion of the South, this must ultimately have divided the Republic; that the people of the South and those of the North are essentially two races of men, with habits of thought and action very unlike; that the Southern States are essentially homogeneous, and perhaps no people in the world is so much so as that which composes almost their entire population; there being among them but a very inconsiderable percentage of foreign blood, except in Louisiana; and none of them having much in common with the character and habits of New England, and of the States chiefly populated by the swarms that have Bowed forth from that teeming hive while the immense and incessant influx of Teutonic and Celtic blood into the North, plays no unimportant part in making it and the South more and more two separate and distinct peoples.

They begin to say that this North, so unlike the South, and with its different theory of the government, is becoming too strong for us; that the present form of government has lasted its full time, and separation is a merely natural process; since the country is too large and has too many varied interests for us longer to continue one household; that the Union never was anything more than a truce, maintained by continual bribery of New England, on the part of the other States, from the very first, with protective tariffs, the carrying trade, fishing bounties, and other gratuities that she has continually clamored for.

If we add to this the fixed determination of the North to intermeddle with slavery, and the equally fixed resolution of the South not to permit such interference, which, while dangerous, doubles the wrong by coupling it with insult, it is not strange that Southern statesmen begin to think and say that it is well that separation has come now, before the North has become strong enough to prevent it, and the South too weak to resist, with her public men debauched perhaps by the manifold bribes that a great nation can offer to avarice and ambition; and before Mexico had been occupied by the North or a foreign power.

There is still a possibility of reconstruction and reunion. But it will not last long unless wise men have control on both sides; and it will disappear at once and forever, if resort is had to the arbitrament of arms. Surely no man of ordinary intellect can be so blind as not to see that if from disunion civil war results, that will amply justify disunion, because, as there is neither desire nor motive on the part of the South to aggress upon the North, hostilities must be initiated by those who were lately our allies, must be unjustifiable, malicious, revengeful—springing either from a determination to intermeddle with slavery after they have ceased to be responsible for it, and so to excite servile insurrection, with all its multiplied hideous horrors; or from a fixed purpose to whip us back into the Union, in order that we may afterwards be their serfs. In either case, hostilities thus initiated will prove that the alliance between us and them was unnatural and unfit, and its longer continuance dangerous and disgraceful to us.

If disunion is *not* followed by war, there is no reason why it should entail upon us any serious disasters. The Southern States are large enough for an empire, and wealthy and populous enough to maintain a government that all the world must respect. And surely no true man in the South will believe that there is not wisdom enough or patriotism enough among its people, to enable them to construct, set on foot and maintain a constitutional government, republican and conservative.

I can see only one mode in which peace can be maintained. The border States ought to hesitate no longer. If they do, coercion will be attempted by the Northern States, and they will be parties to it. They should at once unite with the States that have seceded and are yet to secede, meet them in convention, and aid in framing a Constitution, and setting on foot a Government. When thus united, the matter will have assumed quite a different aspect from that which it wears at present. There will no longer be half a dozen seceded States, but a new and powerful Confederacy, to attempt to coerce which would be simple fatuity. A war against it would be too expensive a luxury for the North to indulge in, and would moreover defeat its own purpose; since it would not only render a restoration of the present Union impossible, but would also make enmities eternal, which otherwise would be only evanescent. A treaty of amity and reciprocity, easily made if no blood is shed, will keep open the door, at least, for complete reconciliation, and in the mean time make an alliance more profitable to each country than an inharmonious Union; and when their people were no longer responsible, as they now think or pretend they are, for slavery within our limits; when the outrages they now perpetrate with impunity would be acts justifying war, those among them who regarded their substantial interests would *compel* the fanatical and rascally to attend to their own affairs, and let our property alone.

I do not see how war is otherwise to be avoided, or reconstruction hoped for. The delay of the Border States encourages the Republicans. As soon as Lincoln is inaugurated, he cannot help but attempt to coerce the seceding States, if the Border States still delay. *Laws will be passed in time, giving him men and money*, and requiring "the enforcement of the laws, and the collection of the revenue." Emboldened by the hesitation of Virginia, Kentucky, Tennessee, and Maryland, we can see that the Republicans become more insolent, and speak in bolder tones of rebellion and coercion. Thersites Hale talks bravely, Lincoln objects to any compromise; and the very fact that any States have seceded is ignored. The names of their members are still called in both Houses.

Action, action, action, is necessary. The Southern States must make common cause. Blame South Carolina as much as you will; the attitude of the North, and all the acts of the Republican party, go very far to prove, even to those most reluctant to believe it, that the separation of the Southern States has not occurred a day too soon.

Lincoln, who declares against any compromise, selects *Seward* for his Secretary of State. Sumner laughs in the Senate as the Southern States withdraw; and Lovejoy exults at the prospect of letting slip the dogs of war. The *New York Journal of Commerce* well says—

"Much of the zeal which is manifested among certain classes all over the North, including many notorious law-breakers, for the faithful execution of the laws in South Carolina and other seceding States, is only an out-cropping of that intense hatred against the South which thirty years' cultivation has produced. At first, such malignity is measurably satisfied by hard words and foul imputations. But as it becomes more fiendish and diabolical, it craves higher-seasoned food. It longs to get at its victim with a butcher-knife. It thirsts for blood. John Brownism affords a temporary relief, but it is a hazardous business, and too circumscribed. Murder by wholesale is what is wanted by the class of fanatics to whom we allude; and a WAR which would make the slaughter legal [recollect their sacred regard for law], and not expose their own precious lives to danger, would be just the thing. A war, too, ostensibly to preserve the Union and enforce the laws! Could anything be more exactly in point?

"But this is not all. The view of these fanatics is not confined to the butchery of masters, it looks also to insurrection among the slaves. It is John Brownism on a large scale. And what an opportunity to inaugurate it with the power and purse of the Government to support the movement!"

More has been done in the last six weeks to satisfy the people of the South that the mass of the people of the north are their enemies, and that the continuance or restoration of fraternal relations with them is simply impossible, than had been done in ten years before.

Whatever we may have thought or wished, Fate has been too strong for us; the die is cast, and the act *done*. The Past is no longer ours. The Present and the Future alone belong to us. It is profitless to inquire who are to blame for the present condition of affairs, or to disclaim responsibility on our individual part. Inexorable circumstances ever mould our destinies, and of these the acts of other men are a great part. It is the condition of human life that their acts should affect us potently for weal or woe. We have now only to accept the responsibility, look the Present steadily in the face, and take precautions and make provision for the Future.

Reconciliation, by means of amendments to the Constitution to be made or agreed to by the North, being simply impossible for the present; first for want of time, and next because they cannot be carried by three-fourths of the States, only one possible mode remains. If the Southern States adopt the Constitution, with no other amendments than such as are necessary for their protection, and as experience has shown to be necessary, with none that can be unfair or injurious to the Northern States if they establish and set on foot a government under the Constitution so amended, and invite the other States to unite with them under it, a restoration of the Union, and a better Union are possible. There is, in my opinion, no other hope whatever.

In the meantime, since the States that have seceded will surely frame a Constitution and establish a government, the Border States, including Arkansas, are called upon to decide what course of action on their part will be most consistent with their honor, and most conduce to their safety. Statesman must know when to abandon the Impossible, how dear soever to him it may be, and how much soever his consistency is involved, and turn wholly to that which is Practicable. Shall Arkansas share the fortunes of her sister States, from whom most of her people come, who have heretofore defended the same Constitution against a common enemy, and who are connected with her by all the ties of one blood, the same habits of thought, the same prepossessions and customs, the same interests, and a common destiny? Will she stand aloof, and await the issue of the struggle, before determining with which side she will cast in her fortunes? Or will she adhere to the North, and become a party to all that may be done in order to subjugate the seceding States? Will she assist to do that? Would she even look on as a neutral, and without striking even one good blow in their behalf, see them crushed under the brutal heel of Power, or lashed back into the Union?

If Arkansas and the other Border States mean to unite with the Seceding States, in case proper guarantees are not given by the North, they may as well do so at once. If any compromise is patched up, somebody will be sold. No such guarantees can be had. Accept such as you can get; and you will soon see what convenient things words are, to cheat withal. Surely you will not let the Seceding States alone make a final Constitution for the Southern United States. It is not possible that any Southern State can be willing to consent to that; can desire to be placed in such position as that they must either simply accept or simply reject that Constitution, after having had no voice in settling its provisions? Surely that would be beneath the dignity even of a young State like Arkansas, and much more beneath that of Virginia. For even Arkansas, let us hope, has sons whose wisdom and judgment might be of some value, and whose opinions might exercise some influence and command some attention. It will surely be very unfortunate if the sober, wise, conservative counsels of Virginia, Maryland, Kentucky, and other of the Border States, should not be heard. It is of the utmost importance that *all* of the Southern States should cooperate in making the new Constitution, lest rash experiments should be tried and the old landmarks injudiciously removed.

The fourth of March is near at hand. If Arkansas is then found in the Union, she will be a party to whatever may have been or may then be done by the Government of the United States. Its acts of coercion, its denials of the rights of the States, its claims of more than Imperial powers, will be her acts, her denials, her claims. When the Senate is convened by the new President, if her Senators answer to their names, as I hope they will *not*, whatever *she* does, they will find themselves, seven States at least occupying no seats there, in a miserable minority; and yet Arkansas will be a party to whatever acts of oppression may be done there by the nineteen Northern States, and the jubilant Abolitionists and Republicans who will then fill that gaudy gilded chamber.

It must not be forgotten, that, if the South returns into the Union, she too will have to make, by implication as strong as express agreement, certain concessions on her part. She will never afterwards be permitted to protest against protective tariffs, nor against laws securing the coasting and carrying trade to Northern bottoms; nor against fishing bounties; nor against a homestead law, to give land to the landless, offer bounties to foreign emigration, and carry out Seward's project of peopling the Territories with foreigners in preference to the native-born; nor against grants of land and money to build a Northern Pacific Railroad withal; nor against internal improvements in the Northern States by the General Government; nor against the erection of light-houses, and the construction of harbors, breakwaters, forts on the Northern Lakes and North Atlantic Seaboard; nor against the making of hot-beds, in which to force new States into a precocious maturity; nor against the acquisition of British America; in short, that we shall in all the future never escape the necessity of aiding with all our might in building up and strengthening the North, until, a hundred-armed Briareus, only the feeble barrier of its good faith shall restrain it from strangling us in its embrace.

If this, or much of it, will probably be the fruit of even a compromise and settlement, we may readily imagine how powerless to resist in all these respects we shall be, how ludicrous any future attempt to resist will be, if we stand by and permit the seceding States to be subjugated by the Federal Power. After that, it would be supremely absurd for us to whisper even to ourselves in our chambers, that this government is the result of a compact between the States. The Virginia and Kentucky doctrines of 1798 would have become utterly obsolete; and the most ultra Federalism the universal orthodoxy.

We cannot separate from the cotton growing States. As well expect a limb severed from the human body, to live. "Sink or swim, survive or perish," our destiny and theirs must be one. We must manfully accept our destiny, meet the danger half-way, and if overcome by it, *deserve*, at least, to have conquered.

The sober truth is, that a revolution of some kind had become as indispensable as thunder storms are to purify the stagnant atmosphere. The body politic had become sick, almost unto death. Self had become everything, and the Country nothing. Corruption, and the prostitution of public office and place to private profit had become so almost universal, and so little disgraceful, that without a great change it was not possible for the Republic to endure.

The Government had become a great market-house, in which everything was bought and sold. It was well said, a year or two since, in the Senate, that ours was the most corrupt Government on the face of the earth. I am not sure but that all the distresses and disasters, the ruin and reverses that may be consequent on a long war will be well repaid by the patriotism, long unknown, which under these stimulants and the pressure of public and private adversities, will be developed and become common in the South by the return to the simple habits of our fathers; by the capacity, now unsuspected, in multitudes of men, to make great sacrifices for their country; by the disappearance from public life of the pestilent small Demagogues who infest all stations, and bring to the discharge of the duties of place and office, only ignorance and incompetency, and often dishonesty; and by the upraising by God of great men in their places.

It is only in the shocks and conflicts caused by great questions that great intellects rise and rule; and it is by them that the attention of the people, habitually little given to profound reflection, is kept fixed upon public affairs, and their interest in those affairs maintained. When there are no such questions, that excite and arouse the passions, and alarm those to whom the interest and honor of the country are dear, then in the stagnant waters corruption breeds; small questions make the turning points of politics; and as they can as well be dealt with by small intellects as by great ones, those busy and bestir themselves, and after a little, push the truly great men from their places, and all becomes, in deliberation as well as action, trivial and contemptible; the petty intrigue, the low cabal, place put up for sale and power, held in unwashed and unworthy hands, prostrated to the most ignoble purposes. Great occasions and great controversies alone produce greatness in a nation. When these die out, all is petty squabbling and low maneuvering.

If the worst should come, and reconstruction of the Union be at the last found to be impossible, there will still be no reason for despair. Let the occasion and the State's necessity demand Wisdom and Patriotism, and it will be found that men are as wise and patriotic now as they were eighty years ago. Who is there that is willing to admit even to himself that the Southern States are not wise enough to make and strong enough to maintain a free government? When they meet in Convention to frame one, they will, fortunately, not *have* to discover the great principles of Constitutional Government. These are already embodied in our present great Charter; and the experience of seventy years has developed its few defects, and shown in what respects and how it needs amendments.

Let us concur in making these amendments, or adopting this Constitution, in establishing a Government for the Southern States. Let us arm, and perfect our military organization. Let us invite the North again to unite with us, and offer them, if they decline, a treaty of amity and reciprocity, peace and the mutual benefits that flow from friendly intercourse. And having thus done our duty, and provided for every emergency, we may tranquilly await the result, sure in any event that we shall not be dishonored.

It is the common cry that the dissolution of this Union will be the signal failure of our experiment of free government; and make us a by-word and an object of contempt all over the world. On the contrary, we are now proving that our institutions are not a failure. The world never saw such a drama as is now being enacted here. Without anarchy, without disorder, without interruption of the free and ordinary course of the laws, without martial law or suspension of the habeas corpus act, or troops to prevent or punish popular excesses, or even an increase of the police, the separation of a great Confederation of Sovereign States goes quietly on, with all the forms of law, all the solemnities of deliberation, all the decorum that could characterize the most ordinary proceedings in a period of profound peace.

Here only, in all the world, could such a spectacle be exhibited. If war results from it, it will not be by our fault; but in consequence of Northern avarice reluctant to let those who have so long been its tributaries go free, and resolute to substitute another government for that which our forefathers made. And, whatever their determination, if the present Union be not restored, and we are such men as have heretofore built up empires, we shall establish a new Republic, that shall outlast us and our children, and vying with its Northern Ally or Rival in arts and arms, surpassing the proudest glories of their common Ancestor, shall still prove to the world that the great experiment has *not* failed, and that men *are* capable of governing themselves.

WILLIAM C. RIVES

Speech on the Proceedings of the Peace Conference and the State of the Union, Delivered in Richmond, Virginia, March 8, 1861

(Richmond: The Whig Book and Job Office, 1861)

William Cabell Rives (1793–1868) was born into a distinguished political family in Amherst County, Virginia. He studied at Hampden-Sidney College, graduated from the College of William and Mary, and read law under Thomas Jefferson. After serving as an aide to General John H. Cocke during the War of 1812, for a time he practiced law. His public responsibilities led him to the Virginia Constitutional Convention of 1816, to the House of Delegates, to the U.S. Congress, and later to leadership in the U.S. Senate and to a number of ambassadorial posts. He wrote The Life of James Madison *(3 vols., 1855–68). A Unionist and a man of conservative values, Rives was a member of the Washington Peace Conference of February 1861 and voted against secession in the Virginia Convention. Nevertheless, after Virginia seceded he held office in the Provisional Confederate Congress and in the first Congress, but he resigned in 1862. Rives's reasoned pamphlet included in this volume was devoted to peace, as he guaranteed Southerners that the North planned to honor the legal right of property in slaves. He discussed the power of a Border state alliance, insisted that noncotton slave states supported the Border state interests on navigation and trade on the Mississippi River, and insisted that feuds, quarrels, and divided interests soon would break up the newly founded Confederacy. See Drew McCoy,* The Last of the Fathers: James Madison and the Republican Legacy *(New York: Cambridge University Press, 1989), esp. 325–59; see also, Robert G. Gunderson, "William C. Rives and the 'Old Gentlemen's Convention,'"* Journal of Southern History *22 (November 1956): 459–76. Rives's family papers are in the Library of Congress.*

The questions which the Convention at Washington was assembled to adjust, all related to the delicate but fruitful topic of domestic servitude as it exists in the Southern States of the Confederacy. According to a just theory of the Constitution, this subject cannot be legitimately brought within the sphere of the General Government, but in two specified cases—first, to pass the necessary laws to give effect to the constitutional guarantee for the rendition of fugitives from service or labor; and, secondly, to prohibit and repress the African slave trade after the expiration of the period of twenty years for which it was tolerated, by the compromise of the Constitution, at the special instance of two of the Southern States— South Carolina and Georgia.

Although this is the full extent of the power given by the Constitution to the national authorities to act upon the question of domestic servitude, cunning and ambitious devices have been contrived, from time to time, by politicians on the one side or the other, to bring it into the arena of national politics, as a means of forming or strengthening party combinations by arousing sectional interests, passions and prejudices. It is not my purpose now to inquire which of the two great parties of the country has been most to blame in the political agitation of this question. It is sufficient for the purposes of this meeting, for me to state that the various forms under which the question has been agitated have brought into discussion the powers of Congress over the institution of slavery in the Territories of the Union—in the District of Columbia—in forts, arsenals and other places over which the General Government has exclusive jurisdiction within the limits of the several states—over the transfer of slaves from one slaveholding State to another—and, finally, over the institution in the States themselves, so far as it might, in the remoteness of time, be affected by an amendment of the Constitution concurred in by the requisite three-fourths of the States; to which must be added the evasion or inexecution of the fugitive slave act.

It was for the final and satisfactory settlement of these various and exciting questions that Virginia, animated by her well-known loyalty to the Union, and with that true statesmanship which in every great crisis, has directed her public councils, invited her sister States to meet her in Convention at Washington. Her Commissioners received no special instructions, nor were they tied down to any particular plan of adjustment as an *ultimatum* or *sine qua non*. We were referred in general to the proposition brought forward by the patriotic and distinguished Senator of Kentucky, Mr. Crittenden, with two modifications added thereto by the legislature, as constituting the basis of such an adjustment as would, in the opinion of the Legislature, be accepted by the people of Virginia. It was the principles of that adjustment that we kept steadily in view; and I think I shall be able to satisfy you that everything of substance in Mr. Crittenden's proposition has been unequivocally secured in the proposition of the Peace Conference, under a form of words more analagous to the precedents of our constitutional history, while several stipulations of great value and importance to the Southern States, not contained in the propositions of Mr. Crittenden, are engrafted upon the plan of adjustment which received the sanction of the Conference at Washington.[1]

The first section of both propositions relates to the territorial question, which has been the *pons asinorum* of this whole controversy. To avoid the difficulties and disputes inseparable from a joint and undivided interest in the common inheritance under the regulation of Congress, both plans propose a recurrence to the patriarchal expedient—"Let there be no strife between me and thee—if thou wilt take the left hand, then I will go to the right—if thou depart to the right hand, then I will go to the left." For this purpose it was proposed by both to re-establish permanently and unchangeably, under the sanctions of a solemn constitutional compact, the Missouri Compromise line of thirty-six degrees thirty minutes, extending it through the whole territory of the United States, and declaring that north of that line slavery, or involuntary servitude, is prohibited, and south it is recognized as existing, with suitable provisions for its maintenance and vindication, so long as the country remains in a territorial condition. Whenever any territory, north or south of the designated line, shall contain a population equal to that required for a member of Congress, it is to be admitted into the Union on an equal footing with the original States with or without slavery or involuntary servitude, as the Constitution of such new State itself shall provide.

In carrying out these principles, common to both propositions, that of Mr. Crittenden uses the following language: "In all the Territory South of the said line of latitude, slavery of the African race is hereby recognized as existing, and shall not be interfered with by Congress, but shall be protected as property by all the departments of the Territorial Government during its continuance." In the proposition of the Peace Conference, the same object is accomplished by a different form of words, pursuing the language of the Constitution, but with a force and effect equally, if not more complete than the terms employed in Mr. Crittenden's proposition. The language used in the proposition of the Peace Conference is this—"In the present Territory South of that line, the status of persons held to involuntary service or labor, as it now exists, shall not be changed; nor shall any law be passed by Congress or the Territorial Legislature to hinder or pre-

1. For comparison of the Crittendon Compromise and the Washington Peace Conference compromise see Robert G. Gunderson, *Old Gentlemen's Convention: The Washington Peace Conference of 1861* (Madison: University of Wisconsin Press, 1961).

vent the taking of such persons from any of the States of the Union to said Territory; nor to impair the rights arising from the said relation; but the same shall be subject to judicial cognizance in the Federal Courts, according to the course of the common law."

It must be borne in mind that by an act of the Territorial Legislature of New Mexico, which includes all the territory south of the parallel of thirty-six degrees, thirty minutes the amplest provision is already made for the protection of the rights connected with slavery. Its very title is "an act for the protection of property in slaves," and in fulfilment of its avowed purpose it furnishes every safeguard usually found in the codes of slaveholding communities, for the vindication and enforcement of the rights of the master. It is unnecessary here to do more than indicate the general character of this Territorial law, as the discussions, which will soon take place in the Convention now assembled in this city, must bring all its details fully to the knowledge of the public. Slavery also already exists in point of fact in this territory, though as yet, it is understood, to a very limited extent.

Taken in connection with this state of the law and the fact, as now existing in the territory south of thirty-six degrees thirty minutes, what more complete protection can be given to the institution of slavery or involuntary servitude there, than is furnished by the proposition of the Peace Conference? It explicitly declares that the "status of person held to involuntary service or labor, as it now exists"—that is, the condition of persons in a state of slavery as now exiting in the Territory, both in law and in fact—"shall not be changed"; nor "shall any law be passed to hinder or prevent the taking of such persons to said Territory, nor to impair the rights arising from the said relation; but the same shall be subject to the cognizance of the federal courts, according to the course of the common law." I shall hereafter allude to this last clause, as a very perverse handle seems to have been made of it to excite the prejudices of persons not familiar with the legal and well established import of the terms used in reference to the common law. For the present, I invite your attention, fellow citizens, to the general scope of this provision—its fullness, its precision, its completeness for every purpose of legal protection, as well with regard to the holding of slaves in security in the Territory, as to the right of taking them there from any part of the Union.

But it is objected that the word slave or slavery is not used in the proposition of the Peace Conference. Neither is it used in the Constitution. In both, the relation is described as that of "persons held to service or labor under the laws of the State," where it exists. This description is in itself far more just and appropriate in a solemn constitutional instrument than the use of an absolute term, from which, in the more familiar historical examples of it, inferences might be drawn very different from the nature of the institution as it existed and still exists in the States of the American Union.

In the Roman civilization, such as it was, from which the historical ideas of slavery were most generally derived, the master had the power of life and death over his slave, and the practice was for each master to fix his brand upon the cheek of his slaves, though of the same race with himself. No wonder that the wise and great men who framed the Constitution of the United States should have wished to guard against inferences and associations such as these by the pretermission of a word that might have led to them. There is recorded evidence that the pretermission was the result of consideration and design, especially on the part of the representatives of the Southern States, who were most interested in the legal, as well as humanitarian, character of the institution as it exists in the United States.

It will be seen, on reference to the history of the Constitution as it has come down to us from the most authentic sources, that, after the first draft of the instrument was reported by the committee of detail, General Pinckney, of South Carolina, desired "some further provision in favor of property in slaves"; whereupon his colleague, Mr. Pierce Butler, proposed a clause providing, in express terms, for the surrender of "fugitive slaves," but immediately withdrew it. On the following day he submitted a proposition for the rendition of "persons held to service or labor under the laws of one State, escaping into another," in the very words, with one or two insignificant variations, in which it now forms a part of the Constitution, and it was unanimously adopted.

But it seems we have grown wiser than the Constitution itself, as well as our fathers who framed it; and there are those who insist that the inexorable *shibboleth* shall be pronounced, however ample, unequivocal and precise are the guarantees otherwise given for all the rights connected with the legal servitude of the African race as it exists in the Southern States of the Confederacy, and as it is recognized and provided for by the proposed arrangement with regard to a partition of the common Territories of the Union. But, in an age of sober reason, a demand resting upon a single word, excluded from the Constitution, when all which that word justly imports is abundantly conceded and secured, can never be made the *sine qua non* of the preservation of our glorious frame of government and of our plighted faith, by a loyal and high-minded people.

Let us now, fellow-citizens, run a brief parallel between the proposition of Mr. Crittenden and that of the Peace Conference, and see which, when analyzed, furnishes the best legal security for the rights connected with African servitude. Both of them recognize the institution as existing in the Territory south of thirty-six degrees thirty minutes. The proposition of Mr. Crittenden seems to recognize it simply as a fact, and adds, negatively, that "it shall not be interfered with by Congress." The proposition of the Peace Conference, in declaring that the "status of persons held to involuntary service or labor, as it now exists, shall not be changed," recognizes both the law and the fact, as it is the law which defines and fixes the status, and farther ensures a known and efficient protection, by declaring that that law, so fixing the status, shall not be changed. Mr. Crittenden's proposition declares that slavery shall be protected as property by all the departments of the Territorial Government during its existence. The proposition of the Peace Conference ensures and establishes that protection, in the most ample manner, beforehand, by declaring that the Territorial law which gives it shall not be changed; and adds that "the rights arising from the relation of involuntary service or labor shall not be impaired either by Congress or the Territorial Legislature, but the same shall be subject to judicial cognizance in the Federal Courts, according to the course of the common law."

The proposition of the Peace Conference thus covers the rights of the master under the double shield of federal and territorial protection, while that of Mr. Crittenden provides for territorial protection only. The cognizance of the Federal Courts furnishes a most important security, as a long line of decisions of the Supreme Court of the United States, among which may be mentioned the celebrated Amistad case, and the case of Groves and Slaughter, as well as the Dred Scott case, recognize and affirm, in the fullest and most unequivocal manner, the right of property in slaves. The Proposition of the Peace Conference throws open, also, the whole arsenal of remedies furnished by the plastic genius of the common law for the assertion and vindication of those rights.

Thus far, fellow-citizens, I think you will agree with me that the proposition of the Peace Conference furnishes a more ample and efficient legal protection for the rights of the slaveholder in the allotted territory than the proposition of Mr. Crittenden. But the determined opponents of the adjustment recommended by the Peace Conference profess to find an important advantage in Mr. Crittenden's proposition, inasmuch as it declares, *in totidem verbis* "slavery of the African race to be *property*."

Undoubtedly, slaves are property. They are made so by the laws of every community in which slavery exists. They are expressly declared to be so by repeated and solemn decisions of the Supreme Court. But they are something besides property. They are also *persons*, sustaining the legal relations and responsibilities of persons. They are punishable by the laws for crimes which they may commit. They are protected by the laws from crimes which may be committed against them. There are also moral relations between the master and slave, which none are more ready to recognize than the Southern slaveholder himself, and which give to the institution, as it exists in the South, its patriarchal and domestic character.[2]

Is not some regard due to the profound and comprehensive policy which adjusted, with so much skill and foresight, the entire frame-work of the Constitution; so that, whatever new provision we engraft upon it for the security of our rights, the essential harmony and consistency of its parts be not broken up? While adhering to the language of the Constitution, the proposition of the Peace Conference, I think I have shown you, recognizes in the most unequivocal manner the legal rights of property in slaves, and provides the amplest possible protection for those rights—a recognition repeated and reinforced by other parts of the plan, which provide, in certain cases, for the payment of the money value of the slave, and guard against his disproportioned taxation in comparison with other property.

So entire and complete is the recognition and protection thus given to the rights of property in slaves, that when a motion was made, in one stage of the proceedings, to substitute, on this point, language taken from Mr. Crittenden's proposition for that of the Peace Conference, four out of seven of the slaveholding States represented in the Convention, voted in the negative, while several of the delegates of the three remaining States which voted otherwise, were, doubtless, influenced mainly by the consideration that their constituents had already expressed their approbation of the terms of Mr. Crittenden's proposition. For myself, I am free to declare that, voting as I did, from deference to the opinions expressed by the Legislature of Virginia, in favor of the language of Mr. Crittenden's proposition, my deliberate opinion was, and is, that it gives, in no respect, any better protection to the rights of the slaveholder than does the proposition of the Peace Conference; while the latter has the advantage of being conceived in language more in harmony with the well considered precedents of our constitutional history.

Let us now advert to another difference between the amended proposition of Mr. Crittenden and that of the Peace Conference, which has been much dwelt upon, but very inconsiderately, as it seems to me, by the adversaries of the latter. The amended proposition of Mr. Crittenden applies

2. Rives was citing Madison in *Federalist* no. 54 on slaves as property and persons.

the Missouri compromise line to future as well as existing territory; and this, in the excited zeal of those who advocate everything in preference to the Peace Conference adjustment, seems to be considered as tantamount to the actual acquisition of territory south of 36°30′, and the perpetual establishment of slavery therein; whereas, the very declaration that territory hereafter acquired south of that line is to be slave territory would operate in itself as a perpetual interdict upon any such acquisition. Under the present arrangement of the Constitution, whether territory is to be acquired by treaty, requiring two-thirds of the Senate, or by a majority of the two Houses, as was irregularly done in the case of Texas—the power of acquiring now rests with the Northern States; and can it be believed, that they would ever, of their own free will, acquire territory south of 36°30′, when, in virtue of a preexisting constitutional compact, the territory would be *ipso facto* slave territory, the moment it is acquired?

Besides the unseemly spectacle, in the eyes of the world, of undertaking to parcel out our neighbors' territory among ourselves, before we have acquired it, it appeared to many of us in the Convention at Washington that it would be far better for the interests of the South, as well as for the paramount harmony and equal rights of both sections, to frame a new organic rule for the acquisition of territory, and make it a part of the Constitution, by which the concurring assent of both sections should be made necessary for such acquisition.

Under such a rule, all projects for the aggrandizement of one section at the expense of the other would be arrested; and new territory would be acquired, only where a clear national interest demanded it. If, for example, the Northern States should wish hereafter to acquire the Canadas or other adjacent British possessions, from motives of geographical preponderance, such a rule would put it at once in the power of the South to prevent it; and, vice versa, if the Southern States should, without any sufficient national consideration, desire to extend our territorial limits in the direction of Mexico and Central America, the North would equally have it in its power, by the same provision, to arrest its accomplishment. While each section would thus be armed, according to the just theory of a well-balanced Confederate Government, with a constitutional power of defending its distinctive interests against the ambitious or irregular encroachments of the other, the proposed rule would, in no case, prevent the acquisition of territory, where it was called for by considerations of a national character.

The door would be left open in every case for deliberation, for compromise, for amicable arrangement. If it should ever become the interest of the Northern States, as it well might be, in order to extend the market for their manufactures and the field for the employment of their navigation, to enlarge the national limits, by honorable negotiation, on the side of Mexico, the South might say, we will not consent to it, unless you admit us to a fair participation of the territory with our peculiar institutions. Or, if the Northern States should desire territorial enlargement in their own vicinity, the South might say, we cannot agree to it, unless you allow us a corresponding expansion, by fair and honorable means, in our quarter.

Such were the considerations which led to the second section in the plan of adjustment proposed by the Peace Conference, making it henceforward a constitutional rule that territory should be acquired only by concurring majorities of the Senators both of the slaveholding and of the non-slaveholding sections, and that no treaty for the acquisition of territory should be valid unless the votes of a majority of the Senators of each section should be given as a part of the two-thirds majority of the whole body required for the ratification of treaties. The practical operation of Mr. Crittenden's amended proposition, in declaring beforehand that all future acquired territory, south of thirty-six degrees thirty minutes, should be slave territory, would be to array the Northern States in solid phalanx against any such acquisition, and thereby render it impossible. The plan of the Peace Conference, by leaving the destination of new territory, in each particular case, an open question, and by giving each section a check upon the other, would invite mutual concessions and equitable arrangements, and secure to the South a far better chance of future expansion, if its interests should require it.

This well timed conception formed originally a part of what was called the Kentucky Resolutions, submitted by Mr. Guthrie; but the committee of a member for each State, to whom all the various propositions were referred, substituted in place of it a provision requiring four-fifths of all the members of the Senate for the ratification of treaties by which territory is acquired. My able and eloquent colleague, whose cheering presence I am happy to have the benefit of this evening (Judge Summers) then brought forward, in an improved and perfected form, the proposition originally submitted by the Kentucky delegation. On the first trial of it in the Convention, it was rejected by a majority of one or two votes; but, a reconsideration being moved, it was afterwards carried by a majority of twelve to six. To his tact, forethought, and good temper, fellow-citizens, you are indebted for what I cannot but consider a decided improvement upon the amended proposition of my honored friend, the distinguished Senator of

Kentucky, and which, if it should ever become a part of the Constitution by the national sanction, will be, in other respects, a most important addition to the checks and balances of our federative system.

I proceed now to the third section of the proposition of the Peace Conference, which covers, by one comprehensive declaration, the same ground with the second, third, and fourth articles, and a part of the sixth article of Mr. Crittenden's proposition. It relates to the long disputed questions of the power of Congress to abolish or interfere with slavery in the District of Columbia, or in forts, arsenals, and other places over which the United States exercise exclusive jurisdiction within the limits of the respective States, and the power also to regulate, control, and restrain the transfer of slaves from one slaveholding State to another.

This last power I have heard earnestly contended for on the floor of the Senate of the United States, as included in the power to regulate commerce among the States, by even so high an authority on constitutional law as Mr. Webster, when it became my duty to meet him in most unequal contest, so far as the strength of the champions was concerned, but with a firm conviction that an invincible ally, truth, was on my side. The same opinion was generally entertained, at a period not long past, by the public men of the North; and although it has gradually given way to discussion, and to intimations of opinion by individual judges from the bench of the Supreme Court, the question has never yet, so far as I am informed, been solemnly and judicially settled by that august tribunal. In like manner, it is within the recollection of all of us that the power to abolish or prohibit slavery in the District of Columbia, and by parity of reason, within the forts and arsenals over which the United States exercise exclusive jurisdiction, has been almost universally asserted in the non-slaveholding States; and petitions for the exercise of that power were, for a long time, one of the most offensive and dangerous forms of anti-slavery agitation.

The adjustment recommended by the Peace Conference proposes to cut off, now and forever, all these sources of agitation and controversy, by an article to be incorporated into the fundamental compact of the States, declaring, in explicit terms, that neither the Constitution, nor any amendment thereof, shall ever hereafter be construed to give Congress any of the powers referred to. Looking forward, at the same time, to the possible contingency that the non-slaveholding States may, at some remote period, form so large a majority of the States of the Union as to enable them, by the requisite three-fourths, to carry an amendment of the Constitution affecting the institution of slavery in the Southern States, the proposition of the Peace Conference further provides by its sixth section, taken in connection with the one we are now considering, that no such amendment shall ever be made without the unanimous consent of all the States. No more absolute security than this can possibly be given against an interference with the domestic institutions of the South.

In providing these various guarantees, the proposition of the Peace Conference, while keeping steadily in view the same objects as the proposition of Mr. Crittenden, does not always employ the same language. The reasons of this difference of phraseology have been, already, I trust, sufficiently justified and explained. That the language employed is appropriate and effective for its purposes, we are authorized to conclude from the fact, which will be attested by the journal of the Conference, that the comprehensive and important section we have just been reviewing, received the unanimous votes of all the slaveholding States represented in the Conference, and with but a single individual dissent of any member of their delegations recorded.

I come now to a comparison of the proposition of the Peace Conference with that of Mr. Crittenden, which calls for a few words of explanation and development. Mr. Crittenden's proposition established the principle that where the officer of the law is prevented by violence or the intimidation of a mob from executing the act for the rendition of fugitive slaves, the United States should pay to the owner the full value of his slave, and made it the duty of Congress to provide for such payment. The same principle and obligation are established in almost the same words, and under the sanctions of a solemn constitutional amendment, by the proposition of the Peace Conference. But Mr. Crittenden's proposition, after the establishment of this fundamental principle, proceeded to declare that the United States, when they shall have paid the owner for the value of his slave, should have the right, in their own name, to sue the county in which the violence or intimidation had taken place, for the recovery of the amount so paid, with interest and damages thereon; and that the county should in like manner, for its indemnity, have recourse over against the individual wrong-doers. These details were omitted in the proposition of the Peace Conference, mainly, it is to be presumed, from the consideration that they formed more properly the subject of legislative enactment than the matter of a general constitutional provision.

But, in the farther progress of the proceeding, an addition was made to this portion of the proposition of the Peace Conference, the history of which it is proper I should give you. After the adoption of the principle that the United States should pay to the owner the value of his slave, in case of rescue by violence or the intimidation of a mob, it was moved on the other side of the Convention that the United States should make full compensation to a citizen of any State who, in any other State, should suffer in his person and property from mobs or riotous assemblies. Though this motion involved the obnoxious principle of a general supervision of the national authorities over the internal administration and police of the several States, it had a certain air of reciprocity, which subjected our friends from the non-slaveholding States, who had stood firmly by us, to more or less embarrassment in voting against it, as they did, and, by their votes, defeated it. They deemed it necessary, therefore, to their position at home, after the issue thus made, that they should, in some form, show their adherence to the principle of the equal rights and privileges of the citizens of all the States.

From this consideration, one of the delegates of New Jersey, who had distinguished himself throughout by his ardent and gallant support of the Constitutional rights of the South, moved to re-affirm an acknowledged principle of the Constitution, by declaring that Congress shall provide, in the words of that instrument, for securing "to the citizens of each State the privileges and immunities of citizens in the several States." Believing the provision to be unnecessary, five of the slaveholding States, Virginia among the number, voted against it. The two remaining slave States, with all the border free States, who had stood firmly with us in every stage of our protracted struggle, seeing in the provision nothing but the affirmance of an unquestioned Constitutional principle, voted for it, and, added to the other States represented in the Convention, carried it by a majority of sixteen States to five.

It has been alleged by the more violent opponents of the Peace Conference that, under this provision, free negroes, who are invested with the quality of citizens, by the laws of some of the non-slaveholding States, would be entitled to claim the privileges of citizens in the Southern States. But, surely, after the decision of the Dred Scott case, which turned specially and indisputably upon this very question, and in which a large majority of the court (two only, out of nine judges, as well as I recollect, dissenting) held in the strongest terms that free negroes are not to be regarded, in any sense, as citizens under the provisions of the Constitution of the United States, such a claim could never be seriously made. Nothing, I am persuaded, could be more contrary to the loyal intentions of the honorable mover of the proposition, and of a decided majority of those who voted for it, than any such perversion of its terms; and should there appear to be any real danger of so manifest a misinterpretation, the proposition itself would, I doubt not, be frankly abandoned.[3]

The subject of the African slave trade is dealt with nearly after the same manner by the proposition of the Peace Conference and that of Mr. Crittenden. Both of them make it the duty of Congress to pass effectual laws to prevent the importation of slaves (to which the Peace Conference proposition adds Coolies) into the United States; and the latter adds also a perpetual constitutional prohibition of the "foreign slave trade," meaning thereby a perpetual interdict to American citizens, of a participation in the African slave trade as carried on to foreign countries as well as to the United States.

Both propositions, finally, provide for giving a special character of permanence and stability to all the foregoing proposed amendments of the Constitution intended to preclude the interference of the General Government with the subject of slavery, by declaring that they shall not be hereafter changed, except by the unanimous consent of all the States. Those original clauses of the Constitution also, which relate to the apportionment of representatives among the States, and to the rendition of fugitives from service or labor, are placed under the same guarantee of permanence and immutability. In thus following the example set by the Constitution itself with regard to the inviolability of the equal representation of the States in the Senate, the most effectual means are taken to give lasting security to the constitutional rights of the South, and to close forever those unhappy controversies which have hitherto divided the Confederacy and arrayed one section against another.

Let me now, fellow-citizens, call your attention to some provisions of great interest to the Southern States contained in the proposition of the Peace Conference, which are not to be found at all in that of Mr. Crittenden. In the first instance, there is an express declaration in the plan of the Peace Conference, that Congress shall have no power to impose any higher rate of taxation on slaves than on land—a subject with regard to which the proposition of Mr. Crittenden is silent. And yet it is easy to see how much the interests of the South might be injured, and their domestic institutions crippled, by an unfriendly exercise of the power of taxation in this regard,

3. Implications of the Dred Scott decision for the Peace Conference proceedings may be found in Don Fehrenbacher, *Slavery, Law, and Politics: The Dred Scott Case in Historical Perspective* (New York: Oxford University Press, 1981).

if it were not restrained by a constitutional prohibition, such as that which the Peace Conference proposes.

Again, the proposition of Mr. Crittenden, with respect to the transfer of slaves from one slaveholding State to another, simply declares that Congress shall have no power to prohibit or hinder such transportation. The proposition of the Peace Conference not only contains the same explicit declaration, but, over and beyond it, secures the right, in cases of transportation by water, of touching at ports and shores within the limits of the free States, and of actually landing, in case of necessity, with slaves, without prejudice to the master's rights of property from the adverse operation of the laws of the State, under whose jurisdiction they are thus temporarily brought.

The practical value of this stipulation will be more particularly felt along the shores of the Ohio, and of the Mississippi above the mouth of the Ohio. Having been one of the Commissioners of Virginia to treat with the Commissioners of the State of Ohio in 1848 respecting the common boundary and jurisdiction of the two States along that river, I am enabled experimentally to appreciate the importance of the provision in question. If gentlemen will look into the history of that negotiation, as they will find it among the published legislative documents of the period, they will see that it was the steady refusal of the Ohio Commissioners to give any guarantee against the operation of their State laws on the rights of property in slaves, when temporarily brought under the jurisdiction of that State by touching on her side of the river, which occasioned the final rupture of the negotiation. What it was then found impossible to obtain from a single nonslaveholding State by negotiation is secured from all by a permanent Constitutional provision, under the terms of the Peace Conference adjustment.

The proposition of the Peace Conference also contains a provision, giving increased facilities for the reclamation of fugitive slaves, to which there is no corresponding provision in the proposition of Mr. Crittenden. In a case which came before the Supreme Court of the United States some fifteen or twenty years ago, to which the Commonwealth of Pennsylvania was a party, it was held by a majority of the Court that, according to a proper construction of the second section of the fourth article of the Constitution, all measures for the surrender of fugitive slaves are under the exclusive cognizance and control of the Federal Government and its authorities, and that it is not competent for the States to pass any laws or take any action on the subject, even in aid of the surrender. This decision was dissented from by the Chief Justice and two or three of the other Judges, nor has it given, at any time, entire satisfaction to the legal mind of the country; but it has, nevertheless, been considered as definitely settling the law of the land.

Its immediate effect was to lead to a repeal of the laws which had been passed by several of the non-slaveholding States, in good faith, to facilitate and cooperate in the fulfillment of this provision of the Constitution, and, in lieu of it, to beget a spirit of jealousy and opposition to the action of the Federal authorities. The opinion has, of late, been widely entertained that it would be a good thing again to open the way for the cooperative action of such of the States as should be animated with loyal dispositions. For this purpose, the proposition of the Peace Conference provides that hereafter the Constitution shall not be construed to prevent any of the States, by appropriate legislation, and through the action of their judicial and ministerial officers, from enforcing the delivery of fugitives from labor, and thus supplies an important additional security for the rights of the South, wherever the obligations of the Constitution upon all the parties are frankly recognized, over and above what is contained in the proposition of Mr. Crittenden.

There are other points of comparison of the same kind, to which I might yet farther call your attention. But I have said enough, I trust, to satisfy you that the proposition of the Peace Conference, so inconsiderately denounced, furnishes, at least, as ample and complete protection for all the rights and interests of the South as any scheme of adjustment that has been offered to the consideration of the country. When, indeed, all the complex relations of the subject, and the degree to which sectional passions and prejudices have been aroused by a long continued political struggle of unprecedented violence, are considered, every candid man must regard it as a matter of surprise, as well as congratulation, that so satisfactory an adjustment should have been reached at last.

By the proposed plan, every possible approach by which the rights and interests of the South could be threatened or assailed—every conceivable avenue through which the agitation of the slavery question could be renewed—is forever cut off and hermetically closed. The controversy respecting the territories is finally laid to rest and irrevocably terminated by an impassable line of demarcation, established with all the sanctions of a constitutional provision. Congress is perpetually interdicted from any interference with the subject of slavery in the District of Columbia, and in other places over which it has exclusive jurisdiction within the limits of any of the States, unless with the consent of the communities and States concerned; and, in a spirit of the most abundant caution, it is provided that no future amendment of the Constitution shall ever be made by which the institution of slavery can be affected in any of the States where it exists, but with the unanimous consent of those States and of all the others. Congress is, also, forever barred from any attempt to interfere with the transfer of slaves from one slaveholding State to another, or, in the exercise of its power of direct taxation, to impose any unequal or disproportionate burthen on the owners of slaves. At the same time, new and important guarantees are given for the fulfilment of the existing obligations of the Constitution with regard to the restitution of fugitives from service or labor.

It is not possible to find, in the history or political institutions of any country, a case in which the peculiar and exposed interests and rights of one part of the nation are more completely fenced round and guarded from encroachment by the other. And this is as it should be. The interests in question are of a most sensitive and delicate character, and have been the chosen object of a reckless crusade waged against them under the joint banners of fanaticism and political ambition. It was the bounden duty of the other States, as loyal parties to a compact of which the fundamental principle is the absolute security of the domestic institutions of the several States, to give ample and unequivocal guarantees for this object, and to ensure thereby quiet and repose to the mind of the South.

Such, I believe, was the honest and sincere purpose of a decided majority of the Peace Conference at Washington. Recent and bitter experience had brought home to them the indispensable necessity of putting an end, at once and forever, to anti-slavery agitation—as itself the sole and dangerous parent of an "irrepressible conflict" between two social systems, which could otherwise live, not only in peace and harmony under the paternal shield of the Constitution, but with mutual and signal benefit to each other. It was their wish and intention, in what they did, to bury under a perpetual constitutional interdict every question with which the political agitation of slavery had been hitherto connected, or on which it could hereafter contrive to fasten; and to bury them so deep that neither the hand of fanaticism, nor of intrigue, nor of ambition, could ever reach them more.

This feeling animated and directed the whole line of border free States, co-terminus with the slave States, stretching from the shores of the Atlantic to the banks of the Mississippi. New Jersey, with her large, national heart, formed amid the historic battle fields of the Revolution—Pennsylvania, with her firm and massive constancy in the Union and the Constitution—the youthful giant States of the Northwest, Ohio, Illinois and Indiana, with a loyalty not forgetful of their mother Commonwealth, and mindful of the great and growing influence they must ever exercise in the councils of an undivided confederacy, stood, on every important question, for the rights of the South. They felt that upon them and the border slave States must fall the brunt of those interminable conflicts which, both history and reason show, would inevitably spring from separation; and in their conduct and in their language they faithfully exemplified the operation of that great law of common interest and sympathy, which make of the central States, on both sides of the line, the special guardians and natural conservators of the Union.

Unfortunately, the same spirit of fraternity and wise conciliation was not exhibited by all the other States represented in the Convention; and this produced our difficulties. But I am happy to be able to say, that even the spirit of Massachusetts was modified before the close of the session; so much so, that a distinguished member of her delegation, who delivered a fervent anti-slavery speech, in the first day of the Convention, rose, in one of the later debates, to disavow a doctrine broached by one of his colleagues, as too ultra for him. On one occasion, and upon a question of considerable interest to the South, New York, too, actually recorded her vote in our favor; and the minority of her delegation, who stood firmly and nobly with us, boldly proclaimed on the floor of the Convention that, when the question should be carried before the people of that great State, a popular majority of a hundred and fifty thousand would declare itself in favor of such an adjustment as the Convention finally recommended.

I have an unshaken confidence that the people, almost everywhere, will declare themselves in favor of this adjustment. The great desideratum now is to take the question out of the hands of politicians. It is their interest, as it is their vocation, to keep alive and foment agitation and division, as the element in which and by which they live and have their being. It is the interest of the people, on the other hand, to put an end to discord, and to promote the return of good feeling, and of mutual kindness and confidence, as the indispensable conditions of the general prosperity and happiness.

I received, fellow-citizens, just at the moment of coming here to meet you, a letter from a leading and noble-hearted member of the recent Convention at Washington from the State of Pennsylvania, who bears the name and official title, as he possesses the Roman virtues, of one of whom we were all accustomed to respect and to reverence in his day—the late Judge White, of Tennessee. Though the letter is entirely of a private character, I cannot deny myself the gratification of reading to you a brief extract from it, as justifying and confirming the confidence I have expressed in the temper of the popular mind, even where there have been recently large party majorities apparently, though not really, adverse to the just claims of the South.[4]

"I learnt," he says, "that the intelligence of our agreement was greeted in the Senate chamber at Harrisburg with three cheers; and I found, from conversing with the members, that it had given general satisfaction. Wherever I stopped, I found the same feeling to prevail. In this county, which is an old Whig county, and which gave Mr. Lincoln a majority of about two thousand six hundred, I am certain that the vote would be more than two to one in favor of conciliation. In short, from all that I can learn, the measures we adopted would be carried by an immense majority in Pennsylvania."

Shall we then, fellow-citizens, just as we are in sight of the promised land, turn back to wander and lose ourselves hopelessly in the dreary and perplexed wilderness of secession? Shall Virginia, when she has a fair prospect of ultimately winning back to the bosom of the Union her disaffected sisters, bolt out herself, and thus render the breach complete and irreparable? The time is gone by for the reckless game of precipitation. It is no longer in the power of a conclave of Senators at Washington by telegram, to get up revolutions to order, saying to their sovereign but obedient States, *go out*, and they go. Even here, if I mistake not, the same thing was practised, when the commissioners of a Southern State telegraphed to their constituents — "the Legislature of Virginia have passed resolutions against coercion — *go out promptly.*"

Fellow-citizens, the time has come for reason, for deliberation, for sober and wise discretion. At whose bidding is Virginia to go out? At that of South Carolina, whose occupation, for months past, has been to taunt, to revile, to depreciate her? At that of the other Cotton States, who rashly followed the example of South Carolina in renouncing the ties which bound her to her sister States, and without the slightest regard to the well-known opinions of Virginia, plunged the country into revolution and anarchy, of which the annihilation of a thousand millions of the national wealth and capital, and the universal derangement and distress which have attended it, grave as these evils are, are not to be counted as the most serious consequences?

If the seceded States had not deserted Virginia and the other border slave States in a manly constitutional struggle for the security and vindication of their common rights; if they had remained, with undismayed firmness at their posts in the national councils; reinforced by that noble

4. Thomas White of Pennsylvania was a delegate to the Washington Peace Conference and an old friend of Rives.

and gallant body of men in the North, who have ever stood by the South in its demand of constitutional equality and justice, they would have had the absolute control of the Government, through the Legislative department—have repelled every encroachment, if such had been attempted—and rendered the experiment of a sectional administration far too barren and thorny ever to be thought of again. And all this would have been accomplished by peaceful constitutional agencies, without any serious jar in the regular machinery of the Government, and without compromising the steady and onward march of the national prosperity and greatness.

Now that Virginia has been so cruelly, not to say wantonly, abandoned by the cotton States in this great constitutional struggle in a common cause, her first duty is to look, with calm and collected composure, to her own true position, as it is prescribed to her by the consideration of her own interest and honor. Let it be understood, once for all, that she is mistress of her own destinies; and that she is neither to be dragged into disunion by precipitation, nor awed into submission by coercion. There are questions of grave import to be maturely weighed and resolved, before she makes up her mind to dissolve a Union, which her greatest and wisest men were the chief agents in constructing, and embarks her fortune with a new confederacy against which their most solemn counsels have warned her.

When the Union shall be dissolved, as is proposed, by the line which separates the slaveholding from the non-slaveholding States, and Virginia finds herself in immediate contact with or in close proximity to States that would then be foreign States to her, without either the obligation or the disposition to surrender fugitive slaves, what prospect could she have of retaining that description of her property and labor? Would not such a state of things be virtually a proclamation of freedom, which, by successive advances and encroachments, would deprive her wholly of her slaves?

How could she and her sister border slave States sustain the collisions and war that would follow, along a frontier of several thousand miles, without a crushing weight of military establishments and of taxes that would be alike fatal to their liberties, ruinous to their resources, and destructive to all the arts of civilization and peace?

Were it possible, as it clearly is not, to surmount these dangers, she must still inquire how her diversified interests, exposed to the competition of the rest of the world, could be reconciled with the inexorable policy of a confederacy built up on the two leading and exclusive ideas of increasing the profits of the cotton culture, and diminishing the value of the labor employed in it, to the utmost practicable extent?

These are some of the questions, deeply involving the interest and safety of Virginia, which must be solved, and satisfactorily solved, before she ventures upon the irrevocable step that she is now summoned to take; and they are questions to be solved neither in hot haste nor upon compulsion.

We are sometimes flippantly told that Virginia must go with the North or the South; and then we are triumphantly asked, which we will do. I say, we will go with neither, for separation. I recognize no such alternative. Our business is to reconcile and reunite North and South; and, in the meantime, let Virginia stand, where nature has placed her, with her sister border slave States, under which denomination I include the noble and loyal States of North Carolina and Tennessee, as well as Arkansas, Missouri, Kentucky, Maryland and Delaware. These States are dove-tailed into each other by geographical, commercial and social relations, and by a pervading community of interests and pursuits, which renders them inseparable. "Whom God hath joined together let no man put asunder."

When we look at them collectively, they present in their noble bays and rivers, in their canals and railroads, in their soil and climate, in their agricultural and mineral wealth, in their commerce and manufactures, in their capacities for future development and improvement, more varied and complete elements for a prosperous and self-sufficing national existence than any separate aggregation of States of our glorious Union; if unhappily, according to the speculations of political theorists, it should be finally resolved into divers and rival confederacies. But I do not now speak of the border slave States with reference to such a contingency. I speak of them as they are, as members of the Union, and necessarily wielding, by their united and harmonious action, a potent influence upon the destinies of the Union, and upon the policy of their sister States both of the North and the South.

Virginia stands at the head of these border slave States. She is their leader and standard bearer, and they frankly and generously recognize her as such. I often, fellow-citizens, take up the map of my country to contemplate its magnificent proportions, to study the relations of its various parts, and to ponder over those great and glorious destinies which a gracious Providence seemed to have, and, I believe, still has, in reserve for us. I never do so without being struck with blended awe and admiration at the proud and imposing attitude of Virginia, as she presents herself to the eye upon the chart of the Confederacy.

Look at her there, in the center of the Union, with her broad base resting upon her solid and faithful supporters, North Carolina and Tennessee—lifting her grand and colossal form, like another Atlas or Teneriffe, to her proud elevation, flanked on the one hand by Maryland, on the other by Kentucky—and then shooting her towering pinnacle into the Northern sky, insinuating herself between the two great Commonwealths of Pennsylvania and Ohio, as if to mingle with and hold them all together with a firmer and closer cohesion. In her very geographical position and connection, we read her mission and her duty.

Let Virginia, in family council with her sister border slave States, agree upon such constitutional guarantees as are proper and necessary for the security of the South; and let them, then, with their united voices, call upon the other States, by the double ties of justice and fraternity, to signify their assent to those guarantees at the earliest possible moment. Happily, we have, in the resolutions of the Peace Conference, a plan of adjustment which has already received the sanction of many of the Northern States through their delegates in that assembly; and, with such modifications as may appear necessary upon a candid and deliberate revision, they could be promptly submitted for the direct action of the people of the several States. There can be no reason to doubt their speedy and cordial acceptance by the people of the border free States, with Rhode Island, and, I believe, Connecticut and New York; and others of the Northern States would soon follow the example.

With regard to the seceded States, however indisposed their leaders may be at the present moment, in the flush of their newly-acquired power, to listen to any terms of reconciliation, a little farther experience and reflection, acting upon the dormant attachments to the Union which still subsist in large masses of their population, could hardly fail to secure from those masses an acquiescence in any plan of adjustment that has the sanction of the border slave States, so much more nearly and deeply interested than they are in the questions connected with the security of slavery in the Union.

But however this may be, there are necessary laws, springing from the inherent relation of things, which must have their effect. When a plan of adjustment shall have been concurred in by both the border slave and the border free States, then the slave States in the valley of the Mississippi, interested in the free navigation and commerce of that river, will cordially unite with the powerful free States above them, in such a pressure upon Louisiana as must bring her back into the Union. It is impossible that the States, lying upon the upper parts of the Mississippi and its tributaries can, for any length of time, acquiesce in the possession of its mouth by a power foreign to them.[5]

5. Here Rives came dangerously close to recommending a Border state alliance

It is in vain that the Southern Confederacy proclaim the free navigation of the Mississippi as a general thesis. Look at the bill on the subject recently passed by the Congress at Montgomery, and you will see that, while they declare the principle of the freedom of the river, they, at the same time, prescribe multiplied regulations with regard to the trade upon it coming from or destined to States beyond the limits of the Confederacy, the neglect or violation of any one of which involves the forfeiture of vessel and cargo, or other heavy penalties. These are vexations and annoyances which cannot but be sorely felt; and the time will come, and come soon, in case of an adjustment of existing controversies satisfactory to the border States, when Tennessee, Kentucky, Arkansas, Missouri and Western Virginia will earnestly unite with Pennsylvania, Ohio, Indiana, Illinois and Iowa in deprecating and opposing a foreign jurisdiction at the mouth of the Mississippi.

This united pressure, concurring with internal causes, will, I firmly believe, induce Louisiana, at no distant day, to return into the Union; and when she returns, the State of Mississippi must and will follow. Here, then, the line of the seceded States is broken at its centre. Texas will be isolated on the west, Alabama, Georgia, Florida and South Carolina on the east; and what rational motive can any of these States have to continue in such a condition of segregation, when, in the meantime, every reasonable guarantee shall have been obtained for the security of their rights in the Union?

I look forward, then, with no small degree of confidence, to the ultimate return of the seceded States into the Union, as the consequence of the line of action now to be inaugurated by the border slave States. Deeply deploring the course of the seceded States—looking upon their conduct, as I must ever do, as compromising the interests of American greatness, freedom and progress more gravely than anything which has ever occurred in our history—I shall yet hail their return with sincere joy, and lively, renovated hopes for the future.

The great question for us, now, is what Virginia is to do? Shall she, too, secede, and renouncing all hope or wish for the preservation of the Union, become the tail of a Southern Confederacy? Or shall she place herself at the head of the serried Macedonian phalanx of her sister border slave States, and with their concert and cooperation, open the way to the reintegration of the Union, which, though, deprived for a time, of some of its pillars, is yet solid and unshaken in its foundations?

This ancient Commonwealth of ours, fellow-citizens, has played a great

---

similar to that recommended by John Pendleton Kennedy and Robert J. Breckinridge.

role in history. She has yet a great role to play. If we revert to her past, we shall see that she has been the proud and acknowledged leader in all those marked and characteristic movements which, at various periods of our history, have looked to the Union of America, for American liberty and greatness. In 1774, she was the first to propose a Congress of deputies from all the colonies to deliberate upon the "united interests of America." In 1776, she was the first to move the declaration of American independence by the united act of the assembled States. In 1777, she was the first to sign those articles of Confederation which pledged the States to "a firm and perpetual association with each other for their common defence, the security of their liberties and their mutual and general welfare."

In 1785, when those articles were found inadequate for their object, it was she who proposed the Convention at Annapolis to strengthen and enlarge them; and, in 1786, she again led the way in the appointment of deputies to the Convention at Philadelphia, for the purpose of forming a new Constitution, more "adequate to the exigencies of the Union"; and it was she in that Convention, more than any or all others, who, by the wisdom and influence of her sons, formed the Constitution under which we now live, and have hitherto lived in unparalleled prosperity and happiness for near three-quarters of a century. A watchful and even jealous guardian, at all times, of the rights of the States; she has never failed to rally to the support of the Union whenever it has been threatened by disaffection in any quarter, whether at the North or the South—as well against New England in 1808 and 1814, as against South Carolina in 1833 and 1850.

She cannot, then, without blotting out all her past history, now join in the unnatural work of subverting those glorious institutions which she has had so large and noble a part in building up and strengthening. Her heart, her mind, her best efforts in the council and the field, have ever been devoted to the great cause of American, Continental liberty and Union. "No pent-up Utica" has narrowed and confined her powers. Her Washington, her Jefferson, her Madison, her Pendleton, her Wythe, her Marshall, and a long list of her illustrious sons have spent the prime of their days in laboring for the development of a high, national destiny, one and indivisible, and their last prayers have been breathed for the perpetuity of the American Union.

You must not only trample in the dust the stars and stripes, the consecrated symbol of our national power and renown—as some have already done in the sacrilegious madness of the hour—but Virginia must first strike from her calendar all those immortal names I have mentioned, with their compatriot worthies; she must raze to the ground the proudest monuments of her glory; before she can enter upon the dreary and untrodden paths to which she is beckoned. Let her not obey the inauspicious summons. Let her persevere in the paths which our fathers trod, under the guidance of patriots and sages and heroes whom they reverenced, as they trusted. It is hers to preserve this glorious Union, which she so largely contributed to form. She has a moral power to do it, which no other State possesses.

But if, in an ill-omened hour, she shall incline to other counsel, let her remember that the process of dissolution and division once commenced has no assignable limits—that a new and separate Confederacy, sprung from secession, must soon fall to pieces under the operation of the same disintegrating principle—that endless feuds and strifes will follow—and that we have no warrant for believing that the laws of history, as we read them in the throes and convulsions of revolutionary France, or in the anarchy and turbulence of our Mexican and South American neighbors, will be suddenly reversed in our favor.[6]

6. Internal discord was a theme in a number of these pamphlets. For the best recent thesis on the antebellum background of this subject see William W. Freehling, *The Road to Disunion, 1776–1854* (New York: Oxford University Press, 1992).

PART IV. *Appendixes*

APPENDIX A

Other Pamphlets on Secession

These pamphlets that were not selected to print and study in detail have much merit in that they add to the overall view of the kinds of arguments made on either side of the Southern secession issue. In general they are similar in tone, phrasing, and opinion to those in the group selected for publication. The authors of these pamphlets belong to the same professions as those of the pamphlets produced in full but include a larger percentage of clergy and state convention delegates. The chronological and regional pattern is also similar, but more Upper South pamphlets are discussed here simply because more of them exist than for any other region. Additional pamphlets located at the Virginia State Historical Library and in the Southern Historical Collection will supplement this list.

PAMPHLETS PUBLISHED BEFORE 1860

William Harper, *Speech Before the Charleston State Rights and Free Association . . . Explaining the Remedy of Nullification*

(Charleston: E. J. Van Brunt, 1832), 12 pages

This was political tract number ten of the Association. In one of many attempts to explain to Southerners the doctrine of "state interposition," on April 1, 1832, South Carolina's chancellor focused on the necessity for a state to protect its vital interests against majority rule. Harper insisted that the idea of the United States as a confederacy of separate states came from Thomas Jefferson, that the right to secede was inherent in the Constitution, but that he was more interested in political necessity than proof of legal right. Harper claimed that an irresponsible majority interest led him to call for the weaker interest to assume the power to protect itself.

John Townsend, *The Southern States, Their Present Peril, and Their Certain Remedy. Why Do They Not Right Themselves? And So Fulfill Their Glorious Destiny*

(Charleston: Edward C. Councell, 1850), 31 pages

In 1850, Townsend, who would become a secession polemicist, suggested prophetically that the spoken word on the views and sentiments of the Southern people and their leaders had less of an impact on the public than had the

[375

written word. He hoped to alert his fellow Southerners to the dangers before them, so he charged Northern moderates with being secret radicals who
planned to use political force against the slave states. His call for a Southern
convention was an admission that South Carolina could not proceed with secession alone and that her destiny was inextricably entwined with the other
slave states.

Muscoe R. H. Garnett, *The Union, Past and Future: How It Works and How To Save It*

(Washington: John T. Towers 1850), 32 pages

Writing in support of a united Southern front in defense of political equality
in the Union, the Virginia congressman recounted the growth of Northern
political power, the North's internal labor problems, and predicted what would
happen to the country if the South was forced to secede. Garnett attacked paci-
fist Southerners who had made territorial concessions that enabled Northern
population to expand and led to majority control of the federal government.
In this widely read and cited pamphlet, he described a future North without
Southern trade rights and tax revenues, which would lead to internal discord
because the "tide of emigration" would continue to produce children in the
face of unemployment and loss of Southern food crops. The South, therefore,
had to work out its own destiny, which meant either its political equality in the
nation or its independence.

Christopher G. Memminger, *The Mission of South Carolina to Virginia*

(Baltimore: James Lucas and Sons, 1860), 34 pages

First published in January 1860 and reprinted during the 1860–61 secession
crisis in the December 1860 issue of *De Bow's Review*, Memminger's message
to the Virginia legislature used the "outrage" at Harpers Ferry as an excuse
to call for a Southern convention. Memminger, an agent of the state of South
Carolina, claimed that John Brown had attempted to divide Southern whites
over slavery, and that the North's response to his capture had revealed its hostility to the South. In addition, the growth of Northern political power, which
Memminger carefully described concession by concession, had brought South
Carolinians finally to call for a united slave state front. He predicted that
the overwhelming population majority of the free states, aided and abetted
by religious and academic antislavery fanatics, inevitably would elect a sectional president committed to remaking the Supreme Court, using patronage
to created additional political allegiances, and controlling future public ex-

penditures, all to the South's detriment. A Southern conference, Memminger promised, could use the threat of the South's commercial independence and restriction of Northern imports to control the North's abuse of federal political power. If economic resistance failed, the conference had to "take our destinies into our own hands."

William T. Avery, *Aggressions and Disunionism of the Republican Party*

(Washington: Lemuel Towers, 1860), 8 pages

Anticipating later arguments over disunion, on April 23, 1860, the Tennessee congressman accused the Republican Party of forcing the slaveholding states to contemplate secession. That party, Avery claimed, advocated disobedience to the fugitive slave laws, wanted to change the composition of the United States Supreme Court, opposed slavery in the District of Columbia, and used Hinton R. Helper's *Impending Crisis* as a wedge to divide Southerners. He urged the Southern Opposition Party (mainly former Whigs and Unionists) to unite with the Democrats in the upcoming presidential election, as it was now time "to look to set our house in order."

John J. Crittenden, *The Union, the Constitution, and the Laws*

(Washington: William H. Moore Printer, 1860), 16 pages

In a Louisville speech of August 2, 1860, which was published as a pamphlet by the National Union Executive Committee with the request to "please circulate" (and it did in great numbers), the devoted Southern Unionist laid out his plans to ameliorate tensions over the expansion of slavery. He launched a diatribe against the national political parties, who he claimed were irresponsible in their desire to win the presidential election at the expense of the Union. But Crittenden also believed in the will of the majority and vowed to uphold the people's choice. Mistakenly, he predicted that whoever would take over the powers of the federal government would abide by the national will for peace.

Albert G. Brown, *Letter . . . on The Interest of Non-Slaveholders in the Perpetuation of African Slavery*

(Carrollton, Miss.: Mississippian Book and Job Office, 1860), 7 pages

In this somewhat disjointed and illogical letter to his constituents, dated September 27, 1860, the Mississippi congressman replied to their concerns about whether nonslaveholders were willing to defend the South in the upcoming "fearful conflict." Admonishing slaveowners for their lackadaisical attitude toward the sectional crisis, he nevertheless assured them of the unity among nonslaveowners in defense of slavery. Brown discussed the material interests of all Southerners in their dependence on the marketplace and the need for slaveowners to employ nonslaveholders and purchase their agricultural surplus. Although he was unclear on the crucial issue of white labor in slave society, he contrasted the job security of nonslaveholders with working conditions in the North, where workers were fired at will. Most important, he assured his constituents, nonslaveholders were certain to remain loyal because of their social interest in slavery. Brown described poor Northern whites doing degrading menial labor, comparing them to slaves, who did the same kind of work in the South. He asserted that "color, and not birth, fortune, family or occupation draws the line." (Brown's theory of "perfect social equality" based on the color line anticipated the efforts of De Bow and others who revealed their genuine fear of poor whites' behavior in the forthcoming hostilities.)

William D. Porter, *State Sovereignty and the Doctrine of Coercion*

(Charleston: Evans and Cogswell, 1860), 24 pages

In the second of the 1860 Association tracts Porter described the results of the Republican victory in the presidential race as subversive to the Southern "social polity . . . with a view to their demoralization and ultimate ruin." Republican success, he claimed, meant that the government would be used to dishonor, cripple, and destroy the South through systematic injury and oppression. Porter asked Southerners: "Will you suffer that yoke to be fastened upon your necks and still claim to be men and freemen?" He called for Southern to remember their heritage of liberty, claiming that under a Republican administration Southern children could be dishonored and shamed. Porter's vivid images and language soon were spread throughout the slave states. (Also see William D. Porter, *State Pride. An Oration Delivered Before the Calliopean and Polytechnic Societies of the State Military School, at Charleston* (Charleston: Evans and Cogswell, 1860). Delivered on April 5, 1860, this speech also anticipated events and established a pattern in which Southern radicals conjured views of future calamity.)

John Townsend, *The Doom of Slavery in the Union: Its Safety Out of It*

(Charleston: Evans and Cogswell, 1860), 25 pages

Reprinted many times, the fourth of the 1860 Association pamphlets was originally Townsend's presidential address to the Edisto Island Vigilance Association, which meant to alarm the protectors of slavery. Declaring, "we will be ruled by ourselves," he was convinced that the Republican Party planned to use violence and the law to abolish slavery. Citing extracts from the March 1860 edition of *De Bow's Review*, Townsend described the South as a hopeless minority in the federal government, growing constantly weaker, and soon unable to stop aggressive invasion and manipulation of the Constitution. The result, he graphically described, was loss of "four thousand million dollars"; valueless land prices; disruption of agricultural labor; a reign of black sloth, idleness, plunder, and murder; and deprivation of political rights for planter and non-slaveholder alike. The only way out of this dominolike cataclysm, he insisted, was for South Carolina to secede immediately. (Townsend also published *The South Alone, Should Govern the South*, which originally appeared in the *Charleston Mercury*, as pamphlet number one of the 1860 Association, whereupon it soon entered its fourth edition.)

John Robertson, *Letters on the Subject of Southern Wrongs and Remedies*

(Richmond: n.p., 1861), 55 pages

These articles, which were published in the Richmond *Enquirer* and *Richmond Whig* over the period from October to December 1860 and republished as one pamphlet early in 1861, represent how many Virginians evaluated the events of 1860 that led to the secession crisis. The author, a former congressman and judge who witnessed with frustration his fellow Virginians apathy toward the dangers that confronted them, attempted to show them how little protection they could expect from the federal government. Robertson castigated the Northern public for attacking the Southern labor system as sinful and a crime and predicted they could cause a bloody race war. He proposed calling a Southern convention (using an argument similar to that of Christopher Memminger described above) that would create a united effort before the Border states allied with the North. Spurred by fear of loss in the upcoming presidential election and certain that the victorious Republicans would use the federal government against slavery, Robertson asked Virginian's what had happened to the brave tradition of resistance their ancestors had given to his generation. In his last article, dated December 1860, he unrealistically demanded a compromise measure in the U.S. Senate that would give the Southern region a veto on Northern actions.

Rev. W. C. Dana, *A Sermon Delivered in the Central Presbyterian Church, Charleston, S.C., Nov. 21st, 1860 . . .*

(Charleston: Steam Power Presses of Evans and Cogswell, 1860), 12 pages

(This and the following two pamphlets, which were sermons preached at the request of Governor William Henry Gist, while hardly original or profound, taken together reveal how the scriptures were used to defend slavery and support secession during those crucial early days after the presidential election of 1860. Indeed, a separate volume of sermon pamphlets could show the enormous impact of Southern churches on the secession movement.) The secession crisis for Dana and other South Carolina clergy led to a call for divine assistance and protection. Through faith, they asserted, the people of South Carolina would reject the naked power of a hostile government and the majority of the Northern people determined to destroy slavery.

Rev. Thomas Smyth, D.D., *The Sin and the Curse; or the Union, the True Source of Disunion, and Our Duty in the Present Crisis*

(Charleston: Steam Power Press of Evans and Cogswell, 1860), 15 pages

Smyth preached this sermon to his congregation at Second Presbyterian Church on November 21, 1860; then church officials requested to publish it. The dour Scotsman called for prayer and fasting in order for the people and their leaders to realize how long Northern government had tried to undermine slavery. Under the influence of anti-Christians, levelers, and anarchists Northern churches had assisted politicians in resisting the scriptures, which recognized and regulated slavery. Smyth hoped that the secession crisis had led individual Southerners back to the church and its helpful arm.

Rev. William O. Prentiss, *A Sermon Preached at St. Peter's Church, Charleston, On Wednesday, November 21, 1860*

(Charleston: Steam Power Press of Evans and Cogswell, 1860), 20 pages

In his parish and later before the South Carolina legislature, Prentiss preached on what he saw as the end of civilization and the birth of a new slave culture, or, what he called, "the hearse and the cradle." At times the Episcopal priest bordered on paranoia, as when he insisted William Henry Seward had plotted to destroy Southern slavery in order to become dictator after a class war in the North. At its core, however, the pamphlet revealed Prentiss's thoughts on Northern religious errors, which he claimed had brought on the destruction of the country, especially because the clergy had followed the laity in the false belief that the scriptures favored democracy. He concluded his speech with the admonition that Southern leaders could not draw back, for they were fighting a battle of life and death, and he predicted that on the Southern republic's natal day, "authors of Revolution will be canonized."

James H. Thornwell, *National Sins. A Fast Day Sermon, preached in the Presbyterian Church, Columbia, November 21, 1860*

(Columbia: The Southern Guardian, 1860), 40 pages

This widely reprinted pamphlet revealed how Christian leaders, usually reluctant to interfere in the civil and political sphere, accepted the task to preach on national sin in order to protect the interests of slaveholding society. Thornwell did so by insisting that the federal political system and the North's treatment of labor was sinful and would need to be reformed if the Union were to be saved. He asserted that the federal government had always relied on honor and good faith for support from the country, and the Northern attack on slavery had broken that faith. Thornwell described corrupt and excessive use of power, focusing on the false belief in "a pure democracy," where the majority attacked the interests of a minority. To bring the sermon back to the issue of Christian duty and obligation he insisted that the North had its own labor problems that might lead to vicious control of labor. Thus, he reasoned, all slaveowners had to acknowledge their personal responsibility to protect the "person of the slave."

Charles Anderson, *On the State of the Country*

(Washington: Lemuel Towers, 1860), 16 pages

During a meeting in San Antonio, Texas, held to discuss the merits of Southern secession, Anderson, a recent settler in Texas, rose to protest what he called the unthinking movement toward secession and the view that all would be well because England planned to protect the South. After agreeing that sufficient cause existed for "dissolution of our Government," he claimed that many Northern states continued to enforce the Fugitive Slave Law and that President-elect Lincoln could not interfere with slavery in the Lower South. Anderson warned that formation of a Southern Confederacy inevitably meant war without assistance from any European power.

William H. Holcombe, *The Alternative: A Separate Nationality, or the Africanization of the South*

(New Orleans: Delta Mammouth Job Office, 1860), ca. 12 pages.

De Bow's Review warmly reviewed this pamphlet, and *The Southern Literary Messenger* of February 1861, reprinted it, thus spreading Holcombe's message of the need for Southern secession throughout the slaveholding states. A poet, accomplished author, and physician, Holcombe believed that the "real quarrel" between North and South was over the North's desire to use force to end slavery. The Republican victory in 1860, he asserted, meant the South no longer was equal in the Union, that Northern church leaders hated Southerners, and that the South would have race warfare. The only way for the "victims of consolidated despotism" to defend honor and duty, was to secede but try to avoid civil war.

Judge Oran M. Roberts, *Speech . . . Upon the "Impending Crisis"*

(n.p., n.d.), 32 pages

Roberts responded to the request of the citizens of Austin, Texas, to publish the text of a speech he delivered there on December 3, 1860. He did so because he believed Texas's honor, rights, and liberty were at stake, and Texans had to choose between joining a Confederate South or becoming a separate nation. He believed the secession issue was based on the continuance or abolition of slavery, that slavery represented the labor system crucial to the economy, and that it promoted equality in the superior white race. With the majority victory of the Northern states he predicted enlarged powers of the federal government would institute a "siege" of the slave states. That scheme of continued aggression, Roberts claimed, was revealed in the North's attempts to abolish slavery in the District of Columbia, refusal of Northern states to honor the Fugitive Slave Law, the North's purposeful forced emigration of antislavery whites into the Border slave states, and its continuous movement against Border slavery so as to hem slavery along the South Atlantic and Gulf Coasts "where it will destroy itself."

Hon. Louis T. Wigfall, *Speech, in Reply to Mr. Douglas on Mr. Powell's Resolution. Delivered in the Senate of the United States, December 11 and 12, 1860*

(Washington: Lemuel Towers, 1860), 32 pages

In this discursive and rambling monologue, which the radical Senator from Texas had bound as a pamphlet and sent to the Gulf South, Wigfall captured the tension, and frustration of those who sought compromise on the protection of slave property. Wigfall asked why Southerners should discuss their demands when nothing had been offered them? He charged that Northerners sent outsiders called the "Mystic Reds" to Texas with poison, plans to burn plantations, and guns to arm slaves. His state, he claimed, had become an armed camp, prepared to defend itself against abolitionists at any cost. Wigfall wondered why he and others remained in hopeless Washington with a dominant Republican congress that every day insulted the values of Southerners, going so far as mocking "chivalry," a term South Carolinians used to describe their principles and their actions.

A. H. Handy, *Speech of . . . , Commissioner to Maryland, from the State of Mississippi . . . on the First Day of January 1861*

(Jackson: Mississippian Book and Job Printing Office, 1861), 23 pages

The Mississippi convention sent Handy to his native state of Maryland to explain to all those who had "sacred Memories" of unity why Mississippi planned to secede. His pamphlet, which was meant to influence events back home as much as it was to do so in Maryland, voiced his concern with the Republican Party victory because it meant subversion of the federal government with the intent to destroy slavery. To make the case Handy quoted from Lincoln, Seward, and the Republican Party platform on the irrepressibility of the sectional conflict over slavery. He rejected the congressional peace movement and the call for a general Southern states convention as too late to protect the "sacred covenant" of slavery. Handy was determined to establish the right and the necessity for secession.

Rt. Rev. Augustin M. Verot, *Slavery and Abolitionism: Being the Substance of a Sermon, Preached in the Church of St. Augustine, Florida, on the 4th Day of January, 1861*

(New Orleans: The Catholic "Propagator," 1861), 23 pages

This pamphlet, published in early 1861, was reprinted on December 8, 1861, because the issues raised in it continued to trouble the new Confederacy. Verot, Roman Catholic bishop of St. Augustine and Savannah, linked abolitionists to anti-Catholic Know-Nothings and defended separation from such bigoted fanatics. He expected the Southern Confederacy to rest on morality and social order, and he called for a slave code to justify slavery. Verot believed that the North was debased, especially in its treatment of immigrants, and he wanted to be certain that Southerners would not behave the same way toward their slaves. He called masters to a strict and rigorous duty, to avoid sexual contact with slaves, to support slave marriage, to defend the slave family by outlawing the sale of slaves, and to oppose the reopening of the iniquitous slave trade, so destructive to both white and black lives.

Edwin T. Winkler, *Duties of the Citizen Soldier. A Sermon, Delivered in the first Baptist Church of Charleston, S.C. . . . January 6, 1861*

(Charleston: A. J. Burke, 1861), 14 pages

This sermon to the Charleston Moultrie Guards reached an audience that wished to reprint it for distribution to all of the military of the state. Winkler defended secession as an act against the tyranny of a government that "insulted our methods of industry." To the "warriors for justice" he preached on sacrifice, devotion, heroism, virtue, patriotism, and temperance and concluded with images of troops preparing to defend their new republic "that rises from the chaos of these times. . . ."

Joseph R. R. Wilson, D.D., *Mutual Relations of Masters and Slaves as Taught in the Bible*

(Augusta: Steam Press of the Chronicle and Sentinel, 1861), 21 pages

On January 6, 1861, Wilson preached in the First Presbyterian Church and published his sermon at the request of his parishioners. He began with the biblical argument for slavery to refute the charges of fanatical and infidel enemies. But he insisted that Southern stewards of the slaves had to "guard their tempers" so that they may avoid unnecessary severity in treatment of the slaves. He spoke of the obligation to resist godlessness among the slaves and of that "divine management" that contributes to uplift, exalt, and enrich the superior race.

James B. Owen, *The Right, Cause, and Necessity for Secession*

(Apalachicola, Florida: n.p., 1861), 32 pages

Owen, the minister and Florida state political leader, too ill to deliver his speech on January 6, 1861 before the state secession convention in support of the resolution on secession, had it printed and distributed among all the delegates and other interested parties. After token deference to the historical right of secession, largely taken from the works of John C. Calhoun, Owen turned to the present crisis and to the necessity for immediate action. For him, the results of the presidential election of 1860 meant that an antislavery, anti-

Southern, despotic free state majority was in charge, and it was determined to use the expanding federal government to tax Southern consumers, encourage foreign labor to settle in the North and thus contribute to a diminished percent of Southern population in the nation, and refuse to reopen the slave trade, which meant further decline in Southern numbers and political power. Thus, he reasoned, it had become necessary for Southerners to shape their own destiny lest further loss of Border slave state support and growth of the number of Northern spies in the Lower South contribute to a weakening of the slave states. Owen concluded with the vision of a separate South of free markets that would save on state expenditures; of an influx of labor and capital; and of building commerce, transportation, and cities in a diversified slave-based society.

Williamson A. W. Cobb, *Personal Explanation . . . Delivered in the House of Representatives, January 7, 1861*

(Washington, D.C.: W. H. Moore, 1861), 8 pages

Cobb of Alabama printed and had bound together two of his last congressional speeches as messages to send home to explain his activities to his constituents. In the first message, he claimed that the wisdom, discretion, and ability of the people of Alabama had guided his movements and that they all were aware that the Republican Party leaders had refused to compromise on the protection of slave property. In the second message, dated January 30, 1861, he made his farewell to Congress. Cobb again proclaimed that he followed the lead of seceded Alabama, and that the vacant seats of Southern congressmen meant that others had supported their states' actions as well. He warned that compromise was impossible because Northern politicians refused Southern rights to equality in the Union.

Governor Albert Moore, *Message . . . to the House of Representatives of Alabama, January 14, 1861*

(Montgomery, Alabama: Shorter and Reid, 1861), 16 pages

Moore had 5,880 copies of this message on war preparations printed and distributed. He expected all Alabamians to rally against the coercive federal government. In response to Northern aggression, he had taken possession of the federal forts in Mobile harbor and a federal arsenal. Moore asked the legislature to allow him to borrow from the state banks (the letters to the bankers were appended to the printed message), to raise an army and purchase weapons, to give the governor's office additional secretarial assistance, to appoint a Military Board of Professionals, and to provide for the care of the state's poor families. In addition he wanted an appropriation to finance the expedition he had sent to Florida to aid in the capture of Fort Pickens in Pensacola Harbor.

John Hemphill, *Speech . . . On the State of the Union. Delivered in the Senate of the United States, January 28, 1861*

(Washington: Lemuel Towers, 1861), 16 pages

This one-time South Carolina nullifier and an adopted Texan versed in constitutional theory argued vigorously that secession was not rebellion but a right of each state. Tired and fearful, Hemphill acknowledged that the Northern government could reject his historical proof of the peaceful right of withdrawal, declare the South in rebellion, and attempt to force the slave states back into the Union. He refused to itemize Southern grievances that had brought on secession, but he maintained that Texas had joined the United States out of fear that England planned to abolish slavery there, only to find the North behaving the same way. A pugnacious Hemphill then warned Northerners that if war came, they could not be certain that bloodshed or internal unrest would only happen in the South. He predicted that slaves would continue to work peacefully in the fields while Northerners would have to draft farmers, and he asserted that "assaults can be best repelled by assuming the offensive."

Leonidas W. Spratt, *The Philosophy of Secession: A Southern View*

(Charleston: n.p., 1861), ca. 12 pages.

Longtime advocate of reopening the slave trade, *Charleston* Mercury editor Leonidas Spratt published in the February 13, 1861, issue this letter to John W. Perkins, a Louisiana delegate to the Montgomery convention, then later published it as a pamphlet. (The *National Intelligencer* of February 19, 1861, thought it important enough to republish.) Spratt's argument addressed the deep divisions in the Southern states over the growth of slavery, and he was attempting to reconcile those differences. He began by explaining that Southern and Northern tensions resulted from the differences between two forms of society: one based on slave labor, the other on lower-class, immigrant, free labor. Spratt insisted that if the slave trade had never been suppressed, the slave states would have had the population, political power, and wealth to protect themselves. For those Southerners who insisted on the dispersal of the dense slave population into the territories out of fear of racial strife, Spratt described the harmony between the large slave and small white populations in coastal South Carolina. He charged Virginia with courting slave trade with the Lower South yet remaining in the Union, and he expressed his fear that the decline in the slave population and rise in foreign workers in the Upper South meant that

that section no longer identified with the labor system that defined Southern society. Spratt, in short, worried that the new Confederacy would divide into antagonistic societies, with a growing immigrant labor system at odds with a predominant slave labor system.

Addresses Delivered Before the Virginia State Convention by the Hon. Fulton Anderson, Commissioner from Mississippi, Hon. Henry L. Benning, Commissioner from Georgia, and Hon. John S. Preston, Commissioner from South Carolina, February 1861

(Richmond: Wyatt M. Elliott, 1861), 66 pages

The commissioners to the Virginia convention from the Lower South states presented their credentials on February 14 and delivered their speeches on February 18 and 19, 1861. On March 4, 1861, a resolution was adopted to print 3,040 copies of those addresses "for equal distribution among members of the convention," many of whom sent them to other important political leaders. Seemingly too late to influence events back home in Mississippi, Georgia, and South Carolina but not too late to fortify resolve in the Lower South, the pamphlets illustrate how the Lower South sought to influence the Upper South's secession movement.

Anderson of Mississippi proclaimed it too late to discuss the right of secession or whether Southern actions were revolutionary and could lead to violent warfare. Instead, he explained that an avowedly hostile federal government had forced the Southern people to take "their interest and their honor into their own keeping. . . ." He invited Virginians "to come out of the house of your enemies" and join your friends, kin, and those with like interests in the protection of slavery.

Benning of Georgia began with the straightforward assertion that Georgia had seceded to "prevent the abolition of slavery." For him the Republican Party permanently controlled the Northern states, and its political philosophy alleged that consolidated government replaced confederated government, thus making "the numerical majority . . . sovereign." He asked what the Lower South had to offer the Upper South in those perilous times. Benning suggested military protection would allow Virginia to develop fully its manufacturing potential and to build large urban centers of commerce and trade with the Lower South. Flatly, he claimed that the North would not allow Virginia to grow as a manufacturing center, because it would not buy what Virginians produced. Tellingly, he threatened Virginians with refusing to allow them to sell slaves South, which would result in a dangerous black population concentrated in only parts of the state and would make slaves vulnerable to the clutches of Northern abolitionists.

Preston of South Carolina also maintained that he had not been sent to make the argument "in proof of the right of secession," but instead was sent to explain what had caused his state to act. He attempted to show that secession was hardly a precipitant movement but was a response to thirty years of Lower South grievances. Understanding how Virginians thought of themselves, he drew on their historic ties to and leadership of the slave states and promised that Virginia would lead the new Southern Confederacy. Relying on that religious imagery so close to the values of Virginians Preston concluded: "With demonic rage, they have set the Lamb of God between their seed and our own seed."

William J. Grayson, *Reply to Professor Hodge on the "State of the Country"*

(Charleston: Evans and Cogswell, 1861), 32 pages

This pamphlet by the South Carolina poet and political thinker William J. Grayson, which was written in reply to the supposedly pro-Southern Princeton theology professor Charles Hodge, captures just how far apart on the secession issue even moderate intellectual leaders had grown. Hodge had written in the September 1860 issue of the *Southern Presbyterian Review* that there were no reasons to dissolve the Union because Northerners generally tolerated slavery, opposed those who desired to keep slaves out of the territories, and supported the Fugitive Slave Law. Grayson refuted him with examples of Northern institutional political action, such as the personal liberty laws adopted by state legislatures, and warned of the consequences of containing slave population. He was outraged by Hodge's assertions that Southerners had seceded only for economic reasons. For Grayson, Northern repudiation of Southern social values and revulsion toward its manners and moral code permanently divided the two sections. He concluded that the only issue the so-called Northern moderates were concerned about was whether they would allow the slave states to depart in peace.

Claudian B. Northrup, *Political Remarks by "N"*

(Charleston: Evans and Cogswell, 1861), 27 pages

Written in mid-March 1861 for a column for the Charleston *Courier* but deemed too inflammatory and discursive to publish, Northrup's friends printed the articles as a single pamphlet. For Northrup, secession would not lead to civil war because Northern leaders were cowards and Northern society was weak. After making cursory comments on Southerners as fierce and self-reliant warriors, he described Northern divisions that would sap their will to fight. Northerners simply had no social bonds of family, no confidence, no will to sacrifice; the rich were selfish and unwilling to pay for war; and recent German and Irish immigrants were clashing with the Protestant farm population.

Benjamin M. Palmer, *A Vindication of Secession*

(Columbia, S.C.: Southern Guardian Press, 1861), 44 pages

This response to pamphlets written by Rev. Robert J. Breckinridge (see his pamphlet included in this volume) appeared in the April 1861 issue of *Southern Presbyterian Review* and was published as a pamphlet during the final stages of the Fort Sumter crisis. Palmer accused Breckinridge of trying to persuade the Border and Upper South states to remain with the Union and of providing them with a distorted view of the secession process. Palmer attempted to convince the Upper South that secession had been achieved democratically because popularly elected conventions had voted to secede, delegates had met in a united convention to write a conservative constitution and form a moderate government, and the constitution and the new government had received popular support in each state. Palmer also claimed that business continued as usual, that the new confederacy strengthened and remained united, and that Yankee treachery caused the Fort Sumter crisis. He explained that secession was necessary because Northern and Southern society functioned differently, their systems of labor were different, and most of all, the Northern numerical majority would control the federal government. In his claiming that Southerners were not anarchists, Palmer raised an early revision of the causes of secession by insisting that sectional tensions would have grown even if slavery had never existed.

PAMPHLETS FROM THE UPPER SOUTH

Truman M. Post, *Our National Union: A Thanksgiving Discourse, Delivered in the First Trinitarian Congregational Church, November 29, 1860*

(St. Louis: R. P. Studley Printer, 1860), 20 pages

This Missouri Unionist who was uncomfortable with using his pulpit to deal with what he called a social controversy nevertheless pointed out that the Border states' best interests kept them in the Union. Post insisted that the Upper South's great commerce and dynamic internal growth would give way to disruptive and cruel border warfare if secession were successful. He warned with great passion, that disunion would not be peaceful or orderly, it would be anarchy.

George Thompson, *Secession is Revolution; The Dangers of the South; The Barrier States, Their Position, Character, and Duty: Delivered . . . December 1, 1860*

(Wheeling, Va.: n.p., 1861), 28 pages

In an attack on the expansionist Lower South, this Virginian from Wheeling claimed that most of the slave states rejected reopening the slave trade for fear of "aggregated danger in a limited and circumscribed space" and that expansion into Mexico and Central America was impossible because their inhabitants would not accept slaves in their midst. Thompson confronted proposed secession among the "barrier" or Border slave states. He identified neither with Northern antislavery radicals nor Lower South secessionists and maintained that if the "barrier" states stood with the Union they could achieve the compromises necessary to ameliorate the tense situation. Thompson suggested that no real crisis existed, that the federal government had done nothing against the South, and that his beloved state of Virginia and Democratic Party, if true to their heritage, would support local rights against strong government and thus save the Union.

Samuel S. Nicholas, *South Carolina, Disunion, and a Mississippi Valley Confederacy*

[Louisville?: 1860?], 15 pages

This Kentucky lawyer, judge, and political essayist wanted to keep the Border South within the Union or to form a separate Mississippi Valley Confederacy. He suggested that radical South Carolina had long plotted to secede, had used Lincoln's election as a false excuse to act, and had used the images of a "house divided" and a "higher law" to argue for a separate Confederacy. Nicholas believed that South Carolina and other cotton states' coercion of the Upper South only revealed the divisions among the slave states themselves, and he asserted that economic rivalry soon would force the Southwest to form a separate Western Confederacy.

Bedford Brown, *Remarks of . . . Made in the Senate of North Carolina, on December 19, 1860*

(n.p., n.d.), 16 pages

Brown attempted to establish conditions under which North Carolina could remain in the Union. His great fear was that the army would become the government and make judgments about the national interest in military terms. He called for a Southern convention, which he claimed would offset the rising hostility and chaos of individual state action, and urged that, if necessary, North Carolina should "seek safety in a separate form of government."

William T. Avery, *Letter . . . to His Constituents*

(Washington, D.C.: n.p., 1860), 8 pages

In this short letter posted on December 27, 1860, the Tennessee congressman explained to his constituents the actions of the congressional committees that were recently formed to achieve sectional compromise. He indicated that he had nothing to hide from the voters, who ultimately made the decisions about the future of the state. Northern congressmen, Avery remonstrated, were defiant, destructive, and determined in their opposition to compromise. He claimed that Tennesseans could choose one of three courses of action: they could join the North, form a Border state Confederacy, or go with the Lower South. Avery advised his constituents that the Lower South planned to make Tennessee into a manufacturing hub, and he warned them of the increasing economic competition coming from Border states, where slavery was on the decline.

Bishop (Rt. Rev.) Thomas Atkinson, *On the Causes of Our National Sins. A Sermon delivered at St. James Church, Wilmington, North Carolina, Friday, January 4, 1861*

(Wilmington: "Herald" Book and Job Office, 1861), 14 pages

In response to President James Buchanan's appeal for a national day of fasting and reflection, Episcopal Bishop Atkinson asked his flock to consider the consequences of a war that would paralyze the country's commercial life. Using biblical language and imagery he cautioned that "Family hatred is the most vehement of all hatred, and civil war is the most cruel of all wars." The Unionist bishop insisted that secessionists rejected reverence for the law and obedience to a rightful authority.

Rev. John H. Chew, *God's Judgments Teaching Righteousness*

(Washington, D.C.: R. A. Waters, 1861), 13 pages

On January 4, 1861, the rector of St. Matthew's parish in Prince George's County, Maryland, described the deplorable economic and social unrest that the mere threat of civil war already had produced, and invoked past unity of the country to confront present discord. If government required repair, Chew declared, then calm, dispassion, and caution were needed to ensure that civil authority was not repudiated without careful consideration.

J. H. Freligh, *The True Position, Interests and Policy of the South*

(Memphis: W. M. Hutton and Co., Printers, 1861), 35 pages

Written for the Memphis press, this collection of secessionist essays on the crisis of the Union and the best policy for the slave states was republished in pamphlet form in early January 1861 in order to reach a wider and specifically targeted Southern audience. Freligh stated that slave states would secede because they had common interests, institutions, and opinions, as well as a moral sense of the people. Predicting that twenty-six free states would coerce eleven slave states and certain that the Northern people would abrogate any laws political leaders passed to guarantee the future of slavery, he chastised Southerners for dividing over their best interests or even thinking of submitting to compromise. A separate South, Freligh reasoned, would grow because it was buttressed by rich land, foreign alliances through commercial trade, economic self-sufficiency, a protective tariff to aid Upper South manufactures, the Southern national legislature's prevention of the rapid sale of slaves South, which would promote the harmony of Southern slave labor, and by a Northern people hostile to slave runaways because of their desire to limit black population growth there.

Hon. John J. Crittenden, *Speech . . . On His Resolutions, Delivered in the Senate of the United States January 7, 1861*

(Washington, D.C.: n.p., 1861), 8 pages

A moderate, Crittenden explained why he sought accommodation over the territorial issue, and wondered, "Is there in this compromise anything repulsive to any section of the country?" To Northern politicians he advised against attempts to divide the Southern people over the extension of slavery. This man of peace saved his harshest comments to respond to the self-righteous, religious language used by his radical opponents. For example, he stated, "you have no right . . . to insist, . . . that I shall substitute my conscience for yours; or that you shall condemn my conscience, and put the penalty upon it of forfeiture of my political rights, if I continue to act upon it." For him, the only means to preserve the Union were "proper terms of equal respect and equal regard."

Robert W. Johnson and Thomas C. Hindman, *To the People of Arkansas*

(Washington, D.C.: W. H. Moore Printer, 1861), 7 pages

In an effort to persuade the Arkansas legislature to call a secession convention, on January 8, 1861, Congressmen Johnson and Hindman described the reasons for their support of secession, arguing that the Republican Congress refused compromise on the territorial issue. If the spread of slavery into new territories was prohibited, they reasoned, the rapidly growing slave population confined to the existing territories would lead to race war, where either blacks would be exterminated or whites would be forced to leave. They claimed that Northern state governments were building militias, and the federal government had begun to reinforce federal forts in the South. The authors concluded that the only way to restore harmony in the country was to create a united and powerful slaveholding nation that would bargain for its rights.

Hon. Daniel C. DeJarnette, *Secession of South Carolina*

(Washington, D.C.: Office of the Congressional Globe, 1861), 7 pages

In response to Northern rejection of South Carolina's secession, the Virginia congressman DeJarnette spoke on January 10, 1861, on a state's right to leave the Union, claiming that the right went beyond being abstract or hypothetical to being necessary for self-protection. He asked whether Northerners would allow peaceful secession or declare the Lower South in rebellion or insurrection as an excuse to use force to restore the Union. The main intent of this pamphlet, which was sent to Virginia in large numbers, was to ask Virginians where they stood on the secession issue, while assuaging their fears that civil conflict would not follow secession. The answer to his question was never in doubt, however; Virginians planned to join South Carolina because of interest, honor, and inclination. Besides, DeJarnette asserted, unified slave states in a new government would be strong enough to resist Northern aggression and force compromise on slavery.

Muscoe R. H. Garnett, *The State of the Union. Speech . . . Delivered in the House of Representatives, January 16, 1861*

(Washington: M. Gill, Witherow, Printers, 1861), 16 pages

Frustrated over the delay on compromise and believing Northerners would not accept constitutional guarantees for the protection of slaves, Garnett attempted to influence the secession movement in Virginia. He insisted that the Republican victory had resulted in the creation of popular antislavery majorities in almost all of the Northern states and state legislatures, which threatened to end slavery. Furthermore, two sections divided by character, institutions, and race (here he referred to Northern immigrants as part of a racial minority) meant that the minority section would be a victim of Northern control of taxation, the treasury Department, the military, territorial government, and future expenditures for the country's growth. Garnett cited the example of the homestead bill to show that the North had the power to continue to lure immigrants to the west and thus destroy the need for slave labor. The result would be the end of slavery and chaos for Southern society. For Garnett, talk of a Border confederacy merely postponed the Upper South's inevitable joining of the Southern Confederacy.

James H. Thomas, *State of the Union*

(Washington: Office of the Congressional Globe, 1861), 7 pages

Joining the debate over the Western territories, on January 17, 1861, Tennessee's Thomas declared that he feared secession but that he supported it because Northerners were determined to end slavery and thus heap ruin and dishonor on the Southern people. He recounted how antislavery sentiment had grown in schools and the pulpit until Northern morality rejected slavery outright, which in turn gave rise to the Republican Party. At the core of Thomas's hostile feeling was his belief that Northerners were refusing to allow descendants of Revolutionary War heroes to move west, but they were encouraging the western migration of the descendants of the Germans who fought for England in the Revolution. In emotional comments directed at his neutral constituents, he predicted a civil war in which recently raised funds would be used to pin the Union back together with the bayonets of federal troops.

Sherrard Clemens, *State of the Union. Speech . . . in the House of Representatives, January 22, 1861*

(Washington: Office of the Congressional Globe, 1861), 8 pages

This worried supporter of the peace movement in Virginia sought to defuse talk of secession in his state by asserting that Virginians would have little in common with a Gulf State Confederacy. Clemens invoked the historic ties of Virginia to the Union, then turned to the crucial issue of slavery and Southern economic interests. He opposed reopening the slave trade and forming an expansive Gulf Coast alliance, which was intent on establishing trade south to Mexico, and charged that Virginia and other Border slave states would become mere economic appendages of the Lower South.

James Lyons, *Four Essays on the Right and Propriety of Secession by Southern States*

(Richmond: Ritchie and Dunnavant, Printers, 1861), 56 pages

This pamphlet, published sometime around late January 1861, was written by James Lyons, a prominent Richmond lawyer, who was attempting to persuade Virginians to join the Lower South in secession. Lyons equated the defense of the familiar values of honor, justice, and equality with the need to protect slave property. If the state did not secede, Lyons asserted, the North would wage civil war against a weak Lower South. And if Virginia united with the states that already had seceded, he continued, then the rest of the Border states would follow, and the slave states would then be strong enough to prevent the archtraitor General Winfield Scott from invading their land and killing their people.

Lazarus W. Powell, *Speech of . . . on the State of the Union*

(Washington: Congressional Globe Office, 1861), 16 pages

On January 22, 1861, this Kentuckian, who was a member of the Senate Committee of Thirteen, discussed the merits and reasoning of the Crittenden Compromise. A committed Unionist who remained in the United States Senate throughout the Civil War, Powell suggested that Northerners actually gained from the Compromise and that the South only required constitutional guarantees for slavery. However, Powell also voiced his support of the Border state Unionists who attacked radical Republican antislavery leaders, accused northern Border states of forming invading bands and stealing slaves, and demanded that no black man be permitted to vote or hold public office.

Emerson Etheridge, *State of the Union*

(Washington: Henry Polkinhorn, 1861), 13 pages

On January 23, 1861, in support of his own resolution on compromise, this Tennessean, vowed to hold the Union together at all cost. Although from time to time he added levity to his speech (there are many pauses for laughter in the pamphlet version of the speech), Etheridge was deadly serious when he claimed that poor-quality congressional leadership had ignored popular feelings and had shown its weakness through blunders over compromise. He claimed that Border states had little in common with the Gulf South and his region would be destroyed if it joined with that section. For him, slavery could not be protected in a separate Confederacy, and Southern interests were best defended in the Union.

Albert Rust, *Speech of . . . on The State of the Union*

(Washington: Lemuel Towers, 1861), 16 pages

On January 24, 1861, amidst interruptions and angry accusations, the Arkansas member of the House Committee of Thirty-three explained why compromise had failed and what Southerners should do about it. The Upper South, Rust declared, wanted conciliation; Northern Republicans, however, were implacable on the Chicago platform. He charged that Northerners were sending home pamphlets taken from the speeches of Southern Unionists to persuade the people that the South was deeply divided and thus prepared to give up on slave extension. (This accusation resulted in a heated exchange with John S. Millson of Virginia.) But Rust believed that most Northerners desired compromise, and he insisted that a united South could bargain to restore the Union on its own terms. His feelings were summed up in his plea, "Force us not to remain in a political family perpetually discordant."

John A. Gilmer, *State of the Union. Delivered in the House of Representatives, January 26, 1861*

(Washington: H. Polkinhorn, 1861), 8 pages

This Unionist called territorial compromise crucial to the preservation of the nation and tried to put his fellow congressmen (and the citizens of North Carolina) in a frame of mind to work for peace. He believed the territorial issue had been settled long before the secession crisis began because climate, soil, and the types of crops grown in a particular region actually determined where slaves could be used. But because of the increased agitation over the expansion issue, the harsh debates that continued without resolution, and Thomas Clingman and other fellow North Carolinians' rejection of Crittenden's proposal (see pamphlet included in this volume), Gilmer called for renewed attempts at compromise. If that failed, the conflicted and loyal leader acknowledged, his duty was to follow his state into what surely was to be a bloody civil war.

James M. Harris, *State of the Union*

(Washington: H. Polkinhorn, 1861), 8 pages

After a harsh disagreement with a fellow Maryland congressman over how to save the Union, on January 29, 1861, Harris fixed blame on the North and on South Carolina for increased sectional tensions. He regretted poor political leadership and party competition and attacked the Lower South's scheming men who desired to rise in public life through creation of a separate nation. Harris's principle concern, however, was the economic plight of Maryland, which was tied to Virginia and the other Border states but was apprehensive about an alliance with the cotton states. To prevent Maryland from being forced to make a decision in a state convention, this Unionist attempted to cajole and then threaten Northerners to rise above party interest and pass with haste the Crittenden compromises.

John W. Stevenson, *On the State of the Union*

(Washington: Lemuel Towers, 1861), 16 pages

Commenting on the House Committee report, on January 30, 1861, the Kentucky congressman placed the blame for the five states leaving the Union squarely on Republicans, who he claimed had stifled all attempts to compromise. Stevenson accused them of wishing to destroy equality among states and subverting the sacred right of protection within the Union. In an attempt to force compromise he proposed an amendment that would create two classes in the U.S. Senate by region and interest so that a separate majority in each would be necessary to pass any substantive legislation. But realizing that compromise was impossible, he stated that no Northern troops would dare cross Kentucky and that common interests linked the Border states with slave states. Stevenson said his loyalties lay with his adopted states (he was born in Virginia), and he planned to follow the will of the people of Kentucky.

William B. Stokes, *The State of the Union*

(Washington: Lemuel Towers, 1861), 12 pages

The future Union General spoke on February 1, 1861, to warn the people of Tennessee of the dangers of joining with the seceded states. Stokes accused the radical Democrats of the Lower South of causing secession, or, what he called, the revolution of a lawless mob and band of armed men bent on seizing property. He insisted that Louisiana had blockaded the Mississippi River, although Rust of Arkansas denied that it had done so, that the Gulf states had refused any compromise, and that the Lower South had abandoned Tennessee and the other Border states to a long and unprotected free state boundary. He charged that the Southern League leaders who had encouraged secession were lazy, nonslaveowning paternalists out to control hardworking Southerners. Drawing on earlier remarks of his North Carolina ally, John Gilmer, Stokes claimed the act of secession would destroy slavery.

Robert Hatton, *State of the Union*

(Washington: Congressional Globe, 1861), 8 pages

In a rambling speech on February 8, 1861, the Tennessee congressman, who was eventually killed during the Civil War for a cause he long had opposed, attacked "crazy enthusiasts," both Northern and Southern, for leading the country to the brink of civil conflict. He called on Northerners to make concessions by removing personal liberty laws and passing compromise measures on slave expansion into the territories, an issue he believed both sides had raised to a furor far beyond its merit. Hatton pleaded with Southerners to resist secessionists, understand that secession could not stop slaves from escaping northward, cease writing insurrectionary pamphlets, and realize that only the federal government was able to keep abolitionists from invading the slave states. He repeated the Border state charge that the Lower South had deserted his fellow Tennesseans on the Western territory issue, and planned instead to plot war with Mexico in order to add to their own slave lands. Hatton concluded that he feared citizens would someday declare with shame that "he was a member of the 36th Congress."

William N. H. Smith, *The Crisis, its Responsibilities and Perils*

(Washington: W. H. Moore Printer, 1861), 16 pages

On February 8, 1861, the Yale educated North Carolinian addressed his colleagues in the U.S. House of Representatives to persuade them to adopt the Crittenden amendment, not because of the right of slave expansion, but because it supported the principle of equality in the Union. Smith insisted on the historical right of property in slaves and asserted that Republican leaders had permanently divided the sections of the nation by refusing to accept that right. He charged that victory in the presidential election had given Republicans the means to prevent the federal government from protecting the South's slaveholding population. Smith concluded that his constituents held him personally accountable for inaction and that they were about to take their fate into their own hands.

Zebulon B. Vance, *To the Citizens of the Eighth Congressional District of North Carolina*

(Washington: H. Polkinhorn, Printer, 1861), 7 pages

This Unionist congressman wrote a message to his worried constituents on February 13, 1861, to explain his position on compromise. Vance told them that Republican acceptance of a constitutional amendment on slave property could keep the Upper South in the Union. He insisted that the Upper South joining the newly formed Confederacy would be harmful to that region because slaves would escape to the North, slaveowners would move to the Lower South, the Upper South would have to pay a higher proportion of the taxes needed to sustain the new government, and Northern states would became even more recalcitrant over slave expansion. He predicted that once disunion had been achieved there was no assurance that the Confederate states would remain together.

Thomas Ruffin, *State Rights and State Equality*

(Washington: H. Polkinhorn's Steam Job Press, 1861), 8 pages

On February 20, 1861, Congressman Ruffin ostensibly joined the debate over the House Committee of Thirty-three's report on the compromise over slave expansion into federal territory when he made this speech but was actually addressing the North Carolinians who were soon to assemble in convention. He charged that the Northerners who controlled Congress were a hostile, unprincipled, reckless majority who had no intention of giving in to the South. Tired of discussion of the rights or merits of secession, Ruffin claimed that the Union had dishonored and humiliated the Upper South and asked whether there would be abject submission or manly secession. He warned his fellow Southerners that the North was preparing for war and used as proof the Fort Sumter conflict, enlarged troop numbers in Maryland and the District of Columbia, and the "iron law of taxes" used to buy weapons and pay for troops.

Samuel McD. Moore, *Substance of a Speech . . . in the Convention of Virginia, on His Resolutions on Federal Relations*

(Richmond: Whig Book and Job Office, 1861), 24 pages

To explain his resolutions of February 24, 1861, delegate Moore of Rockbridge wrote a pamphlet that delineated brilliantly the serious material disagreements between the Upper and Lower South. He feared that Virginia would become subservient in the Southern Confederacy, and he vowed to become an expatriate if that happened. Moore claimed that the Lower South was insensitive to Virginia's need to enforce the fugitive slave law, that to reopen the slave trade would bankrupt the state by lowering slave prices, that the Lower South threatened to keep a neutral Virginia from selling slaves South, and that Virginians would bear the brunt of the tax burden to maintain a Confederate army. Above all, Moore asserted, Lower South demands for free trade would mean the end of tariff protection for Virginia's new industrialists and would force the white working classes, who the Lower South disapproved of, to emigrate.

William L. Goggin, *Speech . . . on Federal Relations, in the Convention of Virginia*

(Richmond: Whig Book and Job Office, 1861), 31 pages

On February 26 and 27, 1861, in a rambling speech full of the bluster of patriotism and confusion over how Upper South states should act, delegate Goggin attempted to review Virginia's political choices. Goggin maintained that the state could remain with the Union, join the new Confederacy, or set up as a separate nation. Grievances against the Lower South's cotton trade policies, which would destroy foreign sales of Virginia tobacco, Goggin said, led him to think about the state's valuable cattle and wheat trade Virginia had established with the Northeastern states. But if Virginians must join the Lower South, he insisted they have fair trading rights in the Confederacy.

John S. Carlile, *Speech . . . in the Virginia State Convention*

(Richmond: Whig Book and Job Office, 1861), 29 pages

On March 7, 1861, the delegate from Harrison spoke on the convention's secession resolution and suggested his state was on a collision course with the federal government. Expressing dislike for South Carolina and the other cotton states, he characterized John Preston's speech before the convention (see above comments on the speech) as an attack on free labor in the Upper South because of his assertion that "none but a subject race will labor in the South." Carlile denounced Robert M. T. Hunter for scuttling the Peace Conference (see Hunter's pamphlet reproduced in this volume) and Goggin for untoward attacks on the Republican Party (see comments above). What had pushed him to such hostility against his fellow leaders, Carlile maintained, was fear that if a rich and well-located state like Virginia joined the Confederacy, it would be forced to stand guard for "king cotton" and be condemned to "self-murder" since Union troops were certain to invade the state.

PAMPHLETS PUBLISHED AFTER APRIL 1861

Lazarus W. Powell, *Speech . . . on Executive Usurpation*

(Washington: Congressional Globe Office, 1861), 15 pages

On July 11, 1861, the Unionist senator from Kentucky opposed the President forcing Congress to appropriate funds for the Federal army. He drew a grim portrait of a President who ignored the country's growing debt, its destruction of commerce, and its rising unemployment in order to pursue war rather than attempt further peace negotiations. Speaking for many of his Border state colleagues and surely directly to his fellow Kentuckians, Powell insisted that civil war could never reunite the country, that Southern secession was an accomplished fact, and that Border state leaders were certain to reopen the debate on secession if the military crossed into their home territories.

John S. Carlile, *Speech . . . on the Bill to Confiscate the Property and Free the Slaves of Rebels; Delivered in the Senate of the United States, March 11, 1862*

(Washington: Congressional Globe Office, 1862), 13 pages

In a desperate speech, the Unionist senator from Virginia insisted he wanted to address present dangers, because the people of the South too often talked of future results. He attacked both abolitionists and secessionists, as he had done before, and claimed they had brought on the disastrous insurrectionary war. Reflecting on the perilous situation in Virginia, Carlile spoke about his personal sacrifice and threats made against his life and discussed violent internal civil warfare. Carlile maintained that the unconstitutional act of abolishing slavery meant that Tennessee and other Border states where the war would be fought would divide over being forced to fight against slavery. (Although he remained opposed to secession, Carlile's loyalty to slave society placed him in an impossible situation during the rest of the Civil War. His speech concludes the debate among Southerners about whether secession was the best means to save slave culture.)

Alexander H. Stephens, "Cornerstone Address"

Alexander H. Stephens (1812–83) was born in Wilkes County, Georgia, and orphaned at an early age. Sickly throughout his life, he showed indefatigable courage and endurance, graduating number one in his class at Franklin College (University of Georgia) and pursuing a splendid legal and political career. Regarded as an excellent debater and parliamentarian, Stephens early entered the Georgia legislature, and from 1843 until 1859 he served as a Whig member of the U.S. Congress. A Unionist, he made a famous speech against calling a Georgia convention and voted for secession only after he knew Georgia would leave the Union. Reluctantly, he served at the Montgomery convention, assisted in writing a conservative Confederate Constitution, and became vice president of the Confederacy. Stephens soon turned against the Confederate government, attended the Hampton Roads peace conference on February 3, 1865, and wrote a brilliant book, *A Constitutional View of the Late War Between the States*, 2 vols. (Philadelphia: The National Publishing Co., 1868, 1870). He reentered Congress and was elected governor of Georgia just before his death. In his address,[1] delivered on March 21, 1861, Stephens sought to unite other slave and Border states and encouraged them to join the newly formed Confederacy by praising the conservatism of the Constitution, pointing out similarities of interests between them, and claiming that the Confederacy could protect their interests because of their few debts and many natural resources. He also wanted a national convention to allow the slave states to present their grievances against the Union. Most important, Stephens's central idea that racial inferiority was the cornerstone of southern life became the cause for which all southerners were willing to fight. The most recent biography of this conflicted man is Thomas E. Schott, *Alexander H. Stephens of Georgia, A Biography* (Baton Rouge: Louisiana State University Press, 1988); see also the collection of Stephens's writings in Myrta L. Avery, *Recollections of Alexander H. Stephens* (New York: Doubleday, 1910). The largest collection of Stephens's papers is at the Library of Congress.

[2] I very much regret that everyone who desires cannot hear what I have to say,

1. No complete text of this important address exists. This version was taken from the March 22, 1861, edition of the *Savannah Republican* as reprinted in Frank Moore, ed., *The Rebellion Record: A Diary of American Events*, 12 vols. (New York: G. P. Putnam, 1862–1867), 1:44–49.

2. Before Stephens began his speech, he thanked the mayor of Savannah and

not that I have any display to make or anything very entertaining to present, but such views as I have to give, I wish *all* not only in this city, but in this State, and throughout our Confederated Republic, could hear, who have a desire to hear them.

I was remarking that we are passing through one of the greatest revolutions in the annals of the world—seven States have, within the last three months, thrown off an old Government and formed a new. This revolution has been signally marked, up to this time, by the fact of its having been accomplished without the loss of a single drop of blood. This new Constitution, or form of government, constitutes the subject to which your attention will be partly invited.

In reference to it, I make this first general remark: It amply secures all our ancient rights, franchises, and privileges. All the great principles of Magna Charta are retained in it. No citizen is deprived of life, liberty, or property, but by the judgment of his peers, under the laws of the land. The great principle of religious liberty, which was the honor and pride of the old Constitution, is still maintained and secured. All the essentials of the old Constitution, which have endeared it to the hearts of the American people, have been preserved and perpetuated. Some changes have been made—of these, I shall speak presently. Some of these I should have preferred not to have seen made, but these perhaps meet the cordial approbation of a majority of this audience, if not an overwhelming majority of the people of the Confederacy. Of them, therefore, I will not speak. But other important changes do meet my cordial approbation. They form great improvements upon the old Constitution. So, taking the whole new Constitution, I have no hesitancy in giving it as my judgment, that it is decidedly better than the old. Allow me to allude to some of these improvements. The question of building up class interest, or fostering one branch of industry to the prejudice of another, under the exercise of the revenue power, which gave us so much trouble under the old Constitution, is put at rest forever under the new. We allow the imposition of no duty with a view of giving advantage to one class of persons, in any trade or business, over those of another. All, under our system, stand upon the same broad principles of perfect equality. Honest labor and enterprise are left free and unrestricted in whatever pursuit they may be engaged in. This subject came well-nigh causing a rupture of the old Union, under the lead of the gallant Palmetto State, which lies on our border, in 1833.[3]

This old thorn of the tariff, which occasioned the cause of so much irritation in the old body politic, is removed forever from the new. Again, the subject of

---

prefaced his lecture with these words: "We are in the midst of one of the greatest epochs in our history. The last ninety days will mark one of the most memorable eras in the history of modern civilization."

3. Stephens was referring to the South Carolina Nullification movement.

internal improvements, under the power of Congress to regulate commerce, is put at rest under our system. The power claimed by construction under the old Constitution, was at least a doubtful one—it rested solely upon construction. We of the South, generally apart from considerations of Constitutional principles, opposed its exercise upon grounds of expediency and justice. Notwithstanding this opposition, millions of money, in the common Treasury had been drawn for such purposes. Our opposition sprung from no hostility to commerce, or all necessary aids for facilitating it. With us it was simply a question, upon *whom* the burden should fall. In Georgia, for instance, we had done as much for the cause of internal improvements of as any other portion of the country, according to population and means. We have stretched out lines of railroads from the seaboard to the mountains, dug down the hills and filled up the valleys, at a cost of not less than $25,000,000. All this was done to open up an outlet for our products of the interior, and those to the west of us, to reach the marts of the world. No State was in greater need of such facilities than Georgia; but we had not asked that these works should be made by appropriations out of the common treasury. The cost of the grading, the superstructure and equipments of our roads was borne by those who entered upon the enterprise. Nay, more—not only the cost of the iron, no small item in the aggregate cost, was borne in the same way, but we were compelled to pay into the common treasury several millions of dollars for the privilege of importing the iron after the price was paid for it abroad. What justice was there in taking this money, which our people paid into the common Treasury on the importation of our iron, and applying it to the improvement of rivers and harbors elsewhere?

The true principle is to subject commerce of every locality to whatever burdens may be necessary to facilitate it. If the Charleston harbor needs improvement, let the commerce of Charleston bear the burden. If the mouth of the Savannah river has to be cleared out, let the sea-going navigation which is benefited by it bear the burden. So with the mouths of the Alabama and Mississippi rivers. Just as the products of the interior—our cotton, wheat, corn, and other articles—have to bear the necessary rates of freight over our railroads to reach the seas. This is again the broad principle of perfect equality and justice. And it is specially held forth and established in our new Constitution.

Another feature to which I will allude, is that the new Constitution provides that Cabinet Ministers and heads of Departments shall have the privilege of seats upon the floor of the Senate and House of Representatives—shall have a right to participate in the debates and discussions upon the various subjects of administration. I should have preferred that this provision should have gone further, and allowed the President to select his constitutional advisers from the Senate and House of Representatives. That would have conformed entirely to the practice in the British Parliament, which, in my judgment, is one of the wisest provisions in the British Constitution. It is the only feature that saves that Government. It is that which gives it stability in its facility to change its administration. Ours, as it is, is a great approximation to the right principle.

Under the old Constitution, a Secretary of the Treasury, for instance, had no opportunity, save by his annual reports, of presenting any scheme or plan of finance or other matter. He had no opportunity of explaining, expounding, enforcing or defending his views of policy; his only resort was through the medium of an organ. In the British Parliament the Premier brings in his budget, and stands before the nation responsible for its every item. If it is indefensible, he falls before the attacks upon it, as he ought to. This will now be the case to a limited extent, under our system. Our heads of Departments can speak for themselves and the Administration in behalf of its entire policy, without resorting to the indirect and highly objectionable medium of the newspaper. It is to be greatly hoped, that under our system we shall never have what is known as a Government organ.

Another change in the Constitution relates to the length of the tenure of the Presidential office. In the new Constitution it is six years instead of four, and the President rendered ineligible for a re-election. This is certainly a decidedly conservative change. It will remove from the incumbent all temptation to use his office or exert the powers confided to him for any objects of personal ambition. The only incentive to that higher ambition which should move and actuate one holding such high trusts in his hands, will be the good of the people, the advancement, prosperity, happiness, safety, honor, and true glory of the Confederacy.

But not to be tedious in enumerating the numerous changes for the better, allow me to allude to one other—though last, not least: the new Constitution has put at rest *forever* all the agitating question relating to our peculiar institutions—African slavery as it exists among us—the proper *status* of the negro in our form of civilization. *This was the immediate cause of the late rupture and present revolution.* Jefferson, in his forecast, had anticipated this, as the "rock upon which the old Union would split." He was right. What was conjecture with him, is now a realized fact. But whether he fully comprehended the great truth upon which that rock *stood* and *stands*, may be doubted. *The prevailing ideas entertained by him and most of the leading statesmen at the time of the formation of the old Constitution were, that the enslavement of the African was in violation, of the laws of nature; that it was wrong in principle, socially, morally and politically.* It was an evil they knew not well how to deal with; but the general opinion of the men of that day was, that, somehow or other, in the order of Providence, the institution would be evanescent and pass away. This idea, though not incorporated in the Constitution, was the prevailing idea at the time. The Constitution, it is true, secured every essential guarantee to the institution while it should last, and hence no argument can be justly used against the constitutional guarantees thus secured, because of the common sentiment of the day. *Those ideas, however, were fundamentally wrong. They rested upon the assumption of the equality of races. This was an error.* It was a sandy foundation, and the idea of a Government built upon it—when the "storm came and wind blew, it *fell.*"

Our new Government is founded upon exactly the opposite ideas; its foundations are laid, its cornerstone rests, upon the great truth that the negro is not equal to the white man; that slavery, subordination to the superior race, is his natural and moral condition. This, our new Government, is the first, in the history of the world, based upon this great physical, philosophical, and moral truth. This truth has been slow in the process of its development, like all other truths in the various departments of science. It is so even amongst us. Many who hear me, perhaps, can recollect well that this truth was not generally admitted, even within their day. The errors of the past generation still clung to many as late as twenty years ago. Those at the North who still cling to these errors with a zeal above knowledge, we justly denominate fanatics. All fanaticism springs from an aberration of the mind; from a defect in reasoning. It is a species of insanity. One of the most striking characteristics of insanity, in many instances, is, forming correct conclusions from fancied or erroneous premises; so with the *anti-slavery* fanatics: their conclusions are right if their premises are. They assume that the negro is equal, and hence conclude that he is entitled to equal privileges and rights, with the white man. If their premises were correct, their conclusions would be logical and just; but their premises being wrong, their whole argument fails. I recollect once of having heard a gentleman from one of the Northern States, of great power and ability, announce in the House of Representatives, with imposing effect, that we of the South would be compelled, ultimately, to yield upon this subject of slavery; that it was as impossible to war successfully against a principle in politics, as it was in physics or mechanics. That the principle would ultimately prevail. That we, in maintaining slavery as it exists with us, were warring against a principle—a principle founded in nature, the principle of the equality of man. The reply I made to him was, that upon his own grounds we should succeed, and that he and his associates in their crusade against our institutions would ultimately fail. The truth announced, that it was a impossible to war successfully against a principle in politics as well as in physics and mechanics, I admitted, but told him it was he and those acting with him who were warring against a principle. They were attempting to make things equal which the Creator had made unequal.

In the conflict thus far, success has been on our side, complete throughout the length and breadth of the Confederate States. It is upon this, as I have stated, our social fabric is firmly planted; and I cannot permit myself to doubt the ultimate success of a full recognition of this principle throughout the civilized and enlightened world.

As I have stated, the truth of this principle may be slow in development, as all truths are, and ever have been, in the various branches of science. It was so with the principles announced by Galileo—it was so with Adam Smith and his principles of political economy. It was so with Harvey, and his theory of the circulation of the blood. It is stated that not a single one of the medical profession, living at the time of the announcement of the truths made by him, admitted them. Now, they are universally acknowledged. May we not therefore look with confidence to the ultimate universal acknowledgment of the truths upon which our system rests? It is the first Government ever instituted upon principles in strict conformity to nature, and the ordination of Providence, in furnishing the material of human society. Many Governments have been founded upon the principles of certain classes; but the classes thus enslaved, were of the same race, and in violation of the laws of nature. Our system commits no such violation of nature's laws. The negro by nature, or by the curse against Canaan, is fitted for that condition which he occupies in our system. The architect, in the construction of buildings, lays the foundation with the proper material—the granite—then comes the brick or marble. The substratum of our society is made of the material fitted by nature for it, and by experience we know that it is the best, not only for the superior but for the inferior race, that it should be so. It is, indeed, in conformity with the Creator. *It is not for us to inquire into the wisdom of His ordinances or to question them.* For His own purposes He has made one race to differ from another, as He has made "one star to differ from another in glory."

The great objects of humanity are best attained, when conformed to his laws and degrees, in the formation of Governments as well as in all things else. Our Confederacy is founded upon principles in strict conformity with these laws. This stone which was rejected by the first builders "*is become the chief stone of the corner*" in our new edifice.

I have been asked, what of the future? It has been apprehended by some, that we would have arrayed against us the civilized world. I care not who or how many they may be, when we stand upon the eternal principles of truth we are obliged and must triumph.

Thousands of people, who begin to understand these truths, are not yet completely out of the shell; they do not see them in their length and breadth. We hear much of the civilization and christianization of the barbarous tribes of Africa. In my judgment, those ends will never be obtained but by first teaching them the lesson taught to Adam, that "in the sweat of thy brow shalt thou eat bread," and teaching them to work, and feed, and clothe themselves.

But to pass on. Some have propounded the inquiry, whether it is practicable for us to go on with the Confederacy without further accessions. Have we the means and ability to maintain nationality among the Powers of the earth? On this point I would barely say, that as anxious as we all have been, and are, for the Border States, with institutions similar with ours, to join us, still we are abundantly able to maintain our position, even if they should ultimately make up their minds not to cast their destiny with ours. That they ultimately will join us, be compelled to do it, is my confident belief; but we can get on very well without them, even if they should not.

We have all the essential elements of a high national career. The idea has been given out at the North, and even in the Border States, that we are too small and too weak to maintain a separate nationality. This is a great mistake. In extent of territory we embrace 564,000 square miles and upwards. This is upwards of 200,000 square miles more than was included within the limits of the original Thirteen States. It is an area of country more than double the territory of France or the Austrian Empire. France, in round numbers, has but 212,000 square miles. Ours is greater than all France, Spain, Portugal and Great Britain, including England, Ireland, and Scotland together. In population, we have upwards of 5,000,000, according to the census of 1860; this includes white and black. The entire population, including white and black, of the original Thirteen States, was less than 4,000,000 in 1790, and still less in 1776, when the independence of our fathers was achieved. If they, with a less population, dared maintain their independence against the greatest power on earth, shall we have any apprehension of maintaining ours now?

In point of material wealth and resources, we are greatly in advance of them. The taxable property of the Confederate States cannot be less than $22,000,000,000. This, I think I venture but little in saying, may be considered as five times more than the colonies possessed at the time they achieved their independence. Georgia alone possessed last year, according to the report of our comptroller general, $672,000,000 of taxable property. The debts of the seven Confederate States sum up in the aggregate less than $18,000,000; while the existing debts of the other of the late United States sum up in the aggregate the enormous amount of $174,000,000. This is without taking into the account the heavy city debts, corporation debts, and railroad debts, which press, and will continue to press, a heavy incubus upon the resources of those States. These debts, added to others, make a sum total not much under $500,000,000. With such an area of territory—with such an amount of population—with a climate and soil unsurpassed by any on the face of the earth—with such resources already at our command—with productions which control the commerce of the world—who can entertain any apprehensions as to our success, whether others join us or not.

It is true, I believe, I state but the common sentiment, when I declare my earnest desire that the border States should join us. The differences of opinion that existed among us anterior to secession related more to the policy in securing that result by cooperation than from any difference upon the ultimate security we all looked to in common.

These differences of opinion were more in reference to policy than principle, and as Mr. Jefferson said in his inaugural, in 1801, after the heated contest preceding his election, there might be differences in opinion without differences on principle, and that all, to some extent had been Federalists and all Republicans; so it may now be said of us, that whatever differences of opinion as to the best policy in having a cooperation with our border sister Slave States, if the worst come to the worst, that as we were all cooperationists, we are now all for independence, whether they come or not.

In this connection, I take this occasion to state that I was not without grave and serious apprehensions that if the worst came to the worst, and cutting loose from the old Government would be the only remedy for our safety and security, it would be attended with much more serious ills than it has been as yet. Thus far we have seen none of those incidents which usually attend revolutions. No such material as such convulsions usually throw up has been seen. Wisdom, prudence, and patriotism have marked every step of our progress thus far. This augurs well for the future, and it is a matter of sincere gratification to me that I am enabled to make the declaration of the men I met in the Congress at Montgomery (I may be pardoned for saying this) an abler, wiser, a more conservative, deliberate, determined, resolute, and patriotic body of men I never met in my life. Their works speak for them; the Provisional Government speaks for them; the constitution of the permanent Government will be a lasting monument of their worth, merit, and statesmanship.

But to return to the question of the future. What is to be the result of this revolution?

Will every thing, commenced so well, continue as it has begun? In reply to this anxious inquiry I can only say, it all depends upon ourselves. A young man starting out in life on his majority, with health, talent, and ability, under a favoring Providence, may be said to be the architect of his own fortunes. His destinies are in his own hands. He may make for himself a name of honor or dishonor, according to his own acts. If he plants himself upon truth, integrity, honor, and uprightness, with industry, patience, and energy, he cannot fail of success. So it is with us: we are a young Republic, just entering upon the arena of nations; we will be the architect of our own fortunes. Our destiny, under Providence, is in our own hands. With wisdom, prudence, and statesmanship on the part of our public men, and intelligence, virtue, and patriotism on the part of the people, success, to the full measure of our most sanguine hopes, may be looked for. But if we become divided—if schisms arise—if dissensions spring up—if factions are engendered—if party spirit, nourished by unholy personal ambition, shall rear its hydra head, I have no good to prophesy for you. Without intelligence, virtue, integrity, and patriotism on the part of the people, no Republic or representative government can be durable or stable.

We have intelligence, and virtue, and patriotism. All that is required is to cultivate and perpetuate these. Intelligence will not do without virtue. France was a nation of philosophers. These philosophers became Jacobins. They lacked that virtue, that devotion to moral principle, and that patriotism which is essential to good government. Organized upon principles of perfect justice and right—seeking amity and friendship with all other powers—I see no obstacle in the way of our upward and onward progress. Our growth by accessions from other States, will depend greatly upon whether we present to the world, as I trust we shall, a better government than that to which they belong. If we do this, North Carolina, Tennessee, and Arkansas can not hesitate long; neither can Virginia, Kentucky, and Missouri. They will necessarily gravitate to us by an imperious law. We made ample provision in our constitution for the admission of other States; it is more guarded, and wisely so, I think, than the old Constitution on the same subject, but not too guarded to receive them as fast as it may be proper. Looking to the distant future, and perhaps not very distant either, it is not beyond the range of possibility, and even probability, that all the great States of the north-west shall gravitate this way as well as Tennessee, Kentucky, Missouri, Arkansas, & c. Should they do so, our doors are wide enough to receive them, *but not until they are ready to assimilate with us in principle.* The process of disintegration in the old Union may be expected to go on with almost absolute certainty. We are now the nucleus of growing power, which, if we are true to ourselves, our destiny, and our high mission, will become the controlling power on this continent. To what extent accessions will go on in the process of time, or where it will end, the future will determine. So far as it concerns States of the old Union, they will be upon no such principle of *reconstruction* as now spoken of, but upon *reorganization* and new assimilation. Such are some of the glimpses of the future as I catch them.

But at first we must necessarily meet with the inconveniences, and difficulties, and embarrassments incident to all changes of government. These will be felt in our postal affairs and changes in the channels of trade. These inconveniences, it is to be hoped, will be but temporary, and must be borne with patience and forbearance.

As to whether we shall have war with our late confederates, or whether all matters of difference between us shall be amicably settled, I can only say, that *the prospect for a peaceful adjustment is better, so far as I am informed, than it has been.*

The prospect of war, is at least not so threatening as it had been. The idea of coercion shadowed forth in President Lincoln's inaugural, seems not to be followed up thus far so vigorously as was expected. What course will be pursued towards Fort Pickens, and the other forts on the Gulf, is not so well understood. It is to be greatly desired that all of them should be surrendered. Our object is *Peace*, not only with the North, but with the world. All matters relating to the public property, public liabilities of the Union when we were members of it, we are ready and willing to adjust and settle, upon the principles of right, equality, and good faith. War can be of no more benefit to the North, than to us. The idea of coercing us, or subjugating us, is utterly preposterous. Whether the intention of evacuating Fort Sumter, is to be received as an evidence of a desire for a peaceful solution of our difficulties with the United States, or the result of necessity, I will not undertake to say. I would fain hope the former. Rumors are afloat, however, that it is the result of necessity. All I can say to you, therefore, on that point is, keep your armor bright, and your powder dry.

The surest way to secure peace, is to show your ability to maintain your rights. The principles and position of the present Administration of the United States—the Republican Party—present some puzzling questions. While it is a fixed principle with them, never to allow the increase of a foot of Slave Territory, they seem to be equally determined not to part with an inch "of the accursed soil." Notwithstanding their clamor against the institution, they seem to be equally opposed to getting more, or letting go what they have got. They were ready to fight on the accession of Texas, and are equally ready to fight now on her secession. Why is this? How can this strange paradox be accounted for? There seems to be but one rational solution—and that is, notwithstanding their professions of humanity, they are disinclined to give up the benefits they derive from slave labor. Their philanthropy yields to their interest. The idea of enforcing the laws, has but one object, and that is a collection of the taxes, raised by slave labor to swell the fund necessary to meet their heavy appropriations. The spoils is what they are after—though they come from the labor of the slave. . . . [4]

Our fathers have guarded the assessment of taxes, by insisting that representation and taxation should go together. This was inherited from the mother country, England. It was one of the principles upon which the Revolution had been fought. Our fathers also provided in the old Constitution that all appropriation bills should originate in the Representative branch of Congress; but

4. The *Savannah Republican* reporter summarized for his readers Stephens's views of the "profligacy of appropriations" by the United States Congress. Stephens said he supported a "clause prohibiting Congress from appropriating any money from the Treasury except by a two-thirds vote. . . ."

our new Constitution went a step further, and guarded not only the pockets of the people, but also the public money, after it was taken from their pockets. . . . [5]

That as the admission of States by Congress under the Constitution was an act of legislation, and in the nature of a contract or compact between the States admitted and the others admitting, *why should not this contract or compact be regarded as of like character with all other civil contracts—liable to be rescinded by mutual agreement of both parties?* The seceding States have rescinded it on their part. Why cannot the whole question be settled, if the North desire peace, simply by the Congress, in both branches, with the concurrence of the President, giving their consent to the separation, and a recognition of independence? This he merely offered as a suggestion, as one of the ways in which it might be done with much less violence to constructions of the Constitution than many other acts of that Government. The difficulty has to be solved in some way or other—this may be regarded as a fixed fact.

In olden times the olive branch was considered the emblem of peace, we will send to the nations of the earth another and far more potential emblem of the same, the Cotton Plant. The present duties were levied with a view of meeting the present necessities and exigencies, in preparation for war, if need by; but if we have peace, and he hoped we might, and trade should resume its proper course, a *duty of ten per cent. upon foreign importations, it was thought, might be sufficient to meet the expenditures of the Government.* If some articles should be left on the free list, as they now are, such as breadstuffs, & c., then, of course, duties upon others would have to be higher—but in no event to an extent to embarrass trade and commerce.

If, we are true to ourselves, true to our cause, true to our destiny, true to our high mission, in presenting to the world the highest type of civilization ever exhibited by man—there will be found in our Lexicon no such word as FAIL.

5. Stephens here turned to the issue of how to have a "peaceful solution of the controversy with the old government." His suggestions are what follow.

366, 375-77, 379-86, 388-91, 394-402, 409, 411. *See also* individual pamphlet authors

Security in the Union, 153, 156

Seward, William Henry, 42, 46, 97, 119, 138, 212, 285, 317, 328, 344, 347, 380, 383

Slave code, 383

Slavery, 14, 16, 20-21, 26-28, 31, 37, 39-44, 46, 52-55, 63, 67, 69, 71, 74-76, 78, 80-82, 84, 86, 88-98, 115, 138, 145-46, 149, 179-91, 193, 207-9, 217, 219, 223, 225, 228, 236-42, 244-47, 253-54, 256-60, 264-66, 284-85, 288-89, 296, 298-304, 310-11, 313-15, 317-18, 321, 324, 327, 329-30, 340, 342-43, 350-54, 356, 358, 361, 363-65, 370, 376-90, 392, 399, 405-6; as labor system, 382; biblical argument in favor of, 384; confinement of and class war, 393; Southern Confederacy could not protect, 395; effect of secession on, 397. *See also* individual pamphlet authors

Slave society, 378

Smith, Adam, 407

Smith, Robert H., 195; on U.S. Constitution, 195-203; on Congress of the Confederate States of America, 196, 199; on British Constitution, 201-2; on defects in U.S. Constitution, 204-5; on Constitution of the Confederate States of America, 204-12; on U.S. Constitution's protection of slavery in the territories, 206-12; on reopening of African slave trade, 207-9

South Carolina, 3, 14, 63, 78-79, 82, 101-4, 106-12, 115, 122-23, 132, 142, 157-59, 163-64, 211, 217, 221, 223-24, 227, 229, 247, 250, 252-54, 256-59, 289, 297, 305, 310-12, 314-15, 319, 321, 322, 324, 337, 344, 350, 353, 367, 371-72, 375-76, 379-80, 386-89, 391, 394, 398, 401

Southern convention, 280, 376, 377-79

Southern Literary Messenger, 382

Southern nonslaveholders, 377-78

Southern Presbyterian Review, 63, 157, 389-90

Southern Unionists, 397

Spoils and patronage, 268

State of nature, 8

Stephens, Alexander H., 85, 88, 325, 402; on Confederate States Constitution, 402-5, 410-12; on slaves subordinate to superior race, 406-7; predicts no civil war, 410-11; on Republican Party, 411

Supreme Court, 8-12, 74, 107, 110, 134, 148, 167-68, 253-54, 270-71, 300, 308, 326, 334-35, 337, 354, 358, 362, 376-77

Tennessee, 79, 82, 110, 119, 121, 126, 128, 132, 143, 179-80, 218, 256, 259, 284, 305, 311, 316, 323, 326, 344, 366, 368-70, 377, 392, 395, 398-99, 410

Texas, 25, 29, 80-81, 102, 143, 154-56, 211, 234, 256, 290, 319, 326, 330, 337, 356, 371, 381-83, 386, 411

Thornwell, James H., 63, 157, 381; on South Carolina, 157, 158-59; on North's repeal of U.S. Constitution, 159-60; on disunion, 160-61, 175; on Lincoln, 162, 170, 173-74; on U.S. Constitution and slavery, 162-75; on Virginia, 175

Treason, 5, 41, 109, 113, 132, 136, 139-40, 149, 151, 306, 309, 325, 335

Trescot, William Henry, 14; on slavery, 14, 16, 20-21, 26-28, 31; on condition of England, 15, 18, 20-24, 30; on commerce, 16, 19, 23-24, 28-30, 32; on federal government, 17; on foreign relations, 23-24, 26, 30; on civil war, 27-28

U.S. Constitution, xiii, xxvi, 3-4, 6, 7, 9-12, 22, 25, 35-37, 39-42, 45-46, 48, 54, 56, 74, 76, 90, 92-94, 96, 98-99, 102, 104-14, 116, 118-22, 126-28, 134,

136-37, 144-45, 148-49, 151, 153-
54, 159-60, 162-64, 166-71, 173-75,
181, 183, 185, 187, 189, 190-12, 219-
20, 222, 228, 240, 242-44, 251-52,
255-56, 261, 263-64, 266, 269-71,
273-76, 279, 281, 285-86, 288, 300,
305-9, 312, 317-20, 324-25, 328, 332-
33, 335-36, 338, 341, 343-46, 349-53,
355-56, 358, 360-61, 363-65, 372,
375, 377, 379, 402-5, 410-12. *See also*
individual pamphlet authors

Vindication, 16, 163, 305, 317, 325, 351-
52, 354, 367

Virginia, 25, 27, 31, 40-41, 55, 80-81,
127, 175, 179-80, 189, 210, 218, 235,
256, 259, 262, 273, 290, 292-93, 295,
300, 307, 311, 331, 340, 344, 346, 347,
349-50, 355, 360, 362, 366-69, 371,
372, 375-76, 387-88, 391, 394-98,
401, 410

Washington Peace Conference, 350-51;
compared to Crittenden Compromise, 354-56, 359-61
Webster, Daniel, 7, 9-11, 41, 104, 111,
128, 273, 287, 301, 304, 329, 358
White working classes, 400